1995

CHRIST THE LORD

CHRIST THE LORD

Studies in Christology presented to Donald Guthrie

Edited by Harold H. Rowdon
Senior Lecturer in Church History, London Bible College

Inter-Varsity Press

INTER-VARSITY PRESS

38 De Montfort Street, Leicester LE1 7GP, England

Box F, Downers Grove, Illinois 60515, U.S.A.

Distributed in Canada through InterVarsity Press,
1875 Leslie St., Unit 10, Don Mills, Ontario M3B 2M5

© Inter-Varsity Press, Leicester, 1982

First published 1982

British Library Cataloguing in Publication Data
Christ the Lord
    1. Guthrie, Donald   2. Jesus Christ – Addresses,essays, lectures
I. Rowdon, Harold H.   II. Guthrie, Donald
    273   BT 202
ISBN: 0–85111–744–9

Library of Congress Cataloging in Publication Data
Main entry under title:

Christ the Lord

    "A select bibliography of the writings of Donald Guthrie": P.
    Includes bibliographical references.
    1. Jesus Christ – Person and offices – Addresses, essays, lectures.   2. Bible.   N.T. –
Criticism, interpretation, etc. – Addresses, essays, lectures.   3. Guthrie, Donald, 1916–
– Addresses, essays, lectures.
    I. Guthrie, Donald, 1916–   .II. Rowdon, Harold Hamlyn.
BT202.C54   232   82–171
ISBN: 0–87784–955–2   AACR2

Phototypesetting in 11/13 Garamond by Nuprint Services Limited, Harpenden, Hertfordshire
Printed and bound by Weatherby Bookbinding, Wellingborough, Northants.

*Inter-Varsity Press is the publishing division of the Universities and Colleges Christian Fellowship
(formerly the Inter-Varsity Fellowship), a student movement linking Christian Unions in universities and
colleges throughout the British Isles, and a member movement of the International Fellowship of Evangelical
Students. For information about local and national activities in Great Britain write to
UCCF, 38 De Montfort Street, Leicester LE1 7GP.*
*InterVarsity Press, U.S.A., is the book-publishing division of Inter-Varsity Christian Fellowship,
a student movement active on campus at hundreds of universities, colleges and schools of nursing.
For information about local and regional activities, write
IVCF, 233 Langdon St., Madison, WI 53703.*

CONTENTS

vi

DONALD GUTHRIE:
AN APPRECIATION

Dear Donald,

The essays published in this volume are offered as a tribute to you from some of your colleagues, students and friends, as well as a modest contribution to theological scholarship.

To have interacted with you has been one of the choicest experiences of our lives. We have admired your careful scholarship, the skilful nature of your oral teaching, the lucidity of your writings, and the fair and charitable way in which you consistently present the position of those whose arguments have failed to convince you. Above all, we praise God for your humility, the warmth of your unobtrusive spirituality, your love for God and man, and your marked ability to wear your learning lightly and to adapt to the level of those with whom you are communicating.

Your life and work have been very closely linked with the London Bible College. One of its first students, you received the honour of being invited to join the teaching staff before you had graduated (subject to a successful performance in the final examinations!). Rapidly, you made your mark on the college, whether in the classroom, the chapel, the senior common room or the board room. Your sagacious contributions to discussions of the academic board and more latterly of the governing body of the college were instrumental in furthering its progress, whether in academic affairs (as in the submission of courses to the Council for National Academic Awards) or in more mundane matters (such as the planning of additional accommodation for an expanding college). It has not escaped our notice that one of the questions that you consistently ask of a proposed change is: 'Will it benefit the students?'

We have observed that your concern for your students goes far beyond their intellectual needs. You have given yourself unstintingly to their total development as rounded persons. With deep insight you have been able to guide students towards spiritual maturity and total integrity. Endowed with a capacity for fun and entertainment largely unsuspected by the general public, you have a rare gift for helping students to relax. (We remember that you were the inspiration – and the star performer – of the evening of entertainment given by the teaching staff to the students and their friends, one hectic summer term.) Your concern for the student with personal problems matches that for the student with high academic potential.

In addition to your work as lecturer in New Testament studies which continued from 1949 to your retirement in 1982 you served as registrar for advanced studies from 1964 to 1979. In this capacity you guided the college into the area of post-graduate work. It was fitting that you should have been available to play a full part in the planning of a taught M.A. course before your retirement. Between 1965 and 1980 you edited a journal, *Vox Evangelica,* the only journal of its kind to be issued by a theological college in this country. We remember the gentle cajoling with which you secured articles from members of the teaching staff. It came as no surprise when you were appointed in 1978 to serve as vice-principal of London Bible College.

Your work has not been confined to a single institution, massive though the contribution to your chosen college has been. For a whole year you combined full-time teaching at London Bible College with part-time teaching at Spurgeon's College. You served as visiting lecturer at the Winona Lake School of Theology in the United States of America in 1964 and 1968 and at the Freie Theologische Akademie, Seeheim, West Germany, in 1975 and 1978. You gave one of the earlier Tyndale Lectures ('The Pastoral Epistles and the Mind of Paul') and have been deeply involved in the work of the Tyndale Fellowship and the Theological Students Fellowship. Your editorial work has been done, not only in connection with *Vox Evangelica* but also with *The Lion Handbook to the Bible, The New Bible Commentary Revised,* and *The Illustrated Bible Dictionary.* Your expertise has also been made freely available to such bodies as *The Scripture Gift Mission* whose concern is with the translation and distribution of Scripture.

We have noted that your writings fall into two well-defined categories. There are the technical works, including the magisterial surveys, *New Testament Introduction* and, now, *New Testament Theology,* which are used as reference works and textbooks around the world. But there are also books like *Jesus the Messiah* and *The Apostles* which mediate fine biblical scholarship to the general public.

It is the same in your preaching. We suspect that there are few things that you enjoy more than expounding a passage of Scripture to a church congregation, bringing out its meaning and applying its teaching with a rare touch of humour. We enjoy listening to you doing it.

With gratitude to God for every remembrance of you, the editor and contributors to this volume dedicate it to their much-loved teacher, colleague and friend. It is appropriate that their work is designed to make a positive contribution to the contemporary scholarly debate about the person of Christ. For you are a man who is totally devoted to Jesus Christ and to positive scholarship. It is our prayer that you will be given many years of happy and productive retirement in which to share your deep knowledge and rich experience with the worldwide audience to which you have spoken so often in the past. Though deprived of the day-to-day fellowship of classroom, common room and chapel which, we believe, has meant so much to you in the past, you will still be able to enjoy the companionship of your wife, Mary, whose support has been yours for so many years and whom we are proud to number among our friends, and of the family circle with which God has enriched your lives.

HAROLD ROWDON

A SELECT BIBLIOGRAPHY OF THE WRITINGS OF DONALD GUTHRIE

'Tertullian and Pseudonymity', *Expository Times* 67, 1956, pp.341f.

The Pastoral Epistles and the Mind of Paul (Tyndale Press, 1956).

The Pastoral Epistles (Tyndale New Testament Commentary, 1957).

The Epistle to the Hebrews in Recent Thought (London Bible College Annual Lecture, 1958).

Contributions to Baker's *Dictionary of Theology* (Baker Book House, Grand Rapids, 1960).

New Testament Introduction: The Pauline Epistles (Tyndale Press, 1960).

'Pseudepigrapha', 'Pseudonymity', 'Romans', 'The Pastoral Epistles', 'Hebrews' in *The New Bible Dictionary* (IVF, 1962).

'The Development of the Idea of Canonical Pseudepigrapha in New Testament Criticism', *Vox Evangelica* 1, 1962, pp.43–49. Reproduced in *The Authorship and Integrity of the New Testament,* SPCK Theological Collections 4, 1965, pp.14–39.

New Testament Introduction: Hebrews to Revelation (Tyndale Press, 1962).

'Recent Literature on the Acts of the Apostles', *Vox Evangelica* 2, 1963, pp.33–49.

Epistles from Prison (Lutterworth Bible Guides, 1963).

'Recent Literature on Petrine Epistles', *Themelios* 1.1, 1962, pp.13–23.

'Some Recent Books on the Gospels', *Vox Evangelica* 4, 1965, pp.43–54.

New Testament Introduction: The Gospels and Acts (Tyndale Press, 1965).

'Oral Tradition in New Testament Times', *Themelios* 3.3, 1966, pp.24–30.

'The Importance of Signs in the Fourth Gospel', *Vox Evangelica* 5, 1967, pp.72–83.

'Form Criticism', *Themelios* 5.1, 1968, pp.8–14.

Galatians, Century Bible, New Series (Nelson, 1969).

Commentary on 'John', 'Colossians', 'Philemon', in *The New Bible Commentary Revised* (IVP, 1970).

'The Pauline Epistles', *The New Bible Commentary Revised* (IVP, 1970), pp.71–76.

A Shorter Life of Christ (Zondervan, Grand Rapids, 1970).

New Testament Introduction, One-volume revised edition (Tyndale Press, 1970).

'Acts and Epistles in Apocryphal Writings' in W. W. Gasque and R. P. Martin (eds.), *Apostolic History and the Gospels* (Paternoster, 1970), pp. 328–345.

Jesus the Messiah (Zondervan, Grand Rapids, 1972).

Contributions to Baker's *Dictionary of Christian Ethics* (Baker Book House, Grand Rapids, 1973).

Contributions to *The Lion Handbook to the Bible* (Lion, 1973).

'The New Testament Approach to Social Responsibility', *Vox Evangelica* 8, 1973, pp.40–59.

'Paul the Preacher and his Preaching', *Fraternal*, 1974, No. 169, pp.22–29.

'History and the Gospels', *Themelios* 10.1, 1974, pp.11–19.

Contributions to *New International Dictionary of the Christian Church* (Zondervan, Grand Rapids, 1974).

'Jesus Christ', 'New Testament', 'Biblical Criticism', 'Canon of the New Testament', 'Johannine Theology', 'Pastoral Epistles' and some minor articles in *Pictorial Encyclopedia of the Bible* (Zondervan, Grand Rapids, 1975).

The Apostles (Zondervan, Grand Rapids, 1975).

Contributions to *The Illustrated Bible Dictionary* (IVP, 1980).

New Testament Theology (IVP, 1981).

'The Lamb in the Structure of the Book of Revelation', *Vox Evangelica* 12, 1981, pp.64–71.

Forthcoming

Hebrews (Tyndale New Testament Commentary).

Manual on *The Teaching of the New Testament*.

Article on 'The Emergence of Criticism: A Critique of Criticism'.

Editorships

Editor, *Vox Evangelica* (1965–1979).

New Testament Editor, *The New Bible Commentary Revised* (IVP, 1970).

New Testament Editor, *The Lion Handbook to the Bible* (Lion, 1973).

Consulting Editor, *The Illustrated Bible Dictionary* (IVP, 1980).

ABBREVIATIONS

BASOR	*Bulletin of the American Schools of Oriental Research*
BHS	*Biblia Hebraica Stuttgartensia*
Bib	*Biblica*
BJRL	*Bulletin of the John Rylands Library*
BZ	*Biblische Zeitschrift*
CBQ	*Catholic Biblical Quarterly*
CD	*Church Dogmatics*
CSEL	*Corpus Scriptorum Ecclesiasticorum Latinorum*
EQ	*Evangelical Quarterly*
ExpT	*Expository Times*
FRLANT	*Forschungen zur Religion und Literatur des Alten und Neuen Testaments*
ICC	*International Critical Commentary*
IRM	*International Review of Missions*
JAOS	*Journal of the American Oriental Society*
JBL	*Journal of Biblical Literature*
JETS	*Journal of the Evangelical Theological Society*
JJS	*Journal of Jewish Studies*
JSNT	*Journal for the Study of the New Testament*
JSOT	*Journal for the Study of the Old Testament*
JSS	*Journal of Semitic Studies*
JTS	*Journal of Theological Studies*
LXX	The Septuagint (Greek translation of the Old Testament)
MPG	J. P. Migne, *Patrologiae cursus completus, series Graeca*
MPL	J. P. Migne, *Patrologiae cursus completus, series Latina*
MT	Massoretic Text
NovT	*Novum Testamentum*
NTS	*New Testament Studies*

OTS	*Oudtestamentische Studiën*
P.B.I.	Pontifical Biblical Institute
PEQ	*Palestine Exploration Quarterly*
PTR	*Princeton Theological Review*
RB	*Revue Biblique*
RHPR	*Revue d'Histoire et de Philosophie Religieuses*
RQ	*Revue de Qumran*
SB	H. L. Strack and P. Billerbeck, *Kommentar zum Neuen Testament aus Talmud und Midrasch*, 6 vols., 1926–61
SJT	*Scottish Journal of Theology*
SNTS	*Society for New Testament Studies*
SNTSMS	*SNTS* Monograph Series
TB	*Tyndale Bulletin*
TDNT	G. Kittell and G. Friedrich (ed.), *Theologisches Wörterbuch zum Neuen Testament*, 1932–74; ET *Theological Dictionary of the New Testament*, ed. G. W. Bromiley, 10 vols., 1964–76.
TDOT	G. J. Botterweck and H. Ringgren (ed.), *Theologisches Wörterbuch zum Alten Testament*, 1970– ; ET *Theological Dictionary of the Old Testament*, ed. J. T. Willis, 1974–
TWNT	see *TDNT*
TZ	*Theologische Zeitschrift*
UBS	United Bible Societies
VT	*Vetus Testamentum*
ZDMG	*Zeitschrift der Deutschen Morgenländischen Gesellschaft*
ZKG	*Zeitschrift für Kirchengeschichte*
ZNW	*Zeitschrift für die Neutestamentliche Wissenschaft*
ZTK	*Zeitschrift für Theologie und Kirche*

INCARNATIONAL CHRISTOLOGY IN THE NEW TESTAMENT

I. Howard Marshall

From an early date belief 'in one God the Father Almighty, . . . And in one Lord Jesus Christ, the only-begotten Son of God, . . . Who . . . came down from heaven, And was incarnate by the Holy Ghost of the Virgin Mary' (the Nicene Creed) has been an accepted part of Christian belief, as expressed in creeds and confessions. Within the last few years, however, this belief has been subjected to strong criticism by a group of British theologians who have argued that it is no longer a meaningful belief for today, and that it can and ought to be jettisoned.[1] They have argued that it is not a central doctrine in the New Testament, although they have not succeeded in denying its presence altogether. More recently, the American Roman Catholic scholar R. E. Brown has stated that, while the incarnation is truly characteristic of Johannine Christianity, it is not characteristic of about 90% of the remainder of the New Testament.[2] Even so conservative a scholar as J. D. G. Dunn has found a full-blown doctrine of the incarnation present in only one passage in the New Testament.[3]

Assertions that the incarnation is not a New Testament doctrine or that it is a dispensable doctrine in modern Christianity may be disquieting to some of us, while to others they may simply give open expression to their own secret uncertainties and doubts. Whatever be the frame of mind with which we read such comments, however, they need to be taken seriously and examined dispassionately. In the space at my disposal there is room simply to take up one aspect of the problem, namely how far there is a doctrine of incarnation in the New Testament itself.

---

[1] J. Hick (ed.), *The Myth of God Incarnate* (SCM, 1977).

[2] R. E. Brown, review in *CBQ* 42, 1980, p.413. *Cf.* M. Wiles: 'Incarnation, in its full and proper sense, is not something directly presented in scripture' (J. Hick, *op. cit.*, p.3).

[3] J. D. G. Dunn, *Christology in the Making* (SCM, 1980), p.241.

1

I

The word 'incarnation' is not a New Testament word any more than is Trinity or eschatology or Christology. Such words, however, have been found useful in the discussion of New Testament theology because they deal with identifiable subjects. Sometimes they are the names of concepts which became important in the later history of theology, so that it becomes profitable to compare later teaching with that of the New Testament and to correct the former by the latter. If dogmatics exists to test the preaching of the church by the Word of God, so New Testament theology exists to test dogmatics by the Word of God as it is revealed in Scripture.

Some words used in later theology may not have a counterpart in New Testament teaching or may have a different connotation from that which they have in the New Testament. J. Carmignac has suggested with good reason that the common use of the term 'eschatology' can lead to misunderstanding of the teaching of the New Testament and wrong identification of its theological concerns.[4] A study of Christology in the light of the New Testament may show that the interests of the New Testament writers were different from those of later dogmaticians. A study of the New Testament to see what it says about 'incarnation' may possibly lead to the conclusion that 'incarnation' is an inappropriate category to use in analysing New Testament teaching, or that New Testament teaching suggests a different understanding and definition of the concept from that current in later centuries, or again that 'incarnation' is not a wholly satisfactory term to sum up this aspect of New Testament teaching and could be replaced by a more appropriate one. That is to say, the term 'incarnation' directs us to certain aspects of New Testament teaching which historically formed the basis for its use in the church, but the teaching of the New Testament in these and other passages may lead us to a new apprehension of the concept and alterations in our existing ideas. We must always be alert to such possibilities, and also to the temptation to express New Testament ideas in our own way which does not in fact do justice to them.

II

The traditional basis of the doctrine of the incarnation is John 1:14 where the prologue of the Gospel comes to a climax in the statement that the Word who had been from the beginning with God and was active in the work of creation and was the light and life of men became flesh and dwelt among us. It is

---

[4] J. Carmignac, 'Les Dangers de l'Eschatologie', *NTS* 17, 1970–71, pp. 365–390.

noteworthy that the subject of the passage is the Word or Logos. It is the career of the Logos which is being described, and not until verse 17 is the name Jesus Christ used for the first time, thereby identifying the Word who became flesh with the historical figure of that name. From that point onwards John ceases to use the term Logos and writes about Jesus, using his name and a variety of Jewish messianic titles to refer to him.

For John, then, the Word became a particular person, Jesus, who existed in human form. The Word is clearly a personal being,[5] a phrase by which I mean that the qualities which we generally regard as being characteristic of human beings as persons are possessed by him. He has intelligence, emotions and will. He is like a person rather than like a dumb animal or a thing.[6] Above all, he is described as the only[7] (*sc.* Son) of God, so that, insofar as we think of the Father as a personal being, so also must we think of the Word as having the same sort of being. He is said to share the glory which is the prerogative of God. He is the Father's partner in his activities, and yet in some way he is subordinate to the Father.

To say that this being became flesh is the problematic statement, since John does not give us any immediate, nearer description of what he means. We have to consider the clause in the context of the Gospel as a whole. John does not mean that the Word turned into flesh or that it merely assumed a fleshly clothing like a Greek god who could instantly transform himself into a human bodily form and move about among men, his real nature and identity being hidden from them except, perhaps, when he demonstrated supernatural powers. It would be truer to say that John opposes such views. Rather, the Word took on a fleshly form of existence. He was, therefore, still the Word.

As such, he could display miraculous powers. We should not overlook this element, even though it has caused one writer to suggest that the Johannine Jesus walks through the world with his feet several inches from the ground.[8] In this way, it is implied, he was not a real man at all, but simply a heavenly being

---

[5] This is true at least for the prologue in its present form. We are not concerned here with possible earlier stages in composition.

[6] The language of persons, as applied to God, is analogical. The point is that analogies drawn from our experience of persons are far more appropriate than those drawn from experience of other entities, whether or not they are entirely adequate to express the nature of God. Put otherwise, we in fact possess no better language than that of persons to express our understanding of God, and nothing in our experience of God suggests that this language is misleading.

[7] Despite the retention of 'only begotten' by some biblical translations and commentators, the translation 'only' for *monogenēs* is probably to be preferred. See I. H. Marshall, *The Epistles of John* (Eerdmans, 1978), p.214 n. 8.

[8] E. Käsemann, *The Testament of Jesus* (SCM, 1968).

masquerading as a man. But in fact this same Gospel presents Jesus as a man who could ask questions to remove his own ignorance and who could feel such human emotions as hunger and sadness, and there is no suggestion that these emotions were faked for the occasion by somebody who was impassible. However, John suggests that the important evidences of divinity in Jesus are to be seen not so much in his mighty acts, though these are not unimportant, but in his revelation of divine glory through loving and humble service. It is the moral attributes which matter: grace and truth came through Jesus Christ. That is to say, the revelation of God in Jesus is seen primarily in his moral attributes and his teaching. Some would like to argue that, as the Word made flesh, Jesus should have been *in all respects* just like any other man, but this is surely an absurd presupposition. The problem, rather, is whether the evidence that he was the Logos constituted a denial of the real humanity of Jesus.

For John, then, Jesus is undoubtedly the personal Word of God now adopting a fleshly form of existence. When we talk of incarnation, this is what is meant by it, for it is here that the New Testament offers the closest linguistic equivalent to the term 'incarnation': *ho logos sarx egeneto.*

III

Our next task is to see whether similar teaching is to be found elsewhere. We must beware, of course, of assuming that similarity of expression necessarily means identity of ideas expressed, and so we must proceed with due caution.

The Epistles of John are commonly regarded as having been written, if not by the author of the Gospel himself, at least by somebody of a closely similar outlook, and subsequently to the Gospel. Here two things claim our interest.

First, there is a series of statements in which the writer defends the confession that Jesus is the Christ (1 Jn. 2:22) or the Son (1 Jn. 2:22f.) or that Jesus Christ has come in the flesh (1 Jn. 4:2; *cf.* 2 Jn. 7). There is general agreement that for the writer the terms Son and Christ are close in meaning, and that by these statements he wishes (i) to identify Jesus as the Son of God and (ii) to affirm that this person Jesus Christ came in the flesh. The negative to these statements would be to deny that Jesus was the Son of God and that this person came in the flesh.

If we ask what such a denial would mean, it seems most likely that the deniers whom the writer had in mind held that a divine power, presumably a spiritual 'Son of God', came upon the man Jesus at his baptism and then departed before the crucifixion. This is the view combated in 1 John 5:6 where the writer emphasizes that Jesus Christ came with the water and with the blood.[9] If this interpretation is correct, John's opponents believed in a merely temporary possession of Jesus by a spiritual power, and they denied that it was the Son of God who died on the cross. Clearly John wished to say that this was not what he understood by the relation between Jesus and the Son. He obviously believed that there was a real and lasting union between the Son of God and the flesh of Jesus, while his opponents probably shared the later gnostic disbelief in the impossibility of a real incarnation and laid stress on the importance of the divine spirit over against human materiality. Thus in the face of opposition to the idea John affirmed the necessity of belief in Jesus Christ, the Son of God, as truly come in the flesh. It may well be also that John believed that even after the resurrection the union of the Son of God with the man Jesus still continued; the heavenly being worshipped by the church was Jesus and not a disincarnate Son of God.[10]

Second, 1 John begins with a statement about that which was from the beginning and which could be seen, heard and handled, namely the word of life. The language used is somewhat equivocal. The word of life could well mean the Christian message, the gospel, which conveys life to those who accept it, but the references to seeing and touching cannot refer to anything other than the concrete manifestation of the Word in Jesus. Both aspects of meaning are present, and it is probable that the writer has chosen this enigmatic and even awkward manner of expression in order to bring out the identity between the Word preached to his readers and the Word incarnate who had been personally known by the apostles.[11] If so, the important thing is that he writes about the Word being manifested in such a way as to be heard, seen and handled. He presupposes the concept of incarnation found in John 1.

Thus the same concept of incarnation as in the Gospel is present in 1 and 2 John, and indeed it is the principal Christological idea in these Epistles. This is a matter of great significance. The Gospel is concerned to present the historical, earthly person, Jesus, and it is in this context that the concept of incarnation might seem to be most at home. But the Epistles are written to people who had never known the earthly Jesus, whose belief was centred on the heavenly Son of God who would one day appear in glory; and it is in this context that the writer finds it necessary to stress that this Son of God truly came in the flesh and died as an atoning sacrifice for sin. For him there could be no separation of contemporary Christian belief and practice from its historical roots in the

[9] K. Wengst, *Häresie und Orthodoxie im Spiegel des ersten Johannesbriefes* (Gütersloh: Mohn, 1976), gives the latest defence of this view.

[10] For the theological importance of this doctrine see D. M. Baillie, *God was in Christ* (Faber, 1948), pp. 96–98.

[11] I. H. Marshall, *op. cit.*, pp. 99–108.

earthly manifestation of the Word or Son in Jesus in fleshly form. The concept of incarnation fundamentally shapes the Christology of the Johannine Epistles and forms the key idea around which John's other statements can be logically organized.

IV

Within the Pauline writings Philippians 2:6–11 is a passage which is often regarded as expressing an earlier formulation of Christian faith about Jesus, although this view is by no means firmly established.[12] The passage speaks of One who was in the form of God, but emptied himself, taking the form of a servant, being born in the likeness of men, and being found in human form. The word 'flesh' is not used here, but the equivalent term 'man' is used. A Being who was in the form of God became in likeness and appearance as a man.

Two different views have been taken of this statement. On the one hand, J. D. G. Dunn follows a number of scholars in arguing that the passage contrasts Jesus with Adam and refers to the way in which the man Jesus rejected the temptation to which Adam fell prey but rather took on himself the lot of fallen Adam. There is no reference to pre-existence or incarnation. On the other hand, S. Kim defends the more traditional interpretation of the passage as a reference to the act of choice of a pre-existent Being in becoming man and submitting to death.[13] For Kim the starting-point of Paul's thought is his conviction, born of his experience at his conversion, that he saw the exalted Christ in glory as the image of God; it was from this experience that he came to see Christ as the Last Adam and also as personified Wisdom. In the light of the total evidence from Paul's writings adduced by Kim there seems to be no reason to deny the traditional interpretation of Philippians 2:6–11 and adopt Dunn's view unless there are convincing reasons for excluding the former possibility and preferring the latter. But Dunn's case is not compelling.[14] In particular, his interpretation does not do justice to the force of the recapitulatory phrase 'and being found in form as man' (Phil. 2:8) which is very odd if it refers to a person who had never been anything else but a man; again the *contrast* clearly expressed between 'being in the form of God' and 'becoming in the form of men' is extremely odd if the contrast is between two stages in the career of a man. We accept, therefore, the traditional view of the passage.

The fact that Christ is said to have become *like* a man is not to be taken to

---

[12] For Pauline authorship of the hymn see S. Kim, *The Origin of Paul's Gospel* (Tübingen: J. C. B. Mohr, 1981), pp. 147–149.

[13] J. D. G. Dunn, *op. cit.*, pp. 114–121; S. Kim, *op. cit.*, ch. 6.

[14] See N. T. Wright's review in *Churchman* 95, no. 2, 1981, pp. 170–172.

mean that the Being merely took on the outward form of a man, but rather to indicate that in becoming a man he did not cease to be what he originally was. To say that the Being was transformed into a man would have been misleading. In order to become like a man he had to empty himself, a verb which is best taken to refer to the abandonment of the glorious and lordly prerogatives which go along with equality with God in order to take on the humble form of a servant and to die. The point is, not that Christ gave up any divine attributes, but simply that he did not behave as one who was equal with God might have been expected to behave, but as a humble servant.

Our modern tendency is to insist that Jesus was every bit a man, just the same as one of us. This may perhaps cause us to do less than justice to the New Testament representation of him as primarily the Son of God who took on the form of man. Where modern discussion emphasizes the fullness of his humanity, the New Testament emphasizes the fullness of his divinity.

Other Pauline passages speak of Jesus in similar terms. In 2 Corinthians 8:9 we have the same thought in a different terminology. Here again Dunn wishes to reinterpret the passage in terms of the man Jesus deliberately renouncing his spiritual communion with God in order to endure the 'poverty' of desolation on the cross for our sakes.[15] But Dunn ignores the way in which heavenly glory can be described in terms of riches (Phil. 4:19; *cf.* Eph. 1:18; 3:16; Col. 1:27), and this provides the more obvious background for Paul's statement.

Galatians 4:4 states that God sent his Son, born of a woman. Similarly, in Romans 8:3 God sent his own Son in the likeness of sinful flesh. Both statements are taken by Dunn to refer simply to the oneness of Jesus with the human race so that he might deliver mankind from bondage and sin and grant them his own sonship in exchange; the language of 'sending' is like that in Mark 12:6 and need not refer to pre-existence – indeed, it is unlikely to do so, argues Dunn, since these statements are soteriological and do not give the necessary theological backing for presenting the novel idea of incarnation to Paul's readers.[16] But this reinterpretation does not do justice to the texts. In his earliest Epistles Paul assumes that the exalted Jesus is on a par with the Father in a way which suggests that a lofty Christology formed part of his missionary preaching and catechetical instruction. To say that God sent his *Son, born* of a woman, suggests a different 'field of meaning' for 'sent' from that in Mark 12:6. Further, as Dunn admits, Galatians 4:4 contains language similar to that used in Wisdom 9:10 about the pre-existent figure of Wisdom. Even if this passage contains nothing more than a literary personification of Wisdom, there

---

[15] J. D. G. Dunn, *op. cit.*, pp. 121–123.
[16] *Ibid.*, pp. 36–44.

was nothing to prevent Paul using it to express the real pre-existence of the Son of God. Again, if Dunn's view is correct, it raises problems as to the point of time at which the Son of God came into existence for Paul. The background of Jewish thought about heavenly intermediaries argues strongly against the possibility that the coming into existence of the Son of God and the birth of Jesus (still less his resurrection) were simultaneous.

The evidence, then, favours the view that for Paul the Son of God existed before his earthly manifestation through his birth as a man. It is against this background of thought that the use of the term 'flesh' in Romans 8:3 takes on significance. In the New Testament generally 'flesh' is the physical substance of which human beings and animals are made; it is variously associated with bones and blood and sometimes contrasted with spirit. It is the stuff of which we are made and thus indicates our corporeality; to be flesh is the opposite of being a ghost or a spirit (Lk. 24:39). In this sense the term is ethically neutral, although it conveys the ideas of physical corruptibility and mortality. But, since the body, made of flesh, is the seat of passions and desires which can lead a person into sin, the term 'flesh' came to be used, especially by Paul, in an ethically bad sense, so that 'to live according to the flesh' is Pauline terminology for living a sinful life in disobedience to God. In Romans 8:3 Paul makes it clear that he is thinking of the flesh as that aspect of man which is prone to sinfulness, and he emphasizes that it was in the likeness of this flesh that God's own Son came in order that he might condemn sin in the flesh. Since elsewhere Paul makes it quite clear that Jesus himself did not sin, we are right to take this verse to mean that he assumed a nature that was like our human sinful nature, and yet did not himself sin (2 Cor. 5:21).[17]

We find the same thought in Colossians 1:22 where Paul states that the One who was in the image of God and through whom all things were created reconciled us to God *in his body of flesh* by death. He had a fully physical, human body, and it was in this incarnate form that he died.[18] The reference to this physical body would be uncalled for if Jesus were simply a man; the phrase is meaningful only as a way of emphasizing the fact that the One described in the preceding 'hymn' became incarnate in order to die on the cross. Further on in the same letter Christ is said to be the One in whom the whole fullness of deity dwells bodily (Col. 2:9). The tense here is present, indicating that the reference

[17] 'While the Son of God truly assumed *sarx hamartias*, He never became *sarx hamartias* and nothing more, nor even *sarx hamartias* indwelt by the Holy Spirit and nothing more (as a Christian might be described as being), but always remained Himself.' C. E. B. Cranfield, *The Epistle to the Romans* 1 (T. & T. Clark, 1975), p.381.

[18] The same thought appears in Eph. 2:16 where Christ reconciled us to God *in one body* through the cross.

is to the heavenly Lord. Over against any suggestion that the power of God was scattered among several beings Paul emphasizes that it is all to be found in Christ, and in him in bodily fashion, *i.e.* assuming a bodily form. Here, then, we certainly have the concept of incarnation, of all the nature and power of God being present in a human person.[19] Neither Colossians 1:22 nor 2:9 taken by itself necessarily points to the personal pre-existence of the divine Being incarnate in Jesus, but this thought is demanded by the language of the 'hymn' in 1:15–20; here it is extremely difficult to take the language to refer to anything other than the personal activity of the One who is the image of God in creation; Dunn's attempt to make the wording mean merely that the power which God exercised in creation is now fully revealed and embodied in Christ is quite unconvincing.[20]

It is clear that Paul uses incarnational language of Jesus; he uses the actual word 'flesh' to refer to the manner of the Son's presence in Jesus, and he identifies the Son as the personal agent of God in creation. But was this a central concept for Paul? The following points may be made.

First, Paul rarely discusses the person of Jesus as a topic in its own right. Not until we come to Colossians was this one of the points at issue between Paul and his readers. It follows that the amount of material in Paul which is directly Christological is scanty; Paul's Christological statements are made almost casually and implicitly in discussions of other topics.

Second, although Paul does not use the term 'Son' very often, it is a major Christological term for him. He uses it when he wishes to make important assertions about Jesus and especially to express his relationship to the Father.[21] When he does not use this term, he speaks of Jesus as the first-born of God or as being in the divine image.

Third, Paul thinks of the Son as coming into the world from the Father and as having been active in the creation of the world.[22]

Fourth, Paul speaks of Jesus as the Son of God and as a man who was born into a human family, with a human mother, physically descended from a human ancestor, David, and having human brothers. Paul does not stress the

---

[19] Col. 2:10 adds 'and you have come to fulness of life in him' (literally, 'and in him you are made full'), but the fact that Paul can write in such terms of believers in no way weakens the force of what he says in the previous verse about Christ or suggests that he sees no difference between Christ and Christians.

[20] J. D. G. Dunn, *op. cit.,* pp. 187–194.

[21] M. Hengel, *The Son of God* (SCM, 1976), pp. 7–15.

[22] 1 Cor. 8:6 should probably be taken in this sense, despite the attempt by J. D. G. Dunn, *op. cit.,* pp. 179–183, to deny that Christ is here being identified with a pre-existent being who was active at creation.

humanity of Jesus as such; he can simply assume it. Where he does direct attention to it is when he draws contrasts between the fatal results of Adam's sin for the human race and the beneficial results of Jesus' act of righteousness, and here he contrasts the one man Adam and 'that one man Jesus Christ' (Rom. 5:15, 17–19). The thought is hammered home by deliberate repetition, and Dunn is right to stress that for Paul the contrast between Adam and Christ was of central significance. Similarly, Paul contrasts the way in which the first man Adam merely became a living being, whereas the last Adam, the second man, became a source of life for others (1 Cor. 15:46-48). Here, however, it is plain that Jesus is more than just a man, for he is a life-giving spirit, the man from heaven. This phrase incidentally shows that for Paul, as for John, the heavenly Lord remains a man.

Fifth, this tension between Jesus as the Son of God and as the second man finds its resolution in a doctrine of incarnation, that is, that the Son of God has come into the world as a man. This suggests that here we have an organizing principle which not only enables us to make sense of Paul's theology but also is of theological importance to him. Paul emphasizes both that it was as a man that Jesus died in solidarity with us and at the same time that it was God who was active in Christ reconciling the world to himself.

V

The same understanding of Jesus is to be found in the Pastoral Epistles, although these writings have an ecclesiastical and pastoral concern and are not directly theological.[23] Incarnational language is found in 1 Timothy 3:16 which describes how 'he was manifested in the flesh'. Although no subject is expressed (the AV 'God was manifest' follows a late text), the language is based on that used elsewhere to describe how the Son of God was incarnate. The thought is of an epiphany in human form, and the implication is that a divine or heavenly subject is intended. The reference is certainly to the earthly life of Jesus and not to his resurrection appearances.[24] In the light of this verse the saying that Christ Jesus came into the world to save sinners (1 Tim. 1:15) probably also implies the pre-existence of the Saviour. The writer also takes over the common Christian belief in the human descent of Jesus from David

---

[23] The Pastoral Epistles are treated separately from the other Pauline Epistles in view of the doubts of many scholars that they stem directly from Paul; see, however, D. Guthrie, *The Pastoral Epistles* (Tyndale Press, 1957) for a defence of their Pauline authorship.

[24] See R. H. Gundry, 'The Form, Meaning and Background of the Hymn quoted in 1 Timothy 3:16', in W. W. Gasque and R. P. Martin (eds.), *Apostolic History and the Gospel* (Paternoster Press, 1970), pp. 203–222.

(2 Tim. 2:8). The heavenly and earthly origins of the Saviour can thus be mentioned on different occasions without any sense of conflict or incongruity. The factor binding these two aspects of his person together is the manifestation of the Son of God in the flesh.

Hebrews also teaches both the divine sonship and the humanity of Jesus. The pre-existent, creative activity of the Son is dominant in the opening verses of the book (1:1–3) and is quickly followed by a description of how he himself took the same nature of flesh and blood as the people whom he came to deliver. He had to be made, says the author, like his brothers in every respect. The Son experienced 'the days of his flesh' and shared in human suffering on the cross before being exalted to heaven. The pattern of thought is the same as we have found elsewhere, but there is an increased stress on the suffering of Jesus in the flesh and his consequent qualification to be sympathetic to mankind in its weakness. For the author it is important that the Saviour is both the Son, God's final messenger to mankind, and also truly man, able to stand alongside his brothers. Since the Son is regarded as pre-existent, his entry into the world is by partaking of flesh and blood, *i.e.* by incarnation.[25]

Finally, in our survey of the Epistles we may note that 1 Peter states that Christ suffered and died in the flesh (3:18; 4:1). The writer also speaks of him as One who was predestined before the foundation of the world, but made manifest at the end of the times (1:20). This appears to be a remnant of incarnational language; Peter does not lay stress on it, but simply makes use of a stereotyped traditional terminology which reflects an existing incarnational theology.[26]

VI

We have found substantial evidence of incarnational language and thinking in the Epistles. But what of the Synoptic Gospels and Acts? Although the Gospels are essentially accounts of the earthly life of Jesus, nevertheless they are written

---

[25] J. D. G. Dunn again attempts to argue that in Hebrews the pre-existence of the Son is 'perhaps more of an idea and purpose in the mind of God than of a personal divine being' (p. 56) – in other words, Hebrews displays an understanding of pre-existence which is more Platonic than Johannine. When Hebrews uses Wisdom language in 1:1–3, 'it is the act and power of God which properly speaking is what pre-exists; Christ is not so much the pre-existent act and power of God as its eschatological embodiment' (p. 209). This impersonal type of understanding seems very alien to the biblical understanding of God as personal, quite apart from imposing a very artificial interpretation upon the biblical text.

[26] Strictly speaking, 1 Peter does not speak of the pre-existence of Christ, but rather of God's predestination of him as a person to fulfil certain functions.

from a post-resurrection standpoint and may be expected to reflect the church's theological understanding of Jesus. Is this expectation justified?

There is frankly little that can be called incarnational, in the sense of teaching the incarnation of a pre-existent Being, in Mark. The writer presents an account of the ministry and death of Jesus in which a key issue is whether he is the Messiah of Jewish expectation, a ruler descended from David. He shows how Jesus understood himself in terms of the Son of man, but in my view none of the statements made about the Son of man are concerned with his pre-existence or incarnation, unless we are entitled to assume that the phrase itself must have carried these associations. [27] Jesus is also declared to be the Son of God, and clearly this is a very significant term for Mark, but again the title is not used in a way which demands that we think of pre-existence. Mark's Gospel in effect asks: How can this man be the Son of God? It does not solve the problem.

It is different with the other Synoptic Gospels, both of which preface their accounts of the ministry with stories of the birth of Jesus. The account in Luke, which is, one might say, logically prior to that in Matthew, is concerned to show how Mary's son would be a holy child, the Son of God, and does so by means of the annunciation narrative which indicates that through the coming of the Holy Spirit upon the virgin Mary her child would be God's Son. Here we have clearly a doctrine of incarnation, of the physical birth of the Son of God; nothing, however, is said about the pre-existence of the Son. Matthew's account has nothing to add at this point; he justifies the title 'God with us' (Immanuel) for Jesus in that he was Mary's son, conceived by the Holy Spirit.

As for Acts, here Jesus is a man, anointed by God with the Spirit and appointed by him as judge of all men (2:22; 10:38; 17:31). For Acts, Jesus is a man whose life follows a career ordained by God which leads him through crucifixion to exaltation. At the same time this Jesus is God's Son (9:20; 13:33), and it is because he is God's Son, the Holy One, that he does not see corruption but is raised up to new life (2:27). Yet how Jesus can be both man and God's Son is not discussed in Acts. This silence may partly reveal the lack of reflection on it in the evangelistic discourses of the early church, but in the context of Luke's work as a whole it is more probable that the explanation given

---

[27] For a detailed discussion of the pre-existence of the Son of Man see J. D. G. Dunn, *op. cit.*, ch. 3; in opposition to R. G. Hamerton-Kelly, *Pre-existence, Wisdom and the Son of Man* (CUP, 1973), he concludes that the Son of man is not pre-existent in the Synoptic Gospels. I am not sure that we can so easily reject the possibility that the Evangelists and their readers may have interpreted the Son of man as an individual, pre-existent figure (as in 4 Ezra and 1 Enoch) who came from God into the world, but this thought is not made explicit in the Synoptic Gospels (as it is in John).

at the outset of the two-volume work in the birth narrative is meant to provide the background for subsequent Christological statements: Jesus is both the Son of God and the earthly descendant of David, a real man, in virtue of his Spirit-conception in the womb of Mary.

VII

We must now try to draw some conclusions from this material and see what further questions it raises.

1. We have found that the concept of incarnation, *i.e.* that Jesus Christ is the Son of God made flesh, is the principle of Christological explanation in the writings of John, the writings of Paul including the Pastoral Epistles, the Epistle to the Hebrews and 1 Peter. The view that it is found merely on the fringe of the New Testament is a complete travesty of the facts. In the writers who are concerned with theological reflection about the person of Jesus, incarnational thinking is of central importance and forms indeed the organizing principle of their Christology. Moreover, in the case of these writers we have found good reason to believe that for them the Son of God who became incarnate was a pre-existent Being. Here we have found ourselves compelled to part company with the conclusions of J. D. G. Dunn who argues that much of the apparently incarnational language refers not to a pre-existent Being becoming man but rather to the creative and saving power of God, given literary personification by Jewish writers in such concepts as Wisdom and Word, now being fully embodied in Jesus so that he represents all that God is in his relationship to mankind.[28]

2. Such incarnational thinking begins with the pre-existent Son of God and states that he became man or became flesh. It thus deals with the question of how the Son of God became man rather than how a particular man, Jesus, could be the Son of God. Thus this way of thinking arose in a community where Jesus was already confessed as the Son of God. In incarnational theology the Son of God is the subject and Jesus is, as it were, the predicate. The direction of thought gives a Christology 'from above' rather than one 'from below'.[29] It is

---

[28] See especially J. D. G. Dunn, *op. cit.*, pp.211f. I am very conscious that my brief comments in this essay cannot do justice to the detailed arguments of this highly stimulating book.

[29] For this way of putting things see W. Pannenberg, *Jesus – God and Man* (SCM, 1964). The statement above is not meant to suggest that a modern approach to Christology 'from below' is wrong; it is only when Jesus has been identified as the Son of God that it becomes possible to look at things 'from above' – but this step was taken in the earliest days of the church before our written documents.

presupposed that Jesus is the Son of God – an assumption which Paul (for example) takes for granted and never attempts to prove, and which has a firm foundation in the teaching of Jesus, whose filial consciousness is the probable starting-point for the church's thinking.

3. Over against this type of thinking we have that of the Synoptic Gospels and Acts. They share the conviction that Jesus is the Son of God, and indeed provide the evidence from his teaching which led to this confession, but they have nothing corresponding to 'the Word became flesh'. For Matthew and Luke Jesus is Son of God in virtue of his birth by the Spirit; Mark does not raise the question. This poses the problem of whether the New Testament contains two alternative and possibly mutually exclusive explanations of the person of Jesus in terms of incarnation and Spirit-conception. The issue is sharpened by the fact that Jesus does not appear in the Synoptic Gospels to have any consciousness of his pre-existence.

If these two explanations are mutually exclusive, the conclusion might be that both are mythological statements of the mystery of the person of Jesus. It is in fact this kind of suggestion which has led some scholars to argue that incarnational language is not to be taken seriously, still less literally, but is merely one – dispensable – mythological expression of early Christian thinking about Jesus.

The question of the status of incarnational language is too large to be discussed here,[30] and we shall remain on an exegetical level. The basic point that needs to be made is that at least some of the New Testament writers did not regard the two types of approach as mutually exclusive. Thus Paul, who is clearly an incarnationalist, knows and affirms that Jesus was born of a woman. Whatever be the truth in the view of some scholars that this phrase betrays a knowledge of the virgin birth,[31] it is unquestionable that Paul believed that Jesus was born of a human mother, and that he did not simply appear in the world like a Greek god turning himself into a human messenger. The same can be said of John who has the figure of Mary, the mother of Jesus, in his Gospel,

---

[30] It is one of the merits of Dunn's book that he demonstrates conclusively that Christian incarnational thinking was not derived from mythological concepts and is therefore not itself mythological in character. However, he goes too far in defending incarnationalism against this charge by reducing the content of the biblical statements to such propositions as that Jesus fully embodies the creative power and purpose of God. Dunn comes near to denying that divine sonship is a personal category.

[31] J. G. Machen, *The Virgin Birth of Christ* (James Clarke, 1930), pp.259–263, holds that we cannot tell from the evidence whether or not Paul knew of the virgin birth. Some Roman Catholic authors take a more positive view of the evidence; see J. McHugh, *The Mother of Jesus in the New Testament* (Darton, Longman and Todd, 1975), pp.273–277.

and notes the sarcastic Jewish comment '*We* were not born of fornication' (8:41), which may be used with irony by John to express that he and his readers knew otherwise about Jesus. John also knows that the Christ was to be descended from David. The tradition of Jesus' human birth and descent from David is thus entirely compatible with an incarnational understanding of him. Indeed, a thinker who held to incarnationalism would surely see nothing incompatible in Spirit-conception, and indeed is extremely likely to have accepted some such explanation (if he thought about it at all) of how the man Jesus could be the incarnate Son of God. If, then, we start from incarnationalism, there is no great problem about the Spirit-conception of Jesus.

If we start from the other side, from the Spirit-conception and virgin birth, the way is perhaps not so clear. But so far as the birth-stories are concerned, the problem may be that a different question is being asked. Here the centre of interest or starting-point is the child who is to be born. Mary is about to bear a child without having had intercourse with her husband, and the question is: How can this be? The answer is that she is to be the mother of a child who is to be God's Son, and this is to be accomplished by the activity of the Spirit. The question is 'from below': how can this baby be the Son of God? The incarnational type of question is absent.

Despite the lack of interest in this question the Synoptic Gospels certainly present Jesus as the Son of God and they guide us to the centre of his self-consciousness as such. It is precisely this self-consciousness which, even in the absence of any consciousness of pre-existence, makes it unsatisfactory to think of Jesus as merely the embodiment of God's creative and saving power and which drives us on to an incarnational understanding of him as the personal Son of God. The evidence in the Synoptic Gospels not only fits an incarnational understanding of Jesus but positively cries out for it.

4. It is here in all probability that we are to find the origin of the concept of the incarnation. The nearest concept that we have in Judaism is that of Wisdom coming to dwell among mankind. In Sirach 24 Wisdom is personified and describes how she is the word which was spoken by God and dwelt in heaven. She looked for a place in which to settle, and the Creator commanded her: 'Make your home in Jacob; find your heritage in Israel'. So Wisdom settled in Jerusalem. Later in the chapter it is made clear that 'All this is the covenant-book of God Most High, the law which Moses enacted to be the heritage of the assemblies of Jacob'. This shows that Wisdom is a personification of the Torah. Similarly, in 1 Enoch 42 we are told that 'Wisdom went forth to make her dwelling among the children of men, and found no dwelling place. Wisdom returned to her place, and took her seat among the angels.' There is, however, here nothing that resembles the idea of incarnation. The idea of

Wisdom entering into holy souls and making them God's friends and prophets (Wisdom 7:27) is not comparable. At best we can say that language used of Wisdom has come to be used of Jesus.

We shall do better to seek the origin of the doctrine in the church's knowledge of the filial consciousness of Jesus. The recognition that Jesus was the Son of God was the starting-point for reflection which made use of Wisdom and Logos language. At the same time the resurrection of Jesus and the church's understanding of this as his exaltation to the right hand of God exercised a decisive effect in leading to the interpretation of his person in the most exalted terms. Here the comments of C. F. D. Moule on the significance of Jesus' 'post-existence' are extremely important.[32]

5. The theological importance of the incarnation cannot be developed here. On the one hand, the divine Sonship of Jesus is crucial in establishing his role as the representative of God, demonstrating his active, sin-bearing love. On the other hand, his real humanity is equally crucial in that through it he is joined to mankind, bearing human sin as man's substitute and conveying to mankind a share in his own personal relationship with God. He became what we are in order that we might become what he is. But there would have been no point in his becoming what we are if he was not what he is, the eternal Son of God, God incarnate reconciling the world to himself.

[32] C. F. D. Moule, *The Origin of Christology* (CUP, 1977).

THE WORSHIP OF JESUS:
A NEGLECTED FACTOR
IN CHRISTOLOGICAL DEBATE?[1]

R. T. France

The ordinary Christian, and indeed non-Christian, who makes no pretence to theological expertise may well look back to 1963 as the beginning of an era of change; the publication of John Robinson's *Honest to God* in that year made it vividly clear that some leading theologians did not believe Jesus to be more than human, though of course at the top of the human ladder. Perhaps more surprising to those not in the know was the fact that official reaction to that book was muted and equivocal. Did this mean then that Christian belief in the divinity of Jesus had become an optional extra? From that time on theology dropped out of the headlines again, until in 1977 the title, if not the contents, of *The Myth of God Incarnate* revived public interest and showed that the spirit of *Honest to God* was still alive. About the same time a television series presented by one of the authors of that book set out a radically reduced estimate of Jesus to a wider audience than *Honest to God* ever reached, and more recently the same author has produced another book with a title designed to shock, *Taking Leave of God*[2], which undercuts the question whether Jesus is God by questioning

---

[1] Donald Guthrie will recognize this essay as a slightly revised version of a paper read at the London Bible College in November 1980 as the Laing Lecture for that year and, as is customary, subsequently published in *Vox Evangelica* 12, 1981. It was on that occasion that he took the opportunity to suggest to me the possibility of joining him as colleague and eventual successor. I dare to hope that that personal association may excuse the impropriety of offering in his *Festschrift* what is really a second-hand article, which cannot even claim to be antique. Some of the material herein is a development of parts of a more wide-ranging paper presented at the 1980 conference of the Fellowship of European Evangelical Theologians at Altenkirchen, West Germany, and subsequently published under the title 'The Uniqueness of Christ' in *Churchman* 95, 1981, pp.200-217.

[2] D. Cupitt, *Taking Leave of God* (SCM, 1980). See an interesting immediate review by David L. Edwards in the *Church Times* of 3 October 1980.

whether there is such a thing as 'God' for Jesus to be!

But behind the headlines a vast and complex debate has been going on, involving theologians of all types, exegetes, biblical, systematic, and historical theologians, philosophers and apologists. No part of the traditional structure of Christology has remained undisturbed. One of the most popular whipping-boys has been the classical formula of the Council of Chalcedon, which proclaimed Jesus as 'truly God and truly man,... in two natures, without confusion, without change, without division, without separation'. It has been attacked as inadequate, as dry and scholastic, but above all as incredible or indeed meaningless to the ordinary man today.

I do not intend here to try to defend the Chalcedonian Definition, nor to enter directly into the modern Christological debate as such, but to go behind the patristic distinctions and the Greek and Latin tags to the basic question of why the whole exercise was necessary in the first place. For if some of our modern theologians are right there is not much point in discussing just how the two natures could be combined in one person: there are not two natures to combine. The divine Jesus, we are told, is a myth which early Christian piety superimposed on a purely human figure, an expression of reverence which would have seemed preposterous, even blasphemous, to Jesus himself and to his earliest followers. By introducing this unnecessary and, to us, unintelligible category of personal divinity into their assessment of Jesus, they created the gigantic red herring of incarnation which has kept the theologians talking ever since. If only we could get back behind that pious mythology to the real Jesus, we could forget about *homoousios* and Chalcedon and Monophysitism, and start talking the language of modern man.

This scenario, which is fundamental to much current debate on Christology, depends on the assumption of a radical discontinuity at some point between the original Jesus and the alien 'God incarnate' character which was superimposed on him. This is what C. F. D. Moule dubs the 'evolutionary' approach.[3] It supposes that 'when the Christian movement spread beyond Palestinian soil, it began to come under the influence of non-Semitic Saviour-cults and to assimilate some of their ideas'. The worship of Jesus as a divine being thus owed its origin to influences foreign to Jesus' own environment. It thus constitutes the 'evolution' of a new species.

In contrast to this approach, Professor Moule advocates a 'developmental' view, which accepts a difference in scale between the Christology of earliest Christianity and its later forms, but sees the latter as 'attempts to describe what was already there from the beginning'. 'They are analogous not so much to the

---

[3] C. F. D. Moule, *The Origin of Christology* (CUP, 1977), p.2 and throughout the introduction.

emergence of a new species, as to the unfolding (if you like) of flower from bud and the growth of fruit from flower.' On this view incarnational Christology was not a red herring. It was the inevitable consequence of what Jesus was and said and did.

I am not convinced that Moule's evolution/development terminology is the most lucid, particularly for those to whom 'evolution' is a word with emotive connotations in another context, but the dichotomy which he discerns among Christological approaches is true and fundamental. Let me, then, declare myself unashamedly a 'developmentalist'. It is my hope in this essay to indicate some of the evidence for this view in a study of the phenomenon which I have termed 'the worship of Jesus'. But first a few comments on one of the basic characteristics of the 'evolutionary' approach.

The search for 'parallels'

In 1961 the Jewish New Testament scholar Samuel Sandmel gave a presidential address to the Society for Biblical Literature the title of which has been remembered and welcomed by many who never heard or read the address. It was called 'Parallelomania'.[4] It focused in an attack on that crutch of New Testament scholars, Strack and Billerbeck's *Kommentar*. Sandmel questioned the value and relevance of collecting 'parallels' to New Testament passages and ideas from a wide range of Jewish sources of different periods and characters.

Sandmel's salutary warning is perhaps even more relevant to much current Christological discussion than it was in 1961. The tendency is to look for 'parallels' to titles like 'Son of God' or to concepts of incarnation or pre-existence, or the attribution of divine honours to a man, and to regard these parallels as *explanations* of the New Testament data, as showing the sources from which these ideas crept into Christian language, and so precipitated the 'evolution' from the teaching of Jesus and the faith of his early followers to the incarnational theology of the later New Testament writings. The search for parallels extends enthusiastically far beyond the Jewish sources questioned by Sandmel, and draws in material from all over the Mediterranean world and even beyond.

Now I would not dispute for a moment the value of the fullest possible knowledge of the cultural background within which the New Testament came into being, in order to help us to interpret it correctly in its own context rather than on the basis of later Christian tradition. Some of the parallels produced are of immense value in this task, as, for instance, anyone who has had to disentangle the significance of John's *Logos* language will know. But 'parallels'

---

[4] Published in *JBL* 81, 1962, pp. 1–13.

can be abused, and I would suggest a few cautions.

1. *Are the parallels real?* A mere coincidence of words or imagery in itself proves nothing, particularly if those words are used in a quite different way in the supposedly parallel texts. Sometimes 'parallels' are claimed which are so partial as to be worthless. Thus, in the search for Graeco-Roman parallels to the idea of incarnation, to quote such myths as that of Philemon and Baucis (where the gods merely appear in human form) or of Heracles (a mortal who was taken up to heaven to be an immortal)[5] is of little value, since while these myths might provide parallels to respectively docetic and adoptionist views, they contain nothing relating to the New Testament idea of incarnation. There is no real parallel here.

2. *Do the 'parallels' come from a relevant culture?* C. H. Talbert's recent book *What is a Gospel?* is essentially an attempt to fit the Christian Gospels into the milieu of Graeco-Roman biographical writing. In the process he suggests how the Gospel material would appear to 'the average Mediterranean man-in-the-street', 'a Mediterranean man', 'a Hellenistic person'.[6] But the prior question must surely be whether the Gospels were written for such a person, whether their materials were developed in a milieu where his Graeco-Roman cultural background would have any influence, or even be known. The culture in which Christianity arose was a mixed one indeed, but can we assume that the average Galilean was familiar with Ovid? A parallel, however real, is of no importance if it comes from a cultural milieu with which the New Testament writers are unlikely to have been familiar. Thus when Talbert produces his one example of the idea of pre-existence applied to an 'immortal', it turns out to be from Plutarch's account of Romulus; on this basis 'a Mediterranean person who heard Jesus depicted in this way would find it difficult to avoid understanding him in terms of the mythology of immortals'.[7] Maybe (though how many Mediterranean men-in-the-street were familiar with Plutarch?), but what has this to do with the development of the idea of pre-existence in (and before) the writings of *Paul?*[8]

---

[5] See especially C. H. Talbert, *What is a Gospel?* (Fortress, 1977), chapter 2, for a careful setting out of the material about such 'immortals'. A detailed response is included in section IV of D. E. Aune, 'The Problem of the Genre of the Gospels' in R. T. France and D. Wenham (eds.), *Gospel Perspectives* 2 (JSOT Press, Sheffield, 1981), pp.9–60.

[6] C. H. Talbert, *op. cit.*, pp. 39, 41, 42.

[7] *Ibid.*, p.40.

[8] *Cf.* J. Drury, *Tradition & Design in Luke's Gospel* (Darton, Longman and Todd, 1976), pp.27–30 for a similar assumption that the world of Aesop and of Apollonius is the right milieu in which to set the development of NT Christology. For a more sober assessment of the relevance of Graeco-Roman parallels, see M. Hengel, *The Son of God* (SCM, 1976), pp.23-41.

3. *Are the parallels significant?* A similarity of wording or indeed of concept may be found to be real and to be from a relevant milieu, but it may still be of no significance. Thus if, for instance, two Jewish writers (*e.g.* Ben Sira and Paul) each make use of the same Old Testament idea, this is evidence of their coming from the same cultural milieu, but not of any contact or dependence between them. Some of the similarities between the language of Qumran and that of the New Testament come under the same suspicion; are they perhaps evidence simply that both sets of writings belong to first-century Palestine, rather than indicating any relationship of dependence? The similarities are real, but are they significant?

4. *Is a parallel necessarily a source or influence?* This is a development of the last point. It seems sometimes to be assumed that when you have discovered a parallel to a New Testament idea which is earlier in time than the New Testament writing (or later in time, but apparently indicative of a continuing theme), you have thereby 'explained' this feature in the New Testament. The earlier is assumed to be the source of the later, or at least a dominant influence on it. At its worst this approach can depict Christianity as a sponge which soaked up whatever religious ideas were present in its environment, itself contributing nothing but a fresh synthesis of second-hand ideas. Indeed such a view is almost inevitable on the 'evolutionary' approach to Christology, for it makes the determining factor in Christological development not anything which was internal to Christianity or derivable from Jesus, but the more sophisticated religious climate of the world around.[9]

But non-Christian parallels, even if shown to be real and significant, are not necessarily the *source* of Christian religious ideas. Martin Hengel, having set out various Jewish parallels to New Testament 'Son of God' language, helpfully refers to them as 'building material which would be used by the early church in the conception of its christological outlines'.[10] The church had something new and unparalleled to say; Christianity drew its essential message not from surrounding religious influences but from the fact of Jesus. In constructing their theology the early Christians (and indeed Jesus himself) necessarily used as 'building material' the ideas and language of the culture to which they belonged, both to give form to their own growing perception of the significance of Jesus and also to present their message in a way their contemporaries could

[9] A remarkable recent example of this approach is Michael Goulder's chapter 'The Two Roots of the Christian Myth' in J. Hick (ed), *The Myth of God Incarnate* (SCM, 1977), pp.64–86, where he derives the developed Christology of the NT primarily from 'the Samaritan gnostical myth', a source which has escaped most other writers on Christology altogether.

[10] *The Son of God*, p.57.

understand. Traditional language might be drawn on sometimes by way of contrast, to show how Jesus differed from existing religious ideas, sometimes approvingly, to show how he developed and fulfilled them. But all the time the determining factor was Jesus. Sandmel puts the point clearly: 'Only by a supposition of such distinctiveness can I account to myself for the origin and growth of Christianity and its ultimate separation from Judaism.... I am not prepared to believe that the writers of Christian literature only copied sources and never did anything original and creative.'[11] Given such an understanding, while parallels may usefully be studied as 'building materials', we should be very cautious of regarding them as sources.

An example may be taken from the Jewish traditions about Wisdom. The idea of Wisdom as a semi-personified mediator, God's agent in creation, who came from God and made her home among men, to be the channel of God's guidance and his blessings, is a prominent feature in Jewish wisdom literature from Proverbs to Ben Sira and the Wisdom of Solomon, and it is widely accepted that wisdom-language has been an element in the fashioning of New Testament Christology.[12] But when one turns to a specific text where verbal echoes are clear, such as Matthew 11:28–30 with its echoes of Ben Sira 51:23–27 (*cf.* 6:24–31), the difference of essential content is as clear as the indebtedness in regard to words and concepts. Ben Sira calls men to come and learn from him and to take up Wisdom's yoke; Jesus also calls men to come and learn from him, but the yoke he offers is his own. Ben Sira has found for himself by 'labouring a little' the rest which Wisdom gives; Jesus himself gives rest to those who labour. Ben Sira can only point to a mediator other than himself; what is lacking in his call, and central to that of Jesus, is precisely the idea of *incarnation*, the Wisdom of God as a man among men. Important as the 'parallels' in the wisdom-tradition are, none of them offers a *source* for this central and radically new concept of New Testament Christology.

Parallels, then, must be used with caution. Even when they are real and significant, and come from a relevant culture, they still leave us with the question why the Christian writers felt it appropriate to use these particular models in setting out their estimate of Jesus. The 'evolutionary' view suggests that the Christians transferred alien religious ideas to Jesus as if not to be outdone; if others have divine saviour-figures, so must we! I wonder about the psychology such a view implies, and how it squares up to what we know of early Christianity. Does the New Testament really suggest an earnest search for ever

---

[11] *JBL* 81, 1962, (n.4) p.4.

[12] See *e.g.* M. Hengel, *The Son of God,* pp.48–51 for a brief review of the material.

higher models from other religious traditions which might be appropriated and imposed on the purely human Jesus, or does it rather indicate a progressive grappling with the implications of what was already there in the traditions and experiences of his ministry and teaching, in which surrounding cultures may indeed have provided 'building materials', but for which the dynamic was internal to Christianity, a new and essentially unparalleled experience of God in Jesus? It is this latter reading of the New Testament evidence that I now wish to support.

The worship of Jesus

New Testament Christology is a complex study, and allows several different lines of approach, all in their own ways valid and illuminating.

We might start 'at the top', by discussing whether the New Testament calls Jesus 'God'.[13] We would then study a small number of passages where explicit God-language may be applied to Jesus. In that case we will find ourselves disappointed that in many cases the apparent direct attribution of divinity to Jesus melts away in the light of uncertainty about either the text, or the punctuation, or the syntax,[14] leaving us with no undisputed (or almost undisputed!) direct attribution of divinity to Jesus outside the opening and closing declarations of the Gospel of John (Jn. 1:1; 1:18;[15] 20:28).

Or we may focus our attention on the classic Christological passages of the New Testament which, without actually calling Jesus 'God' (except in John's prologue), present conscious theological reflection on his relationship with the Father. Passages such as John 1:1–18; Philippians 2:6–11; Colossians 1:15–20 (*cf.* 2:9); Hebrews 1:1–4 provide ample and rewarding scope for a study of some of the earliest deliberate Christological formulation, and are of course crucially important for any adequate discussion of New Testament Christology.

Thirdly we might take one of the most popular routes in recent discussion, a study of the titles applied to Jesus in the New Testament. This route has the advantage of taking us behind the formal statements to an important indicator of how Christians habitually thought and spoke of Jesus, and as such is an

---

[13] For some examples of this approach see A. W. Wainwright, *The Trinity in the NT* (SPCK, 1962), pp.53–74; R. E. Brown *Jesus: God and Man* (Chapman, 1968), pp.6–28.

[14] See *e.g.* Acts 20:28; Rom. 9:5; Gal. 2:20; Col. 2:2; 2 Thes. 1:12; Tit. 2:13; Heb. 1:8; Jas. 1:1; 2 Pet. 1:1; 1 Jn. 5:20.

[15] Reading *theos*, as surely we must since the publication of papyri 66 and 75; English versions have been slow to catch up with the consensus of textual scholars, but see now GNB and NIV. The textual history of Jn. 1:18 may be traced in a fascinating graphic form in J. Finegan, *Encountering New Testament Manuscripts* (SPCK, 1975), pp. 111–177 (summarized pp. 174-177).

invaluable complement to the study of more formal language.[16]

All these approaches are right and necessary, and all will be presupposed as parallel and complementary to the study which follows. But I believe we can and must go further back, to the underlying attitudes which made it appropriate for the New Testament Christians to use such titles as 'Lord' and 'Son of God', to work out their understanding of his eternal relationship with the Father in theological language, and ultimately to call him 'God'. All these forms of expression are, I believe, the outcrops of an underlying stratum which ran deep in the life and experience of Jesus' first followers, and which may be discerned in many incidental ways in the New Testament writings, a stratum which I have called 'the worship of Jesus'.

I am using 'worship' in a broad sense. My dictionary defines the noun as 'adoration paid, as to a god', and the verb as 'to pay divine honours to'. So I am not speaking only, or even primarily, of formal *acts* of worship, involving prayer and adoration, but of the attitude which treats Jesus as divine. This attitude will of course express itself in formal acts of worship, and these will be included in our study, but I want to consider more generally how the earliest Christians thought of Jesus, what was their experience of him. I want to suggest that to regard him as divine was not a late addition to Christian thought, but existed at least in embryo from the beginning, that the formal Christological language of the New Testament was not a new intellectual idea which then had to be translated into experience, but rather was the ultimate working out in theory of what was already present in Christian experience of Jesus.

In considering this subject one very obvious point must be emphasized: the earliest Christians were *Jews*. Monotheism was the hallmark of Judaism. To be a Jew was to be committed, often fanatically committed, to the maintenance of faith in only one God, in the face of a surrounding hellenistic culture which worshipped many gods, not to mention many semidivine heroes, and a deified emperor. Hellenism had made great inroads in Palestine, to be sure, but not to the extent of modifying the monotheistic fervour of the ordinarily religious Jews out of whom Jesus' first followers were drawn, still less that of the Pharisee, Saul of Tarsus. For a Jew then, as now, to speak of a man of his own times as divine was as impossible as it is for a Muslim to welcome the Christian doctrine of the Trinity or of Jesus as the Son of God. A docetic Christology might be acceptable, for the Old Testament provided sufficient precedent for

---

[16] A useful short introduction to the study of the titles of Jesus is by I. H. Marshall in *The Illustrated Bible Dictionary* (IVP, 1980), pp.771-780. *Cf.* more fully, his *The Origins of New Testament Christology* (IVP, 1976), chapters 4-7.

the appearance of God on earth, particularly in the anthropomorphic 'angel of Yahweh'. But this is poles apart from the idea of *incarnation*. If one thing was clear and undisputed about Jesus as he lived in Palestine, it was that he was truly human. Yet it was this real man whom his Jewish followers began to regard as divine and ultimately came to call explicitly 'God'. It is perhaps impossible for us, with nearly twenty centuries of familiarity with Christian doctrine, to grasp the shocking nature of this belief. But it is important to realize that no Jew would calmly listen to a man being described as divine, and it can only have been with the utmost reluctance that Jesus' Jewish followers, however great their respect and love for their leader, could be brought to use such language. We are told today that incarnational language is incredible and offensive to modern man; if he, with his cultural conditioning, cannot take it, how hard must it have been for first-century Jews to speak like this!

It is in this light that we must understand the fact, mentioned above, that the explicit use of God-language about Jesus is infrequent in the New Testament, and is concentrated in the later writings, and that hardly any such language has avoided textual surgery or syntactical ambiguity. It was such shocking language that, even when the beliefs underlying it were firmly established, it was easier, and perhaps more politic, to express these beliefs in less direct terms. The wonder is not that the New Testament so seldom describes Jesus as God, but that in such a milieu it does so at all. There must have been a very strong compulsion behind such a radical conversion of language.

What then was the driving force behind this remarkable development of thought which produced New Testament Christology and culminated in Chalcedonian orthodoxy? In a word, it was Jesus himself and the impact he made on his followers. New Testament Christology was the theoretical out-working of the prior attitude which I am calling 'the worship of Jesus'. We can now only trace this theme sketchily through some of the earlier strata of New Testament thought and life; its fuller development deserves more extended exposition than is possible here.[17]

[17] An important article by R. J. Bauckham, 'The Worship of Jesus in Apocalyptic Christianity', *NTS* 27, 1980/81, pp.322-341, undergirds the argument of this essay with special reference to the apocalyptic tradition in early Christianity. Bauckham's argument hinges on the conscious distinction drawn in such circles between angels, who must not be worshipped, and God, who must. He finds that Jesus is regularly placed on the divine side of this divide, and argues from this that in the context of a monotheistic Jewish tradition Christian religious practice recognized the divinity of Jesus from a very early date. This he regards as 'a remarkable development' which 'may be seen with hindsight to have set the church already on the road to Nicene theology'.

The ministry of Jesus

I realize, of course, that to take the Gospels at their face-value as a factual report of words and events in the earthly ministry of Jesus is an unfashionable thing to do, the more so when the subject under discussion is so evidently theological an issue as the divinity of Jesus. But it is not possible here to defend the authenticity of every saying under discussion, and I must simply hope that the total impression which I am trying to outline may be found strong enough to survive any doubts which may be felt on individual passages cited. For myself, I have given my reasons elsewhere for believing the Gospel accounts to be essentially historical in character, and to be a reliable record of the content of Jesus' teaching, even when due allowance has been made for the Evangelists' individual interpretation of the material they recorded.[18] Some will prefer to view the material here presented as evidence not for what Jesus said and did, but rather for the attitude to Jesus of Christians in the middle decades of the first century, when the Gospel materials were taking shape; in that case it will testify to a later stage in the development of the Christian attitudes which underlie New Testament Christology, but one which is also important to the theme of this essay.

Now the Gospels do not provide clear evidence that Jesus was worshipped in the formal sense during his lifetime. That requests were addressed to him, including requests for miraculous help (e.g. Mk. 1:40; 5:22f.; Mt. 8:25; 14:30), is not evidence of worship, any more than it would be in the case of anyone else who was known to heal by the power of God. Nor need the fact that many such requests include the address kyrie ('Lord') imply divine honours, despite the clearly divine implications of that title as used later, for kyrie as addressed to a living person was a polite form appropriate to anyone regarded as in some sense superior to the speaker, more deferential than our 'Sir', but far from implying divinity.[19]

Similarly, the mention that suppliants and others 'worshipped' him, as the AV put it (e.g. Mk. 5:6; Mt. 8:2; 9:18), or knelt before him (e.g. Mk. 10:17; Mt. 17:14), while it clearly conveyed more than mere politeness, particularly to Matthew who is fond of the verb proskynein, does not in the historical context of Jesus' ministry necessarily imply what 'worship' means to us; it is more than social politeness, but is not a gesture appropriate only

[18] See my essay 'The Authenticity of the Sayings of Jesus' in C. Brown (ed.), History, Criticism and Faith (IVP, 1976), pp.101-143.

[19] See W. Foerster, TDNT 3, pp.1086, 1093; C. F. D. Moule, The Origin of Christology, p.35. For a fuller discussion of the cultural background see G. Vermes, Jesus the Jew (Collins, 1973), pp.111-127.

to God (see *e.g.* Mt. 18:26; Rev. 3:9).[20]

Indeed, it is not easy to imagine what it would mean, especially in a Jewish milieu, to offer formal worship to a man standing in front of you (*cf.* Acts 10:25f. for a typical Jewish reaction). There is only one incident in Jesus' pre-resurrection ministry where *proskynein* seems to approach what we would call 'worship', and that is in a 'numinous' context where the disciples saw Jesus first as a ghost, and then were led by his miraculous power to confess him as 'Son of God' (Mt. 14:33).[21]

To look for formal worship in the normal circumstances of Jesus' ministry is, then, not likely to be helpful. But the formal worship which began very quickly after his death and resurrection was a response to what they had seen and heard during the ministry, as he presented himself to them, indirectly but unmistakably, as more than a man of God.

Not that Jesus went around proclaiming himself to be God. The feature of his teaching which comes closest to this is his use of Father/Son language, which indicates a unique relationship between Jesus and his Father, different in kind from that by which he encouraged his disciples to approach God as 'our Father'. The claim to an exclusively intimate relationship with God in Matthew 11:27[22] is often suspected as a later formulation because it is regarded as untypical of the Synoptic accounts of Jesus' teaching,[23] but while it is un-doubtedly the most explicit such saying, it is only bringing to clearer expression what all the other Father/Son language implies, and this is a persistent feature of both Synoptic and Johannine records. In any account of the Christological implications of Jesus' own teaching this 'Son of God' language must play a significant role.

Less obvious, but arguably more impressive, is the way Jesus' sayings

[20] See the discussion by C. F. D. Moule, *ibid.*, pp.175f.; for the Jewish background see H. Greeven, *TDNT* 6, pp.760-763. *Cf.* R. J. Bauckham, *art. cit.*, p.324.

[21] In Jn. 9:38 it is not clear how much Christological understanding lay behind the man's '*Kyrie*, I believe'; it relates to Jesus' status as 'Son of man', not to his divinity, and the context suggests rather a confused expression of indebtedness and of Jesus' God-sent authority than any attribution of divine honours to him, though undoubtedly John would want his readers to apply it in a deeper sense.

[22] If J. Jeremias, *New Testament Theology* 1 (SCM, 1971), pp.59-61, is right in his suggestion that 'the son' and 'the father' are here not specific but general, making this a simple observation about human family relationships, the point of such an observation in this context could only be as a 'parable' of the special relationship Jesus claims with his Father, making the same claim by analogy rather than directly.

[23] On the authenticity of this saying see especially J. D. G. Dunn, *Jesus and the Spirit* (SCM, 1975), pp.27-34.

sometimes assume divine functions for himself, or seem to put him in the place of God. It is hard to miss this implication in Jesus' assertion, in the face of the suggestion of blasphemy, of his right to the divine prerogative of forgiving sins (Mk. 2:1–12; *cf.* Lk. 23:43). Similarly, he sees himself as the arbiter of men's destiny (Mt. 7:21–23) and as the judge at the final assize (Mt. 25:31ff.; *cf.* Jn. 5:22f.). He is able to give life (Jn. 5:24; 6:40, 51) because he has life in himself (Jn. 5:26). Meanwhile he teaches on his own authority, unlike other Jewish teachers (Mt. 7:28f., *etc.*), and attributes to his own words the eternal validity of the word of God (Mk. 13:31; *cf.* Is. 40:8). He can even picture himself as the king in an eternal kingdom (Mt. 25:31–34; *cf.* the references to the kingdom of the Son of man, Mt. 13:41; 16:28). He demands of his followers an absolute personal loyalty (Mt. 10:37–39, *etc.*), and offers them rest, which he himself will give (Mt. 11:28–30). To reject or to receive him is to reject or to receive God (Mt. 10:40; Lk. 10:16).

All this, and it is not a complete account, is evidence not of a formal claim to divinity so much as of an assumption of a divine role which is the more impressive because it does not seem to require argument or defence, and which occurs in a wide variety of Gospel traditions, Synoptic as well as Johannine.

It is consistent with this that in Jesus' use of Old Testament texts and imagery we find the same tendency to put himself in the place of God, not ostentatiously, but almost incidentally, as if it were a perfectly natural substitution. Thus the children's praise of Jesus is defended by reference to a psalm about the praise of God (Mt. 21:16; *cf.* Ps. 8:2 [Hebrew 8:3]), his mission to seek and save the lost echoes Ezekiel's prophecy of the divine shepherd (Lk. 19:10; *cf.* Ezk. 34, especially verses 16, 22), the rejected stone (Jesus) becomes the stone on which men stumble, echoing an image of God in Isaiah (Lk. 20:18; *cf.* Is. 8:14f.), and the portrayal of the Son of man as judge and king at the final assize echoes the wording of at least three Old Testament accounts of the appearance of God for judgment (Mt. 25:31–34, echoing Dn. 7:9f.; Joel 3:1–12 [Hebrew 4:1–12]; Zc. 14:5). The equation of John the Baptist as his forerunner with the prediction in Malachi 3:1 and 4:5f. [Hebrew 3:23f.] of the coming of the messenger/Elijah (so Mk. 9:12f.; Mt. 11:10, 14) has similar implications if, as I believe, Malachi's figure is the direct precursor of the coming of God, with no third, 'messianic' figure in view.[24] Similar implications may be discerned in Jesus' use of other Old Testament texts, as of course in many later New Testament allusions.[25] It is also remarkable how many of

---

[24] See on this exegesis J. A. T. Robinson, *Twelve New Testament Studies* (SCM, 1962), pp. 35–37; R. T. France, *Jesus and the Old Testament* (Tyndale Press, 1971), pp. 91f., n. 31.

[25] See my *Jesus and the Old Testament*, pp. 150–159.

Jesus' parables apparently apply to himself figures which are typically used for God in the Old Testament, such as shepherd, king, bridegroom, sower.[26]

What may be said of a man who used such language? The whole of this evidence can hardly be dismissed as later Christian creation in view both of its varied and pervasive nature and of its very unobtrusiveness. It does not look as if it was designed to make a theological point. But if even some of this material is genuine, and if we may assume that Jesus' disciples, however gradually, were able to discern its implications, then we have the raw material in Jesus' own teaching for an increasing awareness that he was more than a prophet, and for that attitude to him which could ultimately result in worshipping him as God.

The primitive church

The New Testament accounts of the church in the period following Jesus' resurrection indicate that this phenomenon of the worship of Jesus developed remarkably quickly. Thus we find Jesus described in Peter's sermons in Acts as saviour (4:12), author of life (3:15; 5:31), giver of repentance and forgiveness (5:31), and judge (10:42; *cf.* 17:31). We find too a significant difference in the use of *kyrios* from that in the Gospels: the vocative *kyrie* addressed to a living person need have no superhuman connotations, but when a man is described after his death as *ho kyrios,* this is a different matter altogether, especially when those references are to his present rather than his past status (Acts 2:36; 4:33; 7:59; 10:36; *etc.*). Such uses immediately bring into view the associations which *ho kyrios* inevitably carried for a Greek-speaking Jew, in that it was the standard LXX translation for the name of God. He could no more use *ho kyrios* without thinking of its divine connotations than we could use 'the Lord' of a human leader today. And this title springs into prominence in Christian preaching immediately after the resurrection; indeed its applicability to Jesus is confirmed by reference to the resurrection (Acts 2:36).

Moreover, alongside the attribution to Jesus in preaching of those divine functions and status which his own teaching had implied, we find from a very early period the beginning of prayer addressed to him, first by Stephen at his martyrdom (Acts 7:59) and then by Ananias in Acts 9:10–17, where verse 17 shows that the 'Lord' addressed is Jesus, and Jesus' followers are already characterized as 'all who call upon his name' (verse 14: *cf.* 9:21; 22:16).[27]

---

[26] See P. B. Payne, in the appendix (pp. 338-341) to his article 'The Authenticity of the Parables of Jesus', in R. T. France and D. Wenham (eds.), *Gospel Perspectives* 2 (JSOT Press, Sheffield, 1981); the material is based on Payne's Ph.D. dissertation (Cambridge, 1975).

[27] See also I. H. Marshall, *Acts: an Introduction and Commentary* (IVP, 1980), p.66 for the possibility that Acts 1:24 records prayer addressed to the ascended Jesus even before Pentecost.

Here then is evidence of the beginning of worship of Jesus in a more formal sense.[28] I realize, of course, that Acts is for many critics as suspect for anachronistic features as are the records of Jesus' ministry, but when the above evidence is compared with what Paul's letters indicate of the nature of Christian devotion to Jesus in the period prior to their writing in the 50s and 60s, there seems good ground for questioning why this account may not fairly represent the impact made by the risen Jesus on his followers, an impact for which his own teaching had prepared the way.

The letters of Paul

Paul's letters are generally agreed to be the earliest completed writings of the Christian movement which have survived. They are thus an essential means of testing the picture of earliest Christianity which the later Gospels and Acts present.

Leaving aside the explicit Christological formulations of Philippians 2 and Colossians 1, and the titles he uses for Jesus, I would like now to sketch briefly the evidence for an underlying attitude of worship towards Jesus both in Paul's own mind and in the churches within which he worked.

It is striking first to note the 'definition' of Christians in 1 Corinthians 1:2 as 'those who call on the name of our Lord Jesus Christ'. Not only does the phrase in itself indicate that prayer to Jesus was a normal and distinguishing characteristic of Christians in the 50s, but 'to call on the name of the Lord' is a regular Old Testament formula for worship and prayer offered to God (Gn. 4:26; 13:4; Ps. 105:1; Je. 10:25; Joel 2:32; *etc.*). Thus the phrase as a whole suggests that Pliny's description of Christian worship about 115 as singing 'to Christ as God' could already have been an outsider's impression sixty years earlier.[29] Indeed this characteristic is apparently earlier still, for the use of the Aramaic formula of prayer to Jesus, *Maranatha* ('Our Lord, come'), in 1 Corinthians 16:22 when writing to a Greek church can only indicate that this formula, like such foreign expressions as 'Hosanna' and 'Hallelujah' today, was hallowed by long usage. When it originated in the Aramaic-speaking church can only be guessed, but to be familiar in Corinth in the 50s it is likely to date from the very early days of the Jerusalem church; in that case Jesus, not long after his death, was being 'called upon' by Christians from his own cultural background.

---

[28] *Cf.* also Matthew's use of *proskynein* in 28:9 and 17 of the reaction of the disciples in the presence of the risen Jesus; they are not now suppliants, but, as in 14:33, overwhelmed by a sense of numinous awe.

[29] If it is legitimate to discern a trinitarian structure in Eph. 5:18–20 ('filled with the Spirit... singing to the Lord... giving thanks to God the Father') this would explicitly describe 'singing to Christ', an even closer approximation to Pliny's observation.

That the worship of the Christian congregations in Paul's day was focused on Jesus is indicated by the fact that believers were baptized 'into Christ' (Rom. 6:3; Gal. 3:27), and that their central act of worship was 'the Lord's supper' (1 Cor. 11:20; *cf.* 10:21). Thus it is not surprising that they can be called 'the churches of Christ' (Rom. 16:16), or that he is described as the head of the whole church (Eph. 1:22f.; 5:23), or as its bridegroom (Eph. 5:25–32).

In this context we must mention the famous Pauline phrase 'in Christ', even if adequate discussion is beyond the scope of this essay. At the least it must point to Jesus as the focus of Christian faith, the one to whom Christians owe their spiritual life, and who claims their total loyalty. Even this aspect of its meaning indicates an attitude to Jesus which approaches what we have called 'worship'. But most interpreters find it impossible to do justice to some of Paul's uses of the phrase without using terms such as 'participation', 'incorporation', or 'mystical union'. C. F. D. Moule devotes the second chapter of *The Origin of Christology* to a careful examination of this idea of 'the corporate Christ', in which he recognizes the difficulty of envisaging what such language means, but concludes that it is an essential part of Paul's thought, indicating that for him Jesus 'was found to be an "inclusive" personality. And this means, in effect, that Paul was led to conceive of Christ as any theist conceives of God: personal, indeed, but transcending the individual category.'[30]

That Paul did in fact think of Jesus in much the same way that he thought of God is confirmed by the salutation with which his letters typically begin, 'Grace to you and peace from God our Father and the Lord Jesus Christ.' Jesus and the Father are jointly the source of blessing, and this is confirmed by prayers such as those in 1 Thessalonians 3:11 and 2 Thessalonians 2:16, which envisage Jesus and the Father acting together to answer the prayer.

So it is not surprising that in Paul's letters the same divine function is credited sometimes to God and sometimes to Jesus. The most remarkable instance of this is, of course, the description of Christ in Colossians 1:16f. as the one in whom and through whom and for whom everything was created, and in whom the whole creation is held together (*cf.* 1 Cor. 8:6). Not only does this passage attribute to Jesus the agency in creation, which is in the Old Testament an exclusively divine prerogative, but it does so in language which echoes closely what Paul says elsewhere of God the Creator in Romans 11:36. Similar transfers of attributes and activities of the Father to Jesus occur elsewhere in Paul's letters. In Romans 14:10–12 we are to stand before the *bēma* of God for judgment, but in 2 Corinthians 5:10 it is before the *bēma* of Christ. The 'kingdom of God' (Col. 4:11, *etc.*) is also described as 'the kingdom of his son'

---

[30] *The Origin of Christology*, p.95.

(Col. 1:13), or even, 'the kingdom of Christ and of God' (Eph. 5:5). The Holy Spirit is generally for Paul the 'Spirit of God' but can also be described as the 'Spirit of Christ' within the very same verse (Rom. 8:9) and is elsewhere 'the Spirit of Jesus Christ' (Phil. 1:19). The 'churches of God' (1 Cor. 11:16; 1 Thes. 2:14) are also the 'churches of Christ' (Rom. 16:16). The 'gospel of God' is also the 'gospel of his Son' (Rom. 1:1 with 1:9; 15:16 with 15:19, *etc.*).

I do not imagine that Paul deliberately set out to parallel what he said about Christ with what he said about God. Many of these are merely incidental turns of phrase. But that is why they are revealing; they suggest that for Paul the functions or attributes of God and of Christ were so interchangeable that it did not really matter which he mentioned – it came to the same thing. The same is true, of course, of his uses of 'the Lord'; it is often impossible to say whether Paul intends this title as a designation of the Father or of Jesus, just as many Christians today would find it hard to say which they meant by 'Lord', and would not feel that it mattered very much. In 2 Corinthians 12:8, for instance, who was the 'Lord' to whom Paul prayed? Normally his prayers are addressed to God, but 'my power' in the answer to Paul's prayer appears to be identical with 'the power of Christ' (verse 9). It seems then that for Paul Jesus was already so much identified with God that the same language was naturally applicable to each.

Now this is amazing! To us it seems natural enough, for we have learned from Paul and from his successors for many centuries. But here was a Pharisaic Jew only some 25 years after the death of the Nazareth carpenter, and even less time since he himself had repudiated him as a blasphemer, already so naturally associating this man with the one true God that he could slip almost unconsciously, it appears, into using the same language about Jesus that he used about God and could attribute to him uniquely divine functions without feeling the need to explain such an outrageous idea. It is this, and we have seen only a sample of the material available, which I regard as convincing evidence that the attitude to Jesus which Paul and his churches shared could fairly be called 'worship'.

The New Testament as a whole

We have been considering evidence that already in the earliest post-Easter period Christians were learning to think and speak of Jesus in much the same way as they thought and spoke of God. We have seen that Jesus' own teaching had laid the foundation for this attitude, and we have seen how it resulted even within a few years of Jesus' death and resurrection in the addressing of prayer and formal worship to Jesus as well as to his Father.

The study could be extended through the rest of the New Testament writings, but we cannot do so here. Let us merely note the natural culmination of this process in the last book of the New Testament, where not only is Jesus ('the Lamb') regularly associated with God in his glory and sovereignty (*e.g.* Rev. 7:14–17; 11:15; 12:10; 14:1, 4; 20:6; 21:22f.; 22:1–4),[31] but worship and praise are offered to him equally with the Father (Rev. 1:5f.; 5:8–14; 7:9–12; 22:3). The great doxologies of Revelation are not a new experiment involving the worship of one previously regarded in a less exalted light, but the proper expression of an attitude to Jesus which had been there from the beginning, increasing no doubt in intensity and in sophistication, but deriving from the impression made by Jesus himself during his earthly ministry.[32]

It is instructive to notice that these great doxologies of Revelation ground their praise of the Lamb on the work of salvation which he has accomplished by his death, and which his worshippers have experienced. A similar pattern has emerged in our study of the earlier New Testament material. The attitude of worship towards Jesus is often directly traceable to the Christians' experience of his saving work. They found in Jesus forgiveness, revelation, new life, and thus they saw him to be fulfilling to them the functions of God himself, and they worshipped him. It was this attitude of worship which in turn found expression in the more explicit and sophisticated Christological language which has remained outside the scope of this study.

I am suggesting, then, that the incarnational Christology of the New Testament had its roots not in philosophical speculation, and still less in the gratuitous imitation of supposedly similar ideas in other religions and cultures, but in Christian experience of Jesus, both in his earthly ministry and in his risen power, and that it was the natural translation of this experience into an attitude of worship which provided the seedbed for New Testament Christology. To fail to explore and account for this attitude of worship, as has much modern discussion of the origins of Christology, is to discard the real life-situation of a warm and experience-centred devotion to Jesus in favour of a process of philosophical speculation which lacks an adequate starting-point in the life of the Christian church.

Some scholars draw a distinction between 'ontological' and 'functional' approaches to Christology. In those terms, I have here suggested a functional origin to New Testament Christology. But this applies only to its origin, not to its ultimate character. The truth about Jesus which was first perceived functionally was then necessarily worked out in ontological terms. This was

---

[31] Note the remarkable use of singular pronouns to refer to 'God and the Lamb' in 22:3f.; *cf.* 11:15; 20:6.

[32] On the worship of Jesus in the book of Revelation see further R. J. Bauckham, *art. cit.*, especially pp.329–331.

surely inevitable for Jews who could hardly think of a man as exercising divine functions without considering what effect this belief had on their monotheism. Functional and ontological approaches to Christology would thus be complementary, and it is perhaps unrealistic to speak in terms of a linear progression from one to the other. Neither could exist for long in isolation. But insofar as a chronological development may be postulated, I believe that it was the functional that gave rise to the ontological. Or, to return to the terminology I have preferred, Christology formulation arose out of worship, and worship arose out of the Christians' experience of Jesus.

Thus a study of the development of New Testament Christology must first take account of the attitude of worship which I have outlined in this paper if it is to have the appropriate background against which to go on to the study of the Christological titles. The full significance in particular of the titles 'Lord' and 'Son of God' is not likely to be revealed by studying their background in Jewish and pagan thought without giving prior consideration to the life and thought and worship of the Christian community which applied them to Jesus. But once this attitude of worship is discerned, it is easier to explain why the use of the titles developed in the direction of a more confident attribution of divine honours to Jesus.

This is the background also for the great Christological affirmations of such passages as Philippians 2:6–11, Colossians 1:15–20, Hebrews 1:1–4, and John 1:1–18. These are seen not as brilliant *tours de force,* formulating hitherto unheard-of ideas, but as the explicit theological working out of an estimate of Jesus which was already established in Christian devotion. The idea of Jesus' pre-existence, which features prominently in these and other New Testament passages, is also a natural inference from the attribution to him of divine functions, especially in creation. The idea of Jesus' 'being sent', 'coming from God', which inevitably implies his pre-existence, is widespread in the New Testament even before Paul set it out more formally in Philippians 2:6.[33]

Given this attitude, too, it was inevitable that the Christians should discuss the relation of Jesus with his Father, resulting in the implicitly trinitarian language and thought which occurs unobtrusively in much of the New Testament and in such passages as John 14–16 gets close to theological formulation. You cannot worship a man who himself worshipped God without having to think out the sort of issues to which trinitarian thought addresses itself.

---

[33] See M. Hengel, *The Son of God,* pp.66-76. Hengel emphasizes how early this element came into NT Christology, by an 'inner necessity'. This is now disputed by J. D. G. Dunn, *Christology in the Making* (SCM, 1980), which was published too late to be noticed in this lecture.

Thus when Jewish Christians ultimately reached the stage of calling Jesus 'God', in spite of all the inhibiting traditions of their culture, this was not a brash new doctrine, but the eventual outcome of a process of Christological development which can be traced throughout New Testament Christianity right back to the teaching and impact of Jesus himself.

Conclusion

This paper has made no pretence to be a comprehensive presentation of the New Testament material relating to the worship of Jesus. Indeed the last few paragraphs have indicated that we have left on one side the main lines of New Testament evidence for belief in his divinity. What I have tried to indicate is that to go straight to these more obvious aspects of Christological language and to debate them either in isolation or in comparison merely with non-Christian 'parallels', is to leave out of account the most relevant and important background against which they must be understood, the thought and devotion of the early Christian community out of which they arose. Here there is scope for much more detailed study, but I have tried to sketch out some pointers to an underlying attitude to Jesus which antedates and gives rise to the more deliberately theological reflection. If we may therefore assert that incarnational Christology did not appear either as a bolt from the blue or as an importation of alien mythological ideas, this must have important implications for both the contents and the orientation of Christological debate insofar as it purports to relate to New Testament Christianity.

The basic fact which lies behind all the theological terms and titles is the worship of the carpenter. That is a phenomenon sufficiently arresting to require explanation, even if they had never progressed to the stage of openly calling him 'God'. This worship was no easy option for pious Jews. If their own monotheistic upbringing rebelled against it, they could be sure it would provoke the violent hostility of their fellow-Jews. Even among Gentiles it was a preposterous idea, as is vividly illustrated by the famous Alexamenos *graffito* from third-century Rome: a young man worshipping a crucified human figure with a donkey's head, over the caption 'Alexamenos worships his god'.[34]

Men do not gratuitously court such opposition and ridicule merely out of a dispassionate search for a new religious ideology. There must have been an irresistible compulsion, so that they could do no other. It is the task of our Christology, as it was of theirs, to account adequately for this compulsion.

In this essay I have tried to suggest something of the thought and experience

[34] Illustrated, *e.g.*, in Michael Green, *Evangelism in the Early Church* (Hodder, 1970), pp. 174f.

which could produce this result. If there is any validity in this presentation, it indicates that modern Christological discussion, if it is to maintain its links with New Testament Christianity rather than set up a new discipline unrelated to historical Christian origins, must begin where Christology itself began, in the worship of Jesus.

SOME REFLECTIONS
ON NEW TESTAMENT HYMNS

Ralph P. Martin

Introduction

In what may be regarded as a notable section of his compendious *New Testament Theology*,[1] Donald Guthrie bids us consider the place and significance of 'the Christological "hymns"' which modern New Testament study has isolated, classified and studied, usually at some depth. In tribute to the honoree of this *Festschrift* the following pages are offered as an attempt to set the New Testament hymns found in the Pauline corpus – and with special attention to the Christological examples – in their historical, cultural and theological framework. It is generally conceded that the heart of Paul's understanding of the person and place of Jesus Christ as the church's Lord and creation's head is to be found in these hymnic ascriptions. So what is being considered should have a distinct bearing on New Testament Christology and give us some pointers in the modern discussion.

The background and early development

The specimens of church life that meet us in the pages of the New Testament literature give evidence of a set of worshipping communities of believing men and women. This is clear from the descriptions in the book of Acts (1:14; 2:42, 46; 4:31; 5:12; 13:1–3; 20:7–12) and from the pastoral remarks of Paul, notably in 1 Corinthians 5:3–8 and chs. 10–14. It might be expected that these chapters and references would contain some allusion to a specific part of the Christian cultus, namely the worship of God in religious song. That is exactly what we find in one of the most revealing of these texts. In 1 Corinthians 14:26 Paul sets down what appears to be an 'order' of public worship:

[1] Donald Guthrie, *New Testament Theology* (IVP, 1981), pp.343–365.

37

What then, brethren? When you come together, each one has a hymn (Greek *psalmos*), a lesson, a revelation, a tongue, or an interpretation.

Three short comments are invited on this verse whose importance can hardly be over-estimated. First, most likely Paul is writing descriptively and assessing the situation as it existed in the Corinthian assembly. He need not be expressing approval of the various items in the list.[2] Rather, in a way analogous to his appeal to the strange practice of 'baptism for the dead' (1 Cor. 15:29) he may simply be reporting what was the case at Corinth. Secondly, the objectivity of the statements in this verse seems to be confirmed by how Paul proceeds: 'let all things be done for edification'. As J. Jervell[3] pointed out, he did not say here, 'let each one bring what he has', but 'what each one has let him bring *to edify the church*'. The overall concern of the apostle was not with the presence or absence of specific elements of corporate worship. Rather his main interest was to ensure that all contributions of whatever nature served to promote the well-being and growth of the entire community (*cf.* 12:7: 'for the common good' and the repeated stress on 'edification' in 10:24; 14:5, 12). As a third observation, we may remark that Paul chose to open the list with a reference to 'the hymn'. Some see here an allusion to synagogue practice based on the rubric to begin the worship of God always with praise; others infer that there must have been special significance for the priority of hymns in Paul's thought of a correct 'order' or sequence.[4] 'All things should be done decently and *in order*' (14:40: where the last words, *kata taxin*, could conceivably reflect a concern for arranging items of worship in what Paul deemed to be the right sequence as distinct from spontaneous contributions offered by the Corinthian believers; *cf.* 1 Clement 40:1 which so interprets 1 Cor. 14:40).

Paul's word *psalmos* has an unusual connotation, since it could be misunderstood by Greek-speaking people as a special type of musical composition: and yet it would be familiar to readers of the LXX who would recognize it as the heading given there to many psalms. The suggestion, made by M. Hengel,[5] is that *psalmos* would be understood on its non-Greek, therefore Jewish, background.

---

[2] Or even actively disapproving of this type of worship because of the dangers leading to confusion and disorder inherent in it, according to A. Robertson and A. Plummer, *A Commentary on 1 Corinthians, ICC* (T. & T. Clark, 1914), p.320.

[3] J. Jervell, *Imago Dei in Gen. i. 26f. im Spätjudentum, in der Gnosis und in den paulinischen Briefen* (FRLANT 76: Vandenhoeck & Ruprecht, 1960), p.206 n.132.

[4] A. Schlatter, *Paulus, der Bote Jesu* (Calwer Verlag, Stuttgart, 1969), p.383: 'the fact that the hymn/song is mentioned first of all perhaps points to the situation where the assembly began with a song'.

[5] Martin Hengel, 'Hymn and Christology' in *Studia Biblica 1978*, III. Papers on Paul and

If Paul's term is deliberately chosen, it would indicate a contribution to Corinthian worship in religious song which was based on the Hebrew psalter.

The origin of the church in the matrix of the Jewish ancestral faith made it inevitable that the first followers of the risen Lord, themselves Jews by birth and tradition, would wish to express their devotion in a way to which they were accustomed. But did the synagogue pattern of worship include the use of religious song? The evidence is hard to interpret, and it is usually concluded that psalm-singing was confined to the Temple and its choirs, while the Palestinian synagogues adopted a severely didactic form of worship based on a sequence of prayers, Scripture lections, homily and confession of Israel's faith.[6] This distinction may well have held for Palestinian Judaism or at least for Judaism in its orthodox centre at Jerusalem. But clearly the practices of sectarian groups, at Qumran and among the Therapeutae according to Philo, did include a celebration in song shared by all the community members. In the world of the Jewish dispersion, the hellenistic synagogues were more open to this type of worship. It may be, as Hengel suggests,[7] that the excluding of hymns from the orthodox synagogues was a response to the use of hymns among groups the Pharisees judged to be heretical.

The evidence of the Lucan canticles (Luke 1:46–55 – the *Magnificat*; 1:68–79 – the *Benedictus*; 2:14 – the *Gloria in excelsis*; 2:29–32 – the *Nunc Dimittis*), certain hymnic fragments in the book of Revelation (*e.g.* 15:3f.) and the early scenes recorded of the Jerusalem church supports the conclusion that messianic psalms were being sung in the Jewish-Christian circles that treasured these compositions. The purport of these compositions, from all we know of them, was partly celebratory but chiefly apologetic, and formed part of the theodicy by which the early Christians sought to justify their conviction that God was sovereign in their affairs in spite of the suffering and opposition they were called upon to endure (see Acts 4:24–31). The theme of the fulfilment of Old Testament prophecy in their day linked these messianic pietists with the Qumran covenanters, with the obvious difference that the Jewish messianists held firmly to the belief that the promised Messiah had come and that his name was Jesus of Nazareth. His sufferings had issued in a triumphant vindication by God (Acts 2:32), attested by Davidic oracles and by their own experience as witnesses. And now Jesus of Nazareth was exalted as head of a messianic community in which alone salvation was offered as a present reality (Acts 2:37–42; 4:10–12). The centre of their proclamation was also the focus of their

---

Other New Testament Authors. Sixth International Congress on Biblical Studies. Oxford 3–7 April 1978, ed. E. A. Livingstone (*JSNT* Supp. Series 3: Sheffield, 1980), pp. 173-197 (174).
    [6] See W. Schrage, art. 'synagogē', *TDNT* 7, pp.798-852.   [7] M. Hengel, *art. cit.*, p.188.

worship: God has glorified his son/servant (Greek *pais*) Jesus, who is now enthroned as the 'stone', disallowed and rejected by the Jewish 'builders' (or leaders) but raised to the place of honour by Israel's God himself (Acts 3:13; 4:11). It is not difficult to detect the way Christian apologetic was already busy at work in exploiting the messianic motifs in such psalms as Psalm 2 (God adopts his son;[8] *cf.* the early hymnic fragment in Rom. 1:3f.), Psalm 22 which foretold the sufferings and reward of the righteous man in Israel,[9] Psalm 45 (the anointed warrior-hero who is now 'lord') and especially the related Psalms 8 and 110.[10] From the early speeches in Acts we may conclude that the leading theme relating to the understanding of Jesus' mission was his rejection and vindication, and to illustrate this nexus the proof-text appealed to was Psalm 118:22:

> The stone the builders cast aside
> Is now the building's strength and pride

(as Moffatt's translation renders the couplet). The same *testimonium* recurs in the Gospel tradition (Mk. 12:10 par.) as well as in 1 Peter (2:7); and Paul is indebted to the same 'complex', or text-plot to do with the 'stoneship' of Christ in Romans 9:33.

The interesting thing to notice is the continuance of the theme of victory in Psalm 118:26 which apparently found its way into early liturgies as an acclamation heralding the triumphant return of Messiah, based on his entry into the holy city (Mk. 11:9 par.), but soon the text came to be associated with his parousia in glory. The evidence for that latter idea is the Aramaic prayer-call *marana tha,* 'Our Lord, come!' found in 1 Corinthians 16:22 and Didache 10:6. The division of the letters in the original term *maranatha* so as to yield the translation just given is all but conclusively proved by some recent discoveries from Qumran's Cave 4 (*i.e.* dated in the Middle Aramaic period).[11] Thus the contention that the earliest believers invoked the risen Jesus as Lord and awaited his return in glorious power rests on a firm linguistic basis.

Two other factors need to be added. M. Hengel's recent discussion argues that *maranatha* was 'an expression of the close relationship which Jesus'

---

[8] For the wider implications of Psalm 2:7 in the NT, see L. C. Allen, 'The Old Testament Background of PRO-'ORIZEIN in the New Testament', *NTS* 17, 1970-71, pp.104-108.

[9] J. Reumann, 'Psalm 22 at the Cross: Lament and Thanksgiving for Jesus Christ', *Interpretation* 28, 1974, pp.39-58.

[10] On the use of Psalm 110 as a Christological 'testimony' see W. R. G. Loader, 'Christ at the Right Hand — Ps. cx. 1 in the New Testament', *NTS* 24, 1978, pp.199-217.

[11] See J. A. Fitzmyer, 'The Aramaic Language and the Study of the New Testament', *JBL* 99, March 1980, pp.5-21 (13).

disciples had with their Lord who had been elevated to share God's throne'.[12] In other words, the prayer-speech, 'Come, our Lord' suggests the incipience of a cultus centred upon the living Lord who was believed to be now exalted in fulfilment of Psalm 110:1. The focus of concentration was clearly set on the glory Jesus Christ had recently received, and his elevation to the divine splendour – clearly seen and heard in Stephen's cry, 'I see the heavens opened, and the Son of man standing at the right hand of God' (Acts 7:56) – eclipsed other aspects of Christ's person at that time. The enthroned Lord was present as 'the glory of God' glimpsed as a known reality (Acts 7:55).[13] And it was not appropriate, for reasons we have yet to explore, to relate his glory to his pre-temporal existence (his 'pre-existence') or his future lordship at the end of the age. The earliest Christology had a vision of the Easter triumph of the crucified Jesus and its immediate after-glow in his being exalted to the Father's presence, whence the blessedness of the new age of messianic salvation flowed down to those men and women who in turn were caught up to share his present reign.

That 'conquering new-born joy' is expressed in the pristine church's sense of 'unbounded gladness' (Greek *agalliasis*). The term in question is, as R. Bultmann[14] has shown, essentially eschatological. That is, the joy refers to a present experience that reached out to grasp the wonder of what God had promised to do at the end-time when his kingdom would come and his will would prevail over the earth. For these believers, living as they were sure at 'the turning point of the ages', God's age-old promises of his rule's coming in power were known as present fact since God had raised Jesus out of defeat and death into new life and had given him glory (1 Pet. 1:21). It was not to be wondered at therefore that they could rejoice with a joy both unutterable and exalted (1 Pet. 1:8) in keeping with their knowledge of the enthroned Lord.

Yet he was no distant figure. The prayer *maranatha* is suggestively set in the context of the eucharist where also 'they broke bread... with glad (Greek *en agalliasei*) and generous hearts' (Acts 2:46f.). The Aramaic watchword thus found its natural setting as an invocation for 'the coming of the Lord to His people in a visitation which prefigures the final advent'.[15]

---

[12] M. Hengel, 'Hymn and Christology' (as in n.5), p.185.

[13] This verse could well be translated, Stephen 'saw the glory of God, that is (Greek *kai*) Jesus standing at the right hand of God', a possibility suggested in R. P. Martin, *Carmen Christi: Philippians ii. 5–11 in Recent Interpretation and in the Setting of Early Christian Worship*, SNTSMS 4 (CUP, 1967), p.111, and now accepted by N. Turner, *Christian Words* (T. & T. Clark, 1980), p.198, n.14.   [14] R. Bultmann, art. 'agalliaomai', 'agalliasis', *TDNT* 1, pp.19-21.

[15] G. Wainwright, *Doxology. The Praise of God in Worship, Doctrine and Life* (Epworth Press/OUP, NY, 1980), p.72.

So far then we have considered one specimen of 'religious song', patterned on the Old Testament Psalter and expressing in a conscious tribute to the messianic types already available the fulfilment of Israel's hope for a coming saviour. He was hailed as Jesus of Nazareth who after the humiliation of rejection and death was now raised to his Father's presence where he enjoyed the divine glory. He will come again from that seat to consummate God's purposes (for Israel); and in the meanwhile – and it may be as a prelude to his advent – he was appealed to to 'come' and visit his people who 'broke bread' as a sign of their joyful participation in the new age of the messianic banquet soon to be spread and shared (based on Is. 25, as O. Hofius has shown).[16] Such examples of 'psalms' applied to Christ may well be accurately called 'messianic' tributes, or 'Christ psalms'.

The setting in the Graeco-Roman world

Associated with the influence and work of the proto-martyr Stephen and his followers, the early Christian mission reached out to offer its message to those who lived in Graeco-Roman society.[17] In that world the singing of hymns to the deities of contemporary religious cults was already an established practice. The use of hymns in corporate and private worship in that culture went back a long way; but it reached its high-point at a time when the finest and most sensitive spirits in late classical civilization were becoming conscious of their need of 'salvation'. The immediate occasion was the onset of pessimism and despair, caused partly by Greek science that offered a naturalistic explanation of the universe and partly by Eastern astrology that placed a vast distance between human beings and the gods whom Homer and Hesiod described. A valiant attempt to relate the traditional deities to human life was made as an answer to belief in impersonal 'fate', or 'chance' or iron 'necessity' (Greek *heimarmenē*). We see a fine specimen of this religious aspiration in Cleanthes' 'Hymn to Zeus':

> Thou, O Zeus, art praised above all gods: many are thy
> names and thine is all power for ever.

[16] O. Hofius, *Jesu Tischgemeinschaft mit den Sündern* (Calwer Verlag, Stuttgart, 1976), pp. 16-25.

[17] I accept M. Hengel's far-reaching conclusion that in the earliest Christianity there were already two groups: an Aramaic-speaking congregation of Jewish messianists (the so-called *Urgemeinde*) and also, maybe from the start, a Greek-speaking congregation led by the Seven and with Stephen as prominent as spokesperson for a missionary theology. So-called 'hellenistic Christianity' on this view was part of the earliest church and not a later development due to the mission to Gentiles. See Hengel, 'Zwischen Jesus und Paulus. Die "Hellenisten", die "Sieben" und Stephanus (Apg 6,1-15, 7,54 – 8,3)', *ZTK* 72, 1975, pp. 151-206; and *cf.* I. H. Marshall, 'Palestinian and Hellenistic Christianity: Some Critical Comments', *NTS* 19, 1972-73, pp. 271-287.

> The beginning of the world was from thee: and with law
> thou rulest over all things.
> Unto thee may all flesh speak: for we are thy offspring.
> Therefore will I raise a hymn to thee: and will ever sing
> of thy power.

Written by Cleanthes (*c.* 331–232 BC) this poem represents a lofty state-ment of Stoic belief in the rule of 'law' which governs the universe, and a readiness to apply the idea of Zeus as father and king of the gods to humankind (see Acts 17:28 for a similar connection made in Paul's Athenian sermon). But the Stoic lacked a firm conviction regarding God as personal, and the hymn does not really break out of the imprisoning circle of 'fate' in which all human lives are enmeshed. In fact, this same 'Hymn to Zeus' trails off in a sad identification of the father of the gods and human beings with fate itself. The noble sentiments here expressed serve only to show the need for some confidence in a personal God whose ways are known and can be trusted.

An even more poignant example of the limitations of contemporary religious aspiration is seen in pagan prayers as they are expressed in personal hymns. The scope of such prayers is largely self-centred and the devotee's range of interest does not step outside the circle of egocentricity, as we may observe in the suppliant's appeal to the deity Serapis in Aelius Aristides' 'Hymn to Serapis'. This composition contains some lofty thoughts but without the involvement of personal religion.[18]

New Testament examples of hymnic prayer are quite different as they focus on 'objective' realities which are at the same time intimately related to the believer's experience in the Christian community: the coming of God's king-dom, the progress of the gospel in the world, and the upbuilding of the church. To the extent that these specimens of hymnic prayer-speech (as Paul calls them at least by allusion in 1 Cor. 14:15) celebrate the good news of what God has done in history and especially in the sending, ministry, saving work and triumph of his son Jesus Christ, they stand in the liturgical tradition of the Old Testament.[19] The confession of Israel's God, of which the credo in Deuteronomy 26:5b–9 has been treated as a distillation of cultic praise, centred on several themes of 'didactic exposition'. G. von Rad's study isolated four such themes: the patriarchs, the oppression in Egypt, the march to and entry into Canaan,

---

[18] So G. Delling, *Worship in the New Testament* (Darton, Longman and Todd, 1962), p. 114; A.-J. Festugière, *Personal Religion among the Greeks* (University of California Press, 1960), p. 99.

[19] For what follows see J. I. Durham, 'Credo, Ancient Israelite', in *The Interpreter's Dictionary of the Bible. Supplementary Volume,* ed. K. Crim (Abingdon Press, 1976), pp. 197-199. He gives the bibliography of G. von Rad and M. Noth.

the promised land and home of Israel. Martin Noth wished to enlarge the number of items to include the encounter at Sinai. We note that in each case Yahweh's power is praised as it had been revealed and experienced in events of Israel's historical memory. The might of Israel's God is rehearsed in dramatic fashion and in so doing the faithful Israelite brought the past events over into the present. What God did long ago was re-enacted in the credal recitation and 'contemporized' in a grateful recall.

The basic idea is one of 'remembering' construed in this dynamic way and is carried over into the new Israel and its worship. The events of the 'new exodus' were similarly there rehearsed and recalled in a dramatic re-telling. At this point we are touching upon the shift in an understanding of New Testament canticles that focus on Christ's saving achievement. Unlike the earlier species of 'messianic psalms' these hymns seem – from all the evidence at our disposal – to have been created *de novo* as spontaneous creations of gifted, Spirit-filled members of the community (1 Cor. 14:15; Col. 3:16f.; Eph. 5:18–20), who may be further identified as 'prophets'. If this title is accurate, it suggests that their role was one of instruction and 'exhortation' (*paraklēsis*), according to 1 Corinthians 14:3. And their ministry was intended to 'build up' the congregations, and to do so in one specific regard, namely to ward off erroneous teaching by a positive statement, at services of worship, of how the faith was to be understood and applied with particular reference to Christ's redeeming mission.

We have several extensive pericopes in Paul where, on lexical, stylistic and contextual grounds, we may well suspect that he has taken over and set into the 'flow' of his epistolary correspondence these pre-formed liturgical passages. The more obvious examples in the Pauline corpus are those mentioned by Donald Guthrie: Philippians 2:6–11; Colossians 1:15–20; 1 Timothy 3:16, though the list can be considerably extended. Ph. Vielhauer nominates six accepted hymnic passages, while R. Deichgräber offers five examples of the genre, 'Christ-hymn'. Extending the survey to include Paul and the rest of the New Testament, M. Hengel speaks of 'a dozen christological texts originating within a 50 to 60 year period (40–100 AD)'.[20] After that terminal point at the close of the century there are several well-known references to *carmina Christi* in Pliny, the Letters of Ignatius,[21] and the Odes of Solomon (an early Christian

[20] Ph. Vielhauer, *Geschichte der urchristlichen Literatur* (de Gruyter, 1975), pp.40–47; R. Deichgräber, *Gotteshymnus und Christushymnus in der frühen Christenheit* (Vandenhoeck & Ruprecht, 1967), pp.118-155; M. Hengel, *art. cit.*, p.186.
[21] Pliny, *Ep.* x. 96 (which I have considered in *Carmen Christi* [as in n.13], pp.1-9) and Ignatius, *ad Eph.* 19, the 'Song of the Star' (cf. *ad Eph.* 4).

'hymnbook'). Interestingly, by the time of Justin, at the mid-second century, the flow of such compositions has apparently been checked. The form of the Christian *synaxis* or gathering for public worship at Rome is patterned on the synagogue 'liturgy of the word', to which is then added the 'liturgy of the upper room'. There is less scope for the free rein of the Spirit to inspire spontaneous effusions, though 'prayer' may be free even if led by the president at the Lord's table, 'according to his ability'.

The significance of 'Hymns to Christ'

The teasing question is to know what purpose was served by these Christological hymns. The examples we may point to in Paul's writing suggest that they were well-known in the various churches – else why did Paul take them over, sometimes with slight, if important, adaptation?[22] They were clearly fresh creations, and not simply a reworking of ancient Jewish or messianic texts, though their imagery and idiom have identifiable echoes drawn from the biblical literature. They were also more extensive in length and scope than either the messianic psalms or the fragments of credal statements that can be spotted very obviously in Paul's pastoral discussions in such places as Romans 10:9f.; 1 Corinthians 12:3; 15:3ff. and Colossians 2:6; these are all variations on the credal motif 'Jesus is Lord'. We still need to enquire what may have been the 'catalyst' for the creation of the more elaborate 'hymns to Christ'. Granted as a truism that 'the praise of the community is the response to God's saving act',[23] thus making Christian hymns reflexive and expressive of gratitude to God for all he had done for the world's reconciliation and the church's salvation, we still need to ask why 'Christ hymns' arose in the form they took. Believers, we may be confident, would want to express their praise to the redeemer and to respond to the prompting of the Spirit within their lives. The delicate issue is to ascertain why their hymnic praise to Christ took the shape it evidently did, namely in celebration of what Christ was and did before creation, and in his mission of incarnation and reconciliation that led to a universal acknowledgment that he is now installed as Lord of all worlds and ruler of every agency, heavenly, human and demonic.

The reason, we submit, may be traced to a serious threat to the Pauline kerygma associated with a religious attitude known generically as *gnōsis*. As

[22] Usually such additions serve to anchor redemption in historical events such as Jesus' true incarnation as man and his atoning death on the cross. These saving events assure to the church a place in the new age based on forgiveness of sins. For a discussion of the principle of 'tradition' and 'redaction' in Paul's use of the hymns, see R. P. Martin, *Reconciliation: A Study of Paul's Theology* (Marshall, Morgan and Scott/John Knox Press, 1981), esp. ch.7 (on Col. 1:15-20).

[23] R. Deichgräber, *loc. cit.*, p.201.

early as the situation in 1 Corinthians (or even earlier in Galatians and 1 Thessalonians, it has been claimed),[24] a rival understanding of the Christian message arose, partly drawn from the prevailing Graeco-Roman religious scene and partly as an attempt to turn the church into a hellenistic conventicle. The fullest example is seen in the crisis which prompted the writing of Colossians and maybe the Pastorals and Ephesians. Moreover some emphases in Paul's own preaching may have been recruited and subtly altered to fit into a version of the kerygma Paul no longer wanted to own. Gnostic teachers offered a teaching which quickly challenged the apostolic message as Paul delivered it, and imposed their presence on the churches of the Pauline mission. The tenets of this 'alternative gospel' are seen in a denial of the lordship of Christ as the sole intermediary between God and the world, the insidious relaxing of the moral fibre which led Christians to be indifferent to bodily lusts and sins, and the uncertainty that underlay the meaning of life since the star-gods still held sway and needed to be placated. It is not accidental that the main specimens of New Testament hymns address the various situations in which the presence of gnostic ideas has been suspected and form the polemical counter-thrust to heretical teaching in the areas of doctrine and morals.

Paul's response is directed to these threats which form a network of ideas and practices that are built on a single notion, namely a dualism that separated God from the world. In gnostic thought, God is pure spirit who, by definition, is both untouched by matter and has no direct dealings with the material order. The creation of the universe was relegated to the work of an inferior deity, sometimes linked with the God of the Old Testament. The inter-stellar space between the high God and the world was thought to be populated with a system of emanations or aeons in a connected series, stretching from God to the point at which contact with matter, which was regarded as evil, was just possible. In the Colossian teaching which threatened the church in Lycus valley Christ was evidently given a role as one aeon in a hierarchy, and treated as himself part of the network spun off from the emanating power of the high God.

The 'fulness' (Greek *plērōma*) of aeons that filled the region between heaven and earth was somehow thought to contain 'elemental spirits' which in turn the Colossians needed to venerate (Col. 2:8, 18). Nor was there any assurance that a person's destiny was secure, since the regimen of 'decrees' (Greek *dogmata:* Col. 2:20f.) imposed an ascetic way of life which, being essentially negative, gave no certainty of salvation nor inspired confidence that these astral deities had been successfully overcome. Life's mystery remained to haunt the devotee and he was virtually imprisoned in a mesh of superstition, fear and uncertainty,

---

[24] By W. Schmithals, *Paul and the Gnostics* (Abingdon Press, 1972).

with no way to break the iron grip of astrological control and cultic taboos. What was needed – as we learn from contemporary aretalogies (*i.e.* tributes of praise offered to deities in the mystery religions) – was fellowship with a mighty god or goddess who would lift his or her adherents out of this imprisoning circle and give assurance of salvation and new life. Not surprisingly the delivering deity was hailed as 'lord' (Greek *kyrios*) and 'saviour' (Greek *sōtēr*).

Paul's use of the traditional hymns directed to Christ exactly met the need of his congregations. The ruling idea in such Christological tributes as survive is a portrayal of the odyssey of Christ. His 'course' is surveyed from his life in the Father's presence where he 'functions' as God's *alter ego* or 'image' to include his descent and humiliation in obedience and on to his exaltation in heaven where he received the accolade of a title and a new dignity as ruler of all (*kosmokratōr*). The imagery is one of descent/ascent which replaces the Judaic model of rejection/vindication current in the earlier Christianity.

. But the real point of distinction has more to do with an exploration of the *cosmological role* attributed to the person of Christ. There is a double way in which that adjective came to be applied. First, his pre-existence and pre-temporal activity in creation were made the frontispiece of the hymns. The existence of Christ is taken back to speak of a relationship with God he enjoyed 'in the beginning'. Whether the raw materials of this idea derive from wisdom speculation or from the idea of a heavenly man or from an idealized picture of Adam we cannot really say:[25] what counts is that, as a direct response to the

[25] James D. G. Dunn, *Christology in the Making* (SCM/Westminster Press, 1980), pp. 114-128 devotes a closely reasoned section to Philippians 2:6-11 in the context of Paul's Adam Christology. The thesis he follows and defends is that the hymn uses the model of 'first Adam/last Adam' in that sequence. So there is no need to postulate a pre-temporal existence of Christ, a thought traditionally seen in 2:6a: 'being in the form of God' and so explaining the incarnational allusion in v. 7: 'being born in the likeness of men.' Dunn's position sets up a simple equation: what the Adam of Genesis 1–3 lost, namely his possession of divine 'glory', has been restored to the last Adam, Jesus Christ whose 'glory' is described in 2:9-11. The frontispiece of 2:6a plays no role, Dunn contends, in portraying the 'glory' from which Christ came, nor does it make allusion to his pre-existent state.

Dunn's chief polemic is directed against all attempts at seeing a 'heavenly man' doctrine based on gnostic teaching or derived from Philo's exegesis of Genesis 1 – 2 or drawn from speculation concerning the pre-existence of wisdom. His denials are probably soundly made, and his recourse to the single model of a two Adams teaching is perhaps justified. But has not his championing this line been secured at too high a price, when he proceeds to deny the element of pre-existence behind v. 6a? Granted the Pauline 'order' is first Adam/last Adam, there are several places in the Pauline corpus where the effect of Christ's reconciling work is to restore man's destiny as 'the divine glory' *which was Christ's in the beginning*. See Col. 3:10 (on the meaning of *eikōn* here, see R. P. Martin, *Colossians: the Church's Lord and the Christian's Liberty* [Paternoster, 1972, pp. 115-117]), Ephesians 4:13, 24 as well as the references to the 'image of God' which is *both*

threatening charge that Christ was part of an angelic hierarchy and so linked more with the creation than the Creator, the early church in its outreach to Gentiles came quickly to trace back his being to the very life of God himself. This was done not in a developed way nor, at this stage, as a piece of theologizing, but by attributing to the cosmic Christ an active share in the glory of God (Phil. 2:6) and a role in the creating of the world (Col. 1:15f.). His protological significance was seen as a necessary part of his true being, since only if he existed 'with God' and 'as God' in the beginning (as John 1:1 puts it) was he able to be linked with creation not as part of it but as its maker and groundplan. And only on the assumption of his pre-existent relationship with God could these confessional texts speak meaningfully of Christ's 'being sent' (Gal. 4:4; Rom. 8:3, 32) or alternatively of his 'choosing' to accept the humility of incarnation and obedience (2 Cor. 8:9; Phil. 2:6–8).[26]

Secondly, at the conclusion of his earthly life (and it may be after his willingness to enter the realm of the dead)[27] he took his place in God's presence by receiving universal homage and the acclamation of cosmic spirit-powers that confessed his lordship and so were forced to abandon their title to control over human destiny. This eschatological dimension, heralding the dawn of a new age already glimpsed as a present reality – since 'Jesus Christ is Lord' – would be important to assure believers that their lives were safe under the protection of the regnant Christ. The church that sang the text of Philippians 2:6–11 knew itself to be living in that new world where, all external appearances to the contrary notwithstanding, the astral powers were defeated and Christ the sole ruler of all the worlds was truly Lord. His lordship was no theoretical proposition, nor even a part of their credal profession; it was the living assurance they needed to face their contemporary world with its many 'gods and lords' (1 Cor. 8:5f.) and to rebut the false ideas, both theological and practical, that their lives were the playthings of 'fate' or 'chance' or in the grip of iron determinism. The enthronement of Jesus Christ 'to the glory of God *the Father*' (Phil. 2:11) gave confidence that God had brought victory out of defeat, installed his son as world-ruler, and now wore the face of Jesus Christ whose characteristic name

what redeemed humankind has (1 Cor. 11:7; Rom. 8:29; 2 Cor. 3:18), *and* what Christ was 'in the beginning' (Col. 1:15; 2 Cor. 4:4-6). Only on the basis of the second member of this equation can the hope implied in the first statement be adequately sustained.

[26] This contention is the point of M. Hengel's dictum that the two decades of AD 30-50 (*i.e.* the pre-Pauline era, when the hymns were formulated) were more decisive in innovative and ultimately determinative Christology than the next seven centuries (*The Son of God* [SCM, 1976], p.2).

[27] See R. P. Martin, *Reconciliation* (as in n. 22), pp.66f. for the possibility of a *descensus ad inferos* teaching in Philippians 2:8.

for God was 'Father' (note how the hymn ends with *the Father,* as though to betoken a restoration of men and women to God's family).

Conclusion

The Christological 'hymns', as Donald Guthrie calls them, in the event turn out to be soteriological tributes paid to the cosmic salvation wrought by the redeemer. His salvific work is seen as that of bringing together the two orders of existence ('flesh'/'spirit' in 1 Tim. 3:16) – the celestial and the terrestrial – and his reconciliation is described in a cosmic, transcendental setting. The person of Jesus Christ is set forth in relation to his work as reconciler and world ruler. But inasmuch as he accomplished what God alone could do – the making of the world, the pacification of the hostile powers that had mysteriously broken away from their created order, and the enthronement of a true lordship – and had received from the Father's hand the right to rule human life and to be the judge and criterion of history (as in Rev. 5), it was a short step for the early Christians to go further into Christology. This way of viewing the relation of Christology to Jesus' work suggests that it was *in worship* that the decisive step was made of setting the exalted Christ on a level with God as the recipient of the church's praise. Hymnology and Christology thus merged in the worship of one Lord, soon to be hailed after the close of the New Testament canon as worthy of hymns 'as to God' (Pliny's report of Bithynian Christians at Sunday worship, AD 112).[28]

It was this close drawing together of the persons of the Godhead which laid the foundation for the trinitarian creeds, and raised a bulwark against classical gnosticism in the late second century: yet it has been suggested in this essay that the incipient presence of what became gnosticism led to the creation of these inspired hymns. Just as the occasion of false ideas and customs at the Lord's supper at Corinth prompted Paul to give authoritative teaching in rebuttal and correction, so the rise of aberrant notions touching on the person and place of Jesus Christ in the universe and human life occasioned, under God, a new type of hymnic utterance. Where 'messianic psalms' played their role in defining and defending the church's belief in the fulfilment of Old Testament types and prefigurements, it required a new species – the 'hymn to Christ' – to open fruitful avenues of Christological and soteriological enquiry that set the church from its early days on a course that led eventually to Chalcedon and the *Te Deum:*

> Thou art the King of Glory, O Christ,
> Thou art the everlasting Son of the Father.

[28] As in n. 21.

49

THE BACKGROUND
TO THE SON OF MAN SAYINGS

F. F. Bruce

In his *New Testament Theology* Donald Guthrie concludes a discussion of the Son of man in the Gospels with the observation 'that the title Son of man applied to Jesus made no important impact on early Christian theological thinking and that there is no evidence of a Son of man Christology. . . . The title itself was displaced, but the basic ideas it was intended to express lived on in other forms.'[1] None would have agreed more cordially with that last statement than the late T. W. Manson, who cherished at the back of his mind a project (to be undertaken, perhaps, when he retired) of writing a comprehensive 'Son of man' theology. His untimely death robbed us of a work which might well have crowned his earlier studies.

The problems of the use of 'the Son of man' in the Gospels continue to fascinate New Testament scholars,[2] not least the problem of the almost entire

---

[1] D. Guthrie, *New Testament Theology* (IVP, 1981), p.291.

[2] Some recent contributions (in addition to those cited in following footnotes) are M. Black, 'Jesus and the Son of Man', *JSNT,* issue 1, 1978, pp.4ff.; J. Bowker, 'The Son of Man', *JTS,* n.s., 28, 1977, pp.19ff.; J. Coppens, *Le Fils de l'Homme* (Louvain UP, 1981); J. A. Fitzmyer, 'Another View of the "Son of Man" Debate', *JSNT,* issue 4, 1979, pp.58ff.; A. J. B. Higgins, *The Son of Man in the Teaching of Jesus* (CUP, 1980); M. D. Hooker, 'Is the Son of Man problem really insoluble?' in *Text and Interpretation: Studies in the New Testament presented to M. Black* (CUP, 1979), pp.155ff.; J. Jeremias, *New Testament Theology* 1 (SCM, 1971), pp.257ff.; R. Leivestad, 'Exit the Apocalyptic Son of Man', *NTS* 18, 1971-72, pp.243ff.; B. Lindars, 'Re-enter the Apocalyptic Son of Man', *NTS* 22, 1975-76, pp.52ff.; 'The New Look on the Son of Man', *BJRL* 63 (1980-81), pp.437ff.; I. H. Marshall, 'The Synoptic Son of Man Sayings in Recent Discussion', *NTS* 12, 1965-66, pp.327ff.; 'The Son of Man in Contemporary Debate', *EQ* 42, 1970, pp.67ff.; *The Origins of New Testament Christology* (IVP, 1976), pp.63ff.; C. F. D. Moule, 'Neglected Features in the Problem of "the Son of Man"', in *Neues Testament und Kirche* (R. Schnackenburg *Festschrift*), ed. J. Gnilka (Herder, Freiburg, 1974), pp.413ff.; R. Pesch and R. Schnackenburg (eds.), *Jesus und der Menschensohn* (A. Vögtle *Festschrift*) (Herder, Freiburg, 1975).

absence of any echo outside the Gospels of an expression which plays such a prominent part within them.

In an incident towards the end of Jesus' ministry as recorded in the Fourth Gospel, he speaks of his shortly being 'lifted up from the earth', and the Jerusalem crowd replies, 'We have heard from the law that the Christ remains for ever. How can you say that the Son of man must be lifted up? Who is this Son of man?' (Jn. 12:34).

The Johannine idiom in this interchange is readily recognized. The *double entendre* of the verb 'lift up' is characteristic of this evangelist. Moreover, there are two surprising features in the crowd's response. Jesus had not said, in the immediately preceding context, 'the Son of man will be lifted up' but 'when I am lifted up' (Jn. 12:32). He had, however, said in verse 23, 'The hour has come for the Son of man to be glorified', and in earlier situations in this Gospel he had spoken of the lifting up of the Son of man (Jn. 3:14; 8:28). From this it might be gathered that his being glorified and his being lifted up are identical. So, indeed, they are: we are dealing with two different ways of expressing the same idea. It is plain from some of the contexts in which the lifting up of the Son of man is mentioned that the verb (Gk. *hypsoō*) refers also to Jesus' being literally 'lifted up' on the cross. And the context in which he says, 'The hour has come for the Son of man to be glorified' (Jn. 12:23), makes it clear that here too the crucifixion is meant.

Also, and even more surprisingly, the crowd seems to identify the Son of man with the Christ or the Messiah, although Jesus has not spoken about the Messiah. To Christians, who believed Jesus to be the Messiah and who were familiar with his use of the term 'the Son of man', the equation 'The Messiah = the Son of man' came naturally; here there may be an antedating of this equation into the setting of Jesus' ministry. Certainly there is no reason to suppose that at the time of the ministry the expression 'the Son of man' was current in Judaism as a synonym of 'the Messiah'.

Nevertheless the crowd's question, 'Who is this Son of man?' was a natural one to ask, and may still be asked by readers of the Gospels as they are repeatedly confronted by it.

'The Son of man' in the Gospels

All four of the evangelists regard 'the Son of man' as a self-designation of Jesus. Sometimes, indeed, a comparison of Gospels or Gospel sources indicates that on his lips it could be taken as a periphrasis for 'I'. The Marcan form of his question at Caesarea Philippi, 'Who do men say that I am?' (Mk. 8:27; *cf.* Lk. 9:18), is replaced in Matthew 16:13 by 'Who do men say that the Son of man is?' On the other hand, 'I' may appear as a later re-wording of 'the Son of man'. The Lucan form of another saying of Jesus, 'every one who acknowledges me before men, the Son of man also will acknowledge before the angels of God' (Lk. 12:8), has a Matthaean counterpart with the simple pronoun: 'every one who acknowledges me before men, I also will acknowledge before my Father who is in heaven' (Mt. 10:32; the locution 'my Father who is in heaven' is distinctively Matthaean). But the following words in Matthew, 'whoever denies me before men, I also will deny before my Father who is in heaven' (Mt. 10:33), correspond to a Marcan saying in which it is the Son of man who will be ashamed of those who are ashamed of Jesus and his words[3] 'in this adulterous and sinful generation' (Mk. 8:38; *cf.* Lk. 9:26).

This oscillation between 'I' and 'the Son of man' is sufficient to make the reader stop and ask before each 'Son of man' saying in the Synoptic record, 'Is this original, or has it replaced an earlier "I"?' However, even when allowance has been made for the possibility of a change from 'I' to 'the Son of man', the fact that sometimes the change seems to have worked the other way confirms the impression made by the spread of the designation 'the Son of man' – the impression that, not only in the Gospels as they stand but in the tradition behind them, 'the Son of man' was a distinctive locution of Jesus, one which he used as a self-designation.

The criteria of authenticity invoked by proponents of modern redaction criticism of the Gospels are not so conclusive as is sometimes supposed; but if one of them, the 'criterion of dissimilarity', be applied to the occurrences of 'the Son of man', the conclusion seems plain (although indeed a number of redaction critics would not concede its validity in this instance).[4] Here is a locution unparalleled in the Judaism of the period and one which, outside the Gospel tradition, was not current in the early church. Its claim to be recognized as an authentic *vox Christi* is thus remarkably strong.

It has often been pointed out that the Greek phrase translated 'the Son of man' in the Gospels, *ho huios tou anthrōpou,* means literally 'the son of the man', which would naturally prompt the question: 'the son of *which* man?' But no such question is prompted by the phrase as used in the Gospels, where it is a conventional rendering of an Aramaic expression, probably *bar ᵉnāšā.* But *bar*

---

[3] The rather weakly attested omission of *logous* from this text (*P*[45 vid] *al*) makes Jesus utter a warning to any one 'who is ashamed of me and mine'. It was regarded as 'probably the true reading' by T. W. Manson, who regarded it as confirming his thesis that 'the "Son of man" here stands for the Remnant, the true Israel of which Jesus is the head' (*The Sayings of Jesus* [SCM, 1949], p. 109). C. K. Barrett finds an echo of the full (and authentic) reading in Paul's 'I am not ashamed of the gospel' (Rom. 1:16) and similar statements in early Christian literature ('I am not ashamed of the gospel', *Analecta Biblica,* 42 [P.B.I., Rome, 1970], pp. 19ff.).

[4] *E.g.* N. Perrin, *Rediscovering the Teaching of Jesus* (SCM, 1967), pp. 164ff.

$^{ie}n\bar{a}\check{s}\bar{a}$ is the regular Aramaic form for 'the man', 'the human being' or even, when the emphatic state (rendered in English by means of the definite article) is used generically, 'a man'. (We may compare John the Baptist's words in Jn. 3:27 NIV: 'a man can receive only what is given him from heaven.') It is argued by M. Casey that this construction and meaning lie behind the Gospel use of *ho huios tou anthrōpou*, the speaker saying something which is true of a man generically and applying it to himself. Thus the statement of Mark 14:21a, 'the Son of man goes as it is written of him', could have originated in Jesus' application to himself of the general principle that 'a man goes (to death) as it is written of him' (*cf.* Heb. 9:27, 'it is appointed for men to die once').[5] G. Vermes has argued, more generally, that the Gospel use goes back to the circumlocutional use of *bar $^{ie}n\bar{a}\check{s}\bar{a}$* ('the man', 'this man') as a substitute for the pronoun 'I', 'me'.[6]

There are indeed some passages in the Gospels where 'the Son of man' on the lips of Jesus seems to mean little more than 'I' – for example, when he compares himself with his forerunner in the words: 'John the Baptist has come eating no bread and drinking no wine;... the Son of man has come eating and drinking...' (Lk. 7:33f.; *cf.* Mt. 11:18f.). Again, there is reason to think here and there that the Greek rendering *ho huios tou anthrōpou* has been used where *bar $^{ie}n\bar{a}\check{s}\bar{a}$* meant simply 'man' – for example, a comparison of the Q saying in Luke 12:10 with its Marcan counterpart in Mark 3:28–30 (the two are conflated in Mt. 12:31f.) suggests that in the original form Jesus contrasted the venial sin of speaking against men with the 'eternal sin' of speaking against the Holy Spirit; 'the Son of man' in the distinctive sense of the expression is not in view.

There are, however, two outstanding situations in which the Son of man (in the distinctive use of the phrase) figures. One of these is his appearing in glory; the other is his suffering.

His appearing in glory
In the Olivet discourse it is said that, after the great tribulation which leads up to the end-time, 'they will see the Son of man coming in clouds with great power and glory. And then he will send out the angels, and gather his elect...' (Mk. 13:26f.). It is difficult to avoid the conclusion that the Son of man coming in clouds harks back to the 'one like a son of man' (Aram. *k^{e}bar $^{ie}n\bar{a}\check{s}$*) who, in Daniel's vision of the day of judgment, comes 'with the clouds of heaven' to be

---

[5] M. Casey, *Son of Man* (SPCK, 1979), pp.224ff.
[6] G. Vermes, 'Appendix E: The use of *bar nāš / bar nāšā* in Jewish Aramaic', in M. Black, *An Aramaic Approach to the Gospels and Acts* (Clarendon, [3]1967), pp.310ff.; *Jesus the Jew* (Collins, 1973), pp.160ff.; '"The Son of Man" Debate', *JSNT,* issue 1, 1978, pp.19ff.

presented before the Ancient of Days and to receive universal and eternal dominion from him (Dn. 7:13f.).

Similar language is used by Jesus in his reply to the high priest's question 'Are you the Christ?' in Mark's trial narrative: 'I am; and you will see the Son of man seated at the right hand of Power, and coming with the clouds of heaven' (Mk. 14:62). It is as though Jesus meant: 'If "Christ" ("Messiah") is the term which you insist on using, then I have no option but to say "Yes"; but if I may choose my own words, I tell you that you will see the Son of man . . .'. In this reply the language of Daniel 7:13f. is fused with that of Psalm 110:1, where one whom the psalmist calls 'my lord' is invited in an oracle to take his seat at Yahweh's right hand until his enemies are subdued beneath his feet.

The other Synoptic traditions add further *logia* to the same effect. The Q counterpart to Mark's Olivet discourse says that on the day when the Son of man is revealed his revelation will be like a flash of lightning illuminating the whole sky; it will be the occasion of sudden judgment such as, in the Old Testament record, was manifested in the flood of Noah's day and in the destruction of Sodom and the neighbouring cities (Lk. 17:24–32). Matthew adds references of his own to the Son of man coming 'with his angels in the glory of his Father' to 'repay every man for what he has done' (Mt. 16:27), coming 'in his glory, and all the angels with him', to 'sit on his glorious throne' (Mt. 25:31). He may even introduce the Son of man in this kind of context where the Synoptic parallels make no mention of him: seeing 'the kingdom of God come with power' (Mk. 9:1; *cf.* Lk. 9:27) becomes for Matthew seeing 'the Son of man coming in his kingdom' (Mt. 16:28).

If Daniel's vision indeed stands behind Gospel references to the Son of man's being invested with glory, some attention to that vision is called for. In the vision Daniel sees four beasts coming up, one after another, from 'the great sea' and exercising dominion for a time. The most fearful of the four has ten horns, among which a 'little horn' sprouts forth, exceeding all predecessors in its ambition to wield unlimited power. Then comes the day of judgment, one who is 'Ancient of Days' takes his seat, and he bestows world dominion on a human, not a bestial, figure – on 'one like a son of man'.

One of the attendants on the Ancient of Days explains the details of the vision to Daniel. 'These four great beasts are four kings who shall arise out of the earth' (Dn. 7:17). But the interpreter does not tell Daniel who the 'one like a son of man' is. He simply says that 'the saints of the Most High (*qaddîsê 'elyônîn*) shall receive the kingdom, and possess the kingdom for ever, for ever and ever' (Dn. 7:18). The 'saints of the Most High' in the interpretation correspond to the 'one like a son of man' in the vision, but the two are not expressly identified.

54

Attempts have been made to establish the background of the figure 'like a son of man' – for example, in the supposed New Year enthronement festival in pre-exilic Israel,[7] or in the Ugaritic scene where Ba'al, the 'rider on the clouds', comes before El, the father of the gods.[8] Such attempts are precarious in themselves and in any case are irrelevant to the understanding of Daniel's vision and to the question of its influence on the thought or language of Jesus and the evangelists.

The 'saints of the Most High' – more fully, 'the people of the saints of the Most High' (Dn. 7:27) – who figure in the interpretation of the vision are most probably those Israelites who remained faithful to the covenant in time of persecution. Weighty arguments have indeed been put forward, by M. Noth and others,[9] for their identification with the holy beings of angelic rank who serve God in his heavenly dwelling. But these arguments are not conclusive. It is unlikely that even one so powerful as the 'little horn' should be able to wage war successfully against *these* holy ones, as it is said to have done against 'the saints' in Daniel 7:21. It is more natural to think of the many *ḥᵃsîdîm* who died rather than commit apostasy under Antiochus Epiphanes. If it is faithful men and women that are intended, then their being given 'the kingdom and the dominion and the greatness of the kingdoms under the whole heaven' (Dn. 7:27) offers itself as an Old Testament background to Jesus' words of encouragement to his followers (not in a 'Son of man' saying): 'Fear not, little flock, for it is your Father's good pleasure to give you the kingdom' (Lk. 12:32).

Since Daniel's 'one like a son of man' is not explicitly identified with the 'saints of the Most High', it might be wiser to say that he represents them than that he symbolizes them. But the relation between him and them in Daniel's vision and its interpretation is independent of the question whether or not the Son of man in the Gospels is (sometimes at least) a corporate entity. Jesus certainly associated his disciples closely with himself in coming glory as in present suffering. His words (partly derived from Q) in the Lucan narrative of the Last Supper are relevant in this regard: 'You are those who have continued with me in my trials; as my Father appointed a kingdom for me, so do I appoint for you that you may eat and drink at my table in my kingdom, and sit on thrones judging the twelve tribes of Israel' (Lk. 22:28–30).

But their association with him in his coming authority depended on their

---

[7] *Cf.* A. Bentzen, *King and Messiah* (Lutterworth, 1955), pp.74f.

[8] *Cf.* C. Colpe, *"Ho huios tou anthrōpou'*, *TDNT*, 8 (Eerdmans, 1972), pp.415-419.

[9] M. Noth, 'The Holy Ones of the Most High', in *The Laws in the Pentateuch and Other Studies* (Oliver & Boyd, 1966), pp.215ff.; *cf.* L. Dequeker, 'The "Saints of the Most High" in Qumran and Daniel', *OTS* 18, 1973, pp.108ff.

continuing with him in his trials. We recall his assurance to James and John, when they professed themselves ready to drink his cup and share his baptism, that they would indeed do so (Mk. 10:38f.). But when his trial reached its climax, they proved unable to stand the test. T. W. Manson remarked that, if it had been James and John, and not the two robbers, that were crucified with Jesus, 'one on his right and one on his left', their request to be enthroned on either side of him (Mk. 10:37) would have been fulfilled and the church's formulation of the doctrine of the atonement might have been somewhat different from what it has been.[10] As it was, Jesus himself at the time fulfilled single-handed 'everything that is written of the Son of man' (Lk. 18:31). The time was to come, however, when he would return from death to gather his demoralized followers together again and lead them as before and associate[11] them even more closely with himself in his continuing ministry. 'The aliveness of Christ,' says C. F. D. Moule, 'existing transcendentally beyond death, is recognized as the prior necessity for the community's corporate existence, and as its source and origin.'[12] Positive evidence is lacking that Jesus ever included his followers *in* the concept of the Son of man, but he did attach them as firmly as possible *to* the Son of man.

His suffering

In these last paragraphs we have already begun to refer to the suffering Son of man.

Alongside those sayings which reflect Daniel's vision of 'one like a son of man' who receives sovereign authority from God, there is a group of sayings, especially in the Marcan record, which speak of the Son of man as suffering. In this record, from the Caesarea Philippi incident onward, Jesus emphasizes repeatedly that 'the Son of man must suffer many things' (Mk. 8:31; 9:31; *cf.* 10:33). The necessity of the Son of man's suffering lies in its being the subject-matter of Scripture: Jesus' consciousness that his own deliberately chosen mission was in accordance with what was written confirmed his resolution to submit to arrest in Gethsemane with the words: 'Let the scriptures be fulfilled' (Mk. 14:49). The other Synoptic evangelists bear similar testimony: Luke, for example, inserts into his description of the lightning-like appearance of the Son of man 'in his day' the caveat: 'But first he must suffer many things and be rejected by this generation' (Lk. 17:25).

The fourth evangelist brings the two groups of Son of man sayings together

---

[10] T. W. Manson, *The Teaching of Jesus* (CUP, ²1935), pp.231ff.

[11] *Cf.* Mk. 14:28.

[12] C. F. D. Moule, *The Origin of Christology* (CUP, 1977), p.70.

in his distinctive idiom.[13] For him the crucifixion of Jesus is the 'lifting up' (*hypsōsis*) or 'glorifying' of the Son of man; it is the moment of disclosure, when the disciples will 'see heaven opened, and the angels of God ascending and descending on the Son of man' (Jn. 1:51).

But in the Synoptic records the two groups of passages remain separated. There is no difficulty in seeing the influence of Daniel 7:13f. on those which speak of the Son of man's glorious advent and judicial authority; but 'how is it written of the Son of man, that he should suffer many things and be treated with contempt?' (Mk. 9:12).

Many have seen a pointer to answering this question in Mark 10:45, where Jesus sets an example before his disciples by impressing on them that 'the Son of man also came not to be served but to serve, and to give his life as a ransom for many'. This saying is reproduced *verbatim* in Matthew 20:28, but is missing from the parallel context in Luke 18 (between verses 34 and 35). Luke has indeed a parallel elsewhere, in the context of the Last Supper, but it is not a Son of man saying and makes no reference to a ransom (Lk. 22:27, 'I am among you as one who serves').

The wording of the Son of man saying in Mark 10:45 has often been held to reflect that of the fourth Isaianic Servant Song (Is. 52:13 – 53:12). It does not, strictly, reflect its wording but it does reflect its thought. The word for 'serve' in Mark 10:45 (*diakoneō*) is not that used to render Hebrew '*ebed* in the Servant Song (*ho pais mou*, Is. 52:13, LXX; *douleuō*, Is. 53:11, LXX), and the word for 'ransom' in Mark 10:45 (*lytron*) is not used to render '*āsām* ('guilt-offering') in Isaiah 53:10 (LXX *peri hamartias*). But the sense of the saying in Mark 10:45 corresponds well to the description of the Servant's self-giving in which he procures righteousness for 'many' and bears the sin of 'many' (Is. 53:11f.). The linking of this saying with Isaiah 52:13 – 53:12 has, indeed, been ably contested:[14] it is pointed out, for example, that to give one's life as a ransom or atonement for others was a familiar concept in the Judaism of the time, as the Maccabaean martyrologies show (*cf.* 2 Macc. 7:37f.; 4 Macc. 6:27–29; 17:22; 18:4). It is not suggested that either Jesus or Mark was familiar with these Greek martyrologies; on the other hand, the book of Isaiah was well known to them both.

---

[13] *Cf.* S. S. Smalley, 'The Johannine Son of Man Sayings', *NTS* 15, 1968-69, pp.278ff.; B. Lindars, 'The Son of Man in the Johannine Christology', in *Christ and Spirit in the New Testament* (C. F. D. Moule *Festschrift*), eds. B. Lindars and S. S. Smalley (CUP, 1973), pp.43ff.

[14] *E.g.* by C. K. Barrett, 'The Background of Mark 10:45', in *New Testament Essays: Studies in Memory of T. W. Manson,* ed. A. J. B. Higgins (Manchester UP, 1959), pp.1ff.; M. D. Hooker, *Jesus and the Servant* (SPCK, 1959).

Moreover, the Son of man's suffering is said to be something that was 'written' concerning him. This is a reference to Hebrew Scripture, in which the books of Maccabees played no part. Where, then, in Hebrew Scripture is it written that the Son of man is to suffer?

It is not so written of Daniel's 'one like a son of man'. True, his counterparts, the saints of the Most High, are targets for the assault of the 'little horn' (Dn. 7:21), and it could easily be inferred that, in a situation dominated by God-defying powers, the 'one like a son of man' would fare ill until the time of divine intervention,[15] but the statement 'it is written' implies more than an inference. In any case, the 'one like a son of man' makes his appearance in Daniel's vision at the moment of the overthrow of the God-defying powers and the vindication of righteousness, and it is probably inappropriate to import him into an earlier phase of the vision where he does not figure. Further, when the activity of the little horn is recapitulated in greater detail, and we might expect Daniel to say that he saw the little horn making war against the 'one like a son of man', he does not say so; he imports a feature from the interpretation and says that the little horn 'made war with the *saints*' (Dn. 7:21), as though deliberately avoiding a suggestion that the 'one like a son of man' was attacked. This could be explained if for Daniel the 'one like a son of man' is not the symbolical personification of the saints but their heavenly representative.

If we look for a figure in Hebrew Scripture who suffers many things and is treated with contempt, the righteous sufferer of Psalms and the suffering Servant of Isaiah come to mind at once. As between these two, the balance is tipped in favour of the Isaianic Servant because his sufferings, unlike those of the righteous sufferer of Psalms, are explicitly said to procure the removal of sin for others. Is the Son of man in the Gospels, then, to be equated with the Servant of Yahweh?

Let it be said at this point that there is some reason to think that the Daniel texts we have been considering, and some others associated with them, had the Isaianic Servant Songs in view and were indeed intended to provide an interpretation of them.

One of the designations of the faithful in the time of trial depicted in Daniel's visions is *maśkîlîm,* the 'wise' or the 'teachers' (*i.e.* those who acquire wisdom or those who impart it, the latter activity naturally following from the former). The reference is especially to those who communicate to others the insight which they themselves have gained into the times of the end; 'none of the wicked shall understand, but the *maśkîlîm* shall understand' (Dn. 12:10).

---

[15] *Cf.* C. F. D. Moule, 'From Defendant to Judge – and Deliverer', *SNTS Bulletin* 3, 1952, pp.40ff.; M. D. Hooker, *The Son of Man in Mark* (SPCK, 1967), pp.11ff.

Daniel himself is given such insight: when Gabriel is about to impart to him the revelation of the seventy heptads, he says, 'I have come out to make you wise (*lᵉhaśkîlᵉkā*) . . . know therefore and understand (*uᵉtaśkēl*) that . . . there are to be seven heptads . . .' (Dn. 9:22, 25).

When the minds of many are shaken by the apostates, 'those who make the people wise (*maśkîlê 'am*) shall make many understand', although their faithfulness involves them in severe persecution (Dn. 11:33). So severe will the persecution be, indeed, that some even of the *maśkîlîm* will fall away, but their defection will but serve to refine those who remain faithful (Dn. 11:35). And when at last the righteous are delivered and the faithful departed are raised to everlasting life, 'the *maśkîlîm* shall shine like the brightness of the firmament, and those who turn many to righteousness (*maṣdîqê hārabbîm*) like the stars for ever and ever' (Dn. 12:1–3).

It would be rash to draw too certain inferences from the coincidence between these instances of the hiph'il conjugation of *śkl* and the opening words of the fourth Servant Song, *hinnēh yaśkîl 'abdî*, 'behold, my servant will deal wisely' (Is. 52:13); but that we have to do with more than a mere coincidence is suggested by the statement in Isaiah 53:11 that the Servant will by his knowledge 'make the many to be accounted righteous' (*yaṣdîq . . . lārabbîm*) – *i.e.* he will fulfil the role assigned to the *maśkîlîm* in Daniel 12:3. But if Daniel is thus providing an interpretation of the figure of the suffering Servant, it is a corporate interpretation.

To revert to the Gospels: there is one exception to the rule that when Jesus speaks of 'the Son of man' both nouns have the article (*ho huios tou anthrōpou*). The exception comes in John 5:27, where the Father delegates judicial functions to the Son, 'because he is Son of man' (*hoti huios anthrōpou estin*). Grammatically, this doubly anarthrous form can be adequately accounted for in terms of Colwell's law: it is the complement with the copulative verb. But exegetically, even if there is no particle *hōs* here, it is not far-fetched to recognize a specific reference to the 'one like a son of man' (*hōs huios anthrōpou*) who is assessor to the Ancient of Days on his judgment-throne (Dn. 7:13f.).

There is, again, one exception to the rule that only in the Gospels, and only on Jesus' lips (apart, of course, from Jn. 12:34, where the crowd takes up his own words), does the expression 'the Son of man' occur in the New Testament. The exception comes in Acts 7:56 where Stephen, at the end of his defence before the Sanhedrin, sees 'the heavens opened, and the Son of man standing at the right hand of God'.[16] The language resembles that of Jesus himself before

---

[16] The expression 'the Son of man' is placed on the lips of James the Just in Hegesippus's account of his martyrdom (Eusebius, *HE* 2.23.13), but this account is modelled on Luke's

the same body: in the Lucan form of his reply to the high priest Jesus says, 'But from now on the Son of man shall be seated at the right hand of the power of God' (Lk. 22:69). The change from 'seated' to 'standing' arrests the attentive reader, and points to the meaning of Stephen's words. The Son of man is Stephen's advocate in the presence of God, and standing is the posture proper for an advocate. Stephen, so to speak, appeals from the judgment of the earthly court to the arbitrament of the heavenly court, where the Son of man stands as his prevailing advocate. It is illuminating to read Stephen's words against the background of the dominical logion of Luke 12:8, 'every one who acknowledges me before men, the Son of man also will acknowledge before the angels of God.'[17]

Whatever the Aramaic phrase was that Jesus used (and it can scarcely have been anything other than *bar* '*e*nāšā), and whatever its significance may have been, there was a time antecedent to the compilation of all our Gospels and their ascertainable sources when *ho huios tou anthrōpou* was fixed as its appropriate Greek equivalent. M. Hengel considers that 'an unequivocal christological conception' must stand behind 'this unusual translation' and he is disposed to believe that Stephen's vision of 'the Son of man' may have had something to do with this development.[18]

Hengel's understanding of the matter underlines the conclusion to which the available evidence in any case points – that 'the Son of man' was not a current title, whether for the Messiah or for any other eschatological figure. When Jewish thinkers devised a title for the figure who is brought to the Ancient of Days, it was not the Son of man but Anani (the 'cloud-man').[19] There does not appear to have been any existing concept of 'the Son of man' which Jesus could have taken over and used either to identify himself or to denote a being distinct from himself. The expression as Jesus used it was evidently original to himself: one reason for his use of it may have been precisely that it was not a current title which would already have had associations in the minds of his hearers. It could well have meant for him 'the one like a son of man' (of Daniel's vision) but he could fill it with such further significance as he chose, and not the least part of the significance with which he filled it was the prophetic picture of the humble and suffering Servant of Yahweh. If the

---

narrative of the trial and death of Stephen.

[17] Cf. B. Lindars, 'Jesus as Advocate: A Contribution to the Christology Debate', *BJRL* 62, 1979-80, pp.476ff.

[18] M. Hengel, 'Zwischen Jesus und Paulus', *ZTK* 72, 1975, pp.151ff. (p.203).

[19] *Tanḥuma Tôl dôt* 20; Anani in this sense is linked with the Anani who ends the catalogue of David's descendants in 1 Ch. 3:24 (and who is identified with the Davidic Messiah).

heavenly voice at his baptism (Mk. 1:11) hailed him in language which he recognized as that of Isaiah 42:1, there was no problem in his associating with that scripture another which similarly begins with 'Behold, my servant' – the scripture which we call the fourth Servant Song. It was this that gave him the assurance that a mission involving suffering and contempt was *written* for 'the Son of man', and that this mission was the Father's will for him.

Evidence from Qumran

The transition from suffering for faithfulness to exercising authority and executing judgment is well attested in the Qumran literature (from *c.* 130 BC onwards), and the phase of suffering for faithfulness is bound up with the portrayal of the Isaianic Servant.

The Servant Songs

Shortly after the publication of the complete Isaiah scroll from Cave 1 at Qumran (1QIs^a), a peculiar reading was noted in Isaiah 52:14. Of the Servant it is said there (in MT) *kēn mišḥat mē'îš mar'ēhû*, 'such was the marring of his appearance, beyond (that of) man.' The common translation treats *mišḥat* as construct state of *mišḥāt*, 'marring' (from root *šḥt*), but there is an awkwardness in that the construct is separated from its following genitive by the comparative expression *mē'îš*. The same awkwardness would persist if *mišḥat* were treated (less probably) as the construct of *mišḥāh*, 'anointing' (from root *mšḥ*), the sense then being 'such was the anointing of his face, beyond (that of) man'. (The awkwardness would be avoided if the word were vocalized *mošḥāt*, hoph'al participle of *šḥt*, the sense then being 'his appearance was marred beyond that of mankind'.) In 1QIs^a, however, the spelling *mšḥty* appears – i.e., probably, *māšaḥtî*, 'I have anointed' (perfect qal of *mšḥ*). It is unlikely that the prophet meant 'I have anointed his face beyond that of mankind', but the curious spelling may reflect a messianic interpretation placed on the figure of the Servant by some members of the Qumran community. D. Barthélemy, indeed, one of the first scholars to draw attention to this spelling, thought it had serious claims to be regarded as original;[20] W. H. Brownlee compared the construction with that of Psalm 45:7 (MT 8), 'God . . . has anointed you with the oil of gladness above your fellows' (*mēḥ^{a}ḇērēḵā*), where a royal anointing is in view.[21]

---

[20] D. Barthélemy, 'Le grand rouleau d'Isaïe trouvé près de la Mer Morte', *RB* 57, 1950, pp.530ff. (pp.546ff.).

[21] W. H. Brownlee, 'The Servant of the Lord in the Qumran Scrolls', *BASOR* 132, Dec. 1953, pp.8ff.

The prophet himself, speaking perhaps in the role of the Servant, claims in Isaiah 61:1, 'Yahweh has anointed me' (*m^{e}šaḥtání*), where a prophetic anointing is in view. But what kind of anointing was in the mind of the editor or scribe responsible for the spelling *māšaḥtî* in Isaiah 52:14? Perhaps a priestly anointing, in view of the following words, 'so shall he *sprinkle* many nations.' Brownlee rightly retained the MT reading *yazzeh* ('will sprinkle'), adding that, according to his understanding of the Qumran interpretation, 'the anointing of the Servant would indicate his consecration for the priestly office, so that he could "sprinkle" others.' It may be, then, that here we have a pointer to an identification of the Servant with the expected priestly Messiah, the 'Messiah of Aaron'.

But this is not the only interpretation of the Servant attested in the Qumran writings. In the *Hôdāyôt* (the 'Hymns of Thanksgiving') the person who speaks in the first person singular – be he (as some have thought) the Rightful Teacher himself or some other spokesman for the community – repeatedly applies to himself the language of all four of what we have come to call the Servant Songs. From the first song (Is. 42:1) possibly comes:

> Thou hast shed [thy] holy spirit on thy servant. (1QH 17.26)

From the second (Is. 49:1ff.):

> For thou knowest me from (better than) my father,
> and from the womb [hast thou set me apart].
> [Yea, from the body of] my mother hast thou dealt
>   bountifully with me,
> and from the breast of her who conceived me have
>   thy tender mercies been on me.
> In the bosom of my nurse [hast thou sustained me],
> and from my youth hast thou enlightened me in the
>   understanding of thy judgments.
> With thy truth hast thou supported me firmly,
> and in thy holy spirit hast thou made me rejoice. (1QH 9.29–32)

From the third (Is. 50:4):

> My tongue is as that of those who are taught [by thee]. (1QH 7.10)

> I could not raise my voice
> [with the tong]ue of those who are taught [by thee],

to revive the spirit of the stumbling,
or to sustain with a word him that is weary.   (1QH 8.35f.)

And from the fourth (Is. 53:4, 10):

[My] dwelling-place is with diseases,
and my resting-place among those that are stricken;
I am as a man forsaken.   (1QH 8.26f.).

Whether the composer was speaking of his personal experience or not, the community probably used these hymns in worship, as an adjunct to the canonical Psalter, and in that case each member who participated in the worship made the composer's language his own.

There is, moreover, evidence to indicate that the Qumran community viewed itself as called corporately to fulfil the Servant's ministry. It believed that by its painstaking study and practice of the divine law, and by its patient endurance of the persecution inflicted on it by the ungodly, it would not only secure its acceptance in God's sight but also accumulate a store of merit sufficient to atone for people and land polluted by the dominion of the wicked. In default of Levitical sin-offerings, sin would be atoned for 'through an upright and humble spirit' (1QS 3.8). When all the prescriptions of the community rule were fulfilled, 'to establish a holy spirit for eternal truth, to make atonement for the guilt of rebellion and for sinful faithlessness, and to obtain favour for the land apart from the flesh of burnt-offerings and the fat of sacrifice, then the oblation of the lips according to right judgment shall be as a sweet savour of righteousness, and the perfectness of one's ways as an acceptable freewill offering' (1QS 9.3–5).

In the *Rule of the Congregation,* which envisages the new order when the rightful regime of the sons of Zadok has been restored, the members of the community are described as 'the men of God's counsel who kept his covenant in the midst of wickedness, so as to make atone[ment for the lan]d' (1QSa. 1.1–3).

With this may be compared what is said of the Servant of Yahweh in the Targum of Jonathan: 'He will make entreaty for our trespasses and for his sake our trespasses will be forgiven; . . . by his instruction peace will flourish over us, and when we follow his words our trespasses will be forgiven us. All we like sheep had been scattered, each in his own way we had gone astray, and it was the Lord's good pleasure to forgive all our trespasses for his sake' (Tg. Is. 53:4–6). There the speakers are the people of Israel, and the Servant for whose sake they have been forgiven is the Messiah; but in the Qumran texts it is not for the sake of one individual, but for the sake of the righteous community, that this forgiveness is bestowed on the nation. Nor is the community's suffering minimized almost to the point of disappearance, as the Servant's suffering is in the Targum.

If the whole community had its mission prescribed in terms of the ministry of the Isaianic Servant, it was possible for some smaller body, acting or speaking in the name of the community, to be referred to in similar terms. [22] In one place the atoning terminology is used of the inner council of twelve laymen and three priests, who are called 'a holy house for Israel, a most holy foundation for Aaron, true witnesses in judgment, the elect ones of God's favour, to make atonement for the land and to requite the wicked with their recompense' (1QS 8.5–7).

In the Old Testament atonement 'for the land' is necessary when it has been polluted by bloodshed, and this atonement can be made only by the blood of those responsible (Nu. 35:33). In the Song of Moses God makes atonement for his people's land by avenging the blood of his servants at the hands of his and their enemies (Dt. 32:43).

Vindication and judgment

When the inner council of the community is said to 'requite the wicked with their recompense, . . . to execute judgment on wickedness, that perversity may be no more' (1QS 8.7, 10), it has an activity prescribed for it which cannot be paralleled in the Servant Songs. Nor can it have been possible for the inner council, or for the community as a whole, to undertake this activity in the days when it was at the mercy of its powerful opponents. But the community looked forward to a time when the roles would be reversed, when God would intervene in justice, and then it would be his chosen instrument to execute judgment on the ungodly.

It would be misleading if we said that the community believed itself called to fill the role of Daniel's 'one like a son of man' as well as that of the Isaianic Servant, for there is no reference in the extant Qumran texts to Daniel's 'one like a son of man', nor does 'son of man' appear anywhere in them except in the regular sense of 'human being'.

Nevertheless, some of the ideas associated with Daniel's 'one like a son of man' and with 'the Son of man' in the Gospels find expression, albeit in

---

[22] It is just possible that in one place an individual is so referred to – in 1QS 4.20f., where it is said that 'God will purify by his truth all the deeds of (a) man, and will cleanse (him) for himself more than (or 'from among') the sons of man'. But the wording is too ambiguous for any certain conclusions to be drawn. Cf. J. A. T. Robinson, 'The Baptism of John and the Qumran Community', in *Twelve New Testament Studies* (SCM, 1962), pp.23f.

different terminology, in the Qumran literature. Here, for example, is the Qumran commentator's explanation of Habakkuk 1:12b ('Thou hast ordained him to execute judgment; and thou, O Rock, hast established him to inflict chastisement'):

> The interpretation of this is that God will not destroy his people by the hand of the nations, but into the hand of his elect will God commit the judgment of all nations, and by the chastisement which they inflict those who have kept his commandments in the time of their distress will condemn all the wicked of his people (1QpHab 5.3–6).

God's 'elect' – 'those who have kept his commandments in the time of their distress' – are presumably the members of the righteous community who have maintained their fidelity in spite of persecution. They are, in the words of the *Community Rule,* 'to condemn all transgressors of the law' as well as 'to make atonement for all volunteers for holiness in Aaron (the priesthood) and for the house of truth in Israel (the laity)' (1QS 5.6f.).

In the *Rule of War* the righteous community is the spearhead of the successful attack on the Gentile oppressors of Israel, but in the Habakkuk commentary it is plain that it will also administer final judgment on evildoers within Israel. It is not unreasonable to conclude that its members identified themselves with the 'saints of the Most High' to whom, in Daniel 7:18, 22, 27, judgment and sovereignty are given.[23]

Melchizedek

Before we leave Qumran, we should glance at the heavenly judge Melchizedek who has given his name to the fragmentary document 11Q Melchizedek, published in 1965.[24]

Quoting the passages about the year of jubilee (Lv. 25:13) and the year of release (Dt. 15:2), this document understands both as references to the return from exile at the time of the end, in the tenth and last year of jubilee, 'the acceptable year of the Lord' (Is. 61:2), when the dispersed of Israel will be gathered home. The proclaimer of restoration and liberty at that time will be Melchizedek, 'for that is the epoch of Melchizedek's "acceptable year"' (line 7).

A scriptural basis for Melchizedek's heavenly ministry is sought in Psalm

---

[23] Judgment is given to them and not merely for them (*cf.* Rev. 20:4); see C. F. D. Moule, *The Origin of Christology*, p.21.

[24] *Cf.* A. S. van der Woude, 'Melchisedek als himmlische Erlösergestalt in den neugefundenen eschatologischen Midraschim aus Qumran Höhle XI', *OTS* 14, 1965, pp.354ff.

82:1, 'God (*'elōhîm*) stands in the congregation of *'Ēl*: he judges among *'elōhîm*.' Melchizedek is promoted to be president of the heavenly court; he sits in judgment on the *'elōhîm*, the spirits of Belial's lot. This is related to the statement of Psalm 7:8, 'God (*'elōhîm*) will judge the nations', through the exegetical device of *gezērāh šawāh* ('equal category'), since *'elōhîm* occurs in the singular in both texts as the subject of the verb 'to judge' (and is taken in both to mean Melchizedek, to whom the Most High has delegated his judicial authority). But Melchizedek's ministry of liberation for the men of his own 'lot', the children of light, is celebrated in Isaiah 52:7, 'How beautiful on the mountains are the feet of him who brings glad tidings, . . . who says to Zion, "Your *'elōhîm* reigns!"' Here also, as in the other two texts, the *'elōhîm* in question is Melchizedek. By passing sentence on the hosts of Belial, Melchizedek inaugurates the age of liberation for the righteous.

There is little enough in the two explicit references to Melchizedek in the Hebrew Bible to provide a basis for this conception of him as a heavenly judge and saviour. Some have tried (unsuccessfully, I think) to relate this conception to the portrayal in Hebrews of the Son of God, enthroned at his Father's right hand, discharging a ministry of intercession as his people's high priest 'after the order of Melchizedek' (*cf*. Ps. 110:4). A distant parallel might be found in Luke 4:18f., where the proclamation of the 'acceptable year of the Lord' is fulfilled in Jesus' ministry on earth, but the other side of the coin, 'the day of vengeance of our God', is designedly missing from Luke's quotation of Isaiah 61:1f. (There is indeed, in Jn. 10:34–36, an argument based on Ps. 82:6, 'I have said, "You are gods"', but that argument bears no resemblance to that of 11Q Melchizedek.)

In the Letter to the Hebrews, Melchizedek, 'made like the Son of God' (Heb. 7:3), is a very great man as men go, but he is not a heavenly figure and it is not by him that salvation and judgment are administered. The closest parallels to 11Q Melchizedek appear in those rabbinical texts where Melchizedek is identified with the archangel Michael, 'head keeper of the gates of righteousness' (*Midrash Hanne'elam Lekh*). (Daniel's 'one like a son of man' has been identified with Michael by one or two scholars, but this is not of much relevance here.)

Other Jewish evidence

The closest resemblances to the Gospel usage of 'the Son of man' are found in documents neither of which is likely to have influenced the Gospels – the Parables of Enoch (1 Enoch 37 – 71) and the Apocalypse of Ezra (2 Esdras 3–14).

The Parables of Enoch

The Parables of Enoch appear to be later than the other sections which make up the composite 'Ethiopic Enoch'. We should be cautious in drawing chronological inferences from the absence of any part of the Parables from the Aramaic fragments of 1 Enoch which have been identified among the Qumran texts; but the comparative lateness of the Parables is suggested by their internal evidence.[25]

In the Parables God is described as 'one who had a head of days' (or, more briefly, 'the Head of days'), whose hair is white like wool (1 Enoch 46:1). This language is clearly based on Daniel 7:9, where God is seen as 'one that was ancient of days' with 'the hair of his head like pure wool'. Alongside the Head of days Enoch sees 'another being whose countenance had the appearance of a man' (46:1). This being is referred to repeatedly in the sequel as 'that Son of Man' – an expression which renders three distinct phrases in the Ethiopic version (so that one may wonder about the precise Greek wording, now lost, which was so translated). It is, however, evidently the same figure that is indicated by all three Ethiopic phrases. Here, beyond doubt, we have the 'one like a son of man' who is brought to the Ancient of Days in Daniel 7:13; but as in Daniel 'one like a son of man' is not a title, so 'that Son of Man' is not a title in the Parables. 'That Son of Man' is simply that particular 'Son of Man' (human figure) whom Enoch saw in the company of the 'Head of days'. In 1 Enoch 46:3 he is called 'the Son of Man who has righteousness' and is apparently identical with the being denoted elsewhere in the Parables as 'the righteous one . . . whose elect works depend on the Lord of spirits' (38:2), the 'elect one of righteousness and faith' who 'dwells under the wings of the Lord of spirits' (39:6f.), the 'anointed one' (Messiah) of the Lord of spirits (48:10; 52:4). He is to be a support to the righteous and 'a light to the nations' (48:4; cf. what is said of the Servant in Is. 49:6), and the executioner of divine judgment on the ungodly (48:8–10).

> From the beginning the Son of Man was hidden
> and the Most High preserved him in the presence of his might
> and revealed him to the elect (62:7).

But on the day of visitation he comes out of his place of concealment and is manifested as vindicator of the righteous and judge of the wicked:

> and pain shall seize them
> when they see that Son of Man
> sitting on his throne of glory (62:5).

---

[25] The date around AD 270 proposed by J. T. Milik, *The Books of Enoch: Aramaic Fragments of Qumrân Cave 4* (Clarendon, 1976), is widely regarded as unacceptably late. See M. A. Knibb, 'The Date of the Parables of Enoch: A Critical Review', *NTS* 25, 1978-79, pp.345ff., who prefers a date in the period following AD 70; also C. L. Mearns, 'Dating the Similitudes of Enoch', *NTS* 25, 1978-79, pp.360ff., who thinks of the late 40s AD.

This Son of Man 'was named before the Lord of spirits, and his name before the Head of days, . . . before the sun and the signs were created, before the stars of heaven were made' (48:2f.). But his name is not divulged until near the end of the Parables: then Enoch is translated to heaven and welcomed by God in the words: '*You* are the Son of Man born for righteousness; righteousness abides over you, and the righteousness of the Head of days does not forsake you' (71:14).

The relation borne by the Son of Man in the Parables of Enoch to the community of righteous and elect ones is comparable to that borne by Daniel's 'one like a son of man' to the saints of the Most High. If he is righteous, so are they (38:1ff., *etc.*); if he is elect, so are they (38:3, *etc.*). While hidden in God's presence from all eternity, he takes historical form on earth from time to time in someone who is outstandingly righteous, such as Enoch. If in another section of 1 Enoch the patriarch is commissioned, because of his righteousness, to pronounce God's judgment on the disobedient angels, in the Parables he has been chosen, for the same reason, to pronounce judgment on *all* the ungodly at the time of the end.

The identification of the Son of Man with Enoch (which may be compared with Enoch's portrayal as the Servant of the Lord in Wisdom 4:10–15 is evidence enough that in the Parables we are not dealing with a Christian work. Yet there are some verbal links between the tradition which finds expression in the Parables and certain strands of the Gospel tradition, especially the distinctively Matthaean strand. We recall Matthew 19:28, where the Q promise that Jesus' followers will 'sit on thrones, judging the twelve tribes of Israel' (*cf.* Lk. 22:30) finds its fulfilment 'in the new world (*palingenesia*), when the Son of man sits on his throne of glory', or the similar words at the beginning of the judgment scene of Matthew 25:31–46: 'When the Son of man comes in his glory, and all the angels with him, then will he sit on his throne of glory.' So in the Parables of Enoch the day of judgment dawns when 'that Son of Man' is seen 'sitting on his throne of glory', having been installed there by the Lord of spirits.[26]

The Apocalypse of Ezra

It is certainly to the period following AD 70 that the Apocalypse of Ezra belongs.

In a dream vision recorded in this apocalypse (2 Esdras 13:1–53) 'something resembling a man' (Syr. *'ēyk dᵉmûtā dᵉbarnāśā*) is seen coming up from the sea: 'that man' flies with the clouds of heaven to judge the ungodly and deliver

[26] There is a brief but helpful account of the Son of Man in 1 Enoch in M. D. Hooker, *The Son of Man in Mark*, pp.33ff.

creation. He is acknowledged by God as 'my son' (verses 32, 37, 52) and described as 'the one whom the Most High has kept for many ages' (verse 26). This language, which in other dream visions in the same work is used of the Messiah (7:28, 29; 12:32), is fairly certainly based on that of Daniel 7:13f., although it is reminiscent also of Enoch's 'hidden' Son of Man. The Semitic original of the Apocalypse of Ezra is lost, as is also the Greek version; it survives in a number of secondary versions (notably Latin, Syriac and Ethiopic) based on the Greek. We can only guess what the Semitic term for the 'man' was (Heb. *ben 'ādām*, perhaps, or Aram. *bar ᵉnāšā*); since the Latin refers to him as *ipse homo* (in the vision, but *vir* in the interpretation),[27] the lost Greek version presumably had *autos ho anthrōpos* (*i.e.* no attempt was made to reproduce the Semitic idiom by some such rendering as *huios anthrōpou* with accompanying pronoun or article).

The Apocalypse of Ezra (a Jewish work) could have had no influence on the development of the Gospel tradition. Its vision of the man from the sea represents an independent line of interpretation of Daniel's vision, parallel to that in the Parables of Enoch.

Aqiba

The identification of the 'man' of Ezra's sixth vision with the Messiah crops up elsewhere in Judaism. Naturally, with the growth of exegetical controversy between Jews and Christians towards the end of the first century, the messianic interpretation of Daniel's 'one like a son of man' was bound to become as unacceptable to Jewish theologians as the messianic interpretation of the Isaianic Servant. But the messianic interpretation of Daniel's figure had already been established in some Jewish circles, and it emerges in the remark attributed to Aqiba that the thrones set for judgment in Daniel 7:9 were two in number – one for God and one for 'David', *i.e.* the Messiah (*cf.* Ps. 122:5, 'There thrones for judgment were set, the thrones of the house of David'). Aqiba's colleagues were shocked to hear him voice an interpretation which by now smacked of profanity, but Aqiba would not have voiced it had it not been of respectable origin.[28]

Summary

Our conclusions, then, are as follows:

---

[27] Similarly the Syriac version has *barnāšā* in the vision but *gaḇrā* in the interpretation. Presumably, then, the Greek version had *anēr* in the interpretation.

[28] See b*Ḥag.* 14a; b*Sanh.* 38b; *cf.* n. 19 above. The LXX reading of Dn. 7:13, in which the 'one like a son of man' (*hōs huios anthrōpou*) arrives 'like an ancient of days' (*hōs palaios hēmerōn*), would call for more serious attention in this connection if its text were more certain.

1. 'The Son of man' was not a current title for the Messiah or any other eschatological figure.

2. Jesus' special use of the expression (as distinct from its general Aramaic use in the sense of 'man', 'the man', or a possible use to replace the pronoun 'I') was derived from the 'one like a son of man' who is divinely vested with authority in Daniel 7:13f. Because it was not a current title, it was not liable to be misunderstood, as current titles were, and Jesus was free to take up the expression and give it what meaning he chose.

3. Jesus enriched the expression by fusing with it the figure of a righteous sufferer, probably the Isaianic Servant, so that he could speak of the suffering of the Son of man as something that was 'written' concerning him. By suffering and vindication Jesus, the Son of man, became his people's deliverer and advocate.

4. A similar fusion of suffering and vindicated figures is found in some Qumran texts, although they use a different vocabulary (in which 'one like a son of man' does not appear), and there is no indication that Jesus or the evangelists were influenced by Qumran thought.

5. The 'Son of Man' in the Parables of Enoch and the 'man' in the Apocalypse of Ezra also hark back to Daniel's 'one like a son of man', but in these works also the expression is not a title, and they represent developments probably later than Jesus and the Gospels and certainly independent of them.

6. A 'Son of man' theology could be nothing other than a theology based on what can be ascertained about Jesus' understanding of his identity and life-mission.

IS DANIEL'S 'SON OF MAN'
MESSIANIC?

Robert D. Rowe

At the climax of the trial of Jesus (according to Mk. 14:61f.), 'the high priest asked him, "Are you the Christ, the Son of the Blessed?" And Jesus said, "I am; and you will see the Son of man seated at the right hand of Power, and coming with the clouds of heaven."' At this answer the high priest tore his cloak, and Jesus was quickly condemned to death.

The reply to the messianic question, 'Are you the Christ?', which Jesus answered in the affirmative, led him not only to mention the phrase 'the Son of man' which he had used so often in his ministry apparently referring to himself, but also to allude to two Old Testament scriptures, Psalm 110:1 and Daniel 7:13.

The Son of man will be seen 'seated at the right hand of Power'. 'Power' is here used as an alternative word for God.[1] The only place in the Old Testament where any individual is represented as being enthroned by the side of God is Psalm 110:1.[2] The messianic king is here invited by Yahweh to sit at his right hand 'till I make your enemies your footstool'.

The Son of man will also be seen 'coming with the clouds of heaven'. Only here and in his prophetic discourse in Matthew 24:30 (*cf.* Mk. 13:26) is Jesus' use of the phrase 'the Son of man' linked clearly with Daniel 7:13, where 'one like a son of man' came 'with the clouds of heaven' to be presented before the Ancient of Days. Jesus is nowhere recorded as alluding to any other Old Testament passage mentioning 'the Son of man' nor to any intertestamental work, such as 1 Enoch.

While the rest of the background to Jesus' usage of 'the Son of man'

---

[1] This is made clear in Lk. 22:69, where 'the power of God' is substituted.

[2] *Cf.* 1 Ch. 28:5; 29:23; 2 Ch. 9:8. Here Solomon is seen as sitting on Yahweh's throne. For a treatment of Ps. 110 in the NT, see D. M. Hay, *Glory at the Right Hand* (Abingdon, 1973).

(including the possibility of the phrase being a circumlocution for 'I', the intertestamental literature and Jewish and other interpretations of Dn. 7:13) must be carefully examined, it would be foolish for us not to give full weight to the only direct clue that the evangelists give us concerning its origin: the allusion in Mark 14:62 (and Mt. 24:30) to Daniel 7:13.

We need to consider as the essential background to Jesus' usage the original meaning and significance (so far as we can ascertain it) of 'one like a son of man' in Daniel 7:13. Also we should bear in mind that Jesus' reference to Daniel 7:13 in Mark 14:62 was in reply to the high priest's messianic question, and was linked in his answer to a clearly messianic verse, Psalm 110:1. We must thus consider whether there is any Old Testament evidence for according a messianic meaning to Daniel 7:13.

Messianic kingship in Israel

The Psalms show David and his royal successors as very significant figures in Israelite worship.[3] The word 'messianic' in this article should be taken to mean their role as kings insofar as that went beyond the merely functional and had religious connotations, among which was the hope of a future ideal ruler.

The so-called 'royal psalms' (of which the most clear examples are Pss. 2; 18; 20; 21; 45; 72; 89; 101; 110; 118; 132; 144) often speak of the reigning earthly king in very exalted language. We have seen that in Psalm 110:1, he is invited to sit at Yahweh's right hand. He is called 'my son' by Yahweh (Ps. 2:7), 'the highest of the kings of the earth', whose throne would last for ever (Ps. 89:27-29); his just reign would bring peace, world dominion and plentiful harvests (Ps. 72:7f., 16).

Until the early years of this century, it was thought that these psalms had only a future meaning, referring to the Messiah in the traditional sense. Then S. Mowinckel demonstrated the importance of the context of the Psalms in Israel's worship at the Jerusalem temple.[4] The royal psalms show the king taking part in the liturgy and ceremonies of the temple and the fact of their inclusion in the Psalter is evidence for their frequent use. They were not merely literary prophecies of a future Messiah; they were spoken, sung and acted out in the presence of the reigning Davidic king. It is probable that Psalms 2 and 110 were coronation psalms, while Psalm 45 is a royal wedding song; there may have been an annual celebration of the king's enthronement as part of the autumn festival.[5]

[3] A. R. Johnson, *Sacral Kingship in Ancient Israel* (University of Wales, [2]1967); J. H. Eaton, *Kingship and the Psalms* (SCM, 1976).

[4] S. Mowinckel, *The Psalms in Israel's Worship* (Blackwell, 1962).

[5] *Cf.* J. H. Eaton, *op. cit.*, p.112.

What then was the reason for the exalted language of the royal psalms, if they did not primarily speak of a future Messiah? To some extent the Israelites were influenced by the courtly style and high kingship ideology of neighbouring peoples, which may have gained an entrance into Israelite thought and worship as a result of David's capture of the Jebusite city of Jerusalem.[6] However, the most important element, giving the distinctive Israelite content to this ideology, can be traced to the personal relationship between God and the king that is marked by Nathan's oracle: Yahweh promises that he will raise up David's offspring after him and establish the throne of his kingdom for ever, and adds, 'I will be his father, and he shall be my son' (2 Sa. 7:12–14).

Thus David was promised that his line would be eternal, and that his descendants would inherit a highly privileged and personal 'father-son' relationship with God. The word 'offspring' (*zar'ᵃkā*) could have either a singular or plural meaning. While a line of kings is anticipated in verses 14–16, David's immediate successor was to build the temple (v. 13). At this early stage, then, Nathan's oracle may have contained the hope of a Messiah, of a single ruler who would live up to the high relationship declared between Yahweh and the king. It is often argued that the messianic hope grew gradually, as people realized that the kings were not fulfilling the high-flown language which was used of them in the royal psalms; so they looked for the coming of a special 'anointed one'.[7] The ideal of kingship, however, as celebrated in the Jerusalem temple, may have had a messianic element in it from the beginning.

Psalm 110 is considered to be an early psalm,[8] and if we give credence to the statement of Jesus that it was composed by David (Mk. 12:35–37), it is possible to surmise that David, reflecting on Nathan's oracle, wrote it as part of the liturgy for the coronation of his son, in the hope that his 'offspring' Solomon might be the Messiah and so fulfil the highest meaning of Yahweh's promise. From then on at each coronation, the people must have wondered to what extent the new king would fulfil the demands of ideal kingship, and whether he or the next king would be the promised Messiah, the embodiment of ideal kingship.[9]

We have noted that one of the most important elements in Israelite kingship

---

[6] *Cf.* H.-J. Kraus, *Worship in Israel* (Blackwell, 1966), p. 181.

[7] *E.g.* S. Mowinckel, *He That Cometh* (Abingdon, 1955); A. Alt, *Essays in Old Testament History and Religion* (Blackwell, 1966), pp. 241–259.

[8] *Cf.* M. Dahood, *Psalms* 3 (Doubleday, 1970), p. 112.

[9] For clear messianic prophecies, arising from Davidic kingship, see, *e.g.*, Is. 9:6f.; 11:1–5; Mi. 5:2–4; Je. 23:5f.; 33:14–16; Ezk. 37:24f.

ideology is the relationship between the king and Yahweh, expressed as sonship (2 Sa. 7:14; Ps. 2:7) and co-enthronement (Ps. 110:1). The kingship of the Davidic king is secondary and subsidiary to the kingship of Yahweh. The so-called 'enthronement psalms' (Pss. 47; 93; 95–99) celebrate the enthronement of Yahweh as universal king, as is shown by the cry, *yhwh mālāk*, 'The LORD reigns' or 'Yahweh has become king' (Pss. 93:1; 96:10; 97:1; 99:1). Psalm 47:5, 9 suggests the physical lifting up of the ark to a place of prominence, representing the enthronement and exaltation of Yahweh. Other psalms, too, speak of Yahweh's kingship, which seems to have been a central theme of Israelite worship and ritual at their principal yearly festival in the autumn.[10] What then is the relationship between the kingship of Yahweh and that of David and his descendants? Is the Davidic kingship related not just to Yahweh generally, as we have seen, but to Yahweh as he is acclaimed king?

Psalm 89 combines a hymn to Yahweh, similar to the enthronement psalms (vv. 5–18) with an exposition of his covenant to David (vv. 19–37). These two sections lead up to the lament of verses 38–51, which deals with God's apparent renunciation of that covenant.[11] While David's throne will endure for ever (vv. 29, 36), the throne of Yahweh is also mentioned, founded on righteousness and justice (v. 14). These latter qualities which are features of Yahweh's kingship (*cf.* Ps. 97:2) are to be granted to the earthly king (Ps. 72:1f.).

In Psalm 2, Yahweh and 'his anointed' are together the victims of a conspiracy by the other earthly kings (v. 2). Yahweh, enthroned in the heavens (v. 4), has installed his earthly representative as king in Jerusalem (v. 6): this is what terrifies the nations and their rulers (v. 5). It is by the agency of the Davidic king in filial relationship to Yahweh that the nations will be conquered and Yahweh's kingship vindicated (vv. 7–9). Also in Psalm 110 the joint sovereignty of Yahweh and the king is shown in that Yahweh must be enthroned for the king to sit at his right hand; the king's authority is clearly dependent on Yahweh's command.

The way in which the king rules is important: he must reflect on earth the righteous kingship of Yahweh in heaven. This is inherent in his sonship, and wrongdoing will be punished by Yahweh (2 Sa. 7:14). Psalm 101 is a statement of intent by the king to keep Yahweh's commandments and practise his justice. As Yahweh's heavenly kingship is concerned for the disadvantaged and the needy (Pss. 68:5f.; 82:3f.), so the Davidic king must defend them from

---

[10] Mowinckel's argument for such an enthronement festival (as part of the feast of Tabernacles) is borne out by Zc. 14:16f.

[11] *Cf.* T. N. D. Mettinger, *King and Messiah: The Civil and Sacral Legitimation of the Israelite Kings* (CWK Gleerup, 1976), p.292.

oppression and give them justice on earth (Ps. 72:2, 4, 12–14). The king should trust in Yahweh, not in his own strength (Pss. 21:7; 118:6–9).

So we have seen, mainly from the Psalms, that the kingship of David and his successors (which we can term 'messianic' on the basis of Nathan's prophecy) was closely linked to and derived its authority from the kingship of Yahweh. The Psalms of course are set in the context of Jewish worship and ritual: outside of the temple, David's royal descendants could, and frequently did, ignore the authority of Yahweh. Such would not be the case however when the Messiah came, and in the ceremonies of the temple a messianic role was probably assigned to all the kings that succeeded David.

We have noted that the kingship of Yahweh was probably celebrated in a dramatic form. A. R. Johnson first emphasized the important part played by the Davidic king in the ceremonies of the temple, which is indicated by the frequent references to him in the Psalms.[12] The number of royal psalms, and thus the extent of the king's involvement in the cult, is increased considerably if we accept the arguments of H. Birkeland that the enemies so often mentioned in psalms of individual lament are national enemies and therefore the subject 'I' of these psalms refers to the king.[13] The logic of this view is not refuted by following the position of H. Gunkel, that though the type of individual laments was in origin royal, it was at an early stage 'democratized' for use by others.[14]

If Birkeland is correct, the king appears in situations of profound suffering, as in Psalm 22. A consistent line of scholarship has maintained the likelihood that the king took part in a temple ritual, perhaps annually at the autumn festival, in which he suffered humiliation before being restored to his throne.[15] There is no need to depend for this on parallels with the Babylonian new year festival. The dramatic language of the psalms suggests, for example, a ritual combat with the nations (Pss. 2:8f.; 48:4–6), which the people *see* (Ps. 48:8); they are celebrating the kingship of Yahweh, probably with the reigning Davidic king as the principal actor. The language of Psalm 89:39, 44 likewise suggests a ritual deprivation of the symbols of kingship (crown, sceptre and

[12] A. R. Johnson, 'The Role of the King in the Jerusalem Cultus', in S. H. Hooke (ed.), *The Labyrinth* (SPCK, 1935), pp.73-111.

[13] H. Birkeland, *The Evildoers in the Book of Psalms* (Jacob Dybwab, 1955).

[14] H. Gunkel & J. Begrich, *Einleitung in die Psalmen* (Vandenhoeck & Ruprecht, 1933), pp.147f.

[15] A. R. Johnson, *art. cit.*, p.100; A. Bentzen, *King and Messiah* (Lutterworth, 1955), pp.25-31; H. Ringgren, *The Messiah in the Old Testament* (SPCK, 1956), pp.54-64; H. Ringgren, *Israelite Religion* (SPCK, 1966), pp.235-237; J. H. Eaton, *Kingship and the Psalms* (SCM, 1976), pp.121f.

Robert D. Rowe

throne) in a form of drama. We have noted that this psalm in its earlier sections celebrates the kingship both of Yahweh and of the Davidic king; thus we may infer a context in the festival for the whole psalm, rather than its being initially a response to a specific historical situation of defeat for the king.

While we cannot be certain exactly what rituals took place in the temple involving the king, some psalms clearly present situations where he is said to experience suffering, whether ritual or real. Further, whatever its antiquity or original significance, the title 'of David' (*l^edāwid*) which appears at the beginning of many of these psalms may have reinforced a connection between Davidic kingship and suffering in the minds of some later interpreters.[16]

From one aspect of the temple ritual involving the Davidic king, namely a drama of humiliation and suffering, we must turn to one of the themes associated with Yahweh's kingship (with which, as we have noted, the king is closely connected). This is Yahweh's creation of all things, his ownership or mastery over the world and his control over nature now and in the future (Pss. 24:1f.; 29:3–10; 74:12–17; 89:8–12; 93:1, 3f.; 95:4f.; 96:5, 10–12; 97:3–6; 98:7f.; 103:22; 145:9f.; 146:6). In all these psalms Yahweh's kingship is mentioned; we should especially note Psalms 96:11–13 and 98:7–9, where the natural world is exhorted to join in a song of praise to Yahweh when he comes to set up his righteous rule over the earth.

Turning now to Psalm 8 (which the heading relates as 'of David'), we find another hymn praising Yahweh for his creation; this suggests it would fit well with the psalms of Yahweh's kingship discussed above. The same word 'majestic' (*'addîr*, vv. 1, 9) is used for Yahweh as well as for the 'mighty' waters that he conquers in Exodus 15:6, 10f. and Psalm 93:4, both passages which celebrate Yahweh's kingship.[17]

The speaker in Psalm 8 is an individual ('I', verse 3), and the hymn emphasizes God's graciousness to man in creation. He is insignificant compared to God's works in the heavens (vv. 3f.), but nevertheless God has given him an exalted position, authority to rule over all other living creatures (vv. 5f.). There is a clear connection of thought between this psalm and Genesis 1:26–28. There God created man 'in his own image', which phrase is closely linked to his appointment as ruler over the rest of creation.[18]

[16] Contrast I. Engnell, *Critical Essays on the Old Testament* (SPCK, 1970), pp.82f., who holds that *l^edāwid* means 'a psalm for the king' to be used by David and his successors in the cult, with the more usual view that it denotes authorship.

[17] It seems that the word primarily means 'broad' or 'powerful'; it is applied to earthly kings (*e.g.* Je. 30:21) as well as to God. *Cf.* G. W. Ahlström, *TDOT* 1 (1974), pp.73f.

[18] H. W. Wolff, *Anthropology of the Old Testament* (SCM, 1974), pp.159-165.

76

After a further mention that Adam was made 'in the likeness of God' in Genesis 5:1 (as in Gn. 1:26, together with 'image'), verse 3 states that Adam became the father of a son 'in his own likeness, after his image'. The use of 'image' with 'likeness' refers back to 1:26f., suggesting that the natural father-son relationship between Adam and Seth is analogous to God's creation of Adam 'in his own image'. A corollary of this is that when the Davidic king is adopted as Yahweh's son (Ps. 2:7), their relationship is similar to that between God and Adam (or 'mankind').

A further connection between 'man made in God's image' and the Davidic king is, of course, rulership. We have seen that the first man was given dominion over God's creation (Gn. 1:26, 28; Ps. 8:6–8), which he exercised by naming the animals (Gn. 2:19f.). There is an ambivalence of meaning between the first man as an individual and mankind in general: in Genesis, the first man Adam is representative of all mankind, while in Psalm 8 *'eno͂š* ('man', v. 4) is probably a collective singular; this is particularized however by its parallelism with *ben 'ādām* ('son of man'), which together with the singular subject 'I' in verse 3 may indicate a representative man rather than any individual out of the whole class of 'mankind'.

Like the Davidic king, 'man' is crowned with glory and honour (v. 5), which are both attributes of Yahweh's kingship (Ps. 145:5); 'man' is clearly presented as a king. Also in verse 5, he has been made 'little less than God': this speaks of his relationship with Yahweh, as well as his high position in creation. The coming Messiah (in the Davidic line) will be called 'Mighty God' (Is. 9:6).

Since (i) 'man' is portrayed as a king in Psalm 8, (ii) the speaker is an individual, and (iii) as a creation-hymn the psalm would fit well with the celebration of Yahweh's kingship (with which the Davidic king was closely connected), we must ask whether this is a royal psalm, for use by the Davidic king as representative of 'mankind'.[19] As Israel was chosen by God from the rest of mankind, it is not illogical that David and his successors, in the same fashion chosen by God to rule Israel, should in God's redemptive purposes represent mankind just as did the first man.

A variant form of Psalm 8:4 appears in Psalm 144:3. Here 'man' is *'ādām* and 'son of man' is *ben 'eno͂š*, a reversal of the words in 8:4 as a poetic variation. Psalm 144, also headed 'of David', is clearly a royal psalm, being similar to Psalm 18.[20] The 'new song' (v. 9) suggests the celebration of Yahweh's creator-kingship at the autumn festival, as in Psalms 96:1 and 98:1.[21] Verses

---

[19] *Cf.* A. Bentzen, *op. cit.*, pp.39-47; H. Ringgren, *The Messiah in the Old Testament* (SCM, 1956), p.20.

[20] A. Weiser, *The Psalms* (SCM, 1962), pp.822-825.   [21] *Cf.* also Pss. 33:3; 40:3; 149:1.

12–15 are a petition for fertility and prosperity, linked in verses 8 and 11 with the righteous rule of the king; this is reminiscent of Psalm 72.

The similarity between Psalms 8:4 and 144:3, taken together with the other evidence we have considered of a connection between the king and 'representative man', makes it very probable that Psalm 8 was a royal psalm to be spoken by the reigning Davidic king taking the part of 'representative man' during the celebration of Yahweh's enthronement.

We must now consider whether there is any supporting evidence elsewhere for this thesis of a link between the Davidic king and 'representative man' in the Jerusalem cult. First, we should note that conceptions of paradise, the abode of the first representative man, appear in the royal psalms (Pss. 72:3, 6f., 16; 144:12–14) and in the messianic prophecy of Isaiah 11:6–9. Secondly, in Psalm 45:2 the king is addressed as 'the fairest of the sons of men' (using the common plural form, *bᵉnê 'adām*). While this no doubt reflects courtly language, it is here used of the king in the cult and it needs only a further small step for the king to be considered 'the leader of mankind' or 'representative man', a role analogous to the first man created by God.

Thirdly, we must consider other occurrences of *'adām, 'ᵉnôš* and *ben 'adām*, especially in the Psalms. *'adām* occurs frequently in the Old Testament as the universal word for 'man' or 'mankind' and its most prominent concern is the relationship between God and man. By contrast, *'îš*, 'man' and *'iššâ*, 'woman', are mostly used in a secular context. *'ᵉnôš* is found mainly in the poetic literature and there appears to be little distinction in meaning from *'adām*, which occurs sixty-two times in the Psalms while *'ᵉnôš* occurs thirteen times.[22] In two instances in the Psalms *'adām* is used in parallel with 'princes': 82:7, concerning God's judgment, and 118:8f., concerning trust in God. This may reflect a tendency when *'adām* is used in a collective sense in relation to God, to assimilate to the word the functions of leadership or kingship.[23]

The singular *ben 'adām* occurs ninety-three times in Ezekiel, and fourteen times in the remainder of the Old Testament (including Dn. 8:17, where the usage is similar to that in Ezekiel). In Ezekiel this characteristic phrase by which the prophet is addressed, first in 2:1 after his majestic vision of God, seems to

---

[22] The references to *'adām* in the Psalms may be further broken down as follows: *bᵉnê 'adām* (plural) 23 times; *ben 'adām* (singular) 3; with *kol* ('all') 4; the remainder 32; *cf.* F. Maass, *TDOT* 1 (1974), pp.75-87, 345-348.

[23] If the king played the role of *'adām* in the cult, it is possible that occurrences of the word in Pss. 32:2; 58:11; 84:5, 12; 94:10f. refer primarily to him, though they were no doubt 'democratized' at some stage for use by the people; alternatively there may have been an influence in some of these verses from wisdom sayings (*e.g.* Pr. 28:14).

emphasize the prophet's frailty and distance from God's greatness; this concept corresponds with Psalm 8:4, but lacks the correlative of man's dignified position in Psalm 8:5–8. Ezekiel was a priest and a prophet, but not a king.

Apart from Ezekiel and Daniel, all the other occurrences of *ben 'ādām* appear in poetic parallelism, mostly with *'enôš or 'îš.* In Psalm 146:3 the phrase is used in parallel with 'princes' in a similar way to Psalm 118:8f., thus strengthening the link mentioned above between *'ādām* and leadership (also seen in Ps. 82:7), albeit in these three passages in a manner indicating disapproval.

ben 'ādām occurs three times in Job (16:21; 25:6; 35:8), none of which are directly related to kingship, and four times in Jeremiah in his oracles against foreign nations (49:18, 33; 50:40; 51:43) referring to places cursed so that they will have no human inhabitants. It is perhaps significant that in the passages in Jeremiah the parallel word used is *'îš,* implying the ordinary secular meaning of 'man' rather than man in relationship to God. The same parallel with *'îš* is found in the prophecy of Balaam (Nu. 23:19), where there is a contrast between God and man, though the emphasis is on the character of God rather than man's position; there is no apparent connection with kingship.

In two verses in Isaiah (51:12; 56:2), *ben 'ādām* is in parallel with *'enôš* (as in Ps. 8:4). In 51:12, Israel is not to be afraid of man who is mortal; the frailty of man in comparison to God's creation (51:13, 16) is reminiscent of Psalm 8:3f.; the inevitability of death also appears in Psalm 82:7 linked with 'princes', as we have noticed. Indeed, the idea of 'fear' implies a ruler or king who is oppressive (just as the 'princes', mentioned in parallel with *'ādām* in Ps. 118:8f. and with *ben 'ādām* in Ps. 146:3, are not to be relied upon).

Isaiah 56:2 ascribes blessing to the man who keeps justice and does righteousness in preparation for the coming of God's salvation (v. 1). While verse 2 is probably 'democratized', referring to any Israelite, 'justice' and 'righteousness' were primarily the duties of the Davidic king (Ps. 72:1f.) and in the proper exercise of his kingship in reliance on Yahweh, Yahweh's salvation was revealed (Pss. 20:5; 21:1). Thus the two occurrences of *ben 'ādām* in Isaiah have ideological links with kingship or leadership, which is not surprising in view of the general similarity of ideas between parts of Isaiah 40 – 66 and the psalms which celebrate Yahweh's kingship.[24]

The third occurrence of *ben 'ādām* in the Psalms (with Pss. 8:4; 146:3 and the

---

[24] Contrast N. H. Snaith, *The Jewish New Year Festival: Its Origin and Development* (SPCK, 1947), p.200, with S. Mowinckel, *The Psalms in Israel's Worship* 2 (Blackwell, 1962), pp.116-118. While agreeing on their similarity of theme, Snaith argues for the dependence of the 'enthronement psalms' on Is. 40 – 55, while Mowinckel holds that the reverse was the case.

synonymous *ben* *'enôs* in Ps. 144:3) is in Psalm 80:17. This is a psalm of national lamentation which conceives of Yahweh as king, since he is 'enthroned upon the cherubim' (v. 1) and is addressed as 'Shepherd', a description commonly applied to kings in the ancient Near East.[25] Israel is pictured as a vine which Yahweh brought out of Egypt; there is a plea to God to look from heaven and 'visit' it (v. 14). A situation of serious national reverse and impending destruction is in view. In verse 17, the prayer becomes more specific: 'let thy hand be upon the man (*'îs*) of thy right hand, the son of man (*ben 'ādām*) whom thou hast made strong for thyself.' There are three major interpretations of this verse:

1. The reference, some conjecture, is to Benjamin, which means 'son of the right hand'; the tribe of Benjamin is mentioned in verse 2. However it is difficult to see why Benjamin should have been picked out at the climax of the psalm; also there is clearly some identification between Israel as the vine and the 'man of thy right hand', which is strange if the latter means the single tribe of Benjamin.

2. According to others, it is another pictorial way of describing Israel, in addition to 'the vine'.[26] One factor influencing this view seems to be verse 15, where the Hebrew text has 'upon the son (*bēn*) whom thou hast made strong for thyself'. If *kannâ* (found only here in the Old Testament) in the parallel clause means 'stock', planted by God's right hand, *bēn* would seem to refer to 'the vine' Israel, and it may then be argued that this is determinative for the very similar second clause in verse 17. LXX, however, took *kannâ* as a verb ('restore') and following this line of interpretation, M. Dahood translates the first clause of verse 15, 'Take care of what your right hand has planted'. He takes *bēn* (v. 15) to mean the king on the basis of Psalm 89 where his 'sonship' is emphasized and the same word for Yahweh's 'strengthening' of him (*'immaṣtâ*) is used in 89:21 as in this clause.[27]

Alternatively, RSV omits the second clause of verse 15, as a variant of verse 17;[28] again, *bēn* (v. 15) could refer to the king even if *kannâ* refers to the vine (= Israel), by a close identification between king and people. Finally, if *bēn* refers to Israel, by analogy with Hosea 11:1 (which we consider unlikely, because of the link with Ps. 89), it is not necessarily determinative for verse 17, since *ben 'ādām* is used there. The main argument against this view is the change of

[25] *Cf.* Gn. 49:24; Pss. 23:1; 78:70–72; Ezk. 34:2ff.; 37:24.

[26] See A. Weiser, *op. cit.,* p.551; D. Kidner, *Psalms 73–150* (IVP, 1975), p.292; C. Colpe, *TDNT* 8, pp.400-477.

[27] M. Dahood, *Psalms 2* (Doubleday, 1968), p.260.

[28] This is followed by A. A. Anderson, *Psalms 2* (Oliphants, 1972), pp.585f.; J. D. G. Dunn, *Christology in the Making* (SCM, 1980), p.70.

imagery in verse 17 from a tree to a 'man'. While the context shows some identification between the two, parallels exist for associating 'the man of thy right hand', whom Yahweh has strengthened, with the king but not with Israel as a collective entity with no leader in view.

3. It is, others argue, a reference to the king who represented Israel as its leader and whose interests could be identified with it; thus a petition for Israel moves easily into one for the king.[29] The language of verse 17 suggests an individual, and 'the man of thy right hand' can be best explained as a reference to Psalm 110:1, where the king is invited to sit at Yahweh's right hand. Yahweh is visualized as enthroned in verse 1, so the idea of the king being enthroned beside him, at his right hand, is not out of place. In conjunction with this, the verbal connection with Psalm 89:21 provides incontrovertible evidence that 80:17 refers to the king: not only does the uncommon usage of *'immaṣtâ* ('made strong', with Yahweh as the subject) follow 89:21, where the object is the Davidic king,[30] but also in both verses the 'hand' of Yahweh is the instrument of blessing. Like 80:1, 89:14 speaks of the 'throne' of Yahweh; 89:13 refers to Yahweh's 'right hand' (*cf.* 80:17) in close conjunction with his throne, as in Psalm 110:1.

Thus, without relying on the evidence we have noted previously linking *ben 'āḏām* with the king, we have established that Psalm 80:17 refers to the king and describes him as *ben 'āḏām*. While this description may function partly to emphasize the human frailty of the king and his need for Yahweh's strengthening, the number of occasions when we have noticed a connection made between *'āḏām* or *ben 'āḏām* and a royal or princely figure (or 'representative man' described in terms of kingship) suggest that in the context of worship, especially in the celebration of Yahweh's kingship and creatorship, the Davidic king was known as *ben 'āḏām;* on the evidence of Psalm 80:17, he would have been recognized by that title.[31]

No great distinction need be made between *'āḏām* and *ben 'āḏām,* except that

---

[29] A. A. Anderson, *op. cit.,* p.586; M. Dahood, *op. cit.* 2, p.260; H.-J. Kraus, *Psalmen* 2 (Neukirchener Verlag, [2]1978), p.724; D. Hill, '"Son of Man" in Psalm 80 v. 17', *Nov T* 15 (1973), pp.261-269.

[30] In Is. 41:10 Israel is the object of *'immaṣtîḵā,* with Yahweh as the subject, but here Israel is cast in the role of 'my servant', who is demonstrated to have royal attributes (Is. 42:1), and may be dependent on Ps. 89:21, since David is called 'my servant' in the previous verse.

[31] Contrast F. H. Borsch, *The Son of Man in Myth and History* (SCM, 1967), pp.114-117, who does not contend that 'Son of man' was necessarily an official title in Jerusalem, though it may possibly have been so at some stage; our suggestion is limited to its use as a title or firm description in the context of the cult, in connection with the king's role at the autumn festival when Yahweh was worshipped as King.

ben 'adām means an individual man (just as the plural *bᵉnê 'adām* means more than one man considered as individuals) and thus in the cult may unambiguously be applied to the king who is an individual as well as representing 'mankind' collectively. The application of the title *ben 'adām* to the king speaks of him representing 'man' both in his frailty (Ps. 8:3f.) and his dignity (8:5–8). This is similar to the way that he is at one with Israel, God's chosen 'vine', as their leader in Psalm 80 in humiliation and defeat (vv. 4–6, 12f.) as well as in the requested vindication (vv. 17f.). We noted above that some of the psalms represent the king as experiencing suffering and humiliation, before his restoration.

From Psalm 80:17, then, we should notice the following points: (i) the king is called *ben 'adām;* (ii) he is so closely associated with Israel that, as we have seen, it is hard to detect when the psalmist moves from speaking of Israel in general, as 'the vine', to the king in particular as their representative; (iii) as *ben 'adām,* he is associated with his people in their tribulation (vv. 5f.), before his exaltation by Yahweh becomes for them the means of 'life' (v. 18); (iv) he is called *ben 'adām* in the context of Yahweh's kingship (v. 1); (v) the connection with Psalm 110:1 implies his enthronement at the right hand of Yahweh, associated with his role as *ben 'adām.*

To summarize our consideration of messianic kingship in Israel, we have seen that in the context of worship the Davidic king was closely associated with the kingship of Yahweh, was sometimes represented as suffering and also played the role of 'representative man' (analogous to the first man) in relation to God; here he acted out, in his person and on behalf of his people Israel, on the one hand the frailty and humiliation of mankind and on the other the kingly authority and exaltation of mankind. In that role he was known as *ben 'adām.*

C. H. Dodd wrote that Psalm 80:17, by identifying ' "God's right-hand Man" (the one who "sits at God's right hand") with the divinely strengthened "Son of Man," might well be regarded as providing direct scriptural justification for the fusion of the two figures in Mark 14:62.'[32] To test Dodd's thesis, we must turn now to Daniel to see what evidence there is that the messianic kingship that we have described, and which is associated with the title *ben 'adām* in Psalm 80:17, is behind the 'one like a son of man' of Daniel 7:13.

Daniel's 'son of man' and messianic kingship

The principal theme of the book of Daniel is the kingship of God: how he intervenes to accomplish his purposes, and brings down earthly kings that flout his authority.

---

[32] C. H. Dodd, *According to the Scriptures* (Collins, 1952), pp. 101f.

In chapter 2 an exiled Israelite interprets God's revelation to a heathen king who rules over the most powerful empire of his day; thus at the time when Israel came under foreign domination, God is shown as revealing his authority to the dominating power and declaring his purposes for the kingdoms of the world in every age, not just for Israel. Nebuchadnezzar's wise men cannot tell him his dream, saying that 'none can show it to the king except the gods, whose dwelling is not with flesh' (2:11). Daniel agrees with their verdict on the basis of their common knowledge, but proclaims a revealing God whom they did not know: 'there is a God in heaven who reveals mysteries' (vv. 27f.). The book contains the account of God's revelations to men and of his interventions on their behalf, both of which show his supreme authority and kingship. Daniel ascribes to God the source of all wisdom, power and authority (vv. 20–23). Whereas the gods of the Chaldeans do not dwell with men, the book shows how the kingship of the 'God of heaven' (2:37, 44) becomes effective on earth.

Daniel's theology of the relationship of God to earthly kings is given in 2:37: 'the God of heaven has given the kingdom, the power, and the might, and the glory' to Nebuchadnezzar, though the latter is called 'king of kings'. In turn, Nebuchadnezzar acknowledges Daniel's God as 'Lord of kings' (2:47). So God is represented as giving authority to kings and also revealing mysteries, presumably to guide the kings and cause them to worship him.

God also 'removes kings and sets up kings' (2:21), as seen especially in chapters 4 and 5. Chapter 4 begins and ends with Nebuchadnezzar's acknowledgement of God's kingdom as everlasting (vv. 3, 34; *cf.* Ps. 145:13) with authority over all in heaven and earth (v. 35). God's heavenly kingdom was seen to be a present reality, for Nebuchadnezzar honours 'the King of heaven' (v. 37).

The same verse shows his ethical appreciation of God ('all his works are right and his ways are just'). Justice is a traditional attribute both of Yahweh's kingship (Ps. 96:10) and of the messianic king (Ps. 72:2). Daniel had warned Nebuchadnezzar after interpreting his second dream: 'break off your sins by practising righteousness, and your iniquities by showing mercy to the oppressed' (4:27). We have noticed from the Psalms that the conduct of the Davidic king was important: as Yahweh was righteous (Pss. 89:14; 97:2; 99:4), so the Davidic king must exercise righteousness (Ps. 72:1–3); as Yahweh provided for the poor and oppressed (Ps. 68:10), so the king must reflect the same concern in practical ways (Ps. 72:2, 4, 12). Thus the standards of Israelite kingship (ruling under the authority of the superior kingship of Yahweh) are applied to the Babylonian king.

The main lesson that Nebuchadnezzar learned, as the result of the temporary insanity that God brought upon him, was that 'the Most High rules the kingdom of men, and gives it to whom he will' (4:17, 25, 32; 5:21; *cf.* 4:26). Nebuchadnezzar had to acknowledge that his authority as king was not supreme; it was subject to God's kingship which made demands both upon his conduct and his attitude. The pride of Nebuchadnezzar, in acknowledging no greater authority or source for his own power, was brought low (4:30; 5:20); he had to learn that, as rulers likely to please him, God looks 'for the lowliest of men', who will put their confidence in the God of heaven (4:17; *cf.* 4:37). Nebuchadnezzar must act as an under-king on behalf of God, an idea strongly linked to the tradition of the Davidic king ruling under the authority of the kingship of Yahweh. An analogy may be made with the rulership given to Daniel and his three friends under the authority of the king (2:48f.; 3:30; 5:29; 6:1–4).

The kingship of Yahweh was seen not only in humbling Nebuchadnezzar and deposing him temporarily (4:31–33; 5:20f.), but also in depriving Belshazzar of his kingship (5:26–28, 30f.) because he had acted presumptuously and did not honour 'the God in whose hand is your breath, and whose are all your ways' (5:23). God's interventions show that his kingdom cannot be ignored; it *must* become effective on earth.

The dream that came to Nebuchadnezzar in chapter 2 is similar in meaning to that given to Daniel in chapter 7. Four successive kingdoms are represented by the different metals constituting the statue in chapter 2, and by four fierce animals coming out of the sea in chapter 7. In each case Nebuchadnezzar's kingdom is the first mentioned and seems to have been the most pleasing to God: he is the head of gold, the most precious metal in the statue (2:38). The first beast that came out of the sea (7:4) was like a lion and had eagle's wings; Nebuchadnezzar's temporary insanity and recovery can be recognized in the plucking off of its wings and the mind of a man being given to it, after it had been made to stand up like a man.[33]

As we shall see later, there is evidence for parts of Daniel being influenced by the throne-vision in Ezekiel 1.[34] There the four living creatures who supported God's throne each had four faces, respectively of a man, a lion, an ox and an eagle. The fact that the beast representing Nebuchadnezzar's kingdom is described in terms of three of these (while the later beasts in Daniel 7 are not represented in Ezekiel 1) may imply God's approval, in part at least. God appears enthroned in Daniel 7:9 and it is possible that just as the four living

---

[33] J. G. Baldwin, *Daniel* (IVP, 1978), p.139.

[34] *Cf.* M. Black, 'The Throne-Theophany Prophetic Commission and the "Son of Man": A Study in Tradition-History', in R. Hamerton-Kelly and R. Scroggs (eds.), *Jews, Greeks and Christians* (E. J. Brill, 1976), pp.57-73.

creatures of Ezekiel 1 supported God's throne in heaven, so the four beasts of Daniel 7 should have 'supported' God's throne (or kingship) on earth; it is because their kingship did not match up to the standards of the king of heaven that they, like Belshazzar, are to be deposed.

The two dreams in chapters 2 and 7 represent history as a search by God to find some individual or people who would faithfully exercise earthly kingship on his behalf; this was the ideal of Davidic kingship, taught to Nebuchadnezzar in chapter 4. Each successive kingdom showed a further decline from God's ideal. Thus a dramatic intervention by God became necessary; in addition to God's heavenly kingdom that was a *present* reality to Nebuchadnezzar (4:3, 34, 37) and had potentially supreme authority on earth (which at times was made effective by God's various interventions), God would in the *future* 'set up a kingdom which shall never be destroyed' (2:44). It is clear that this future kingdom of God will be seen *on earth,* an effective and permanent manifestation of his eternal heavenly kingship.

The instrument of destruction of the statue, which represents the full achievement of human authority apart from God, is a stone, 'cut out by no human hand' (2:34, 45); it afterwards 'became a great mountain and filled the whole earth' (v. 35). In the interpretation of the dream, the destruction of the statue and the growth of the mountain mean the setting up of God's kingdom on earth; what is represented by the stone, however, is not equivalent to God, although it refers to an intervention by God. The function of the stone is taken in chapter 7 by the kingdom being given by God, after the destruction of the beasts, to 'one like a son of man' (7:14), who represents 'the saints of the Most High' (7:18, 22, 27). The destruction of the beasts is not attributed to 'one like a son of man', but 'the saints of the Most High' had been involved in conflict with the final beast (7:21, 25); thus they (and the 'son of man' representing them) were involved in its downfall.

So chapter 2 speaks of the kingdom of God being set up on earth, while chapter 7, in describing the same event, speaks of persons other than God receiving the kingship from him: 'one like a son of man' and 'the saints of the Most High'. The only possible precursor of this dual kingship, which is the climax of the vision in chapter 7, is the kingship of Yahweh, who delegates kingship on earth to the Davidic king, as we have seen in the Psalms. Therefore it seems clear that Daniel 7 has as its background the kingship of the Davidic king. The ideal king who would make God's kingship effective on earth is seen in 'one like a son of man' and 'the saints of the Most High'.

We have observed how Daniel speaks of the kingship of God as a present reality; earthly rulers must take account of it, and it will one day become effective permanently on earth. We must now consider whether there is any indication in Daniel of earthly rulers taking the role of 'representative man' which was assumed by the Davidic king, as expounded in Genesis 1:26–28 and Psalm 8:3–8. The example of Nebuchadnezzar is particularly instructive in this respect. In Daniel 2:38, as well as the sons of men, God had given into his hands 'the beasts of the field, and the birds of the air, making you rule over them all'. The context of God's supremacy and his gift to man of kingship over the animals suggests an allusion to Psalm 8:6–8, though in Jeremiah 27:6 and 28:14 there are references to Yahweh giving to Nebuchadnezzar 'the beasts of the field to serve him'. However, 'the birds of the air' do not appear in the verses in Jeremiah, as they do in Psalm 8:8.

E. W. Heaton considered that Nebuchadnezzar's sovereignty over men and all living creatures may reflect elements of the Babylonian new year festival, when the Epic of Creation was recited at the annual enthronement of the reigning king.[35] If such was the case, we may note a strong resemblance between Israelite and Babylonian kingship traditions at this point, but should surmise that in Daniel (where an Israelite was the interpreter) the dominant influence would have been the celebration of the creator-kingship of Yahweh. L. F. Hartman, while recognizing a dependence on Jeremiah 27:6; 28:14, scorns the idea that Daniel 2:38 contains any allusion to Genesis 1:28 or Psalm 8:6–8, for the reason that 'Nebuchadnezzar is not "mankind"'.[36] However, we have already seen that Nebuchadnezzar's kingship is treated in similar categories to Davidic kingship (*e.g.* Dn. 4:27), and the Davidic king played the role of 'representative man'.

There is a reminiscence of Daniel 2:38 in chapter 4, where the beasts of the field found shade under the tree which symbolized the king, and the birds of the air dwelt in its branches (vv. 12, 14, 21). However, it is the character of God's judgment on Nebuchadnezzar that most clearly recalls Genesis 1:26–28 and Psalm 8:3–8: those passages show the true dignity of man in having dominion over the animal world under the authority and gift of God; man is in an intermediate position between God and the rest of the animal creation. Daniel 4 presents Nebuchadnezzar lifting himself up above man's proper position by denying his dependence on God (v. 30), so that not only is his kingdom over men and beasts taken away from him but he himself is reduced to the level of an animal (vv. 25, 32f.), by way of temporary insanity. When his reason returned to him, he regained his kingdom (v. 36); his mind had been made like that of a beast (5:21) but afterwards he received again the mind of a

[35] E. W. Heaton, *The Book of Daniel* (SCM, 1956), p. 131; *cf.* A. Lacocque, *The Book of Daniel* (SPCK, 1979), p. 50.

[36] L. F. Hartman and A. A. Di Lella, *The Book of Daniel* (Doubleday, 1978), p. 147.

man (*cf.* 7:4). His restoration led not only to his kingship over men and the animal world again (the relationship downwards), but also to his acknowledgement of God's supreme authority (the relationship upwards). He had previously wanted to know the honoured position of 'man's' kingship, as described in Psalm 8:5–8, without recognizing his insignificance and dependence on God, seen in Psalm 8:3f. This omission is now made good by his confession that 'all the inhabitants of the earth are accounted as nothing' before God (Dn. 4:35); this is based on Isaiah 40:17, a creation passage very similar in thought to Psalm 8:3f.

We have seen that in Genesis 1:26–28, 'man' created in God's image was made to have a special relationship with God, and to rule. Daniel shows that earthly kings, as 'representative man', may be eager to rule, but are often unwilling to acknowledge any relationship to God. Instead of allowing their kingship to be 'in the image of God' (as the Davidic kingship was supposed to be, a reflection of Yahweh's kingship on earth), they are represented as constructing in Nebuchadnezzar's first dream a statue (or 'image') of themselves, of a man, which God had to smash to re-establish his supreme authority. In chapter 3, Nebuchadnezzar foolishly set up a great statue, probably similar to that which he saw in his dream, concentrating on himself as the head of gold rather than the fact that God would destroy the whole statue.

We have noted that the dreams in chapters 2 and 7 can be seen as a search by God to find someone to exercise earthly kingship properly on his behalf; we now see that this was the original destiny of 'man' in Genesis 1:26–28 and Psalm 8:3–8. The search is for some individual or people who can fulfil the role of 'man' in reality, as the Davidic king had acted out that role in the temple at Jerusalem. The converse of this is a search by man apart from God for the true significance of his humanity; we have noted that the statue of 'man' that was constructed by the world empires had to be destroyed by God; 'manhood', the absence of it and similarity to it are recurring motifs in Daniel.

The word *'āḏām* does not appear in the Aramaic section of the book of Daniel (2:4 – 7:28); instead the word *'enāš* appears twenty-five times, meaning 'man', 'mankind' or 'a man'. We earlier concluded that *ben 'āḏām* ('son of man') was a title given to the Davidic king in taking the role of 'representative man' in temple worship. The equivalent in Aramaic of this Hebrew phrase is *bar 'enāš*, which appears in Daniel 7:13. According to H. Haag, *bar* ('son') in Aramaic was not as necessary to convey the idea of a single person as *ben* in Hebrew, because *'enāš* alone can mean 'a man' or 'men, mankind'.[37]

---

[37] H. Haag, *TDOT* 2 (1975), p. 161.

It is clear that in Daniel 7, a contrast is being made between the beasts and 'one like a son of man'. A human figure appears subsequent to the animals; the prefix k^e ('like') occurs not only in verse 13 before 'a son of man', but also in verse 4 ('like a lion') and verse 6 ('like a leopard'), while an alternative expression is used for the second beast (v. 5). Thus the meaning of 'like' may merely refer to the appearance of the different figures in the dream, which were not easy to describe exactly. However, if the writer wanted to refer in Aramaic to the appearance of a human being in contrast to the beasts, there was no need for him to use *bar,* since *'enāš* on its own would have been sufficient (as we have seen). In verse 4, the first beast was made to stand upon two feet *ke'enāš* ('like a man'). Exactly the same phrase (without *bar*) could have been used in verse 13, which would have been precisely in line with the form of 'like a lion' (v. 4) and 'like a leopard' (v. 6). The fact that the form in verse 13 is *k^ebar 'enāš* ('like a *son* of man') suggests a deliberate intention to recall the Hebrew *ben 'āḏām,* which was applied to the Davidic king.[38]

Whether *bar 'enāš* means 'a man' or, as we have argued, more particularly 'a son of man', recalling the use of the phrase *ben 'āḏām* in the Jerusalem cult, the contrast between the animals and 'man' in chapter 7 again relates to 'man's' dignified position of kingship in Genesis 1 and Psalm 8. In addition to verse 13, *'enāš* ('man') occurs three times in chapter 7, twice in verse 4 and also in verse 8. We have already commented that verse 4 speaks of Nebuchadnezzar's restoration to the true status of 'man' after his acknowledgement of God's superior kingship. It seems that the kings, represented by the succeeding beasts, do not achieve this true 'manhood' which is gained by recognizing God's authority; however, they exercise dominion which is the other pole of 'man's' status. Thus we imagine that 'man's' search in history for the true significance of his humanity continues simultaneously with God's search for 'man' to fulfil his true role.

'Man's' search seems to be on the verge of success, since the final most powerful king (represented by the little horn) has eyes 'like the eyes of man' (v. 8). This suggests that the final ruler, who speaks words against the Most High (v. 25), will for a time give a plausible impression of fulfilling 'man's' destiny, apart from God. However, just as the statue is destroyed in chapter 2, so 'man's' false ideas of his own position are destroyed along with the fourth beast (7:11). God's search is ended as he delegates the kingship on earth to one who will accept the true role of 'man', ruling under God's authority. It is not by coincidence that he is called 'one like a son of man' (7:13).

[38] *Cf.* R. N. Longenecker, *The Christology of Early Jewish Christianity* (SCM, 1970), p.86, where he holds that *bar 'enāš* here constitutes 'a titular usage, meaning more than just that the figure looked human.'

We have now seen that the Davidic kingship, with authority on earth delegated by God as 'the King of heaven', forms the background to the vision in Daniel 7. We have further seen that this new delegated kingship is represented as fulfilling the original role of 'man' in the creation order (as expounded in Genesis 1:26–28 and Psalm 8:3–8); also *bar* '*e nāš* may well be a deliberate echo of the Hebrew *ben 'ādām,* by which the Davidic king was known when he took the part of 'representative man' in the Jerusalem cult. However, the fact that such ideas and allusions represent the background to the use of *bar* '*e nāš* in Daniel 7:13 does not necessarily mean that the figure appearing in the dream can be described as messianic, the hoped-for future ruler of the Davidic line. To pursue this question, we must look first at the general character of God's interventions in Daniel to see if 'one like a son of man' is represented as an angelic figure, and secondly at other features of the dream in chapter 7 and its interpretation to see whether he is merely a symbol for 'the saints of the Most High'.

In each of the chapters of Daniel 2 – 7 God is shown as intervening in human affairs, and it is interesting to compare his instruments or agents of intervention. In chapter 2, we have seen that the instrument represented in Nebuchadnezzar's dream was a stone 'cut out without a hand being put to it' (vv. 34, 45),[39] the latter phrase implying the heavenly origin of the stone. In the similar vision in chapter 7, we have noted that part at least of the stone's function is represented by 'one like a son of man', and the statement that he came 'with the clouds of heaven' (7:13) likewise suggests a heavenly origin. God is sometimes represented as riding on the clouds (Pss. 68:4; 104:3).

In 3:25, after Daniel's three colleagues had been put into the furnace, four men were seen there, 'and the appearance of the fourth is like a son of the gods'. While the fourth person could be described as 'a man', there was an ambiguity in his appearance which suggested his likeness to an angel. We shall notice other examples of this human-angelic ambiguity in Daniel. That 'a son of the gods' (v. 25) means 'an angel' is shown by verse 28, where he is said to be God's agent in rescuing the three men. Similarly in chapter 6, Daniel says that God sent 'his angel' and shut the lions' mouths (v. 22).

In 4:13, Nebuchadnezzar's judgment is undertaken by 'a watcher, a holy one', which must mean an angelic being, since he comes down from heaven (*cf.* vv. 17, 23), though the same word for 'holy one' is used of 'the saints of the Most High' in 7:18, 22, 25, 27. God's intervention in chapter 5 is in the form of 'the fingers of a man's hand' writing on the wall at Belshazzar's feast (v. 5). Once again, the hand looked human, but clearly it was not, and Daniel says it

---

[39] L. F. Hartman and A. A. Di Lella, *op. cit.,* p.147.

was sent from God's presence (v. 24).

Thus in each of the six interventions by God in chapters 2 – 7, the agent is clearly from heaven, and in three cases (3:25; 5:5; 7:13) a likeness to humanity is mentioned. This material may be supplemented by considering chapters 8 – 12, which are in Hebrew.[40] In 8:25, the little horn who rises up against 'the Prince of princes' (= God) will be broken 'by no human hand', which is similar to the phrase in 2:34, 45. Also in these chapters, Daniel is visited by various heavenly beings and told of the doings of others. As earlier in the book, they are often described as 'men' (8:16; 9:21; 10:5; 12:6f.) or similar to men (8:15; 10:16, 18), though they are clearly angelic. In the perspective of the book of Daniel, the distinction between God's earthly and heavenly servants sometimes seems to break down, as in 8:10–13, where 'the host of heaven' probably refers both to the angels and to the historical Israel (*cf.* 12:3); while in 7:18ff. the 'saints of the Most High', who must represent God's people on earth (as in 11:33, 35; 12:1, 3) because they suffer at the hands of the 'little horn' (7:21, 25),[41] are described, as we have seen, by the same word as the angelic 'holy ones' in 4:13ff.

Gabriel appears as a 'man' (*'îš*) in 9:21, and it is not recorded that his presence had any frightening effect on Daniel, as had his first approach in 8:17f. Since Gabriel is addressed in 8:16, it must be he that is described in verse 15 as 'having the appearance of a man' (the word for 'man' being the less common *geber*). Gabriel is instructed by another heavenly being (v. 16), who speaks with a 'man's' (*'āḏām*) voice between the banks of the river Ulai, where Daniel saw the vision (v. 2). Daniel is addressed as 'son of man' (*ben 'āḏām*, v. 17), in a situation similar to that in Ezekiel 2:1, where the prophet is so addressed after he had seen 'a likeness as it were of a human form' (*kᵉmar'ēh 'āḏām*, Ezk. 1:26) on the throne, referring to God. The same expression, *kᵉmar'ēh 'āḏām*, is used of the heavenly being in Daniel 10:18, while a similar expression, using *bᵉnê 'āḏām* ('sons of men'), occurs in 10:16.

The same heavenly being, who appears in 10:5, called there and in 12:6f. a 'man (*'îš*) clothed in linen' (*cf.* Ezk. 9:2), is described in similar terms to Ezekiel

---

[40] While there is no consensus on the unity of Daniel among scholars, it is difficult to divide the book satisfactorily, since chapter 7 belongs with earlier chapters by language and perhaps chiastic arrangement, while in content it is similar to the later chapters; *cf.* M. Casey, *Son of Man: the Interpretation and Influence of Daniel 7* (SPCK, 1979), pp.7-10. Since the book has an apparent unity in its final form, it is reasonable to look for indications of the meaning of Daniel 7 in the later chapters.

[41] *Contra* J. J. Collins, 'The Son of Man and the Saints of the Most High in the Book of Daniel', *JBL* 93 (1974), pp.50-66, who takes the 'saints of the Most High' as an angelic host.

1:26–28, though the parallels are not exact. The effect on Daniel is very marked (10:8–11, 15–18) and he needed a strengthening touch on three occasions. This is in contrast to the earlier appearances of Gabriel, where the effect was not so severe. Daniel addresses this being as 'my lord' in 10:16f., 19; 12:8, a form of address that is mostly used in the Old Testament to God or to a king (*cf.* Dn. 1:10). It is this being who is assisted by Michael, implying that he is in a superior position to Michael (10:13, 21). The fact that he is represented 'above the waters of the stream' in 12:6 suggests that his was the 'man's' voice between the banks of the river in 8:16. If that is the case, apart from Daniel being called *ben 'ādām* in 8:17, it is only this being who is called or likened to *'ādām* (8:16; 10:16, 18), while the form of the phrases 'one in the likeness of the sons of men' (10:16) and 'one having the appearance of a man' (10:18) suggests that the writer may have identified 'one like a son of man' in 7:13 (also a glorious figure) with this heavenly being in chapter 10. Some commentators consider this heavenly being to be God himself, because of the similarity to Ezekiel 1.[42] However, he might partake of the character of divinity, without being identified completely with God, like the angel of Yahweh in Genesis 16:7ff. and other Old Testament references.[43]

We noted that the use of *keḇar 'enāš* ('like a son of man', Dn. 7:13) suggests a deliberate intention to recall the Hebrew *ben 'ādām*, in the context of 'man's' (*'ādām*) role in relationship to God. The fact that in the Hebrew section of Daniel (apart from the special case of 8:17) *'ādām* is used of only one particular heavenly being, makes an identification likely between that being and *keḇar 'enāš*. However, we cannot be certain, and perhaps the writer was not certain of the exact significance of the visions: heavenly beings could no doubt be similar without being the same. What is clear is that 'one like a son of man' in 7:13, in common with all other agents of God's intervention in Daniel (despite their frequently human appearance), had a heavenly origin, since he came 'with the clouds of heaven'. The book of Daniel shows the kingship of God becoming effective on earth by means of his interventions from heaven, which often take or appear to take human form; this is the forerunner of incarnational theology.

'One like a son of man' in 7:13, we have seen, represents the one who will fulfil the true role of 'man', ruling under God's authority. Yet in order to fulfil this role assigned at creation to 'man' made in the image of God (Gn. 1:26–28), he must in a sense be the reverse of that image: he is 'like a (son of) man', in the image of man, though possessing that heavenly origin and divine power that is the mark of all God's interventions in Daniel. Thus to fulfil 'man's' role in the

---

[42] *E.g.* H. Haag, *TDOT* 2 (1975), p.165.

[43] *Cf.* E. J. Young, *The Prophecy of Daniel* (Eerdmans, 1949), pp.224-229.

image of God, he takes the image of man and adds to it a fresh supply of God's strength; in the figure of 'one like a son of man' it is as if we see a fresh infusion of the divine into 'mankind'. It is proto-incarnational.

Having noticed the heavenly origin of 'one like a son of man' and suggested his possible identification with the heavenly being of Daniel 10, we must consider the suggestion that he should be identified rather with Michael, who is said to 'arise' at the climax of the book in 12:1.[44] Against this identification it may be argued that 'one like a son of man' appears on earth, where the beasts had exercised their rule and the Ancient of Days had come (7:22), while Michael's realm is solely in heaven. He is involved in heavenly conflicts in 10:13, 21, while in 12:1–3 it is the heavenly aspects of the everlasting kingdom that are presented, such as resurrection (v. 2), and the wise shining 'like the stars' (v. 3). He may be a heavenly representative or counterpart of 'one like a son of man', but the latter appears on earth, probably at the same time as Michael arises in heaven (12:1). The rising of Michael suggests that the war in the heavens has been completed, but does not necessarily imply the setting up of a kingdom on earth. If our suggested identification of 'one like a son of man' with the heavenly being of chapter 10 is plausible, Michael there assists him and fights together with him (10:13, 21).

Thus, while the Davidic kingship and the true role of 'man' form the background to Daniel 7, we have now observed, based on our consideration of other instances of God's interventions and revelations in the book, that 'one like a son of man' is represented as a heavenly being, angelic or divine. Does this prohibit a messianic interpretation?

The main reason for doubt, remembering the background we have noted in this chapter of Davidic (messianic) kingship and 'representative man' (under the title of *bar 'eⁿāš*), is not the representation of 'one like a son of man' as a heavenly being (strange as that may seem) but the fact that in the interpretation of the dream (commencing at verse 17) the role of 'one like a son of man' in receiving the kingdom is taken by the 'saints of the Most High' (vv. 18, 22, 27), God's faithful people on earth. Thus it is frequently argued that 'one like a son of man' is not to be seen as an individual, the messianic leader of his people, but is purely a symbol for the people of God, having no separate identity from them. Just as the four beasts in the vision did not exist in reality, it is argued that 'one like a son of man' is not a real being.[45]

---

[44] So J. J. Collins, *The Apocalyptic Vision of the Book of Daniel* (Scholars Press, 1977); A. Lacocque, *The Book of Daniel* (SPCK, 1979), pp. 133f.

[45] M. Casey, *Son of Man* (SPCK, 1979), pp. 24f.; *cf.* M.D. Hooker, *The Son of Man in Mark* (SPCK, 1967), pp. 11-30.

If 'one like a son of man' is merely symbolic of the 'saints of the Most High', he cannot be a 'messianic' figure, since he has no separate existence. If he can be shown to be an individual figure not wholly identified with God's people, then the background factors we have noted together with other features in chapter 7 will imply messianic status. We shall consider three negative arguments against the separate identity and messianic role of 'one like a son of man', to be followed by three positive arguments.

1. It is argued that there is no mention of the Messiah in Daniel, and therefore the author belonged to a group that did not expect the Messiah.[46] Even if it is true that the Messiah is not mentioned elsewhere in Daniel, there is still no need to infer a lack of belief in the Messiah; the early prophetic books, Hosea and Amos, each have only one reference to a messianic figure (Ho. 3:5; Am. 9:11f.). However, 'an anointed one' is mentioned in Daniel 9:25f., called 'a prince' (v. 25), and 'cut off' (v. 26) presumably by an untimely death. While most commentators consider that two 'anointed ones' are mentioned, appearing after successive periods of seven and sixty-two weeks, J. G. Baldwin points out that the time-gap between the command to rebuild and the coming 'anointed one' literally reads 'seven sevens and sixty-two sevens', and thus it may be the same 'anointed one' who after sixty-nine weeks 'comes' (v. 25) and is 'cut off' (v. 26).[47] If that is the case, a single messianic personage who suffers is probably in view. 'To bring in everlasting righteousness' at the end of the seventy weeks (v. 24) implies the setting up of God's eternal kingdom, with which a messianic figure is sometimes associated.[48]

2. The 'saints of the Most High' suffer persecution and apparent defeat at the hands of the final king (vv. 21, 25; cf. Rev. 13:7). It has been argued that the Old Testament does not know of a suffering Messiah, and therefore 'one like a son of man', who is identified with the saints, cannot be the Messiah. We have noted, however, that in some of the psalms the Davidic king is said to experience suffering, while in Psalm 80, as *ben 'ādām*, he is identified with Israel in their tribulation prior to his exaltation.[49] It is more likely that the

---

[46] M. Casey, *op. cit.*, pp. 30f.

[47] J. G. Baldwin, *op. cit.*, pp. 170f.; *cf.* E. J. Young, *op. cit.*, pp.195-221, who takes the last clause of verse 24 to mean the anointing of a 'most holy' one, the Messiah, rather than 'a most holy place' (RSV), since the object is not specified.

[48] N. S. Denham, *The Prince of the Covenant* (unpublished manuscript in London Bible College library, 1953), dates the decree of Cyrus, which he takes to be the beginning of the seventy weeks, in 457 BC, producing detailed arguments to dispute Ptolemy's chronology of the Persian period; the foreword is by F. F. Bruce.

[49] C. F. D. Moule, 'From Defendant to Judge – and Deliverer', reprinted in *The Phenomenon of the New Testament* (SCM, 1967), pp.82-99.

connection of suffering with 'one like a son of man' comes from the Psalms and the role of the king in the Jerusalem temple, rather than from the figure of the 'servant' in Isaiah 53.[50]

3. It is argued that if the Messiah had been in view in Daniel 7:13f., he would hardly have been omitted from the interpretation in the following verses.[51] However, not all aspects of the dream are interpreted: verses 19–22 are an amplification of the dream, rather than part of the interpretation (though the interpretation in verse 18 of the 'saints' receiving the kingdom is incorporated into verse 22). Additional information is given: 'claws of bronze' are mentioned (v. 19); the ten horns are specifically said to be on the head of the fourth beast (v. 20); the little horn 'seemed greater than its fellows' (v. 20); this horn 'made war with the saints, and prevailed over them' (v. 21); the Ancient of Days 'comes' to earth (v. 22). This coming of the Ancient of Days in judgment presumably refers back to verse 9, and contrasts with the later coming of 'one like a son of man' to be enthroned. Since verses 19–22 represent an amplification of the dream rather than the interpretation, the Ancient of Days (like 'one like a son of man') is not mentioned in the interpretation.

Not all aspects of the dream therefore require symbolic interpretation, as do the beasts. Even 'the saints' are not restricted to the interpretation, but appear in the amplification of the dream in verse 21. Thus the relationship between 'one like a son of man' and 'the saints' cannot be merely symbolic; by combining verses 21 and 22 with the first description of the dream, we conclude that the war of the saints is seen to take place before the coming of the son of man, who then receives the kingship as a leader-figure, at the same time as the saints. The interpretation is concerned mainly with the fourth beast (vv. 19, 23) and therefore not every aspect of the dream is explained. In the interpretation of the beasts, they are first called 'four kings' (v. 17). Clearly some individual kings are represented, such as Nebuchadnezzar (v. 4) and perhaps Alexander (v. 6); however, they also represent kingdoms and a plurality of kings, especially the fourth beast with its ten horns. By the same token then 'one like a son of man' may be an individual and also symbolic of the 'saints of the Most High', who like him receive the kingdom.

The positive arguments are as follows:

1. The enthronement of God (v. 9) followed by the granting of kingship to 'one like a son of man' (v. 13) is reminiscent of the coronation of the Davidic

---

[50] Despite a possible allusion to Is. 53:11 in Dn. 12:3; *cf.* F. F. Bruce, *Biblical Exegesis in the Qumran Texts* (Tyndale Press, 1960), pp.62, 65.

[51] M. Casey, *op. cit.*, pp.24f.; J. D. G. Dunn, *op. cit.*, p.69.

king in Psalm 2.[52] The 'wheels' (v. 9) and 'fire' (vv. 9f.) of God's throne may be compared to Ezekiel 1:15ff., 27, but the structure of the dream reflects the celebration of Yahweh's kingship, which we have seen in the Psalms is associated with the Davidic (messianic) king.[53] The fact that kingship is given by the enthroned Ancient of Days to a figure who is closely associated with God's people (represented by the 'saints of the Most High') is sufficient to identify that figure as the Messiah, provided he is not a mere symbol.[54]

In Psalm 110:1, the Davidic king is enthroned at the right hand of Yahweh; this is recalled in Psalm 80:17 where 'the man of thy right hand' is found in parallel with 'the son of man'. Is the 'one like a son of man' in verse 13 observed as being enthroned beside Yahweh? If that is the case, it is likely that he is enthroned as an individual (the leader of his people), because of the difficulty of envisaging the enthronement of all the saints at the side of God. 'Thrones were placed' (v. 9) is plural, and many have wondered whether the second throne is for the son of man; clearly someone or some persons are enthroned beside the Ancient of Days. M. Casey argues that the thrones are for other members of the court who are part of God's retinue, on the basis that 'the court (*dînā'*) sat in judgment' (v. 10);[55] however *dînā'* (literally meaning 'judgment') implies neither singularity or plurality, so may simply refer to 'the judge'. This is the more likely as the myriads are said to be 'standing' in verse 10; also in Micaiah's vision of Yahweh sitting on his throne, all the host of heaven are 'standing beside him' (1 Ki. 22:19). Nowhere is the heavenly host represented as seated beside God, though this is the position of the Davidic king in Psalm 110:1. The likeness of the dream in other respects to the coronation psalms of the Davidic (messianic) king (Pss. 2; 110) leads us to conclude that the second throne is for the son of man.

2. It is difficult to conceive of the 'saints of the Most High' without a leader. The Israelite king could be closely identified with his people (as we saw in Ps. 80); generally in the ancient Near East the link between an individual and the community was stronger than in the Western world today. The king could fully represent his people, and yet still act as a separate individual apart from

---

[52] A. Bentzen, *King and Messiah* (Lutterworth, 1955), pp.74-76; J. A. Emerton, 'The Origin of the Son of Man Imagery', *JTS* 9 (1958), pp.225-242; C. F. D. Moule, *The Origin of Christology* (CUP, 1977), p.26.

[53] E. W. Heaton, *The Book of Daniel* (SCM, 1956), pp.174-176, relates the defeat of the four beasts to creation imagery, as seen in the context of Yahweh's kingship in Ps. 74:12ff. This also fits in with the king taking the role of 'representative man' to fulfil God's creation ordinance in Gn. 1:26–28.

[54] *Cf.* R. H. Fuller, *The Foundations of New Testament Christology* (Collins, 1965), p.36.

[55] M. Casey, *op. cit.*, p.23.

them.[56] We observe today each nation feels the need to have a figurehead, even if he or she has no effective power. It is hard to think of any sizeable organization operating without representative leadership. Thus, since the 'one like a son of man' and the 'saints of the Most High' are both said to receive the kingship, the most natural conclusion is that the individual figure receives the kingship on behalf of his people, especially when other features of his situation (his receipt of the kingship in the manner of a Davidic king, and his title of 'son of man') suggest Messiahship. Having received the kingship, he shares it with the saints, by virtue of his close identification with them.

3. If, as we have seen, 'one like a son of man' who comes 'with the clouds of heaven' is a heavenly being, although he may represent the saints he cannot be merely a symbol for them. If he is just a symbol he is not an agent of God's intervention on earth, unless the people he symbolizes are in fact a heavenly host, which we do not accept because of their earthly suffering. Thus, surprisingly, it is the heavenly origin of the 'one like a son of man' which finally proves his individuality and thus (taken with other indications in the chapter) his messianic role.

This combination in the dream of a heavenly being with the Messiah, which we have described as proto-incarnational, marks a new conception in the Old Testament. Yet it is not completely unprecedented, for we have seen that the Davidic king in his role as 'son of man' was 'little less than God' (Ps. 8:5), created 'in the image of God' (Gn. 1:27), while the future Messiah in David's line would be called 'Mighty God' (Is. 9:6). The question how a heavenly being could become the messianic king, and lead his people through suffering to receive a kingdom, was not answered until the coming of Jesus, who prior to his crucifixion warned the high priest (Mk. 14:62) that he would see 'the Son of man seated at the right hand of Power, and coming with the clouds of heaven'.

[56] *Cf.* I. H. Marshall, *The Origins of New Testament Christology* (IVP, 1976), pp.66f.

CHRISTOLOGICAL AMBIGUITIES IN THE GOSPEL OF MATTHEW

D. A. Carson

Recent study of the Christology embraced by the Gospel of Matthew has usually run along several complementary lines. First, in the age of redaction criticism and the dominance of the two-source hypothesis, careful attention has been given to comparisons (not to say contrasts) between Matthew on the one hand, and Mark and Q on the other.[1] Second, several scholars have focused attention on the meaning and function of particular titles, such as 'Lord',[2] 'Son of God',[3] 'Son of David'[4] and others. Third, others have directed their study to particular passages rich in Christological language and symbolism, and based broad conclusions on their findings. One thinks, for instance, of Michel's seminal study on Matthew 28:16–20,[5] and of the many works that have sprung from it; or, more recently, of Nolan's book on Matthew 1f., which develops a Christology shaped by the Davidic covenant.[6]

---

[1] One may think, for instance, of the seminal essay by G. M. Styler, 'Stages in Christology in the Synoptic Gospels', *NTS* 10, 1963-64, pp.398-409; or of the recent commentary by Robert H. Gundry, *Matthew: A Commentary on His Literary and Theological Art* (Eerdmans, 1981).

[2] On 'Lord', see Gunther Bornkamm, 'Die Sturmstillung im Matthäusevangelium', *Wort und Dienst* 1, 1948, pp.49-54, available in English in G. Bornkamm, G. Barth and H. J. Held, *Tradition and Interpretation in Matthew* (SCM, 1963), pp.52-57 [hereafter *TIM*]; and many others after him.

[3] On 'Son of God', see especially Jack Dean Kingsbury, *Matthew: Structure, Christology, Kingdom* (Fortress, 1975), and the telling critique by David Hill, 'Son and Servant: An essay on Matthean Christology', *JSNT* 6, 1980, pp.2-16.

[4] On 'Son of David', cf. Dennis C. Duling, 'The Therapeutic Son of David: An Element in Matthew's Christological Apologetic', *NTS* 24, 1978, pp.392-410; and for greater background, Christoph Burger, *Jesus als Davidssohn* (Vandenhoeck & Ruprecht, 1970).

[5] O. Michel, 'Der Abschluss des Matthäusevangeliums', *Evangelische Theologie* 10, 1950-51, pp.16-26.

[6] Brian M. Nolan, *The Royal Son of God: The Christology of Matthew 1 – 2 in the Setting of the Gospel* (Vandenhoeck & Ruprecht, 1979).

With few exceptions, however, these studies assume that because the Evangelist is writing from the perspective of faith, and decades after the events (most scholars believe the Gospel of Matthew was written about AD 85; Gundry, not later than AD 63; and others, from theological positions as polarized as those of William Hendriksen and John A. T. Robinson, place the book at various dates before AD 70), he must reflect a theology contemporaneous with his own *Sitz im Leben*. Inevitably, it is presupposed that the Gospel of Matthew is studded with Christological anachronisms.

The purpose of this paper is to call these assumptions into question, and to suggest replacing them with a subtler construction which more fairly reflects the evidence. If this were a book instead of a short article, it would be necessary to embark upon several rather negative discussions. For instance, it would be necessary to begin with the observation that Matthew chose to write a Gospel about Jesus, and to see where that would take us. Was Matthew himself unaware of his putative anachronisms? If so, then must we assume he was anachronistic only sometimes? And exactly how may we distinguish genuine anachronisms, material that is not anachronistic yet not historical, and material that is historical and therefore not anachronistic? On the other hand, if Matthew *was* aware of his alleged anachronisms, then we must adjust our understanding of what a 'Gospel' is; and we would have to ask whether Matthew intended to be *consistently* anachronistic, reflecting his own times, or selectively so; and if the latter, we would need to know how (or if!) he expected his readers to tell the difference. These questions would take us into complex considerations of literary genre, which cannot be probed here.[7]

Behind them lies another nest of questions concerning the power of redaction criticism. How valid is it to conclude that, because some snippet is redactional and not traditional, it is *for that reason* not historical? Or, for that matter, how valid is it to assume that because something is judged traditional, it must therefore be historical? How influential on our redaction criticism is the bevy of fairly speculative 'historical' *Sitze im Leben* which are reconstructed almost exclusively on the grounds of form and redaction criticism? What do we know, after all, of Matthew's community (did he have a community?) except by reconstructions that are no more than deductions based on debatable judgments about why he wrote?

Some of these questions I have explored elsewhere, and shall refrain from repeating myself here.[8] I am far from suggesting that redaction criticism is not

---

[7] I have reviewed the most recent commentary which makes substantial appeal to considerations of literary genre – that of Gundry (see n. 1, *supra*) – in *Trinity Journal* 3, 1982.

[8] 'Redaction Criticism: On the Use and Abuse of a Literary Tool', in *Scripture and Truth,* ed. D. A. Carson and John D. Woodbridge (Zondervan, 1982).

a valuable literary tool, when its severe limitations are carefully borne in mind. Equally, I am not suggesting that Matthew attempts to describe the events in Jesus' day with reportorial disinterest. Matthew's Christology is far more subtle than that. Rather, while revealing his own Christological commitments, both by the flow of his argument and by occasional asides and other remarks which he does *not* put back into the time of Jesus, Matthew carefully avoids outright Christological anachronisms but holds that the frequently ambiguous Christological confessions and claims which transpired in Jesus' day unerringly pointed forward to the full understanding held by the church in the post-resurrection period.

To justify this thesis, I must show three things: first, that at least occasionally Matthew unambiguously reveals his own Christological commitments; second, that the many Christological texts often assumed to be anachronistic are nothing of the kind; and third, that the Evangelist himself intends to show that the confessions and claims which transpired in Jesus' day can only be rightly understood if they are seen to point forward to the full-orbed Christology of his own day. To demonstrate these three comprehensively for each Christological title used by Matthew would require a very thick book. Within the confines of this article I must limit myself to priming the pump: I shall select five of the most prominent Christological terms in the Gospel of Matthew, and sketch out a line of argument which seems to me quite compelling, even if it could be considerably expanded.

Before embarking on this survey, however, it is worth pausing to remark that the third point which must be shown – that the Evangelist himself intends to show that the Christological confessions and claims which transpired in Jesus' day can only be rightly understood if they are seen to point forward to the full-orbed Christology of his own day – bears an intrinsic probability, if we may judge by the Evangelist's treatment of other themes. In a manner somewhat analogous to the Epistle to the Hebrews, which understands laws, institutions and past redemptive events to have a major *prophetic* function in pointing the way to their fulfilment and culmination in Jesus, so Matthew holds that certain major redemptive appointments in the Old Testament (*e.g.*, the exodus, the exile), and certain prophecies surrounding Old Testament figures (especially David), are not only significant in their own right but enjoy a prophetic function fulfilled in Jesus Messiah. The very structure of the Old Testament revelation, he holds, finds its true culmination in Jesus and the events of his ministry, passion and resurrection.[9] Just as those *past* events and

---

[9] I have dealt with these themes at some length, especially Matthew's use of the Old Testament, in my forthcoming commentary on Matthew (Zondervan).

words of a bygone period of salvation history find their fulfilment in the ministry of Jesus, so, it may be argued, do the events and words *during* Jesus' ministry point forward to a maturer understanding achieved by Jesus' disciples only after the resurrection and Pentecost. Again, Matthew quite clearly sees Jesus' ministry in Gentile Galilee, the healing of the (Gentile) centurion's servant and of the (Gentile) Canaanite woman, and the repeated hardness of the Jewish leaders (4:12–17; 8:1–4, 5–13; 15:21–28; 11:20–24; 23:1–39), as unambiguous pointers to world-wide, inter-racial mission, a new extension of the locus of the people of God (24:14; 28:15–20). An Evangelist with such deep sensitivities to the organic connections in redemptive history might almost be *expected* to detect similar connections in the Christological arena.

Christ

We may begin with 'Christ', the rough Greek equivalent to 'Messiah' or 'Anointed One'. In the Old Testament, the term refers to various people who have been 'anointed' to some special function: priests (Lv. 4:3; 6:22), kings (1 Sa. 16:13; 24:10; 2 Sa. 19:21; La. 4:20), the patriarchs ('anointed' meta-phorically; *cf.* Ps. 105:15), and even the pagan king Cyrus (Is. 45:1). As early as Hannah's prayer, 'messiah' is parallel with 'king': 'the LORD will give strength to his *king*, and exalt the power of his *anointed*' (1 Sa. 2:10). With the rising number of Old Testament prophecies regarding King David's line (*e.g.* 2 Sa. 7:12–16; *cf.* Pss. 2:2; 105:15; Is. 45:1; Dn. 9:25f.), 'Messiah' or 'Christ' became one of the favourite designations of a figure who would represent the people of God and bring in the promised eschatological reign.

The Palestine of Jesus' day was ripe with diverse messianic expectations. Some Jews expected two different 'messiahs'. But the link, in Matthew's first verse (1:1), between 'Jesus Christ' and 'the Son of David', makes it fairly clear just what Matthew is claiming. The Evangelist writes from the perspective of faith: the Jesus about whom he writes is the Messiah.

Syntactically, the absence of the article enables us to go further. It is well known that, on the whole, the Epistles use anarthrous *Christos,* reflecting a time when 'Christ' had become almost a proper name (though we may doubt that it ever lost its titular force completely, even in Paul),[10] whereas the Gospels prefer *ho Christos,* suggesting the earlier period, during Jesus' ministry, when 'Christ' was still purely titular, 'the Messiah'.[11] There are other,

---

[10] See especially N. T. Wright, 'The Messiah and the People of God: A Study in Pauline Theology with Particular Reference to the Argument of the Epistle to the Romans' (D. Phil. thesis, Oxford University, 1980), pp.9-55, 247ff.

[11] So, for instance, A. T. Robertson, *A Grammar of the Greek New Testament in the Light of Historical Research* (Broadman, 1934), pp.760f., 795.

syntactical forces which bear on the question of whether or not the word is articular; but the fundamental distinction between the articular and the anarthrous forms can scarcely be disputed, even if it may be questioned in particular instances. Of the approximately seventeen occurrences (there is an important variant reading at 16:21) of *Christos* in Matthew, all are titular except those in 1:1; probably 1:16; certainly 1:18; and possibly the variant at 16:21. In these instances, including the variant, the Evangelist is unambiguously writing from the confessional stance of his own mature reflection, using the form of the name/title common in the church when he writes. But wherever he describes the events of Jesus' ministry, during which 'Christ' was never a name in any real sense, he uses a titular form (which he also uses in 1:17, part of his own editorial aside, probably because he is there drawing attention not to the *person* of 'Messiah' but to the *time* of 'the Messiah'; *cf.* 2:4; 11:2; 16:16, 20; 22:42; 23:10; 24:5, 23; 26:63, 68; 27:17, 22). In short, Matthew ably distinguishes between his *own* linguistic practice and Christological understanding, and that enjoyed by the disciples during the days of Jesus' ministry.

We may go further. The ways these titular usages function in Matthew suggest not only that people during Jesus' ministry never used *Christos* as a personal name (with some residual titular force), but also that *no-one* during Jesus' ministry understood *Christos* or *ho Christos* in the full, Christian sense presupposed by Matthew. Matthew 2:4 finds the Magi asking where the Christ was to be born. Unlike the leaders of Jerusalem, they, at least, wanted to pay him homage; but there is no hint that they understood him to be a *suffering* 'anointed one', as Matthew did. To Peter, the Father supernaturally reveals Jesus' identity as 'the Christ' (16:16, 20); but he, too, has no category for a suffering and dying Christ (16:21–23). None of the disciples is prepared for Good Friday and Easter. At that distinctly *Christian* level, the level at which the Evangelist operates, no-one but Jesus himself understands in advance just what it means to be 'the Christ'.[12] Elsewhere in Matthew, Jesus can refer to 'the Christ', in a titular sense, and focus in on some other aspect of Christological implication (22:42; 23:10). He can warn against false Christs (24:5, 23). When challenged directly by the high priest as to whether or not he is the

---

[12] I am here breaking a trend, developed by Gerhard Barth and popularized in *TIM*, pp. 105ff. He argues that the disciples in Matthew, unlike those pictured in Mark, are characterized by deep understanding which distinguishes them from outsiders. This analysis is mistaken: *cf.* my commentary (as in n.9, *supra*), and especially Andrew H. Trotter, 'Understanding and Stumbling: A Study of the Disciples' Understanding of Jesus and His Teaching in the Gospel of Matthew' (Ph.D. thesis, Cambridge University, 1982).

Christ, Jesus gives an answer 'affirmative in content but reluctant or circumlocutory in formulation'[13] (26:63f.). From the perspective of the high priest, Jesus has spoken blasphemy; from the Evangelist's perspective, however, the high priest's conclusion is not only in error as to Jesus' messianic identity, but, in a deeply ironic way, it is one step in bringing the Christ to the cross and the ransom-death (20:28) which, as any Christian (like Matthew) could clearly see some time after the event, was the Christ's prime purpose in coming. In exactly the same way, the taunting tormentors (26:68) speak better than they know. Even Pilate does (27:17, 22).

The only other passage in Matthew where [ho] Christos is used is 11:2, where, we are told, John 'heard in prison about the deeds of *the Christ*' and sent disciples to question him. At first glance, the passage is rather surprising: Matthew does not normally intrude into his narrative explicit reference to his own Christological convictions. With the exception of the first chapter, he normally prefers to reveal these convictions only by the flow of his narrative. But having established his confessional stance in 1:1, 18, it is scarcely anachronistic for him to let that stance peep through again.

Indeed, there may be an important reason for doing so. Matthew here reminds his readers just who it is the Baptist is doubting. John may doubt; but from Matthew's perspective the time for doubting has passed. The Baptist's doubt, *in his own time,* was understandable. He had preached of one who was to come with both blessing and judgment (3:11f.);[14] but the only reports he was receiving were of blessing, not judgment. And meanwhile, the forerunner of this putative Messiah was languishing month after month in Machaerus. Within this context, Jesus' response is masterful. He points to the evidence of miracles in his ministry, but in the language of Isaiah 35:5f.; 61:1, with possible further allusions to Isaiah 26:19; 29:18f. Isaiah 61:1 is an explicit messianic passage; Isaiah 35:5f., though it has no messianic figure, describes the return of God's people to Zion with accompanying blessings (*e.g.* restoration of sight). Jesus claims that these messianic visions are being fulfilled in the miracles he is performing; and his preaching the good news to the poor (*cf.* also Mt. 5:3) is as explicit a claim to fulfil the messianic promises of Isaiah 61:1ff. as is Luke 4:17–21. The powers of darkness were being undermined; the kingdom

---

[13] David R. Catchpole, 'The Answer of Jesus to Caiaphas (Matt. xxvi.64)', NTS 17, 1970-71, p.226.

[14] *Cf.* James D. G. Dunn, *Jesus and the Spirit* (SCM, 1975), pp.55-60. Dunn's discussion is important. He is interested in asking when the question of Mt. 11:3 would arise. 'The most obvious answer is, *as soon as the note of imminence characteristic of John's preaching was supplanted or at least supplemented by the note of fulfilment characteristic of Jesus' preaching*' (p.59; emphasis his).

was advancing (Mt. 11:12; 12:28). But intriguingly, all four of the passages from Isaiah also contain references to judgment, somewhere in the immediate context. We read, 'Behold, your God will come with vengeance, with the recompense [better: 'retribution', as in NIV] of God' (Is. 35:4). What Isaiah foresaw was not only the proclamation of 'liberty to the captives' but 'the day of vengeance of our God' (Is. 61:1f.).

Thus, Jesus is allusively responding to the Baptist's deepest concerns. The blessings promised for the end have broken out and prove it is here, even though the judgments are delayed. 'And blessed is he who takes no offence at me' (Mt. 11:6), *i.e.* who does not fall away on account of Jesus. The beatitude in this form assumes the interlocutor has begun well and now must avoid stumbling. It is therefore an implicit challenge to John to re-examine his presuppositions about what the Messiah should be and do in the light of Jesus' fulfilment of Scripture, and to bring his understanding and trust into line with him. But by the time Matthew writes, the problem is largely resolved. It has become clear to Matthew, as to all Christians, *though not transparently so to the Baptist because of his place in salvation history*, that Jesus is truly the Messiah, as attested not only by his miracles but by his death and resurrection; and that the promises of retribution and vengeance, at least those not poured out in the bitter cup which Jesus himself drank (26:27, 39),[15] will find their fulfilment when Messiah returns at the end of the age (13:40–43; 24:36–51; 25:1–46). All of this Matthew clearly understands when he uses 'the Christ' in 11:2.

Detailed comparisons between Matthew and Mark in their respective uses of [*ho*] *Christos* would be interesting, but would take us too far afield, and entangle us in the intricacies of the so-called 'messianic secret' debate. I would be prepared to argue that Mark, too, can distinguish between his own confessional stance regarding 'Christ', and the perceptions of people during the period of Jesus' ministry. Matthew, however, carries through the distinction more systematically and subtly.

Son of David

There are three recent studies of Matthew's use of this title. Kingsbury is primarily interested in arguing that 'Son of David' is less significant title for Matthew than many scholars have assumed, and certainly less important than 'Son of God'.[16] Nolan focuses primarily on Matthew 1 – 2, but rightly argues

---

[15] On which see especially C. E. B. Cranfield, 'The Cup Metaphor in Mark xiv.36 and Parallels', *ExpT* 59, 1947-48, pp.137f.

[16] Jack Dean Kingsbury, 'The Title "Son of David" in Matthew's Gospel', *JBL* 95, 1976, pp.591-602.

that Davidic motifs stretch beyond the title itself and gather strength from almost every chapter in the Gospel; but in the end he associates too many Matthean themes with a Davidic Christology and loses control.[17] Duling shows how Matthew frequently associates 'Son of David' with Jesus' *healing* ministry, and attempts to link this with a peculiar Matthean *Sitz im Leben*, in which the Evangelist is opposing certain Jewish conceptions of 'Son of David';[18] but his Jewish sources are not particularly compelling.

If we are careful not to assume that everyone who takes 'Son of David' on his lips is being presented by Matthew as someone who holds a full-blown 'Son of David Christology', we shall be open to a more nuanced interpretation of the evidence. Matthew certainly holds that Jesus is the 'Son of David' and stands in the royal succession (1:1, 6, 17 [*bis*], 20).[19] These verses find no parallel in Mark. For Matthew, the title is not only equivalent to saying that Jesus is the promised Christ (1:1), but that he fulfils the promises God made to David (2 Sa. 7:12–16) and reiterated through the prophets (*e.g.* Is. 9:6f.). For at least some Jews in Jesus' day, 'Son of David' was an accepted messianic title (*cf.* Psalms of Solomon 17:21), and became an important theme in early Christianity, one that was frequently tied up with Christianity's Scriptures (*cf.* Lk. 1:32, 39; Jn. 7:42; Acts 13:23; Rom. 1:3; Rev. 22:16). Matthew opens his Gospel in ways that show he stands in this Christian train.

Matthew's remaining uses of 'Son of David', however, are more subtle; and none is demonstrably anachronistic, while collectively they point toward a fully Christian understanding of the term. The mention of David in Matthew 12:3 (paralleled in Mk. 2:25), in the context of debate with the Pharisees, may presuppose a 'Son of David' Christology in Jesus' mind; but the exegetical factors which bear on the question are too complex to be weighed here. More interesting are the frequent uses of 'Son of David' on the lips of those seeking healing or exorcism ('Have mercy on us, Son of David': Mt. 9:27; 15:22; 20:30f.), heightened by the wondering question of the crowds after one such miracle: 'Can this be the Son of David?' (12:23). The same theme is not unknown in Mark (*cf.* 10:47f.), but is much stronger in Matthew. Hill rightly remarks, 'The use of the Davidic title is less extraordinary in address to Jesus than some think: in Palestine, in the time of Jesus, there was an intense Messianic expectation.'[20] Small wonder: the messianic age was to be a time

[17] B. M. Nolan, as in n.6, *supra.*

[18] *Cf.* n.4, *supra.*

[19] On the significance of the genealogy, see the extended discussion in my commentary (as in n.9).

[20] David Hill, *The Gospel of Matthew* (Marshall, Morgan and Scott, 1972), p. 180.

when 'the eyes of the blind [would be] opened, and the ears of the deaf unstopped', when 'the lame man [would] leap like a hart, and the tongue of the dumb sing for joy' (Is. 35:5) – a point which, as we have seen, Jesus can make in the context of the title *ho Christos,* when he is answering the Baptist's doubts (Mt. 11:4–6).

It appears, therefore, that 'the Christ' and 'the Son of David' overlap considerably in their significance. If 'Son of David' bears distinctive emphasis, it conjures up the image of a king and his kingdom. That is why the same pericope which harbours the question, 'Can this be the Son of David?' (12:23), also records Jesus' conclusion, after the same exorcism: 'But if it is by the Spirit of God that I cast out demons, then *the kingdom of God* has come upon you' (12:28). The anointed one ('the Christ') is the anointed king ('the Son of David'); and if he is exercising his kingly authority to fulfil messianic expectation, then the messianic kingdom ('the kingdom of God') must have dawned.

So, at least, reasoned those who were most in need of Jesus' help. The Pharisees had other interpretations of Jesus' miracles (*e.g.* 12:24). Small wonder the needy were among the first to glimpse Jesus' identity: they had most to gain by their hope. They constituted the complementary side of an important truth: Jesus came to those in need of a physician (9:12f.).

Something similar transpires in Matthew 21:9, 15. There, 'Son of David' is not connected with healing or exorcism; but this title is certainly messianic, and portrays the crowd (21:9) and then the children (21:15 – influenced by the crowd, and less inhibited, even in the temple precincts), as those who recognized Jesus' identity at the time of his triumphal entry. Interestingly, Luke's account (19:38) omits reference to the 'Son of David', but rightly understands its significance: 'Blessed is *the King who comes in the name of the Lord!*' Some scholars reject the authenticity of this event, even though it appears in all four Gospels, or suggest that 'Son of David' could not have been a messianic description, on the grounds that a messianic acclamation on the lips of the people would have forced the authorities to intervene. Perhaps, it is argued, the phrase 'Hosanna to the Son of David' is nothing more than a formula of greeting addressed to pilgrims on their way to the temple. These suggestions are far-fetched. As all the Gospels report the event, the cries *were* messianic. How else shall we explain the fact that the authorities *do* raise objections (21:16)? But the authorities had enough sense not to antagonize the crowds whose hope and expectation were at fever pitch (*cf.* 26:4f., 16). Equally significant is the fact that Jesus is prepared to accept the praise of the children, and defend it (21:16; see further below).

None of this is historically implausible, and many fine points could be addressed in favour of the story's essential authenticity. On the other hand, this should *not* be taken to mean that the crowd, the children or the opposing Jewish leaders saw in 'Son of David' everything that Matthew saw. This is made clear by Matthew 22:41–46 (*cf.* also Mk. 12:35–37; Lk. 20:41–44). All agree that the Jewish leaders accepted the identification of 'the Christ' with 'the Son of David'.[21] The problem is posed by Jesus' question as to how the Messiah can be the Son of David. Psalm 110 opens with the words, 'The LORD said unto my Lord'; this psalm, acknowledged to be Davidic in authorship and messianic in reference, therefore presents the Messiah in a position superior to that of David. How can David's son also be his lord? Matthew records: 'And no one was able to answer him a word, nor from that day did any one dare to ask him any more questions' (22:46). In other words, in Matthew's assessment, Jesus' contemporaries were stuck. Their categories for 'Messiah' and 'Son of David' could not accommodate the scriptural data. A 'Son of David' who would restore something of the grandeur of David's kingdom, eliminate the Roman overlords, and introduce 'messianic' blessings, they could understand; and exuberant crowds might joyfully and hopefully proclaim Jesus to be just such a Messiah. But no-one during Jesus' ministry could integrate into this pattern the notion that this Messiah was also David's *lord*.

Where the Jewish authorities were silenced, modern scholars have chosen to speak and offer diverse interpretations of this pericope. Some hold that the passage *denies* the identification of Messiah with Son of David;[22] but Matthew 1:1 shows that was not Matthew's view, and Matthew 21:16 suggests it was not Jesus' view. Others argue for a two-stage Christology developing in the church: 'Son of David' applies to the span of Jesus' human life, 'Christ' to the risen Lord.[23] Nothing in the text supports this view: it is the imposition of a scheme developed elsewhere. Still others think the passage is concerned to deny all *political* expectations of messiahship without denying Davidic descent.[24] But although political considerations are prominent elsewhere (*e.g.* Jn. 6:15), and are presupposed at several points in Matthew's Gospel, the central issue in this pericope is not political but theological and exegetical.

The point is that, although none of Jesus' contemporaries grasped the answer to the conundrum raised by Jesus, *Matthew knows what the answer is.* Writing after the resurrection and Pentecost, after the period of relative

---

[21] *Cf.* G. F. Moore, *Judaism in the First Centuries of the Christian Era* 2 (Harvard University Press, 1930), pp. 328f.; Joseph A. Fitzmyer, *Essays on the Semitic Background of the New Testament* (Geoffrey Chapman, 1971), pp. 113-126; Donald Guthrie, *New Testament Theology* (IVP, 1981), pp. 253-256.

[22] They follow in the wake of W. Wrede, *The Messianic Secret* (ET James Clarke, 1971), p. 46.

[23] So F. Hahn, *The Titles of Jesus in Christology* (ET Lutterworth, 1969), pp. 247f.

[24] O. Cullmann, *The Christology of the New Testament* (ET SCM, ²1963), pp. 131f.

uncertainty and of traditional Christological categories too narrow to accommodate the evidence, Matthew perceives that Jesus legally stood in the royal line and was in truth David's son (hence the genealogy in Mt. 1, and the frequent references to Davidic fulfilment motifs); yet Jesus was also in fact the Son of God, virgin born, superior to David, the risen Lord, the one through whom all of God's sovereignty is now mediated (28:18–20). From Matthew's perspective, it was easy enough to see how Jesus could be David's lord, while yet being his son.

It follows that there is only one way Matthew could have interpreted the pericope. The enigma Jesus proposes is an invitation, indeed a challenge, to re-think their current Christological presuppositions by measuring them against Scripture. The affirmations of the crowds at the triumphal entry, the children in the temple courts, the blind who desired sight, might all cry out that Jesus is the 'Son of David'; and the Jewish leaders might with equal enthusiasm deny it. As for Jesus, he not only tacitly accepts that he is the Son of David (as in 21:16), but suggests that the Scriptures picture a Son of David who is also David's Lord – and that therefore the conceptions of both supportive crowd and opposing Pharisee are too narrow. The most the acclamations do is affirm part of the truth, and thereby point to the full truth of the matter not fully understood until the period after Jesus' resurrection and exaltation.

Once again, therefore, we have discovered Matthew's capacity for distinguishing between the Christological understanding of Jesus' contemporaries, and his own. Doubtless he wants his readers to see the full significance of 'Christ' and 'Son of David', even as he does; but he does not compromise the authenticity of his account to achieve this end. Rather, he shows how the imperfect understanding and faith of those who at least were right in their identification of Jesus, pointed to the full truth which Jesus alone grasped during the period of his ministry, but which the church came in time to embrace.

Lord

There are so many occurrences of this title in Matthew that even a hasty examination of each passage is not possible in this essay.

To simplify matters a little, the modern trend can be sketched in somewhat as follows. In his essay on the stilling of the storm, Bornkamm[25] noted that in Matthew (8:23–27; *cf.* Mk. 4:35–41; Lk. 8:22–25) the disciples cry, 'Save, *Lord*; we are perishing.' Instead of *Kyrie,* Mark has *Didaskale* and Luke has *epistata.* Bornkamm argues that, unlike Mark and Luke, Matthew has designated

[25] *TIM,* p.55.

Jesus 'not only . . . with a human title of respect, but with a divine predicate of majesty. This is obviously the meaning of *kyrie*'.[26] Indeed, Matthew uses *kyrios* comparatively more often than do the other Synoptists. In a later essay,[27] Bornkamm carried the argument farther, pointing out that in Matthew Pharisees and strangers can refer to Jesus in such terms as *didaskalos*, but the disciples, with the exception of Judas Iscariot, do not: they refer to him as *kyrios*, and this, for Matthew, is a predicate of divine majesty. Stanton remarks, 'Most scholars have accepted this view.'[28] The inevitable implication, of course, is that the Evangelist was anachronistically reading back a view of Jesus not actually found until the time of his own *Sitz im Leben*. Gundry[29] has honed this view yet farther, and argues that the Evangelist was constantly creating scenes or embroidering scenes to present Jesus' full deity and the response of adoring worship. For instance, when the Magi see Jesus and his mother they *pesontes prosekynēsan autō*, which, according to Gundry, means they fell down and worshipped Jesus in the fullest sense, recognizing his deity and kingship. (Gundry, of course, does not think of this as either great insight by the Magi nor blundering anachronism by the Evangelist, since he holds that the story of the Magi has no historical referent, but only theological purpose.)[30]

At first glance, the evidence appears persuasive; but once again, a subtler interpretation more fairly reflects the evidence. Bornkamm neglects to mention that, although in the Gospel of Matthew Jesus' disciples do not address him as *didaskalos*, yet Jesus refers to *himself* in that term, *in the context of discussing his relationship with his followers* (10:25f.; 23:18; 26:18). Some of the 'strangers' who thus address Jesus are, after all, inquirers (8:19; 19:16). Although it is true that Jesus' opponents can address him as *didaskalos* while trying to trip him up (12:38; 22:16, 24, 36), they can also address the disciples and refer to Jesus as '*your* teacher' (9:11; 17:24). I have now given all of Matthew's references to *didaskalos*; and they seem a narrow base to support the weight of the thesis that for Matthew this term is inferior.

Of course, the thesis rests in part on the observation that Matthew is rather fond of *kyrios*, and sometimes prefers it even when the Synoptic parallels preserve something else. But it does not necessarily follow that Matthew is

[26] *Ibid.*

[27] First published as 'Enderwartung und Kirche im Matthäusevangelium', in *The Background of the New Testament and its Eschatology*, ed. W. D. Davies and D. Daube (Cambridge, 1956), p.41; ET in *TIM*, pp.15ff.

[28] Graham N. Stanton, 'The Origin and Purpose of Matthew's Gospel: Matthean Scholarship from 1945 to 1980', *Aufstieg und Niedergang der Römischen Welt* (Walter de Gruyter, 1982), forthcoming.

[29] Robert H. Gundry, *Matthew* (as in n.1, *supra*), pp.31f.

[30] *Cf.* n.7, *supra*, for further discussion of Gundry's approach.

ascribing full deity to Jesus every time he applies *kyrios* to him. Bornkamm does not reckon adequately with the range of Matthean usage. The word often turns up in the parables, where, even if the *kyrios represents* Jesus, it first and foremost refers to a human individual in the parabolic story itself (13:27; 18:25ff.; 20:8; 21:30, 40; 25:11ff.; *cf.* 10:24f.). One of these examples pictures a son addressing his father as *kyrios* (21:30). More impressive yet, Pilate is addressed as *kyrios* by the chief priests and Pharisees (27:63). It follows that *kyrios* is not a technical term for Matthew, and cannot be *assumed* to bear the weight of deity. It may carry only its common force of respect to a superior. Matthew's demonstrable proclivity for it *may* spring from personal usage rather than profound, theological motivation. In two or three instances, as we shall see, *kyrios* as used in Matthew certainly hints at something more than mere respect; but when this occurs, the context calls for such a conclusion. But as far as the stilling of the storm is concerned, it is hard to see why we should think that *kyrios* predicated 'divine majesty' of Jesus, instead of serving as yet another example of the reportorial freedom exhibited by all the Evangelists. After all, the pericope ends with the following question by the astonished disciples: 'What sort of man is this, that even winds and sea obey him?' (8:27). The question is singularly out of place if by *kyrios* they have *already* predicated 'divine majesty' of Jesus. Similarly, it is very doubtful if *proskyneō* by itself or in connection with *piptō* suggests anything more than obeisance, homage: note the usage in 18:26; 20:20.

This is not to say that Matthew entertains no notion of Jesus' deity. Quite the contrary: there is bountiful evidence that the idea is important to him. But he handles the theme with the kind of restraint which makes Jesus' claims all the more plausible. In a number of places, an Old Testament text which refers to Yahweh is applied to Jesus without any sense of impropriety (*e.g.* 3:3; 11:9–11). The same thing occurs in connection with broader themes: for instance, in Matthew 5:11f. the disciples *of Jesus* are likened to the Old Testament prophets *of God,* so far as suffering for righteousness is concerned. In this parallel, Jesus is not likened to prophets (as are the disciples), but to God. Again, in Matthew 7:15–23, Jesus ascribes to himself the ultimate judicial function which belongs to God alone. More broadly, Philip B. Payne has demonstrated at some length how often, in Jesus' parables, images which in the Old Testament are applied exclusively to God now quite clearly stand for Jesus (sower, director of the harvest, rock, shepherd, bridegroom, father, king, vineyard owner, *etc.*).[31] Moreover, in Jesus' quotation of Psalm 110 (in

[31] Philip B. Payne, 'Jesus' Implicit Claim to Deity in His Parables', *Trinity Journal* 2, 1981, pp.3-23.

Mt. 22:41–46), already discussed, the remark of Guthrie seems appropriate: 'If Jesus acknowledged himself to be Messiah, and admitted in the course of the dialogue that the psalmist addresses the Messiah as Lord, it is tantamount to recognizing the title as applicable to himself.'[32] Again, in Jesus' defence of the children's 'Hosannas!', he cites Psalm 8: 'Have you never read, "Out of the mouth of babes and sucklings thou hast brought perfect praise"?' (21:16). This response is a masterpiece. It not only provides a biblical basis for letting the children go on with their exuberant praise, thus stifling, for the moment, the objections of the authorities; but, at the same time, it also encourages thoughtful persons to reflect, especially after the resurrection, that Jesus is saying more than first meets the eye. The children's 'Hosannas', after all, were *not* being directed to God, but to the Son of David, the Messiah. Jesus is therefore not only acknowledging he is the Son of David, but he is daring to justify the praise of the children by applying to himself a passage of the Scripture referring exclusively to God.[33] The same sort of assessment must be made when Jesus forgives sin, a prerogative of God alone (9:1–8).

Now there is no doubt that the post-resurrection church came in time to apply *kyrios* to Jesus in the same way in which the LXX used *kyrios* as a reference to God. But from the evidence I have just outlined, it appears premature either to minimize the Christological implications of Jesus' historical self-disclosure, or to exaggerate the amount of creative tinkering Matthew allegedly performed on the tradition in order to make the *recognition* of Jesus' deity retroactive, as it were, to the period of Jesus' ministry. Rather, Matthew records all kinds of subtle claims regarding Jesus' deity, made by Jesus himself; and he records all kinds of acts of homage or obeisance, each pointing forward to the full understanding which came to the disciples only *after* the resurrection. That no-one really enjoyed such understanding *before* the passion is obvious: otherwise there would have been no passion. Certainly Matthew rather favours *kyrios* and *proskyneō;* doubtless some of the reasons cannot be retrieved with any degree of certainty. But it appears that one of the contributing factors, at least in some of his usages, is that the words are ambiguous. Interpreted narrowly, the words do not permit an anachronistic reading of the church's mature theology back

---

[32] Donald Guthrie, *New Testament Theology*, p.293.

[33] This argument, of course, presupposes that Ps. 8 is not messianic. This is almost certainly the case. Even in the NT, application of Ps. 8 to Jesus (1 Cor 15:27; Heb. 2:6) is due not to any messianic character of the psalm, but to Jesus' role in introducing humanity to the heights God designed for it – as most commentators now acknowledge. The earliest treatment of Ps. 8 as messianic by ancient Jewish authorities is the targum on Ps. 8 (*cf.* F. J. Maloney, 'The Targum on Ps. 8 and the New Testament', *Salesianum* 37, 1975, pp.326-336) which almost certainly postdates the NT.

into Jesus' day; yet at the same time, no reader in Matthew's day could fail to read those same words without recognizing that the full response of worship before Deity is required by his or her full understanding of the Gospel, an understanding achieved in part by being located a little later in the flow of redemptive history than those who knew Jesus in the days of his flesh.

Son of God

It quickly becomes clear that this and related expressions are very important in the Gospel of Matthew (2:15; 3:17; 4:3, 6; 8:29; 14:33; 16:16; 17:5; 26:54; 27:40, 43, 54; *cf.* also certain parables, especially 21:33ff.). Matthew preserves almost all of Mark's references to Son (of God), takes over three from Q material, but adds six of his own. Moreover, the theme is probably related to another, *viz.* God as Father, of great importance to Matthew.

I cannot here enter debate on whether 'Son of God' is the paramount Christological confession in Matthew,[34] nor examine peculiarities in Matthew's treatment of the title (*e.g.* his clear linkage of Jesus the Son with Israel the Son, 2:15; 4:3, 6),[35] nor even examine each passage closely to defend the authenticity of what is purported to have taken place. It is sufficient for my purposes to show that *in principle* there is no historical implausibility in thinking that Jesus during his ministry was confessed as Son of God, that good arguments can be advanced for even the most difficult occurrences, and that in any case the understanding held by the participants during Jesus' lifetime is demonstrably short of that of the Evangelist himself.

Pre-Christian Jewish literature does not provide us with uncontested evidence that 'Son of God' was used as a title for the expected Messiah; but 4QFlor. 10–14 comes close, referring to an apocalyptic figure who is the son of a king, presumably David, and thus picks up Old Testament references to a royal 'son'.[36] Not less important, three Synoptic passages make the connection between 'Son of God' and 'Christ' explicit. In Matthew 26:63f. (*cf.* Mk. 14:61f.; Lk. 22:66f.), the high priest, Caiaphas, says, 'I adjure you by the living God, tell us if you are the *Christ, the Son of God.*' Again, in Luke 4:41, when the demons cry to Jesus, 'You are the *Son of God*', Luke comments that Jesus would not allow them to speak 'because they knew that he was *the Christ*'. The third, and by far the most important and the most complex, is Matthew

---

[34] *Cf.* n.3, *supra.*

[35] For convenient and recent discussion, *cf.* James D. G. Dunn, *Christology in the Making* (SCM, 1980), pp.48-50; Donald Guthrie, *New Testament Theology*, pp.303-312.

[36] *Cf.* Joseph A. Fitzmyer, *A Wandering Aramaean: Collected Aramaic Essays* (Scholars Press, 1978), pp.102-107. For full discussion, *cf.* M. Hengel, *The Son of God* (Fortress, 1976).

16:16 (*cf.* Mk. 8:29; Lk. 9:20), where Matthew's account adds to Peter's famous confession 'You are the Christ' the equally famous apposition, 'the Son of the living God'. The majority of contemporary scholars assign 'the Son of the living God' to Matthean redaction and judge it inauthentic. Recently, however, Meyer has offered substantial reasons for judging the Matthean addition authentic.[37] At the risk of oversimplifying his well-crafted arguments, we may list the most prominent: 1. Matthew's account better explains the genesis of all the other forms, including 'You are the Christ' (Mk.), 'The Christ of God' (Lk.), and 'the Holy One of God' (Jn. 6:69), than can Mark's simpler confession. 2. 'Son of God' may well have had *for Peter* no more than purely messianic significance. If so, it does not, *as far as Peter is concerned*, say much more than *ho Christos*. 3. There are several details in the pericope as a whole which plead Matthean priority (especially in 16:17–19).

Some other passages present various difficult questions, but no reason to doubt their authenticity. It is not entirely clear, for instance, whether the confession of the centurion and his men, 'Truly this was the Son of God!' (27:54), should be taken in a hellenistic, pagan sense (they perceived Jesus to be some kind of 'divine' being, in a pagan sense), or in the Jewish sense (they perceived him to be the Messiah: *cf.* Mt. 16:16 and 26:63). Certainly the lack of an article with *huios* is no impediment to the latter view;[38] and since Pilate's soldiers were probably non-Jewish natives of the land, rather than Romans from far-off pagan lands, it is intrinsically likely that they were familiar with Jewish categories. In any case, there is no historical implausibility in the account.

It appears, then, that Matthew is able to distinguish several things from one another. Demons, soldiers, disciples – all can confess Jesus as 'the Son of God', within the period of Jesus' ministry. By this they do not mean more than that they perceive Jesus to be the Messiah, the Christ; and even their understanding of 'Christ' remains totally inadequate, as we have seen, since it does not include anything of the suffering Servant, or of an ontological connection with Deity. At a second level, Jesus himself reflects a level of self-conscious sonship with his Father which finds its climactic statement in Matthew 11:25–30. I have discussed the critical questions surrounding these difficult verses elsewhere;[39] but at very least they reflect Matthew's recognition that Jesus enjoyed an astonishing reciprocity with his Father. It is one thing to say 'no one knows the Son except the Father'; it is quite another to say 'no one knows the Father except

---

[37] Ben F. Meyer, *The Aims of Jesus* (SCM, 1979), pp. 189-191.

[38] *Cf.* C. F. D. Moule, *An Idiom-Book of New Testament Greek* (Cambridge, 1959), p. 116.

[39] As in n.9, *supra*.

the Son and anyone to whom the Son chooses to reveal him'. But Matthew does not pretend that this was understood by the first disciples; and certainly nothing like it is presented in the form of a confession. As with Jesus' pre-passion references to his death and resurrection, and as with Jesus' bifocal relationship to David, so also here: some Christological truths were not understood until after Jesus' resurrection and exaltation. *And Matthew is able and willing to tell the difference.* This is made especially clear when we look at a third level of Christological understanding, that of Matthew himself. Although 'Son of God' is not used in Matthew 1 – 2, it has often been demonstrated that the account of Jesus' virginal conception is meant to show that Jesus was not only 'Son of David' (1:1–17) but also 'Son of God' (1:18–20).[40] No reader of Matthew's Gospel could go through his text without knowing something that the people of Jesus' day did not know; and thus from Matthew's perspective they would be brought to see how the early confession of Jesus as 'the Son of God' pointed to deeper truths than the first confessors could have recognized.

Son of man

Even more complex ambiguities surround the title 'the Son of man'. Elsewhere I have tried to assess recent research on this topic.[41] Although I cannot argue the case here, it is likely that Jesus chose 'the Son of man' as his favourite self-designation *precisely because it was ambiguous.*[42] It could conceal as well as reveal. At times, it was no more than a self-reference; but always lurking in the background was the eschatological figure of Daniel 7, so that especially toward the end of his ministry, whether alone with his disciples and talking about eschatological matters (24:27, 30), or when under oath at his trial (26:63f.), Jesus could use the title with unambiguous messianic significance. Simultaneously, we should not shy away from the observations of Bowker,[43] who points out how many Semitic contexts (Ezk., Ps.8, the Targums) use the title to make explicit the chasm between frail, mortal man and God himself. This kind of connotation admirably suits a number of Synoptic references where the frailty, suffering and death of the 'Son of man' is in view. It is best to suppose

[40] The issues are complex. *Cf.* R. E. Brown, *The Birth of the Messiah* (Geoffrey Chapman, 1977), pp. 122ff.; Jack Dean Kingsbury, *Matthew*, pp. 42-53; and the classic work of J. Gresham Machen, *The Virgin Birth of Christ* (Marshall, Morgan and Scott, 1930).

[41] See the Excursus '"The Son of Man" as a Christological title' in the commentary referred to in n.9, *supra*.

[42] *Cf.* Richard N. Longenecker, '"Son of Man" Imagery: Some Implications for Theology and Discipleship', *JETS* 18, 1975, pp.8-12; I. Howard Marshall, *The Origins of New Testament Christology* (IVP, 1976), pp.76ff.; E. Schweizer, 'The Son of Man', *JBL* 79, 1960, p.128.

[43] John Bowker, 'The Son of Man', *JTS* 28, 1977, pp.19-48.

that Jesus purposely combined these multiform backgrounds, precisely because his own understanding of messiahship was laced with themes both of royal authority and of suffering and death. It would have been extraordinarily difficult for Jews expecting a purely political Messiah to grasp exactly what the title meant; and just when they might begin to think they had nailed it down, it would show some other hue and slip from their grasp again – *until after the resurrection and exaltation.* At that point, Jesus' disciples could not help but detect in Jesus' frequent pre-passion use of the term a messianic claim. It is a mark of the Evangelists' (including Matthew's) fidelity to the history of redemption that they reserve the expression for the lips of Jesus alone.

Much more could be said about each of these Christological titles; and others (*e.g.* 'servant', 'the coming one') have not even been introduced. But enough has been said to conclude that Matthew successfully attempted to distinguish between his own Christological understanding at the time he wrote, and that of Jesus' contemporaries, including his disciples, during the days of his ministry. Yet at the same time, he set forth his Gospel in such a way that he revealed his own Christological commitments, and showed what conclusions he expected his readers to draw. All of the titles take on new light in the wake of the cross and the empty tomb; and yet the pre-passion usages anticipate and point to the fullness of revelation about to dawn.

In short, close study shows Matthew to be both faithful historian and profound theologian, and very much interested in the question 'how we moved from there to here'. Doubtless this analysis could be developed into a book-length monograph; but it is offered in this form to honour a scholar with high respect for the text of Scripture, a Christian who places little value on uncontrolled speculation, whose cautious scholarship is always reverent and fair, and whose most valued works, while conservative, never stoop to obscurantism or obfuscation. *In multos annos!*

CHRIST'S HEALING MINISTRY AND HIS ATTITUDE TO THE LAW

Gordon J. Wenham

One of the problems that has most perplexed biblical scholars is our Lord's attitude to the law. On the one hand he appears to have openly disregarded some of its ceremonial provisions; on the other he condemns his opponents for not taking the law seriously enough and instructs his disciples to obey its every letter. Various attempts have been made to explain the apparent inconsistency in our Lord's attitude.[1]

The traditional Reformed view is that Christ taught his disciples to obey the moral law of the Old Testament; indeed his ethical teaching is essentially a searching exposition of the ten commandments.[2] However, he rejected the ceremonial law because it was made obsolete by his ministry: in particular, his death on the cross made the temple sacrifices redundant.

As widely recognized, this view has its difficulties. It is not clear that Jesus made a sharp distinction between the moral and ceremonial law.[3] At times he can be very positive about the ceremonial law, encouraging people to offer sacrifice (*e.g.* Mk. 1:44). Although like the Old Testament and first-century Judaism he recognized the special status of the ten commandments (Mk. 10:19), his moral teaching is not merely a reaffirmation of the principles of the decalogue, For example, his redefinition of adultery by excluding polygamy and remarriage after divorce represented a great innovation over against Old Testament standards.[4]

---

[1] For a wider survey of the main approaches see K. Berger, *Die Gesetzesauslegung Jesu* 1 (Neukirchen, 1972), pp.3-11.

[2] *E.g.* D. Guthrie, *Jesus the Messiah* (Pickering & Inglis, 1972), p.85; J. W. Wenham, *Christ and the Bible* (Tyndale Press, 1972), pp.32ff.

[3] R. J. Banks, *Jesus and the Law in the Synoptic Tradition* (CUP, 1975), pp.242f.

[4] *Cf.* G. J. Wenham, 'May Divorced Christians Remarry?', *Churchman* 95, 1981, pp.150-161.

A completely different approach has therefore been advanced by more critical scholarship.[5] This tends to regard the anti-law elements in the Gospel tradition as early and authentic, reflecting Jesus' own rebellious attitude towards the Old Testament. As a charismatic or prophetic figure he called men to repent and to find the pure will of God in total submission to God's demands. Like the Old Testament prophets he found little value in the rigmarole of ritual: it could easily be a cloak for hypocritical religiosity. The Evangelists, and particularly Matthew, were more conservative. They were afraid of antinomianism and insisted that the disciples of Jesus should still respect the law. On this view, then, the mixture of sentiments about the law in the Gospels represents an attempt to moderate Jesus' own radical views and encourage the early church to remain faithful to the moral heritage it had inherited from Judaism.

Again, this view has its problems. Its portrait of Jesus bears a noticeable likeness to the modern liberal theologian. One wonders how far modern seekers for the historical Jesus are simple recreating a Christ in their own image. But more seriously, there is a great problem in postulating such a discontinuity between the teaching of Jesus and the early church.[6] Finally, too, it is doubtful whether the Evangelist Matthew, generally alleged to be the greatest culprit in distorting Jesus' teaching about the law, has been correctly interpreted.[7] If Matthew understood the law to be valid until the death/resurrection of Christ, and the teaching of Jesus to take the place of the law thereafter, many of the supposed contradictions within the Gospel disappear.

To establish Matthew's own view of the law is one thing: to demonstrate that he has correctly interpreted the mind of Christ is quite another and to do this would be quite beyond my competence. I wish to approach the problem from the other end, by trying to set out the purpose and function of the ritual laws within the Old Testament itself. It seems to me that many discussions of Jesus' attitude to the law are vitiated by misunderstanding of the meaning of that law. This essay, then, is an attempt to expound the purity laws[8] in Leviticus 11

[5] *E.g.* J. Jeremias, *New Testament Theology* 1 (SCM, 1971), pp.204ff.; J. Riches, *Jesus and the Transformation of Judaism* (Darton, Longman & Todd, 1980); R. E. Nixon, 'Fulfilling the Law: The Gospels and Acts' in *Law, Morality and the Bible* (ed. B. N. Kaye and G. J. Wenham) (IVP, 1978), pp.53-71 is somewhat closer to the critical view than the Reformed view.

[6] *Cf.* D. Guthrie, *New Testament Introduction: The Gospels and Acts* (Tyndale Press, 1965), pp.199f.; R. T. France, 'The Authenticity of the Sayings of Jesus' in *History, Criticism and Faith* (ed. C. Brown) (IVP, 1976), pp.101-143.

[7] W. D. Davies, *The Sermon on the Mount* (CUP, 1969); J. P. Meier, *Law and History in Matthew's Gospel* (Biblical Institute Press, Rome, 1976).

[8] For a more detailed exposition see G. J. Wenham, *The Book of Leviticus* (Eerdmans, 1979).

– 15 to show that the values they enshrine and the character of the God they declare are indeed the same as those demonstrated in our Lord's healing ministry

Leviticus 11 – 15 sets out various types of uncleanness. Chapter 11 distinguishes clean and unclean animals, *i.e.* it declares which animals may and which may not be eaten. Chapter 12 discusses the uncleanness caused by the discharge following childbirth. Chapters 13 – 14 discuss the uncleanness of 'leprosy': *ṣāra'at* is not modern leprosy or Hansen's disease, but unsightly skin conditions such as psoriasis, favus or severe eczema.[9] Chapter 15 deals with the uncleanness caused by discharges from the reproductive organs.

Why these various conditions should all be defined as unclean has long perplexed commentators. What is the common denominator which causes both a pig and 'leprosy' to be defined as unclean? Three solutions are to be found in recent literature.

Hygienic

The first asserts that the rationale for all these rules is hygiene.[10] Pigs may carry tapeworm, while gonorrhoea (Lv. 15:2-15) is highly infectious. Attractive though this interpretation is to a generation intoxicated with medical progress, it has two main defects. First, not all the unclean conditions or foods are a health risk, while many foods (*e.g.* poisonous plants) or conditions which are dangerous are not listed and may be presumed clean. Second, if unclean is to be identified with unhygienic, why did our Lord abolish this distinction? It is not as though a great advance in medical knowledge can be postulated between the time of Moses and the first century AD. Indeed, to accept a hygienic explanation of these laws is to admit tacitly that the Jews have been right to maintain them and that Christians, at least until this century when advancing medical knowledge made them redundant, have been mistaken to dispense with them.

Cultic

The second suggestion is that the unclean animals represent a rejection of the religious customs of the Canaanites.[11] Pigs were unclean, because some of Israel's neighbours ate them in religious feasts. To show the difference between Yahweh and Baal, Israelites did not eat pigs. Now it could be supposed that in a thousand or more years the danger of religious syncretism had passed, and

---

[9] *Cf.* S. G. Browne, *Leprosy in the Bible* (Christian Medical Fellowship, 1970); E. V. Hulse, 'The Nature of Biblical "Leprosy"', *PEQ* 107, 1975, pp.87-105.

[10] *E.g.* R. K. Harrison, *Leviticus: an Introduction and Commentary* (IVP, 1980), pp.120ff.

[11] *E.g.* M. Noth, *The Laws in the Pentateuch and Other Studies* (Oliver & Boyd, 1966), pp.56ff.

these laws had become irrelevant. Therefore Jesus could let them go without any worry. Unfortunately, this theory fails to explain much of the Old Testament evidence. For example, the bull was a favourite sacrificial animal of the Canaanites, and both they and the Egyptians worshipped gods in the form of bulls. If this theory were correct, one would have expected bulls to be anathema to Israel. In fact, bulls were the most highly prized of Israel's sacrificial animals. There must then be some other principle underlying Israel's acceptance of bulls as clean, but pigs as unclean. Aversion to Canaanite practice may have enhanced their feelings about animals and conditions they regarded as unclean, but these are not a sufficient cause of the original prejudice.

Symbolic

The third possible explanation of these laws is that they are symbolic: that is, they express religious truths through insisting on certain types of action in certain situations. This symbolic interpretation is at once the oldest and the most recent interpretation of these laws. I think a case can be made for supposing that the pre-Christian letter of Aristeas interpreted the laws as symbolic. Acts 10 certainly does, and some of the older commentators looked for symbolic meanings behind the laws. Andrew Bonar[12] said the sheep was a clean beast, because it reminded the Israelite that the LORD was his shepherd! The pig was unclean because it was forever wallowing in the mire of iniquity. This symbolic interpretation, as these examples show, was somewhat capricious. They give me the uneasy feeling of being invented to make a sermon on Leviticus more interesting. And with medical advance in the last century it went out of fashion. Bible lovers thought they could show that Moses was given laws about health care long before Pasteur and Lister discovered their rationale!

But since 1966, the symbolic interpretation has returned to favour in a new and more sophisticated guise. This is not due to the insights of biblical scholars, but to the work of social anthropologists whose study is primitive societies. The concept of clean and unclean, so strange to us, is common in such societies. In a book called *Purity and Danger*, Mary Douglas devoted a chapter to the abominations of Leviticus. This discussed in some detail the laws of Leviticus and showed how a seeming hotch-potch of assorted cultic regulations all bear witness to a systematic coherent view of the world expressed in Leviticus.

According to Mary Douglas[13] and more recently the rabbinic scholar Emanuel

---

[12] A. A. Bonar, *A Commentary on Leviticus* (Banner of Truth, 1966, reprint of 1861), pp. 214f.

[13] M. Douglas, *Purity and Danger* (Routledge & Kegan Paul, 1966); *Implicit Meanings* (Routledge, 1975), pp. 249-275.

Feldman, [14] these laws are symbolic: that is, they are real laws which had to be observed, but in observing them Israel was constantly reminded of certain fundamental theological truths, *e.g.* that God had chosen Israel, that God was the creator and source of life. Since our age professes to despise both symbols and rituals, we tend to find this approach to biblical religion a little strange, and I must therefore begin by defining the function of ritual symbolism in the Old Testament. [15]

We are, of course, familiar with various symbols today: road signs, badges, uniforms, the shape of buildings and the commonest symbols of all, words. Now some symbols are merely extrinsic, just conveying information which you can accept or reject. Certain road signs are clearly in this category; nothing compels you to slow down when you see a 'School' or 'Road Narrows' sign. But other symbols have an intrinsic authority built into them, so that you are almost compelled to act in a certain way. For example, a wedding-ring not only reminds the wearer that he or she is married, but encourages loyalty to the spouse when the couple is parted and reminds others to keep their distance. Uniforms have a similar effect on wearer and observers. The design of churches likewise expresses perceptions about religious realities and invites the worshipper to share them. Medieval cathedrals with the high altar at one end of the church, the congregation at the other and the priest in between express a very clear view of the relationship of God and man. A quite different view is enshrined in the rearranged cathedrals of the Reformation in Switzerland. Here a tall pulpit rises in the middle and the congregation sit all around it. This Reformed design stresses the centrality of the Word of God and man's need to be subject to it. Now the physical shape of the building not only expresses religious truths, it compels anyone who would worship there to assent to these truths (at least silently).

Now it seems to me that the symbolism of the Old Testament cleanness laws is of this latter type. It is not merely extrinsic and informational. Rather it is an intrinsic, effective symbolism. These regulations not only remind you of certain theological truths, they compel you to acknowledge them in daily living. The food laws are a perfect example of this on the anthropological interpretation. They express the truth that Israel is a people chosen by God to be separate and holy; that she is different from all the other nations. But more than that, they served to segregate Israel from these other nations. Since Gentiles did not observe the Old Testament regulations about food, good Jews

[14] E. Feldman, *Biblical and Post-Biblical Defilement and Mourning: Law as Theology* (Ktav, New York, 1977).

[15] *Cf.* my discussion in *Numbers: An Introduction and Commentary* (IVP, 1981), pp.25-39.

did not eat with Gentiles. A friendly Gentile might serve a pig to a Jew or, even more likely, an animal that had not been killed according to the right procedures. This would make him unclean, *i.e.* unfit to worship God. Thus the food laws not only symbolized Israel's difference from the nations, they served to separate them from the nations.

The food laws

Douglas' interpretation of the food laws is based on a comprehensive analysis of Leviticus 11, which follows Genesis 1 in dividing creatures into three groups: those that fly in the sky, *i.e.* birds and flying insects, those that walk on the land, and those that live in the waters, *i.e.* fish and other aquatic creatures. Douglas observed that, in differentiating clean and unclean animals, Leviticus specially emphasizes their means of locomotion. Do land animals have cloven hooves? Do fishes have fins and scales? Do flying insects behave like birds, *i.e.* do they have wings and two legs to hop with? If the answer is yes, *e.g.* grasshoppers, they are clean and therefore may be eaten. If the answer is no, *e.g.* if they use all their legs to travel with, they are unclean and cannot be eaten (Lv. 11:21f.). It seems that a particular mode of travel is taken as the norm for a particular medium: if animals conform to this norm they are clean. If they do not conform, they are unclean.

Soler highlighted the animals' eating habits.[16] Birds of prey that eat carrion and living creatures are unclean. It is the herbivorous sheep and ox that are the model of the clean land animal.

Clean animals may be eaten: unclean animals cannot. When it comes to sacrifice, there are further distinctions: only *domesticated* clean animals can be sacrificed. Since fish were not domesticated in ancient Israel, there were no sacrificial fish. But, among the flying creatures, pigeons and turtle doves could be sacrificed, and among the land animals, sheep, goats and cattle (*e.g.* Lv. 1 – 4).

It thus appears that in the three spheres of air, land and water there are repeating patterns of classification. Douglas illustrated it diagrammatically, here somewhat simplified.

---

[16] J. Soler, 'The Semiotics of Food in the Bible' in R. Forster and O. Ranum (eds.), *Food and Drink in History* 5 (Johns Hopkins University Press, 1979), also published as 'The Dietary Prohibitions of the Hebrews', *New York Review of Books 26.10* (14 June 1979), pp.24-30.

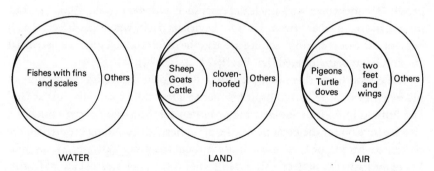

WATER   LAND   AIR

These repeating patterns would be recognized in an agricultural community, and it is intrinsically likely that some significance was perceived in them.

What this significance was, emerges when the Old Testament structure of the human world is examined, for it, too, divides into three concentric domains.

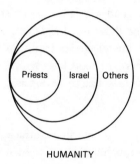

HUMANITY

This leads to the following correspondences:

Priests = sacrificial animals
Israelites = clean animals
Gentiles = unclean animals

That these equations are not merely the invention of an anthropologist's over-fertile imagination may be shown by various texts where men are equated with animals, or animals treated like men. For instance, animals must rest on the sabbath like men and their human slaves (Ex. 20:10). First-born animals, like first-born humans, are to be dedicated to God (Ex. 22:29f.). In poetry[17] Israel is equated with clean animals such as the ox, whereas Canaanites, unclean

---

[17] *Cf.* C. M. Carmichael, 'Some Sayings in Genesis 49', *JBL* 88, 1969, pp.435-444.

people, are identified with unclean beasts such as donkeys (Gn. 49:6, 11). But most striking of all are two texts from Leviticus itself, where the defects which bar a priest from offering sacrifice are also the defects which preclude sacrificial animals from being offered (Lv. 21:18-21; 22:20-24).[18]

These food laws, therefore, pictured to the faithful Israelite the mystery of his redemption. He had to limit his diet to a few chosen animals, just as God had limited himself to one elect nation among all the nations of the world. We also see here one of the great principles of biblical ethics finding expression: the redeemed people of God must imitate their redeemer. 'Be perfect, as your heavenly Father is perfect' (Mt. 5:48); 'Be imitators of me, as I am of Christ' (1 Cor. 11:1). In avoiding certain meats, the Israelite was in effect confessing his faith in the God who had saved him, and was acknowledging his lordship.

In the Gospels Jesus quietly rejects the food laws of the old covenant (Mk. 7:15-19). His attitude here is of a piece with his attitude to the Gentiles during his ministry. Though apparently reluctant to admit non-Jews as his followers, he is nonetheless friendly towards them. This contrasts with the Gentile mission attested in Acts and the Pauline Epistles, which is thoroughly aggressive in evangelizing those outside Israel. And it is in Acts and the Epistles that the food laws are rejected outright. When the kingdom of heaven was opened to all believers, the food laws which symbolized Israel's unique status as the only people of God had to be cast aside.

Bodily uncleanness

However, Jesus mounted a more direct attack on the other uncleanness regulations. We find him touching lepers, women with discharges and human corpses (*e.g.* Mk. 1:41; 5:27, 41). To the significance of these rules we now turn.

A diagrammatic representation of Israel's sacred space reveals a similar pattern to the earlier diagrams representing the distinctions between unclean, clean and sacrificial.

---

[18] Other passages in which parallels between men and animals appear include Gn. 1:22,28-30; 9:5; Ex. 13:2,13; 21:28ff.; Ho. 4:16; 10:11; Am. 4:1.

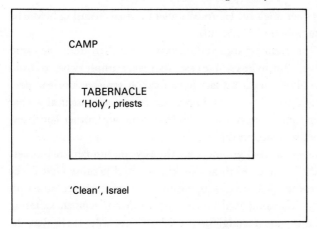

OUTSIDE THE CAMP

'Unclean'
Israelite lepers, etc.
Dead
Gentiles

It was in the holiest part of the tabernacle that God dwelt enthroned over the ark. No-one could enter the holy of holies except the high priest once a year on the day of atonement.

In the Old Testament there are essentially two poles of existence.

Positive	*Negative*
God	Chaos
Life	Death
Order	Disorder
Normality	Deformity
Cleanness	Uncleaness

More precisely, the Old Testament sees a spectrum of conditions ranging from perfect life to death. Between these extremes are found various degrees of disorder. The greater the disorder, the more serious the uncleanness.

Life (Normality)		Increasingly disordered ➤		Death (Total Disorder)
God	*Priests*	*Israelites*	*Gentiles and unclean*	*Dead*
Holy of Holies	*Altar*	*Camp*	*Outside camp*	*Sheol*
	Sacrificial animals	*Clean (Edible)*	*Unclean*	*Dead animals*

Dead animals are specially unclean, in that anyone who touches them becomes unclean. Living unclean animals, *e.g.* donkeys and camels, do not make a man unclean if he touches them, but any dead animal or any human corpse makes the toucher unclean. He must undergo ritual cleansing before he can worship in the temple (Lv. 11:24-40).

In severe cases of uncleanness those afflicted were expelled from the camp (Lv. 13:46; Nu. 5:2-4). But in less severe cases they were simply debarred from worship, more precisely from eating sacrificial food. If someone unclean does eat, he is liable to die (Lv. 7:19-21). So human uncleanness is essentially a bar to worship and severe uncleanness is a bar to fellowship with other Israelites, because one was expelled from the camp.

It is against this general background that the laws on human uncleanness must be understood. Life and death are antithetic. And because God is the creator of life, anything that smacks of death must be excluded from his presence. Thus, since bleeding leads eventually to death, women suffering from bloody discharges are contagiously unclean (Lv. 12; 15:19-30). So menstruation and the postnatal discharge, as well as other types of bleeding, make a woman unclean. Douglas [19] has suggested that sometimes there are moral motives behind uncleanness laws, *e.g.*, making menstruation a contagious form of uncleanness should keep young men from being overfriendly with young females, since the men might become unclean and suffer sudden death if they came to participate in worship. But much more important is the witness that these laws give to the character of God. God is life and nothing which suggests death may enter his presence. Similarly a man suffering from a discharge, perhaps as the result of gonorrhoea, becomes contagiously unclean. He may not be losing blood, but to have something wrong with his life-creating organ is incongruous and indeed incompatible with worship which celebrates God as the giver of life and normality. Furthermore, if the loss of life-sustaining blood makes a person unclean, so does the loss of life-creating semen[20] (Lv. 15:2-18).

Finally, the patchy skin diseases called 'leprosy' made a man look abnormal and therefore unclean. It is the patchy character of these diseases that make a man unclean: if it affected the *whole* body, the man was pronounced clean (Lv. 13:12f.). These symptoms were seen as abnormal, incompatible with wholeness, and therefore unclean. Those affected were expelled from the camp and had to behave like mourners (Lv. 13:45). These regulations thus testified to the

---

[19] *Cf. Purity and Danger*, pp. 129ff.

[20] In my commentary on Leviticus, though I noted some of the ethical safeguards consequent on making sexual intercourse unclean, I was at a loss to interpret the rules symbolically. If, however, the whole system of uncleanness laws is seen as expressing the antithesis between life and death, it becomes more obvious why loss of blood in menstruation or emission of semen are polluting. They involve the loss of potential life. I should now prefer to regard the normal/ abnormal (clean/unclean) contrast as part of the life/death contrast rather than *vice versa*.

character of God: God is the author of life — more than that, the creator of order, normality and wholeness. Anything that conflicted with that was incompatible with worshipping. Therefore those so afflicted must keep out of his presence. But in so doing they were in fact bearing witness even in a back-handed way to what God was like.

Leviticus 14 goes into a long description of the sacrifices and rites needed to cleanse a leper. It must, however, be noted that this cleansing was not curing him. Cleansing took place after healing. He recovered — spontaneously or in response to prayer. No rites are prescribed to cure him; these rituals portray in vivid fashion his reintegration into the elect and holy nation. They do not effect his healing. The Old Testament law does not offer healing to the leper or to anyone else for that matter. If they recover, well and good: if they do not, the law cannot help them.

Conclusion

But the prophets look forward to a day when the blind shall see and the lame leap like a hart. The great innovation of our Lord's ministry was not merely the opening of the kingdom to Gentiles, but healing the lepers, giving sight to the blind and so on. His coming heralds a new age of grace. God's character as the giver of life, wholeness and normality that the Old Testament law declared is not abolished. Rather it is demonstrated dynamically in our Lord's saving ministry. The Old Testament law insisted that it was the duty of the strong and healthy to help the weak and handicapped. Indeed it threatens that God will punish those who exploit the widow, the orphan, the blind and the poor. But the Old Testament law did not offer God's healing of their infirmity. It is this which Jesus brought: therefore in the new age of the gospel these regulations which prevented some people from enjoying worship in the house of God are swept away.

His blatant rejection of the rules covering leprosy, corpses and people with discharges was expressive of the new age of redemption he inaugurated. He deliberately touched the unclean and healed their infirmity. The old law was disparaged because the new era of grace had come. Yet in a real sense there is perfect continuity between the old law and our Lord's healing ministry. Both bear witness to God's character: the God of life and health and normality. While the Old Testament reminds men of these divine attributes by placing certain restrictions on the unclean, Jesus demonstrated God's power over death and other conditions that suggested it. His healing ministry and attitude to the ritual law match perfectly.

Leviticus declares that God is holy and the author of life and health: the Gospels show the same God saving the sick and sinful and giving life to the dead. Although the coming of Jesus thus makes the Old Testament ceremonial law obsolete in one sense, in another it enhances and underlines it most dramatically. There is then a congruity in the Gospels between our Lord's attitude to the moral law and his attitude to the ceremonial law. There is at once both continuity and discontinuity between the Old Testament law and the teaching of Jesus. Both express the mind and will of the holy God. But the new revelation in Christ is both more demanding and more gracious. It is more gracious in that God's character is now shown to be redemptive as well as holy. It is more demanding in that our Lord's ethical requirements go further than those of the already high standards of the old covenant.[21]

[21] In 'Towards a Systematic Approach to OT Ethics' (forthcoming) I explore the way each stage of divine revelation both presupposes and modifies existing ethical insights.

'THIS GENERATION WILL NOT PASS...' A STUDY OF JESUS' FUTURE EXPECTATION IN MARK 13

David Wenham

The Synoptic eschatological discourse bristles with problems. Perhaps the most acute, at least for the thinking Christian, lies in Mark 13:30 (cf. Mt. 24:34; Lk. 21:32): 'Truly I say to you, this generation will not pass away before all these things take place', since this verse follows on from a description of the coming of the Son of man (vv. 24-27) and seems to suggest that Jesus (or at least the Evangelists) expected the second coming within a generation – mistakenly, as we now know.

The purpose of this article is to take a fresh look at this problem.[1] It will be argued that the difficult verse refers not to the second coming, but to the fall of Jerusalem and the preliminaries to the end: these are expected within a generation by Jesus, but the time of the parousia itself is unknown (v. 32).[2]

Our route to this conclusion will be via an examination of the structure of the eschatological discourse in Mark, but we will also bring in the evidence of Matthew and Luke where it is relevant. Matthew and Luke are important at least as early interpretations of Mark's Gospel, but probably also as independent, or partially independent, witnesses to the underlying tradition.

Mark 13:5-23: the troubles preceding the end; 13:24-27: the end itself

The first step in our argument is to note with approval the argument of recent scholars that Mark 13:5-23 is one section of material describing the period

---

[1] For a survey of earlier discussion, see G. R. Beasley-Murray, *Jesus and the Future* (Macmillan, 1954), and the author's own survey in *TSF Bulletin* 71, 1975, pp.6–15 and 72, 1975, pp.1–9.

[2] For an earlier defence of a similar position, see A. R. Moore, *The Parousia in the New Testament* (Brill, 1966), especially pp.131–136.

preceding the end.[3] First, the unity of the section is made clear in Mark by the way he opens and closes the section with very similar warnings against false prophecy. Compare verse 5: '*blepete* that no one leads you astray. Many will come in my name...' with verses 21f.: 'False Christs and false prophets will arise... But *hymeis blepete.*' It is quite possible that this is a deliberate bracketing (*inclusio*); but even if it is not, it is still the case that all the material in between can be lumped together as 'things that will precede the end and that might arouse false eschatological expectation' (*e.g.* wars, persecutions, desolating sacrilege, *etc.*). So the section hangs together thematically. Secondly, Mark's verse 23 seems to mark a major break in the Marcan discourse and to indicate that what precedes belongs together: '*hymeis de blepete: proeirēka hymin panta*'.[4] It is followed by a clear move forward in time: 'But in those days *after* that distress....'

It seems then that Mark's description of the end-times falls into two parts: the things that must precede the end (vv. 5-23), and the end and second coming itself (vv. 24-27). We shall argue later that the recognition of this structural division is one of the keys to understanding the difficult verses about the timing of events at the end of the chapter.

The desolating sacrilege and the accompanying distress
the direct prelude to the second coming

We have argued that Mark 13:5-23 is one section describing the things that must precede the end; but within that section what is the sequence and structure of thought? This is remarkably difficult to ascertain with any assurance. It is particularly hard to decide how much chronological progression there is within the section: there is obviously some sort of crescendo, as we move from the general disasters of war, famine, *etc.* (v. 8) to the disciples' sufferings (vv. 9–13) to the desolation of Jerusalem and the unparalleled disaster (vv. 14–20).

But to what extent is this a chronological, as opposed to a dramatic, progression: do the disciples' sufferings begin *after* the wars, famines, *etc?* Does the murderous inter-family hatred of verses 12f. precede the desolating sacrilege, or is it part of the same thing? It seems quite likely that we have several overlapping descriptions of the same period — the period before the end – so that the distress of the persecuted disciples in verses 12f. is the same as, or part

---

[3] *E.g.* J. Lambrecht, *Die Redaktion der Markus-Apokalypse* (P.B.I., Rome, 1967), p.286; also R. Pesch, *Naherwartungen* (Patmos, Düsseldorf, 1968), pp.74–82.

[4] As already observed, this *blepete* may well be picking up the *blepete* in v. 5. There is another *blepete* in between in v. 9, but it has a different thrust, unconnected with false prophecy.

of, the distress following the setting up of the desolating sacrilege.[5]

But despite these observations it is hard to avoid the conclusion that there is some chronological progress within the section (vv. 5-23). Thus in verse 7 the situation is that 'the end is not yet' (although the birth-pains of the end are being experienced, v.8); but in verse 24 we are told that 'in those days after that tribulation, the sun will be darkened . . . and they will see the Son of man coming'. Between verse 7 and verse 24 we have evidently moved on from a situation where 'the end is not yet' to a situation where we know that 'he is near' (v. 29).

If we try to explain how the situation has changed between verses 7 and 24 – how do we know that we are 'near' in verse 24 rather than in verse 7? – the most obvious change is that the desolating sacrilege event has happened in between. Without attempting to explain the detailed sequence of thought in verses 5-23, we may fairly confidently suggest that within this section of 'things that must precede the end' there are, firstly, certain categories of trouble that will characterize the last days – wars, famines, persecution of the disciples while the gospel is preached; these are the birth-pains of the end time which must happen, but they are 'normal' aspects of the whole period – to be expected, but not of great chronological significance. There is, secondly, the particular disaster of the desolating sacrilege (which we take to be a cryptic reference to the destruction of Jerusalem);[6] this will be accompanied by unparalleled tribulation. Being a particular event rather than a category of suffering, the desolating sacrilege is a chronologically informative sign of the end in the way that the other sufferings are not; before this event we can say that the end 'is not yet', but after it we can no longer say that.

But the desolating sacrilege event is not only significant for the timing of the end in the limited sense that it is something that must happen some time before the end; it is probably significant also more positively in that it leads into the end. This may be suggested by the contrast between the restraining call for calm '*When you hear* of wars . . . do not be alarmed; this must take place, but the end is not yet' (v. 7) and the positive call for action '*When you see* the desolating sacrilege, let the reader understand; then let those in Judea flee . . .' (v. 14); the impression is that in verse 14 the awaited eschatological action is beginning. There may also be a significant verbal link between '*When you see* the desolating sacrilege . . .' (v. 14) and '*When you see* these things taking place, you know that

---

[5] There is a particularly good case for saying that Matthew sees the desolating sacrilege as part of the distressing events he has previously described: note the word *thlipsis* in common in vv. 9 and 21 and the connective *oun* in v. 15. (See my note in *TB* 31, 1980, pp.155–162.). It is also of interest that in Didache 16:3–5 the two sections are mixed up.

[6] See appendix A below.

he is near, at the very gates' (v. 29); if there is, then the desolating sacrilege and the accompanying tribulation are the decisive indicators of the Lord's nearness. But the surest proof of the significance of the desolating sacrilege for the end is the wording of verse 24: 'But in *those days* after *that tribulation* the sun will be darkened . . . they will see the Son of man coming'; here the end seems explicitly tied to the tribulation associated with the desolating sacrilege; compare verse 19 'for in *those days* will be *tribulation*'.[7] This close verbal link between verses 19 and 24 shows that the tribulation associated with the desolating sacrilege is the immediate prelude to the end. This might in any case be suggested by the climactic end-position of verses 14-20 within verses 5-23 and by the importance of the desolating sacrilege as *the* event that must happen before the end: it seems improbable that it is thought of just as an incident which must occur, but after which more routine sufferings may go on. The dynamics of the discourse suggest that verses 19f. describe the historical climax and conclusion of all that has gone before, leading us into the following description of the coming of the Son of man. So we do not have two different divine interventions to save the elect – one in 13:20 (after the desolation of Jerusalem) and one in verses 24-27 (at the parousia); they are one and the same event, the parousia bringing to an end the tribulation associated with the desolation.

Our conclusion, then, is that, although the detailed analysis of verses 5-23 is difficult and at points uncertain, nevertheless the desolating sacrilege and the accompanying events are seen as the direct prelude to the Son of man's coming, Verses 5-23 describe all the different woes that must precede the end; but the decisively important woe that leads to the end is the desolating sacrilege.

The desolation and tribulation are understood to last for an indefinite period of time

One consideration that might appear to argue against our previous conclusion about the significance of the desolating sacrilege is the fact that the description of the sacrilege event is followed immediately by a strong warning against

---

[7] It might be possible to argue that when the second coming is said to follow 'that tribulation', the reference is not specifically to the desolating sacrilege, but to the whole gamut of troubles described in the first half of the discourse. After all, we argued for the unity of vv. 5–23, and Matthew uses the word *thlipsis* in his v. 9 as well as in v. 21. But the verbal links between vv. 19 and 24 in Mark (and between the comparable verses in Matthew), as well as the climactic position of the desolating sacrilege within the chapter, make it hard to avoid a linking of the sacrilege and the end. (The words 'and never shall be' in v. 19 need not tell against this, but simply emphasize the gravity of the tribulation.) What does seem quite probable is that the tribulation of Matthew's vv. 9–14 (and perhaps of Mark's verses 12f.) is the tribulation of the desolating sacrilege period described from a different angle; but this probably strengthens rather than weakens the case for linking the end and the desolating sacrilege period.

Christological speculation. 'And then if any one says to you, "Look, here is the Christ . . .", do not believe it. False Christs . . . will arise . .' (vv. 21-23). As we have seen, this is reminiscent of the opening of the discourse (vv. 5f.), and so the whole block from verses 5-23 seems to come, as it were, under an anti-speculation rubric. Does this not contradict the argument that the desolating sacrilege is seen as an indicator of the nearness of the Lord's coming? If it is true that the desolation of Jerusalem leads into the end, then excited speculation seems justified at that time, despite verses 21f.

But in reply to this, the following two points may be made. The warning against people who proclaim that 'Christ is here' or 'there' need not be taken as a denial of Christ's nearness, but on the contrary may be seen as a warning against those who exploit the fact of his nearness to point people to false Christs. In a situation when Christ is known to be near (*i.e.* after the setting up of the desolating sacrilege), the scope for deceivers to mislead the elect is the greater – hence the need for the warning in verses 21-23.[8] This interpretation of these verses gains support from Matthew's version (24:23-28), since his warning is explicitly against those who try to foist on people wrong ideas of Christ's return, saying that he is 'here', 'there', 'in the wilderness', *etc.*, when in fact Christ's coming will be like lightning and manifest; the objection is not to near expectation, but to disastrously wrong (*e.g.* speculative) use of the expectation.

We may add to that the further argument that, although the Evangelists probably believed the desolation of Jerusalem to be the chronological prelude to the end, this does not mean that they necessarily expected the arrival of the desolating sacrilege to mean an immediate end. It is more likely that they saw the appearance of the sacrilege as inaugurating a final period leading up to the end. Thus diagrammatically we suggest that their understanding will have been as follows:

The appearance of the desolating sacrilege does indeed bring us out of the

---

[8] Note how misleading signs and wonders are specifically associated with the 'man of lawlessness' in 2 Thes. 2 and with the beast in Rev. 13.

'end-is-not-yet' period into the period when the end is near, but the period of desolation is indeterminate.

In favour of this understanding we adduce the following factors:

1. The Danielic background to the language used in Mark 13:14-20. In Daniel the setting up of the desolating sacrilege marks the inauguration of a substantial period of suffering and apostasy (lasting three and a half years – to be understood symbolically). It is a period when patient endurance is called for (Dn. 12:11f.). We cannot assume *a priori* that the Evangelists will have used the Danielic imagery in a Danielic way, but their borrowing from Daniel seems to be much more than just casual echoing of some phraseology. And it may be of interest that the Christian use of the same Danielic ideas in Revelation (*e.g.* 13:5) seems in keeping with the original Danielic understanding of a period or era of evil.

2. The description of the setting up of the sacrilege in Mark (and Matthew) gives no hint that a very short period of 'desolation' is in mind; on the contrary, those in Jerusalem are advised to run away, which might hardly be worth it if the desolation was going to lead to immediate salvation! More seriously, the description in Mark 13:19f. of a distress so severe that 'no human being would have been saved, if the Lord had not shortened the days' sounds like something drawn out and also like something universal – unavoidable even by the elect – rather than local. This may be a hint that the desolation of Jerusalem inaugurates a period of widespread distress and that we are not thinking just of the crisis in Jerusalem. Similarly the reference to the activity of false prophets in verses 21-23 suggests a period of trial. We conclude that Mark – and Matthew – almost certainly do envisage a period of disaster such as is described in Daniel.

3. This understanding is explicit in Luke: he speaks of a period of captivity for the Jews, while Jerusalem is trampled 'until the times of the Gentiles are fulfilled' (21:24). Luke's testimony might be discounted by some on the grounds that his material is secondary; but he only spells out what we take to be implicit in Matthew and Mark.[9]

We conclude that all three Evangelists will probably have seen the fall of Jerusalem not as coming immediately before the end, but as inaugurating a period of 'desolation' and great 'tribulation'. They expect the end after that period. The end is 'near' after AD 70, in that we are in the final lap of the end-times; but how long that lap will last is not specified.

---

[9] For discussion of the Lucan wording, see appendix B below. In the light of Luke's interest in the Gentile mission, his 'times of the Gentiles' may reasonably (though not certainly) be taken to refer to the time of Gentile mission.

The interpretation of 13:28–32: the desolation of Jerusalem in a generation, but the end-time unknown

Our argument so far has been (i) that verses 5–23 of Mark 13 belong together and describe 'things that must happen before the end', the end then being described in verses 24–27; (ii) that within verses 5–23 the setting up of the desolating sacrilege + the accompanying tribulation are the chronologically significant events, leading into the end; (iii) that the appearance of the desolating sacrilege does not necessarily mean a quick end, but inaugurates a period of trouble of uncertain length. Given these conclusions, we can proceed to look at some of the problematic verses at the end of the discourse.

'These things' in the parable of the fig tree = the troubles of verses 5–23

Immediately after the description of the second coming we have the parable of the fig tree, the leaves of which show the nearness of summer; and the application of this is 'So also, when you see these things taking place, you know that he is near, at the very gates' (v. 29; *cf.* Luke's 'that the kingdom of God is near', 21:31). In the light of our preceding analysis, it seems clear that this parable looks back and connects verses 5–23 (the description of the things preceding the end) and verses 24–27 (the description of the end-event). 'These things' must be the troubles described in verses 5–23, and especially the desolating sacrilege complex of events; it is when these things are taking place that he is 'near, at the very gates'.

The only plausible alternative is to interpret 'these things' in terms of the celestial signs (vv. 24f.). But these celestial upheavals are better seen as the accompaniments of the second coming, as indications of the summer's arrival, not of its nearness; the signs of its nearness are the events prior to the celestial disturbances, *i.e.* the desolating sacrilege and the other distressing events going with it.[10]

'All these things' in a generation (v. 30) also = the troubles of verses 5–23

Our conclusion about the probable meaning of 'these things happening' in Mark 13:29 is of obvious importance for the interpretation of verse 30, since this too refers to 'these things happening': 'Truly, I say to you, this generation will not pass away before all these things take place'. Since 'these things' in verse 29 were probably the distressing events of the period before the end (and in particular the desolating sacrilege), the same is probably true of 'these things' in verse 30: 'these things' are the distressing events before the end, not

---

[10] There is a stronger, but not decisive, case for saying that 'these things' in the parallel Lucan verse (21:31) are the celestial upheavals. *Cf.* his v. 28, but also his v. 36.

the end itself, and it is they (and not necessarily the end) that will happen within a generation.

The possible flaw in this argument is Mark's addition of the word 'all' in verse 30. Whereas in verse 29 he referred to 'these things' taking place and being a sign of the Lord's nearness, in verse 30 he refers to '*all* these things'; does the addition of 'all' not indicate that he has now expanded 'these things' to mean the preliminary period of tribulation + the Lord's coming? After all, in verse 29 the time of tribulation and desolation was a sign of the Lord's nearness.

Various considerations tell against this expansive interpretation of 'all these things' in verse 30 and favour our suggested interpretation:

1. It is not obvious that the addition of *panta* (all) makes a change in the reference of *tauta* (these things) likely, despite the common assumption of scholars. If *tauta* in verse 29 are clearly the things that will precede the Lord's coming ('When you see these events taking place, you know that he is near'), it seems likely that *tauta* are the same in the following sentence ('truly I tell you, this generation will not pass until these events – all of them – take place'). We may note in support of this argument that Matthew has the identical phrase in both contexts; there is no expansion of the thought.[11]

2. If 'all these things' that are to happen in a generation in verse 30 include the parousia, there is an uncomfortable tension with verse 32, 'But of that day or that hour no one knows'. There is a tension because verse 30 gives definite information about the time (in a generation), whereas verse 32 is emphatically agnostic; there is also a tension in that the opening phrase, 'but of that day or hour', sounds as though it is introducing reference to a different day from the one just discussed. It may be possible to explain this tension as the result of poor editing (though it is notable that Matthew, as well as Mark, has the contrast). But it is more satisfactory to say that there is a deliberate contrast between 'all *these* things' that will happen in a generation (*i.e.* the troubles referred to in verse 29, notably the desolation of Jerusalem) and '*that* day', concerning which no-one knows ('that day' being, as often, the last day, the day of judgment).

3. Taking verses 30 and 32 respectively of the destruction of Jerusalem and of the second coming makes for a coherent understanding of the whole chapter, as follows:

> (i) Opening discussion and question about the destruction of the temple (vv. 1–4).

---

[11] But contrast Lk. 21:31–32 and compare 21:36.

(ii) Answer, part 1: a description of the whole sequence of events up to and including the end (vv. 5–27).

    a. vv. 5–23:   the things that must happen before the end, culminating in the fall of Jerusalem + the accompanying distress. (A)

    b. vv. 24–27: the second coming. (B)

(iii) Answer, part 2: the timing of the events (vv. 28–32ff.).

    a. vv. 28f.:   the relationship of (A) and (B) – the desolation of Jerusalem indicates the nearness of the second coming.

    b. vv. 30f.:   the time of (A) – the desolation of Jerusalem in a generation.

    c. vv. 32ff.: the time of (B) – the time of the second coming unknown.

The striking thing about this understanding of the chapter is that verses 28–32ff. follow on well from the preceding material in verses 5–27, when understood in this way. We saw that in verses 5–27 the desolation of Jerusalem seems to inaugurate the final lap before the second coming, but it is not stated how long the final period of desolation will last; it is also not said when the desolation will begin. Verses 28–32ff. confirm that 'these things' (notably the desolation of Jerusalem) are a sign of the Lord's nearness and an indication that we are into the last lap; but they also clarify the questions of timing that were unexplained in the earlier verses: thus verse 29 emphatically explains that 'these things' (the desolating sacrilege, *etc.*) will happen in a generation, but verse 31 explains that the timing of the Lord's coming is unknown. As it turns out then, verses 28–32 in a real sense contain *the* answer to the disciples' opening question about 'when' Jesus' predictions would happen. Up to this point in Jesus' reply a description of the end-time has been given, but the question of timing has not been explicitly answered. Now in verses 28–32 the chronological information is given to relate the preceding material to the disciples' question.[12]

---

[12] Perhaps more specifically we should see v. 30 as *the* answer to their question. This may be suggested both by the striking verbal similarity between the disciples' question in v. 4 and Jesus' saying in v. 30, and also by the particular emphasis given to the saying of v. 30 by its introductory *amēn* and by the following v. 31. If it is correct to view v. 30 as picking up the

Conclusions and implications

The last three arguments are sufficient to show that the suggested interpretation of Mark 13:30 is plausible;[13] and we have ended up not only with a satisfactory explanation of Mark 13:30, but also with a coherent explanation of the structure of the whole discourse. If the resulting analysis of the discourse is correct, then the eschatological expectations expressed in it may be summed up as follows: before the end there will be a period of troubles and of mission to the Gentiles, a period culminating in the desolation of Jerusalem and terrible accompanying distress. These things, including the desolation of Jerusalem, will be experienced within a generation; but, although they indicate that the Lord is near, it is not known how long the period of desolation and tribulation will last, nor exactly when will be the glorious coming of the Son of man.[14]

Although this suggested analysis eliminates the 'problem' of Mark 13:30, it still leaves us with the possibly embarrassing implication that from at least AD 70 onwards we have been living in the last period of Jerusalem's desolation and of tribulation; and the Lord has been near 'at the very gates' throughout two millennia.

We cannot discuss this problem here at length, but we will end this paper with three observations that may alleviate the embarrassment.

---

question of v. 4, then this may confirm the correctness of taking v. 30 to refer to the destruction of Jerusalem, since the disciples' question is primarily and explicitly about the predicted destruction (even if it had broader implications).

There is one other structurally important *panta* – in Mk. 13:23. It is tempting to argue that this *panta* is picking up the *panta* of v. 4 and is also a clue to the meaning of the *panta* in v. 30. But, although this would fit in well with our argument, it would be unwise to build on the assumption that so common a word as *panta* must have the same reference in different contexts.

[13] Taking vv. 30 and 32 respectively of the destruction of Jerusalem and of the second coming is in line with evidence from elsewhere in the Gospel tradition, since we find elsewhere an expectation of two distinct judgments, one to fall on Jerusalem and the Jewish people, probably in the near future (*e.g.* Mt. 21:43; Lk. 13:34f.; 19:27, 41–44; 23:28–30), and the other to be universal and unexpected (*e.g.* Mt. 13:36–43; 25:31f.; Lk. 17:22–37, *cf.* Acts 1:7,11). The single most striking parallel to Mk. 13:30 is the 'Q' saying of Mt. 23:35f. (Lk. 11:50f.): 'Truly I say to you, all this will come upon this generation.' This is explicitly referring to the particular judgment to come on the Jews, and given its position in Matthew, there is a strong case for saying that at least Matthew's equivalent of Mk. 13:30 (*i.e.* Mt. 24:34) has the same reference. However, this is not a decisive argument by itself: the later verse could have a broader reference than the earlier one, and there are some other disputed verses that have been taken to show that the second coming, as well as the fall of Jerusalem, was anticipated within a generation (*e.g.* Mk. 9:1; Mt. 10:23).

[14] I am glad to note a hint of this sort of view in Donald Guthrie's *New Testament Theology* (IVP, 1981), p.795: 'In this case the "tribulation" is extended from the fall of Jerusalem to embrace all tribulations between that event and the parousia.' Also for a somewhat similar understanding of the eschatological discourse, see D. A. Carson's forthcoming commentary on Matthew.

The problem of the Lord being 'near' from New Testament times to today is raised not only by my hypothesis, but by much New Testament teaching; and similarly the problem of the period of 'tribulation' lasting from New Testament times to today is one raised not only by my hypothesis, but acutely by the book of Revelation, if the author regarded himself as living in the age of the beast and of the final tribulation (*cf.* 7:14), and also by other New Testament books, *e.g.* 1 John 2:18; 4:3, and 2 Peter.

To judge from various passages, *e.g.* Matthew 24:37–42 (*cf.* Lk. 17:26–35), Luke 21:34–36 (*cf.* 1 Thes. 5:3), the final time of tribulation is not going to be a period of total, unmitigated disaster for everyone; on the contrary, much life goes on as normal, as it did in Sodom and Gomorrah. The church is called to continue to preach the gospel through the period, and the danger facing the church is not only the threat of persecution, but also the temptation to sleep and to join in the world's fun.

The Evangelists' teaching about the nearness of the end is not based on information about how long there is to go between now and the end – information which they quite specifically deny having; it is based on the conviction that the penultimate act in the salvation history drama is the first-century judgment on Jerusalem. Once we have reached that point, we are in the last lap and on the brink of the end; there is no more possibility of saying 'the end is not yet' – the end may now be at any time, though no-one knows, except the Father. If this was their understanding of nearness – in terms of being in the final lap, not in terms of being within a particular known distance of the end – then, although the Evangelists would no doubt have been amazed to think that the last lap could last for almost 2,000 years, they could not have excluded that possibility. And today's Christian need not conclude that they were mistaken in their teaching; on the contrary he can and should accept for himself or herself their teaching that we are in the final lap and that the Lord is at the gates.[15]

---

[15] See F. F. Bruce, *The Epistles of John* (Pickering and Inglis, 1970), p.65, for some helpful remarks on 'nearness'.

David Wenham

Appendix A:
Mark 13:24–27 not the second coming?

Perhaps the most attractive alternative explanation of the problems considered in our paper is that defended by R. T. France in *Jesus and the Old Testament*.[1] According to this, Mark 13:24–27 is not a description of the second coming at all; it is a figurative description of the destruction of Jerusalem, seen as the triumph of the Son of man. For the arguments in favour of the view readers should see France's discussion; here we can only explain briefly why we feel unable to accept his arguments.

1. We concede that the language about the celestial disturbances in verses 24f. could be figurative, as could other similar language about the parousia, *e.g.* in 2 Peter 3. However, we doubt whether in fact the relevant Old Testament background compels us to take the language that way, or whether other Jewish apocalyptic literature supports that interpretation.[2]

2. We concede that the Son of man is not actually said in verses 24–27 to come to the earth; but this in no way excludes the possibility that the coming may be the final judgment. Compare Paul's description of the parousia in 1 Thessalonians 4:16.

3. The view in question does not seem to do justice to the contents and structure of verses 14–27:

(a) It is argued that verses 14–23 all describe the events prior to the fall of Jerusalem (though presumably v. 20 is a look forward to AD 70 in parentheses), and the fall of the city itself actually comes in verses 24ff. But this argument seems to go against our analysis of the chapter, which pointed to there being a major break and turning-point between verses 23 and 24. Verse 24 seems to mark the beginning of something quite new, not just the completion and climax of the sufferings that have been described in verses 14–23. We saw that at the beginning and the end of verses 5–23 there was an emphatic warning against excited speculation about the end and the second coming; in verse 24 we get the impression that we have moved out of that period into the end-time, and there are no

---

[1] IVP, 1971, pp.227-239. For an earlier exposition of the same view see J. M. Kik, *Matthew Twenty-Four. An Exposition* (Swengel: Bible Truth Depot, 1948), and more recently *cf.* S. Brown in *JSNT* 4, 1979, pp.12-14, on Matthew.

[2] See M. Casey, *Son of Man* (SPCK, 1979), p.174, also pp.171-177, for a general critique of France's view. No doubt in the OT cosmic imagery was sometimes used of historical events, but we doubt if all such language can be reduced to the historical.

more warnings against speculation (which we might expect if verses 24–27 are describing AD 70 and not the end).

(b) France maintains that verses 14–23 describe events connected with the siege of Jerusalem, but he fails to find any description of the city's fall in those verses; as a result he is encouraged to see such description in verses 24–27. It is quite probable, however, that the fall of Jerusalem is implied in the earlier verses. One possibility is that the unexplained 'tribulation such as has never been' of verse 19, which makes flight necessary, includes the fall of Jerusalem. In the light of verse 2 this seems a natural enough interpretation, and it is not obvious why the tribulation should be things leading up to, but not including, the destruction. (Indeed it is arguable, as we saw, that verses 19 and 20 describe something larger than only the fall of Jerusalem, not something less and preliminary!) It is true that the destruction is not directly referred to in verses 14–20 – nor is it in verses 24–27; but this may simply be because the Evangelists thought it clearly implied, or because they were being deliberately cautious about direct reference to the event, hence the cryptic allusiveness of verse 14.[3]

---

[3] See further discussion of these verses in Appendix B. It is true that in the Mt./Mk. version there is nothing explicitly military described, and this makes possible the view that the 'sacrilege' of v. 14 is zealot abominations and that the tribulation (v. 19) is that of the period before (and not including) the destruction in AD 70. However, despite the (quite probably deliberate) avoidance of military language, any 'reader who understood' the Danielic background to the Mt./Mk. passage would know that in Dn. the desolating sacrilege was brought by a pagan invader attacking the city of Jerusalem with armed forces: the place of the sanctuary was 'thrown down' (Dn. 8:10f.) and trampled under foot (8:13). Anyone knowing the story of the Maccabees would know that Antiochus destroyed parts at least of the temple (cf. 1 Macc. 1:39; 3:45; 4:38,48). And the very phrase 'desolating sacrilege' should quite probably be interpreted (at least in the LXX of Dn. and in 1 Macc.) as meaning 'a sacrilege that makes desolate', i.e. 'that lays waste'. When then Mt. and Mk. speak of the 'desolating sacrilege', they are referring, albeit obliquely, to a military attack, such as was implied by Jesus' prediction at the start of the ch., 'There will not be left here one stone upon another, that will not be thrown down' (Mk. 13:2). It is at least an interesting coincidence that in the Hebrew of Dn. 8:11 there is a reference to the place of the sanctuary being 'overthrown' (šlk), but in the LXX this is translated: the sanctuary will be 'made desolate' (erēmoō): the overthrow which Jesus predicted is the desolation brought by the pagan invader. Luke in our view correctly brings this out in his 'When you see Jerusalem surrounded by armies, then know that its desolation has come near' (Lk. 21:20).

Of course, it may be argued that the setting up of the desolating sacrilege does not fit the known facts of the Roman attack of AD 70 (whereas it would fit with the zealot abominations), and it may be argued further that the call for flight after any Roman sacrilege had been perpetrated (or even after the Roman armies were surrounding the city; so Lk.) does not make good historical sense. But such arguments probably misunderstand the prophecy, taking it to be a detailed description in advance (or post eventum) of the events of AD 70, whereas, if we may judge from the Danielic language used, it was more probably intended to be a general prediction of a

Luke's equivalent verses to Mark's verses 14–20 (*i.e.* Lk. 21:20–24) are notably different and seem to tell in favour of our view, since Luke explicitly refers to the destruction of Jerusalem where Matthew and Mark have the vaguer reference to unparalleled tribulation. If Luke's version is his interpretation of the Marcan text, he is a witness to our interpretation; if his is an independent and primitive tradition, he is still an important witness in that he has both a description of the destruction of Jerusalem and also a separate description of celestial signs and of the Son of man's coming; it is doubtful if he identifies the destruction and the coming.

(c) On the view in question we are presumably required to see the fall of Jerusalem as the 'shortening of the days for the sake of the elect' (v. 20) and as leading to the 'gathering of the elect' (v. 27). But, although the judgment of the Jews may sometimes have been seen as leading to blessing for the Gentiles,[4] it is not clear that this is what is intended in 13:20b: it is not obvious how the shortening of the Jewish war facilitated Gentile mission, and the elect in 13:20b sound like people caught up in the tribulation, *i.e.* Jews in Palestine (if the siege of Jerusalem is being described). It is notable that in verses 20b and 27 it is the 'elect', not specifically the 'Gentiles' who are referred to. The thought of the gathering and saving of the elect seems much more simply understood of the second coming than of AD 70.[5]

(d) More generally, it seems curious to have the destruction of the holy city viewed as the occasion for the coming of the Son of man with great power and glory. In Daniel 7 the coming of 'one like a son of man' was a glorious moment, marking the end of the pagan emperor's defiling rule; but the destruction of Jerusalem in AD 70 marked the high-point of pagan Rome's attack on the Jews. And, although Jesus and his followers might have regarded the destruction of Jerusalem as their vindication, it seems more likely that they would have seen it as a tragic vindication than as a glorious moment.

---

second Antiochus-type situation, *i.e.* a situation when a pagan destroyer came, desecrated the sanctuary, and the faithful fled to the hills (1 Macc. 2:28).

[4] *Cf.* perhaps Lk. 21:24, though this does not necessarily imply that the times of Gentile blessing began with the fall of Jerusalem; Acts would seem to suggest a different Lucan understanding.

[5] We agree with France, *op.cit.*, pp.236-238, that Mt. 24:30, 'all the tribes of the *gē* shall mourn' could be translated 'all the tribes of the land' (not 'earth'). But it is not clear that this is the natural translation in the context of the cosmic-sized imagery of vv. 29-31, and the other similar NT use of the Zc. citation (Rev. 1:7) is a witness to the interpretation France rejects. Also, compare Mt.'s description of a heavenly sign followed by 'earthly' consternation with Lk. 21:25.

4. The view being considered takes insufficient account of the references to the second coming in the discourse. If it were the case that the exclusive focus of the eschatological discourse was on the question of the fall of Jerusalem, then we might be inclined to take verses 24–27 of the fall. But nearly all scholars are agreed that later in the discourse the 'coming' of the Lord (Mk. 13:35) and the 'parousia' or glorious 'coming of the Son of man with his angels' (Mt. 25:31; 24:37,39,44; *cf.* Lk. 21:36) refer to the second coming; in view of this it is hard, though not impossible, to take the 'coming' of the Son of man in verses 24–27 of anything different. There is also reference to the second coming before verses 24–27: for example, we have the double warning against people proclaiming a near end (vv. 5f. and 21f.), and we are looking forward to the coming of the end throughout the opening section (*cf.* vv. 7,10). In Matthew the situation is even clearer, since in verses 26f. he has 'Q' material about the parousia of the Son of man *'coming* out and *shining'* like lightning from east to west; this immediately precedes his description of the sign of the Son of man *'shining'* in the heaven and of the Son of man *'coming'* on the clouds (vv. 29–31). Matthew expects extraordinary mental agility on the part of his readers if they are to understand that these two heavenly comings of the Son of man are two quite different events.[6]

5. The view does not do justice to the fact that language similar to that found in 13:24–27 is used regularly elsewhere in the New Testament of the parousia. If it could be shown that the language used was clearly and regularly used elsewhere in the Gospels and New Testament of the destruction of Jerusalem, there would be a case for taking it that way here. But none of the possible parallels that can be cited (*e.g.* Mk. 9:1; 14:62; Mt. 10:23) is exegetically unambiguous. We agree that the 'coming' of the Son of man may occasionally be something other than the parousia, but there is no other regular usage.

On the other hand, examples of similar language used of the parousia are frequent: in the Gospels, for example, compare Matthew 13:40f. on the Son of man sending his angels to gather, also 16:27 (*cf.* Mk. 8:38); 25:31; *etc.* In Paul, an early and important witness, the Lord's 'coming' is the second coming, *e.g.* in 1 Corinthians 11:26 and probably 16:22 (*Maranatha*); and in the references to the second coming in 1 and 2 Thessalonians there are a great range of parallels to Mark 13:24–27, so much so that it is probable that Paul and the

---

[6] It might just be arguable that vv. 26f. in Mt. 24 must be something different from vv. 29-31, since the disciples are told not to get excited about the imminence of the parousia in vv. 26f., but then are told that the Son of man is coming immediately in vv. 29-31. But against this see our discussion above.

Synoptists are drawing on the same traditions,[7] which makes his usage of particular importance for our argument. Elsewhere note James 5:8f.; 2 Peter 3:10–12; Revelation 1:7 (*cf.* Mt. 24:30). The list of such examples could be extended;[8] but the point is clear that the total New Testament context of the passage we are considering makes it most unlikely that the readers of the Gospels would have understood the coming of the Son of man in 13:24–27 of anything but the second coming.

6. The view in question might be attractive if it satisfactorily accounted for the structure of the discourse in a way that other views do not. But we have seen that the view does not entirely satisfactorily explain the structure (point 3(a) above) and we have offered an alternative explanation of the structure in the main part of our paper, which tells against this suggestion and makes it unnecessary.

Appendix B: The tradition underlying Mark 13:14-20 and parallels

Our argument about the setting up of the sacrilege inaugurating a final period of time may be confirmed by certain considerations concerning the original form of the discourse lying behind Mark 13:14-20 and parallels.

In this section of the discourse there are several difficulties: the difficulty in the similar Matthean and Marcan versions lies not only in the obscurity of the language about the desolating sacrilege, but also, and for our purposes more significantly, in a tension between the opening and closing verses of the section. The opening verses, 14-18, describe events in Jerusalem and Judea, and Jesus' hearers are urged to flee. We expect next to find a description of the destruction of the temple and city; instead we find in verses 19f. a broad description of unparalleled tribulation, which apparently involves the elect and from which they could presumably not flee. These verses could be taken of the fall of Jerusalem and nothing more; but the generality of the language and the references to 'all flesh' and 'the elect' suggest that we have unexpectedly stepped

[7] See my 'Paul and the Synoptic Apocalypse' in *Gospel Perspectives* 2 (ed. R. T. France and D. Wenham, JSOT Press, 1981), pp.345-375.

[8] We could add the extracanonical evidence of the Didache, since in ch. 16 a description of the last days which is quite closely parallel to Mk. 13:9-23 (par.) is followed by a description of the second coming.

out of the narrow Palestinian arena into something bigger affecting all of humanity and all of the elect (though perhaps including the fall of Jerusalem). Given this tension between verses 14-18 and verses 19f., it is not surprising that some scholars have taken verses 14-20 to be describing the fall of Jerusalem in AD 70, others to be describing a future antichrist, and others to be somehow describing both.

So far as the Lucan version of the same passage is concerned, this is simpler in that it appears to be clearly describing the historical destruction of Jerusalem (and not much more); but its very difference from Matthew and Mark requires explanation. It may be that Luke has rewritten the earlier and more difficult version, in order to be intelligible and, perhaps, in the light of events. But there are reasons to doubt whether Luke has been so creative here, and in any case that explanation would leave the difficulties of Matthew and Mark unexplained.

The alternative solution that we wish to propose is that the Matthew/Mark version and the Lucan version both derive from a common underlying tradition, the contents of which will have been approximately as follows:

1. Warning of desolating sacrilege/armies around Jerusalem. Call to flee . . . .

   (so Mt./Mk./Lk.)

2. For there will be (great) *ananke* on the land and wrath on this people . . . . Jerusalem will be trodden . . . . until the times of the Gentiles are fulfilled.

   (so Lk.)

3. And then there will be (great) *thlipsis* as has not been (*or*, And there will be (in) those days *thlipsis*) . . no human being would be saved . . . but for the sake of the elect, he shortened the days.

   (so Mt./Mk.)

4. And then if anyone says to you, 'Lo, here is the Christ . . .'; warning of false Christs and prophets.

   (so Mt./Mk.)

5. But in those days after that tribulation the sun will be darkened . . . they will see the Son of man. (*Or*, And there will be signs in sun and moon . . . And they will see . . .)

   (so Mt./Mk./Lk.)

What are the arguments that suggest this reconstruction? Essentially the argument is that such a reconstruction accounts well for the present Synoptic texts and their difficulties.

The argument for deriving Matthew/Mark from the proposed original

Matthew and Mark are quite close to each other in this passage and may be considered together. Our reconstruction assumes that Matthew and Mark have reproduced quite accurately the contents of the underlying tradition, with the exception of section 2 which they have omitted. The main argument for this is that it explains the present tension in Matthew and Mark between the opening and closing verses of verses 14-20. Originally the opening verses and the call to flight were followed by a description of the destruction of Jerusalem (being preserved in Luke), but Matthew and Mark have omitted this, going straight on to the following broader section.

It may seem at first sight unlikely that Matthew/Mark would have produced a more difficult text on the basis of a simpler text. But their difficult text does need some explaining, and it is not hard to suggest both how and why they changed the underlying tradition.

So far as the 'how' is concerned, Matthew/Mark have simply jumped from one prediction in the postulated original to a second similar prediction – from *estai ananke* to *estai thlipsis* (or *esontai . . . thlipsis*). The mechanics of the jump and alteration are very straightforward.

As for the 'why' of the alteration, it might have been accidental. If, as seems more probable, it was deliberate compression, it could simply have been for the sake of brevity; but a much more likely explanation is suggested when one notes their earlier cryptic language when referring to the 'desolating sacrilege'. Mark in particular appears to be avoiding any very explicit reference to the temple and its destruction, when he says 'When you see the desolating sacrilege set up where it ought not to be (let the reader understand). . .'. Given the opening of the chapter (vv. 2 and 4), there is little doubt that Mark is here coming on to describe the destruction of the temple, but for some reason he uses quite obscure language at the crucial point: this could be normal apocalyptic obscurity, but it could also be because of the sensitivity of the subject in a particular historical situation. It is quite likely that the same reason(s) would have led him (or his tradition) to omit the direct description of the destruction of Jerusalem which we suspect to have been in his source-tradition.

It is not difficult then to explain the mechanics or the motivation of Matthew/Mark's supposed abbreviation of the postulated underlying text.

And positively in favour of the hypothesis is its ability to explain the tensions in the Matthew/Mark text.

The argument for deriving Luke's text from such an original

The hypothesis suggested involves Luke having retained the verses about the destruction of Jerusalem, which Matthew and Mark omitted. Presumably he did not share the other Synoptists' embarrassment over direct description of the fall of Jerusalem, hence his unashamed reference to armies surrounding the city in verse 20. But what positive arguments are there in favour of this hypothesis so far as Luke is concerned?

There is good reason for seeing Luke 21:23b–24 as a primitive part of the discourse rather than as Lucan adaption of Mark
In addition to the quite well-known arguments of C. H. Dodd and others for the independence and primitiveness of the Lucan tradition here (which have some plausibility),[9] the following points merit attention.

1. There is a small agreement of Matthew and Luke against Mark, which may possibly show their knowledge of a non-Marcan tradition: they have *estai gar anankē megalē* (Luke), *estai gar tote thlipsis megalē* (Matthew), whereas Mark has *esontai gar hai hēmerai ekainai thlipsis*. It is arguable that Luke's *anankē* may derive from the postulated source-tradition, since the evidence of Luke/Acts does not suggest any Lucan aversion to the word *thlipsis* or his fondness for *anankē* used in the sense of 'distress'.[10]

2. There is some reason for thinking that Paul was familiar with the Lucan form of the tradition, and even perhaps with our postulated underlying tradition. Compare the following:

estai... orgē tō laō toutō... achri hou plērōthōsin kairoi ethnōn (Lk. 21:23f.);

pōrōsis apo merous tō Israēl gegonen achris hou to plērōma tōn ethnōn eiselthē (Rom. 11:25);

ephthasen de ep' autous hē orgē eis telos (1 Thes. 2:16).

(Note that 1 Thes. 2:16 comes in the context of a reference to Gentile mission; *cf.* Rom. 11:25.) We have argued elsewhere for the use of common, non-

---

[9] For a convenient summary see I. H. Marshall, *The Gospel of Luke* (Paternoster, 1978), p.771. For C. H. Dodd's discussion see *More New Testament Studies* (Manchester University Press, 1968), pp.69-83.

[10] *Cf.* Acts 7:11. *Contra* J. Zmijewski, *Die Eschatologiereden des LukasEvangeliums* (Peter Hanstein, Bonn, 1972), pp.186f.

Marcan and pre-Pauline traditions in Luke 21, Romans and 1 Thessalonians; and it seems quite likely that the three texts cited above reflect such a tradition (though 1 Thes. 2:16 may also be related to Mt. 23:36).[11]

But, if Paul did know a version of Luke 21:23f., is there any reason to think that he knew it in its Lucan context and adjacent to the desolating sacrilege tradition? This cannot be proved. But: (a) There is evidence for Paul having known a version of the eschatological discourse that included the desolating sacrilege tradition (*cf.* Paul's 'man of lawlessness'), and also some of the particularly Lucan material within the chapter. (b) The saying in question must have had some context. (c) It is probable that in the tradition the saying referred to the destruction of Jerusalem: note the links between 1 Thessalonians 2:14-16 and the 'Q' passage of Matthew 23:32-36//Luke 11:48-51, and note that Matthew has this 'Q' material adjacent to the eschatological discourse. (d) Although it is possible that in Paul's tradition two quite separate things were expected in the near future – a judgment on the Jews of Palestine and the destruction of Jerusalem on the one hand and the coming of the man of lawlessness to the temple on the other – it is simpler to assume that Paul associated the two, as do the Synoptists. (e) It is an interesting possibility that the Thessalonians' excitement about the end 'having come' (2 Thes. 2:2) was partly provoked by Paul's reference in 1 Thessalonians 2:16 to the 'wrath' having come on the Jews of Palestine. Such excitement would be explicable if Paul had taught them a form of the eschatological discourse in which the wrath on the Jews was a key event leading to the end. 2 Thessalonians 2 may then be seen as Paul's clarification of the misunderstanding of 1 Thessalonians 2:16 (where Paul had perhaps been speaking prophetically or spiritually; *cf.* Rom. 11:25): the Thessalonians had correctly remembered that Paul had spoken of wrath on the Jews preceding the end, but they had to be reminded that the wrath would include the appearance of the new Antiochus.[12]

We admit to the speculativeness of some of these suggestions,[13] but we

---

[11] For this and various of the following points see my 'Paul and the Synoptic Apocalypse', especially pp.353-358, 361-365.

[12] *Cf.* 1 Cor. 7:26,29. Paul here speaks of the *enestōsan anankēn*. We have here a further glimpse of Paul's teaching about the eschatological sufferings, and we may appreciate how his readers/hearers might have taken him to mean that the end had come, or virtually come. Note the use of *enistēmi* in 2 Thes. 2:2 (*cf.* 2 Tim. 3:1), and of *anankē* in Lk. 21:23.

[13] If these speculations are correct, then Paul becomes an important and very early witness to our suggested interpretation of the eschatological discourse. He expects a judgment on the Jews of Palestine taking the form of a desecration of the temple by an Antiochus-like figure – one might suppose a Roman emperor – within the near future. (1 Thes. 2:16 may be interpreted of imminent judgment, and in any case *cf.* 2 Thes. 2:6f.) Paul sees the coming of the lawless one as leading to the parousia and as a necessary prelude to the end, but he does not give any indication

consider it reasonable to cite Paul as a probable witness to the primitive origin of Luke 21:23f.

3. The book of Revelation is a further possible witness to the primitiveness of the Lucan tradition in 21:23f., and to the postulated underlying tradition. Thus in Revelation 11:2 there is a reference to the trampling of the temple courts followed by a reference to the 'two witnesses'. These witnesses may be understood as the church in mission and so be linked with the Synoptic references to the evangelism of the nations (including, quite probably, Lk. 21:24); the trampling and the witness last for the same length of time, and presumably the same period, as the reign of the blasphemous beast of Revelation 13:5. The beast is reminiscent of the Matthew/Mark desolating sacrilege, and so Revelation may be said to link together motifs from the Matthew/Mark and the Lucan traditions.

Revelation 13 is itself of particular interest, since after the description of the beast in verses 1-6, which is reminiscent of the Matthew/Mark desolating sacrilege, there is a reference to the beast 'conquering' the saints and (later) to captivity and slaying with the sword (13:7,10), which is reminiscent of Luke's description of the destruction of Jerusalem (21:23f.), and then there is a reference to deceptive signs and wonders, which is reminiscent of the false prophecy that follows the description of the desolating sacrilege in Matthew/Mark.[14] This sandwiching of the Lucan material between the Matthew/Mark material is precisely what we have postulated as the order of contents in the reconstructed pre-Synoptic tradition: the author of Revelation may be drawing on the tradition and interpreting it in his own way.[15]

---

of the length of the lawless one's reign, and he quite specifically does not use the lawless one's arrival as a positive chronological indication of the time of the end, this being quite unpredictable (1 Thes. 5). The one addition to be made to this description of Paul's view is that Rom. 11:25 and perhaps 1 Thes. 2:16 suggest that Paul regards the wrath against the Jews as having begun in terms of their spiritual blindness: is this the beginning of the work of lawlessness described in 2 Thes. 2:7?

[14] Perhaps Rev. 13:7b-8 is an allusion to the universal tribulation of Mk. 13:19f. Yet another possible point of contact is between the Lucan verses and Rev. 6. It has often been noted that the opening of Rev. 6 is similar to the opening of the discourse in Lk. 21, but it has not so often been observed that there is a possible parallel between the fifth seal in Rev. 6, on the one hand, with its description of the suffering of the saints which must last *heōs plērōthōsin kai hoi syndouloi* (6:11) and which will be followed by the celestial signs, and Lk. 21:12-24, on the other hand, which describes the sufferings and desolation that will last *achri hou plērōthōsin kairoi ethnōn* and that will be followed by the celestial signs.

[15] It is possible to claim that the author of Rev. shares the Marcan/Pauline eschatological understanding: he sees the period of the beast, which for him takes the form of the Roman empire, as of uncertain length but as leading up to the end. But, whereas Mark and Paul expect

4. Elsewhere in the eschatological discourse of Luke 21 Luke appears to be reproducing tradition quite faithfully, not writing inventively. It is true that, if Mark is his primary source, Luke edits his source material quite freely in this chapter; but there is nothing else as substantial as 21:23b f. that can confidently be dubbed Lucan 'creation'. His concluding verses (34-36) might be the most obvious candidates, but we have argued elsewhere that these are traditional material, quite possibly part of an early form of the eschatological discourse.[16]

Luke's omission of the Matthew/Mark sayings about tribulation and false prophecy due to his earlier use in chapter 17
One thing that has to be explained on the hypothesis proposed is why Luke omitted that section of the original discourse which Matthew and Mark retained, namely the description of the terrible *thlipsis* and the following warnings of false prophets and false Christs.

This is in fact well explained as due to Luke's desire to avoid repetition of what he has said in Luke 17:22ff. Here Luke portrays first a period of intense distress (17:22): 'Days will come when you will desire to see one of the days of the Son of man and you will not see it'. The form of the distress is not specified, but we deduce from the following passage (18:7f.) that it is something that provokes 'the elect' to cry out day and night for vindication and for the Lord's

---

the desolating sacrilege/man of lawlessness in the future, the author of Rev. (who on the most widely accepted view wrote after AD 70) sees himself as in the age of the beast and of the great distress.

[16] See 'Paul and the Synoptic Apocalypse'. Lk. 21:20 might appear to tell against this: if the reference to the desolating sacrilege found in the parallel verse in Mt./Mk. is primitive, as we suppose, then Lk. may seem to have substituted a fairly straight description of a military invasion for the Danielic original found in Mt. and Mk. If he has, then it may seem natural to explain his vv. 23f. (with their description of the conquest of Jerusalem) in the same way, *i.e.* as a Lucan replacement for the Mt./Mk. reference to unparalleled distress – rather than as distinct, independent tradition. This argument, however, can just as well be used in reverse: if Lk. 21:23f. are primitive material, then 21:20 may also be primitive (though we would not wish to deny that the wording and form of expression may be Lucan in both cases). It is possible that the original read roughly as follows: 'When you see Jerusalem surrounded by armies and the desolating sacrilege standing...'; compare Dn. 11:31, and note that the Lucan picture of military attack is not much less Danielic than the Mt./Mk. picture. If the tradition was such, then Mt./Mk. omitted the military reference, probably because of the sensitivity of the subject, and Lk. the rather obscure reference to the desolating sacrilege. (Even if this suggestion is incorrect and Lk. 21:20 is indeed a wholly Lucan adaptation of the Mt./Mk. tradition, this would not compel us to take 21:23f. the same way. Lk. had an obvious reason for wishing to alter the obscure reference to the desolating sacrilege, but slightly less obvious reason for altering the later reference to the great distress.)

return. Then in 17:23 Luke goes on to refer to the activities of false prophets at that time, who say 'Behold here, behold there...'. The thought here is similar to that in Mark 13:19-22 (par.), where first the great tribulation is described affecting even the elect, and then there is warning about the activities of the false prophets seeking to mislead even the elect and saying 'Behold here... behold there'. Given this notable similarity, it is intelligible that Luke omits the relevant material when he comes to it in chapter 21.[17]

The mechanics of Luke's editing are explicable
It is quite simple to explain Luke's editorial procedure on the hypothesis proposed. Luke found in his source 'And then (in those days) there will be (great) tribulation' (*kai... estai/esontai thlipsis*); he omits this, but carries on with a notably similar construction in his *kai esontai sēmeia...* It is possible to explain either that Luke has taken over the construction of what he has omitted and used it in the description of the heavenly signs, or that he had a source containing the phrase *kai... esontai sēmeia* (perhaps *sēmeia megala en ouranō*),[18] in which case the jump from *kai estai/esontai thlipsis* to *kai esontai sēmeia* would have been easy.

Other evidence for an underlying original
The hypothesis of a fuller and primitive underlying discourse from which the Evangelists have drawn differently is suggested not only by this passage, but even more strongly by the material found at the end of the discourse. It is impossible to prove this within this paper. It must suffice to say that we believe that the differing conclusions to the eschatological discourse in Matthew 24:36 – 25:30, Mark 13:32-37 and Luke 21:34-36 (+ the material in Luke 12:35-48) can be shown to fit together as a single coherent discourse: each of the Evangelists has utilized the material differently; Mark, for example, has extracted a series of exhortations to wakefulness and left out almost everything else.[19] If the Evangelists' different use of an underlying tradition can be

[17] It is, we believe, possible to go a step further and to argue that Lk. 17:22-37 is basically a series of extracts from the eschatological discourse, which Lk. has deliberately used ahead of time in ch. 17 to illustrate the unpredictability theme of 17:20f. This is suggested by evidence of parallel material in Mk. 13, Mt. 24 and Lk. 21. Although we cannot defend this view here, if it is correct, it clearly makes Lk.'s omissions in ch. 21 the more intelligible.

[18] Compare Lk. 21:25 with 21:11f. and Mt. 24:30. Did the original form of the tradition refer (like Joel 2:30f.; cf. 2:10; 3:15) to signs in general and then to specific signs in sun, moon and stars?

[19] It is suggested that the contents of the original discourse ending were as follows: (1) Mt. 24:36//Mk. 13:32; (2) Mt. 24:37-41//Lk. 17:26-30; (3) Lk. 21:34-36; cf. Mk. 13:33; (4) Mt. 25:1-12; (5) Lk. 12:35; (6) Lk. 12:36f.; (7) Mk. 13:35f.//Mt. 24:42; cf. Lk. 12:38; (8) Mt.

demonstrated in this material at the end of the discourse, it is entirely probable that they worked in the same sort of way earlier in the discourse.

Conclusion

We cannot prove that the underlying form of the discourse was as we have proposed; but the hypothesis is a reasonable one, and it adds probability to what we concluded earlier, namely that when Matthew and Mark speak of the second coming occurring '(immediately) after the distress of those days', they are not tying the coming very tightly to the fall of Jerusalem itself, but to a broader period of tribulation associated with the fall that will affect the whole world.

24:43//Lk. 12:39; (9) Mt. 24:44//Lk. 12:40; (10a) Lk. 12:41; (10b) Mk. 13:37; (11) Mt. 24:45-51//Lk. 12:42-46; (12) Mt. 25:13//Mk. 13:33; (13) Mt. 25:14-30; *cf.* Mk. 13:34a; (14) Lk. 12:47f. I have explained the case for this reconstruction in an as yet unpublished paper on 'The Conclusion of the Eschatological Discourse'.

THE LIGHT AND THE STONE:
A CHRISTOLOGICAL STUDY
IN LUKE AND ISAIAH

Geoffrey W. Grogan

The first two chapters of the Gospel of Luke possess many features of special
interest for the student of the New Testament. For example, after the formal
opening (Lk. 1:1–4), we are introduced to a fascinating selection of people, a
group of 'messianic pietists', who 'awaited the arrival of God's Kingdom in a
non-violent, passive way'.[1] The language of this section of the book is full of
semitisms which give it, even in translation, a flavour all its own. A reader
familiar with the phraseology of the Old Testament, reading the Gospel of
Luke for the first time, would feel completely at home in this section of the
book.

Criticism has taken great interest in these two chapters.[2] Critical issues need
not much concern us in this essay, however, since there is general agreement
today that the chapters are a genuine literary product of the apostolic age. It is
with the theology of the writer, not with his sources, that we are concerned.

This study will concentrate attention on the story of Simeon in Luke
2:25–35. The writer's aim is to demonstrate that this passage can be fully
understood only when seen against the background of the book of Isaiah, that it
interprets that book Christologically, and that it implies a somewhat programmatic approach to the history of the Christ as foreshadowed in the pages of
Isaiah.

Simeon and the infant Jesus (Lk. 2:25–27)

The immediate context underlines the fulfilment of the Jewish law by the

---

[1] R. P. Martin, *New Testament Foundations* 1 (Paternoster, 1975), p.91.

[2] The history of the criticism of these chapters needs to be studied in the context of the
criticism of this Gospel as a whole. See D. Guthrie, *New Testament Introduction* (Tyndale Press,
1970), chs. 4–7; R. P. Martin, *New Testament Foundations* 1; I. H. Marshall, *Luke: Historian and
Theologian* (Paternoster, 1970).

parents. It refers to the rites of circumcision and purification (vv. 21f.), and quotes from the Old Testament (vv. 23f.; *cf.* Ex. 13:2, 12, 15; Lv. 12:8).

Attempts to identify Simeon can only be speculative. Although it has no more claim to our credence than other suggestions (in fact, less than some), a quaint passage in the commentary on Luke by a 12th-century Byzantine writer shows, perhaps, his awareness of the importance of the Isaianic background. Euthymius Zigabenus identifies Simeon with one of the translators of LXX. He says that it was he alone who objected to the rendering *parthenos* ('virgin') in Isaiah 7:14, and that he was informed by an angel that he would live to take the virgin's son into his arms.

The phrase *paraklēsin tou Israēl* ('consolation of Israel') immediately reminds the reader of Isaiah. This prophecy, in common with other prophetic writings, contained many warnings of divine judgment, but it also promised a time of comfort for Jerusalem/Israel (Is. 40:1), in a context which speaks of Babylonian captivity (Is. 39:6f.). In fact, the note of divine comfort, once it has been sounded in chapter 40, is often echoed in later chapters (*e.g.* 49:13; 51:3, 12; 52:9; 57:18; 66:13). Occasionally it occurs earlier, notably in Isaiah 12:1, once again in a context which speaks of a return from exile (11:11f.). Of course, the theme is not restricted to passages where its distinctive terminology occurs, and this theme is to be found in many of the book's chapters.

Simeon's conception of how God will console Israel becomes clear in the *Nunc Dimittis,* which too, we shall discover, contains a number of important allusions to Isaiah. This will underline the appropriateness of understanding the phrase chiefly in Isaianic terms.

Luke, in both his volumes, shows a special interest in the Holy Spirit, and in this passage he gives prominence to his work in connection with Simeon. The Holy Spirit was 'upon him', a phrase frequently employed in relation to Old Testament prophecy, especially in historical passages.[3] Perhaps the most significant group of passages in the canonical prophets is to be found in Isaiah. It is true that Isaiah 11:2 relates to a kingly figure, but the qualities with which he is endowed by the Spirit belong largely to the understanding. The Servant of the Lord has a ministry which is partly instructional,[4] and the Spirit is put upon him (Is. 42:1). The figure of the anointed prophet in Isaiah 61:1ff. is particularly interesting. He, too, has the Spirit upon him, and he joyfully proclaims the consolation of God's people. He is sent '... to bind up the brokenhearted, ... to comfort all who mourn; to grant to those who mourn in Zion – to give them a garland instead of ashes, the oil of gladness instead of

---

[3] Nu. 11:17, 25, 29; 24:2; 1 Sa. 10:6, 10; 19:20, 23; 2 Ki. 2:15; 2 Ch. 15:1; 20:14.

[4] Is. 42:6; 49:2, 6; 50:4.

mourning, the mantle of praise instead of a faint spirit . . . ' and so on. Luke shows us Jesus reading from this passage in the Nazareth synagogue and applying it to himself (Lk. 4:16–21). He records it at the very beginning of Jesus' ministry, suggesting, perhaps, that it established a programme for that ministry. If this is so, then Simeon may be viewed as anticipating and pointing to the Spirit-endowed ministry of Jesus, the supreme preacher of divine consolation.

But Jesus is not only the preacher of consolation in Luke's Gospel. He is the Christ of God (Lk. 9:20).[5] As J. A. Motyer says, 'the most sustained treatment of the Davidic-Messianic theme occurs in Isaiah 1 – 37 and in particular in the self-contained unit, chs. 7 – 12.'[6] Other passages from the Old Testament will have influenced Simeon's messianic expectation, but there can be no doubt that the great book of Isaiah would play a major role, especially as 'the consolation of Israel' and 'the Lord's Christ' were so closely linked, if not identified, in his mind.

Is it far-fetched to see significance even in the location of the event? It was in the temple that Isaiah was given his great vision of the glory of God.[7] It was in the temple that the aged Simeon, controlled by the same Spirit of prophecy, saw [8] the fulfilment of the prophecies contained in the book that bears Isaiah's name.

The Nunc Dimittis (Lk. 2:29–32)

Alan Richardson, writing about the *Magnificat, Benedictus* and *Nunc Dimittis*,[9] declares, 'the three hymns are as Jewish as any of the Psalms of the O.T., but they are as Christian as anything in the N.T. in their conviction that the Age of Promise was inaugurated in the hour of Christ's conception by the Holy Spirit.' This is certainly true of them in their present setting in the Gospel of Luke. Whether they are Jewish or Baptist hymns adapted for Christian purposes, or primitive Christian hymns, or whether they are authentic utterances of the inspired prophets to whom Luke attributes them, is an important question, but it does not greatly affect our thesis in this essay. We are not concerned with the *Nunc Dimittis* in itself but in its context, and (because our study will also touch on the story of Anna) with the theology of Luke rather than with that of Simeon. If the *Nunc Dimittis* was uttered by Simeon himself, as the present

[5] *Cf.* also Lk. 2:11; 4:41; 20:41; 22:67; 23:2, 35, 39; 24:26, 46.
[6] 'Messiah', *The Illustrated Bible Dictionary* (IVP, 1980), p.990.
[7] Is. 6.
[8] Note the apparent emphasis on the visual nature of his experience: Lk.2:26,30.
[9] *Introduction to the Theology of the New Testament* (SCM, 1958), p.175.

153

writer believes, it is nevertheless true that Luke has shown his own acceptance of it by incorporating it in his Gospel. It is not only the poem itself, but also its Lucan context, which is steeped in the language of Isaiah.

Simeon has waited long for this moment. '*Nun*' (now') is placed first for emphasis, and may remind us of two dramatic occurrences of the word in the LXX of Isaiah. Westermann comments on the oracle which opens at Isaiah 43:1, '"But now", it begins, to contrast with 42:18–25, a new hour has struck. It comes along with a new word of God, which cancels (40:2) the old guilt (42:18–25), and thus proclaims the dawn of the day of release.'[10] His comment on Isaiah 44:1 reads, 'The assurance of salvation begins with the words, "But now", in contrast to what was said of Israel's past in 43:22–28, in the same way as 43:1ff. contrasts with 42:18–25. Israel is summoned into the new era to hear the new word.'[11] Simeon has lived in eager anticipation of God's new day, and his 'now' is both personal and eschatological.[12]

Simeon thinks of himself as a watchman released by his master (*despotēs*) from his duties. The one for whom he was watching had now arrived. 'But in Simeon's canticle this watchman theme has been combined with that of the last words of the aged or dying.'[13] If the language is reminiscent of anything in LXX, it recalls particularly Genesis 15:15 and 46:30. The latter is particularly significant, for, as Raymond E. Brown points out, 'Here, as in the Nunc Dimittis, there is an emphatic "Now," expressing the sense of a felt fulfilment of promise. This parallel with Jacob/Israel has all the more force because of Jewish speculation that, while Jacob saw Joseph, he was still left yearning for God's salvation (Gen. 49:18). The targums stress that he was "looking for the redemption that God would bring to His people".'[14]

The glad sense of eschatological fulfilment is intensified by Simeon's reference to peace. The reign of the coming Davidic king would give the great blessing of peace to his people (Ps. 72:7; Is. 9:4–7; 11:6–9; Ezk. 34:25). Some writers have laid stress on a possible zealot interest in the Gospel of Luke. J. M. Ford, for example, declares that 'the main purpose of Luke's Gospel (and, perhaps, Acts) is to present a book of consolation for the disappointed zealot, be he Jewish or Jewish Christian.'[15] He also says, 'Simeon, like Zechariah, may have

---

[10] *Isaiah 40–66* (SCM, 1969), *ad loc.*

[11] *Ibid., ad loc.*

[12] Paul is very fond of the '*nun*' of realized eschatology. *Vide* Rom. 3:21; 8:1; 11:30; 16:26; 2 Cor. 6:2, *etc.*

[13] R. E. Brown, *The Birth of the Messiah* (Geoffrey Chapman, 1977), p.457.

[14] *Ibid.* Brown refers his readers to M. McNamara, *The New Testament and the Palestinian Targum to the Pentateuch* (Analecta Biblica 27; Pontifical Biblical Institute, 1966), pp.243-245.

[15] 'Zealotism and the Lukan Infancy Narratives', *Nov T* 18, 1976, p.280.

expected a military leader.'[16] In view of this, it is worth noting that Luke seems to be suggesting here, and in his quotation of the *Gloria in Excelsis* earlier in the chapter, that God's peace has already come, at least in some realized sense, with the advent of the messianic child, so that Simeon's departure takes place not simply in anticipation of it but in the experience of it. There may be battles to be fought against the powers of evil, but peace has already come to those who recognize the Christ. The coming of the child brings peace. This is thoroughly in line with Old Testament prophecy, and especially with Isaiah's vision of the child of the fourfold name (9:6).

What does Simeon mean when he declares this to be *'kata to rhēma sou'* ('according to thy word')? D. R. Jones alludes to the view that the *Nunc Dimittis* is of liturgical provenance and says that in this case the phrase could have referred originally to the priest's word of blessing on the worshippers.[17] On the other hand, remembering that Simeon is virtually presented here as a prophet, we might relate the phrase to a previous unrecorded oracle given to him by the Spirit. This may have been the means through which he was given the certainty of continued life until the advent of the Messiah. If, however, as we intend to argue, the understanding of the book of Isaiah which lies behind this passage is somewhat programmatic, then Simeon may well be saying that the Old Testament word (and especially Isaiah), interpreted to him by the Spirit, had led him to see that God's promised peace would come when the messianic child appeared. In this way we may understand the logic of the word 'for' (*hoti*) which opens verse 30.

We have already noted the emphasis on sight in verse 26, and this recurs in verse 30. Howard Marshall says, 'By the use of the phrase "my eyes" (*cf.* Is. 52:10, *MT;* Lk. 10:23f.) he stresses the reality of his vision of God's salvation.'[18] The book of Isaiah contains a number of significant passages where sight plays an important part. The prophet sees Yahweh in the temple.[19] Isaiah 33 is especially interesting. Here the prophet declares, 'Your eyes will see the king in his beauty' (v. 17), and then, later in the same oracle (v. 22), he continues, 'the LORD is our king; he will save us.' Simeon sees the infant messianic king and announces that he has seen God's salvation.

The Greek word *sōtērion* used here is found only four times in the New Testament, of which three occur in the writings of Luke (Lk. 2:30; 3:6; Acts 28:28; *cf.* Eph. 6:17). In Luke 3:6 it comes in a quotation from Isaiah 40:5, and in Acts 28:28 it immediately follows a somewhat lengthy quotation from

---

[16] *Art. cit.*, p.281.

[17] 'The Background and Character of the Lukan Psalms', *JTS* 19, 1968, p.40.

[18] I. H. Marshall, *The Gospel of Luke* (Paternoster, 1978), *ad loc.*

[19] Is. 6:5, which occurs in a passage apparently applied to Jesus Christ in Jn. 12:40f.

Isaiah 6. It should not surprise us therefore to discover that in Luke 2:30 also it is understood chiefly in Isaianic terms; this we shall see from the two verses that follow.

Simeon appears to identify 'thy salvation' with 'the Lord's Christ'. D. R. Jones points out that 'in the Testaments of the Twelve Patriarchs the salvation looked for is certainly in some sense what might be called the eschatological event and at times seems equivalent to the Messiah.'[20] This would suggest that a personalized concept of salvation was not foreign to Judaism around this period. Of course, the book of Isaiah presents God as himself the salvation of his people: 'Behold, God is my salvation; I will trust, and will not be afraid; for the LORD GOD is my strength and my song, and he has become my salvation.'[21]

D. R. Jones, writing on verse 31, says, 'The idea of the preparation of *salvation* is unique, and in the light of what follows, this must mean the providential preparation of salvation through Israel's history, according to prophecy and promise, until the time of the fulfilment which is now recognized.'[22] Luke uses the verb *hetoimazein* (to prepare) about the ministry of John the Baptist in Luke 1:17, 76; 3:4.[23] Perhaps the use of the word here, in Luke's context, indicates that the Baptist's ministry, although important, is not unique, and that his work represents the climax of the long centuries of divine preparation. This preparation surely includes the book of Isaiah, the language of which permeates the following verse, where the word 'light' stands in apposition to 'thy salvation'.

In what sense, though, had God prepared his salvation 'in the presence of all peoples'? This phrase may simply anticipate the reference to the Gentiles in verse 32. In this case, Simeon is saying that God has planned to reveal his salvation to the whole world.[24] If, however, the preparation relates to the past centuries of prophecy, then it would seem natural for this phrase also to have a past reference.

Perhaps an examination of Isaiah can help us here. This Old Testament book, like other prophetic writings, sets the messianic prophecies within the context of world history. Israel is rarely seen in isolation but rather in its Gentile environment. Either Assyria or Babylon forms the backdrop to much of the book, while Isaiah 13 – 23 comprises the longest series of prophecies

---

[20] *Art. cit.*, p.41.

[21] Is. 12:2; *cf.* Is. 33:2 and, perhaps, Is. 62:11. The idea occurs also in the Psalter, *e.g.* Pss. 27:1; 35:3; 62:2.

[22] *Art. cit.*, p.42.

[23] R. E. Brown makes this point, *op. cit.*, p.439.

[24] *Cf.* Is. 52:10, although this verse speaks of 'nations' rather than 'peoples', and if Simeon's phrase is a conscious allusion to this verse, it is difficult to account for the change of word.

against the Near Eastern nations contained in the Old Testament. Immediately following, chapter 24 views the whole world from the divine perspective. Neither the great king of the future nor the suffering Servant are mere Israelite phenomena. It is not only in the fulfilment but also in the promise, not only in the passages themselves but in their wider historical and prophetic context, that 'all peoples' appear. What is true supremely of Isaiah holds good, of course, for other Old Testament prophetic books.

Christ came to bring light to men. This is an important theme, not only in the birth narratives of Luke,[25] but also in John's statement of the incarnation in his prologue.[26] Like virtually all great concepts applied to Christ in the New Testament, this is rooted in Old Testament thought. Without doubt, Isaiah furnishes the chief element in its background. In the structure of John's Gospel chapter 12 is of great importance, for in it the Evangelist brings his account of Jesus' public ministry to its conclusion, and focuses on the fact that God's light has come into the world in him. In this passage he quotes twice from Isaiah (Is. 53:1; 6:10) and applies each verse to Christ the Light.[27]

In Ephesians 5:14 there is an unidentified quotation, 'Awake, O sleeper, and arise from the dead, and Christ shall give you light.' Alan Richardson has pointed out the inaccuracy of the RSV translation of the quotation formula here:[28] 'it is said' should read 'it says' or 'he says'. Modern writers tend to treat this verse as a quotation from a primitive Christian hymn, perhaps connected with baptism.[29] This formula, however, normally introduces quotations from Old Testament Scripture,[30] and it may well sum up, much in the fashion of Matthew's reference to 'Branch' prophecies (Mt. 2:23), the teaching of the Old Testament along this line. There can be no doubt that Isaiah supplies the bulk of these (*e.g.* Is. 2:5; 9:2,6; 26:19; 42:6; 49:6; 60:1–5, 19f.).

Passages like John 12 and Ephesians 5:14 would certainly incline us to turn to Isaiah for our understanding of Luke 2:32, but there are stronger considerations than these. In a context where almost every phrase is evocative of Isaiah's prophecies,[31] we can hardly fail to see an echo of Isaiah 42:6 and 49:6, especially when, like them, this verse speaks also about Israel. Luke's interest in Isaiah 49:6 is clear, in any case, for he quotes it in Acts 13:47, where he

[25] *E.g.* in Lk. 1:77–79 as well as here.

[26] Jn. 1:4–9; *cf.* 8:12; 9:5; 12:35–46.   [27] Jn. 12:37–41.

[28] 'Scripture, Authority of', *The Interpreter's Dictionary of the Bible* 4 (Abingdon Press, 1962), p.249.

[29] *E.g.* R. P. Martin, *New Testament Foundations* 2 (Paternoster, 1975), pp.262f.

[30] *Vide* especially B. B. Warfield, *The Inspiration and Authority of the Bible* (Presbyterian and Reformed, 1948), ch.7.

[31] R. E. Brown sees this particularly clearly, *op. cit.*, pp.458-462.

relates it to the extension or implementation of Christ's ministry to the Gentiles through the apostles.

A. B. Bruce, among other writers, has pointed out that Luke, who has his own way of presenting the Christian universalism of the gospel, has preserved the distinctively Old Testament flavour of it here.[32] What does he mean by *eis apokalypsin* ('for revelation')? Howard Marshall discusses this.[33] He mentions the view that Luke is referring to nothing more than a salvation to be seen, but not experienced by the Gentiles, and says, 'but Acts 13:47; 26:22f. show that something more than seeing is meant.' In the context of the *Nunc Dimittis,* this 'light', because it is in apposition to 'thy salvation', is surely a saving light; and that is in line with Isaiah 49:6, 'I will give you as a light to the nations, that my salvation may reach to the end of the earth.' It is also worth noting that this theme occurs more often in the oracles of this prophetic book than in any other part of the Old Testament. The reference to the Gentiles is followed by the words, *kai doxan laou sou Israël* ('and for glory to thy people Israel'). The word *doxa* (glory), with its Hebrew equivalent *kābôd,* is rich with meaning. Paul sums up the privileges of Israel in a handful of pregnant terms, and 'glory' is one of these (Rom. 9:4). All that we have seen so far in our passage will incline us to look first in Isaiah for background to the whole phrase here, and we do not look in vain.

We must first notice, however, the grammatical relationship of the second line of verse 32 to the first. The words *phōs eis* ('light for') almost certainly govern both *apokalypsin* ('revelation') and *doxan* ('glory'), so that the light, which is also God's salvation, and which, in the context, is clearly to be identified with 'the Lord's Christ', brings glory to God's people Israel.[34]

The word 'glory' has a number of shades of meaning in Scripture,[35] but in many passages the glory of God has associations with 'brightness' and so with light and revelation, as here in the *Nunc Dimittis.*[36] Given certain conditions, God promises his people, 'Then shall your light break forth like the dawn, and your healing shall spring up speedily; your righteousness shall go before you, the glory of the LORD shall be your rearguard' (Is. 58:8). A later passage is even more significant, however, because of the way it links the glory of God in Israel

[32] 'Gospel of Luke', *Expositor's Greek Testament* 1 (Hodder and Stoughton, 1903), *ad loc.*

[33] *The Gospel of Luke, ad loc.; cf.* R. E. Brown, *op. cit.,* pp.439f.

[34] R. E. Brown discusses the grammatical issue here and comes to the same conclusion, *op. cit.,* p.440.

[35] *Vide* M. R. Gordon, 'Glory', *The Zondervan Pictorial Encyclopedia of the Bible* 2 (Zondervan, 1975), pp.730-735; M. Carrez, 'Glory', *The Vocabulary of the Bible* (Lutterworth, 1958), pp.137-141.

[36] *E.g.* Ezk. 1:28; Lk. 2:9.

with the drawing of the Gentiles to the light. 'Arise, shine; for your light has come, and the glory of the LORD has risen upon you. For behold, darkness shall cover the earth, and thick darkness the peoples; but the LORD will arise upon you, and his glory will be seen upon you. And nations shall come to your light, and kings to the brightness of your rising.... Then you shall see and be radiant' (Is. 60:1–3, 5).

This great passage shows the glory of God so manifest in Israel that it glorifies his people too, and Gentiles are attracted by the brightness of that glory and light. Godet makes an interesting comment in connection with the language of Simeon here. He says, 'The Gentiles are here placed first. Did Simeon already perceive that the salvation of the Jews could only be realised after the enlightenment of the heathen and by this means? We should see what a profound insight this old man had into the moral condition of the generation in which he lived. Guided by all that Isaiah had foretold respecting the future unbelief of Israel, he might have arrived at the conclusion that his people were about to reject the Messiah (v. 35).'[37]

Certainly the order here is unusual and without parallel in the Old Testament, unless it be in a remarkable oracle in Isaiah 19. There judgment is pronounced on Egypt, but it is then declared that salvation will follow. The Egyptians will know the Lord and will be reconciled to their old enemies, the Assyrians. This oracle concludes: 'In that day Israel will be the third with Egypt and Assyria, a blessing in the midst of the earth, whom the LORD of hosts has blessed, saying, "Blessed be Egypt my people, and Assyria the work of my hands, and Israel my heritage "' (vv. 24f.). The passage seems to imply that in some sense Egypt and Assyria will actually take precedence over Israel, for what else can 'third' mean?[38]

Their precedence cannot be in terms of revelation, for whenever in the Old Testament the enlightenment of the Gentiles is contemplated, it always comes through the agency of Israel.[39] It could, however, bear witness to a general precedence in the order of repentance, and so of actual blessing, although it must be said that no emphasis is laid upon this in the passage concerned. Discussing the spiritual history of Israel in Romans, Paul recognizes that the nation's initial rejection of Jesus Christ will result in a postponement of blessing for the people as a whole. 'A hardening has come upon part of Israel, until the full number of the Gentiles come in, and so all Israel will be saved; as it is written, "The Deliverer will come from Zion, he will banish ungodliness

---

[37] *A Commentary on the Gospel of St. Luke* (T. & T. Clark, 1893), *ad loc.*
[38] *Cf. e.g.* the use of the same Hebrew word in Nu. 2:24; Jb. 42:14.
[39] Gn. 12:3; 18:18, *etc.*

from Jacob"; "And this will be my covenant with them when I take away their sins."'[40]

The child of destiny (Lk. 2:33–35)

Luke uses the verb *eulogein* ('to bless') twice in his account of Simeon's encounter with Jesus and his parents. On the first occasion it introduces the *Nunc Dimittis*, on the second it introduces this further oracle. The first is an ascription of praise to God, while the second introduces a warning of suffering. The whole tone of the second oracle is different from the first, and the somewhat surprising character of this is underlined by the word *idou* ('behold'). The word is appropriate here not simply in the setting of the Simeon story but in the plan of the book as a whole, for it introduces the first intimation in it of a destiny of suffering for the infant Jesus.[41]

The verb here translated 'set' (*keimai*) also occurs earlier in the chapter (vv. 12, 16) where the infant Jesus is lying in the manger. It is most unlikely, however, that Luke intends us to apply the word simply to the position of the babe in Simeon's arms. It is much more likely that it means, 'is appointed',[42] so that the function to which we are now introduced is as much part of the divine purpose for him as that described in the *Nunc Dimittis*. His work was meant to reveal man and his thoughts, as well as God and God's thoughts.

Most commentators see in the words, 'the fall and rising again of many in Israel', an allusion to Isaiah 8:14f. The prophet is speaking of 'the LORD of hosts' (v. 13), so that such an allusion implies belief in the deity of Jesus.[43] It should also be noted that this passage occurs in the same general context as the 'child' prophecies of Isaiah 7:10–17 and 8:16 – 9:7. In fact, children – the child of prophecy and the children of the prophet – dominate this section of the book. It will not, therefore, surprise us to find the messianic child and the prophecy of the stone of stumbling linked in this New Testament interpretation. Isaiah 8:14f. develops the stone-of-stumbling imagery fairly fully, but it begins on a more positive note: 'and he will become a sanctuary'. In Isaiah's day the sanctuary for Israel was a building constructed of stone. Isaiah 28:16 may be amplifying this imagery by its reference to the foundation stone laid in Zion by God. Psalm 118:22f. also speaks of a stone established and exalted by God,

---

[40] Rom. 11:25–27. It is of interest to note that LXX quotations of Is. 59:20 and 27:9 are used by the apostle to support his contention at this point.

[41] This point is noted especially by E. E. Ellis, *The Gospel of Luke* (Nelson, 1966), *ad loc.*; *cf.* A. Plummer, *St. Luke* (T. & T. Clark, 1922), *ad loc.*

[42] *Cf.* Phil. 1:16; 1 Thes. 3:3, in both of which the verb is followed as here by the preposition *eis* ('for').

[43] The whole passage plays an important part in the thought of 1 Peter (2:8; 3:14f.).

although rejected by men. So each of the leading 'stone' passages of the Old Testament, quoted and used by the New Testament writers,[44] implies that God is building a definite structure. Simeon utters his prophecy within the temple itself, but we probably should not attach special significance to that in respect of the stone imagery, for the language of his oracle does not in any way draw it out.[45]

Do the words, 'the fall and rising again of many in Israel', refer to two groups or to one? Scholars are not agreed, but the majority favour the former.[46] Marshall, however, argues that the analysis of the phrase into two, with the word *pollōn* ('many') covering both halves of the expression, is awkward. He then says, 'Moreover, if we take the reference to be to one group of people, we obtain a good antithetical parallel with the second *eis* phrase which speaks of the rejection of the Messiah.'[47] Micah 7:8 can supply an Old Testament parallel supporting the reference to one group, and both in this verse itself and in its immediate setting there are linguistic parallels to the Lucan context. For example, Micah speaks of 'the God of my salvation' (Mi. 7:7) and says, 'when I sit in darkness, the LORD will be a light to me' (v. 8). In LXX the verbs for falling and rising are those used in Luke.

We may be able to find evidence supporting a one-group understanding of this passage within the book of Isaiah. It is true that Isaiah 53 is a passage remote from Isaiah 8, but the closing verse of the *Nunc Dimittis* contains, as we have seen, clear allusions to Isaiah 49, an earlier passage in the Servant Song sequence. Presumably, Simeon's two oracles are not to be thought of as completely distinct, but related in some way to each other. If his words do refer simply to one group, then they must imply a conversion of attitude. Such a conversion occurs in Isaiah 53:3–5. It is true that this finds its expression in quite different terms from Simeon's words, but there is a possible linguistic link in the word 'many', which occurs in Isaiah 53:11f. M. D. Hooker[48] has warned us that we should not assume a Servant Song background whenever we come across words and phrases in the New Testament which also occur in the LXX of the Songs, but the saturation of the context with Isaianic language certainly encourages such an assumption at this point.

A passage later in Luke may also support the suggestion we are making. The

---

[44] These passages appear together in 1 Pet. 2:4–8.

[45] *Contra* R. E. Brown, *op. cit.*, p.461, n.48.

[46] *E.g.* J. Jeremias, 'polloi', *TDNT* 6, p.541; R. E. Brown, *op. cit.*, p.461. Brown is very dogmatic when he says, 'the attempts of some commentators to read the fall and rise consecutively (i.e. they shall fall and then rise, as in Micah 7:8) are certainly wrong.'

[47] I. H. Marshall, *The Gospel of Luke, ad loc.*

[48] M. D. Hooker, *Jesus and the Servant* (SPCK, 1959).

parable of the husbandmen (Lk. 20:9–19) ends with the words, 'What then is this that is written: "The very stone which the builders rejected has become the head of the corner"? Every one who falls on that stone will be broken to pieces; but when it falls on any one it will crush him.' This saying clearly belongs to the same general realm of thought as the oracle of Simeon and has the same type of Old Testament background. It is true that the English 'but' translates the weak adversative *de,* rather then the stronger *alla,* and that verse 18 may therefore present two statements of judgment in which the same basic image is employed in different ways.[49] Imaginative penetration of the language, however, might well suggest to the hearer or reader that the second statement implies finality, whereas the first comes short of this. As W. Manson expresses it, 'to fall or trip on the stone – i.e. to find a present cause of stumbling or offence in Christ – is to be broken. But to have the stone fall on one – i.e. to continue impenitent until the Judgment – is to be crushed.'[50] So such a fall need not be final, and the broken man on the ground may rise, healed, to newness of life. The word *anastasin* ('rising again'), which is used so often of the resurrection of Christ in the New Testament, may suggest the spiritual resurrection of those who accept him and his claims.[51]

The child is also to be 'for a sign that is spoken against'. In Isaiah 7:3 and 8:1–4, the prophet's children are 'signs and portents in Israel from the LORD of hosts' (Is. 8:18). The great sign of this section of the book, however, is the child Immanuel (Is. 7:10–17; 8:8, 10). The sign is given by God, after Ahaz has refused the invitation to ask for one. It comes in a context of unbelief and disobedience and it is followed by the threat of judgment. This judgment is not couched in terms of total destruction, and there are gleams of hope in the language used. For example, it is pictured as an overflowing river, whose waters will 'overflow and pass on, reaching even to the neck' (Is. 8:8), but not right over the head. It is in this kind of setting that the prophecy of the 'stone of offence' occurs (Is. 8:14f.).

Just as Ahaz rejected God's offer of a sign in Isaiah's day, so men will speak against his sign in Jesus. Indeed, Luke, like the other Evangelists, presents the rejection of Jesus by the Jewish leaders very much in terms of controversy and verbal antagonism. In Luke 11, this antagonism is expressed both in the comment, 'He casts out demons by Beelzebul, the prince of demons', and also by an unbelieving and inappropriate request for a sign (Lk. 11:15f.). Later in

---

[49] So *e.g.* I. H. Marshall, *The Gospel of Luke, ad loc.*

[50] *The Gospel of Luke* (Hodder & Stoughton, 1930), *ad loc.*; *cf.* N. Geldenhuys, *Commentary on the Gospel of Luke* (Marshall, Morgan and Scott, 1950), *ad loc.*

[51] *Cf.* Rom. 6:5.

the chapter, Jesus says that he is himself God's sign for men in that generation
(Lk. 11:29–32). The close of Luke's second volume contains a reminder that
the church of Christ, too, experiences rejection and verbal antagonism (Acts
28:22).

The words which open Luke 2:35, 'and a sword will pierce through your own
soul also', are parenthetical.[52] It is not surprising that they have proved to be of
special interest to Roman Catholic commentators. R. E. Brown gives a
conspectus of patristic and modern interpretations of these words.[53] If, in fact,
for Luke, the church shares the rejection of Jesus, it is perfectly in harmony
with this for Mary to share his sufferings. We need see no more special
significance in the reference of sufferings to her, particularly in view of the fact
that the whole oracle is addressed to her.

This assumes, of course, that the statement does refer to sufferings. Marshall
represents the views of most modern commentators, when he says, 'The
thought is of the anguish that Mary would share at the general rejection of her
Son, culminating in the passion.'[54] Brown agrees with a number of other
scholars in seeing here an echo of the words of Ezekiel 14:17, which in LXX
contains both *rhomphaia* ('sword'), and the verb *dierchesthai* ('to go through').
In the Ezekiel passage the sword is an instrument of judgment, an image which
occurs several times in Ezekiel. 'The image is of a selective sword of judgment,
destroying some and sparing others, a sword for discrimination and not merely
for punishment (Ezk. 5:1f.; 6:8f.; 12:14–16).'[55] In this discrimination, there
is a separation even of families. Brown quotes passages like Matthew 10:34–36;
Luke 12:51–53 and Luke 8:19–21, and then helpfully comments, 'Indeed her
special anguish, as the sword of discrimination passes through her soul, will
consist in recognizing that the claims of Jesus' heavenly Father outrank any
human attachments between him and his mother, a lesson that she will begin
to learn already in the next scene (2:48–50)...If being an Israelite will not
guarantee a share in Jesus' salvation, neither will being a member of his
family.'[56]

So far, this statement seems an exception to the remainder of Simeon's two
oracles, for it appears not to echo Isaiah in any way. Certainly if we are looking
for linguistic comparisons, this is true. So much New Testament use of the Old
Testament is suggestive, however, and seems to be designed to remind the
biblically literate reader of the rich Old Testament background to Christ in so
many different ways. It seems likely that such a reader would be drawn to think
not only of the Ezekiel passage with its linguistic connections, but also of verses

[52] *Vide* R. E. Brown, *op. cit.*, pp.465f. and note.   [53] *Op. cit.*, pp.462f.
[54] *The Gospel of Luke, ad loc.*   [55] R. E. Brown, *op. cit.*, p.465.   [56] *Op. cit.*, pp.464f.

like Zechariah 12:10, Psalm 22:16 (LXX) and even of Isaiah 53:5. We should note especially the first half of Isaiah 53:5, 'he was wounded for our transgressions'. The Hebrew verb translated 'wounded' means 'to bore through' or 'to pierce'. In LXX this is rendered by the verb *traumatizein*, which, with its cognate noun, is peculiar to Luke in the New Testament.[57] On the face of it, therefore, it would seem unlikely that there is any allusion to Isaiah 53, despite the fact that 'many' in Luke's previous verse reminds us of it.

The immediate context in Isaiah, however, especially Isaiah 53:3f., so harmonizes with the picture of verbal antagonism and rejection presented by Simeon, that we are forced to think again. We remind ourselves that these parenthetic words of Simeon are not, in fact, about Jesus but about Mary, and yet that they owe their place in the oracle to the fact of her involvement in his sufferings. The word *kai* ('also') certainly implies this. It therefore seems likely that the reader is intended to think first of the rejection of the messianic child/servant of the Lord, then of the piercing which, for him, was the final expression of it, and then of the antagonism which his disciples and family, including his mother, would face and which would bring them suffering and social ostracism. The choice of phraseology from Ezekiel rather than from Isaiah 53 may have been dictated by a desire to avoid any suggestion that she actually shared in effecting atonement, or else – and this would fit the Lucan context well – to emphasize the social effects of being on his side. This was, of course, something Mary had to face from the beginning. It is worth noting, incidentally, that Zechariah 13:7 has the word *rhomphaia* for 'sword' and that its context speaks of wounding in the house of friends and of a divine discrimination among the people.

Simeon's second oracle closes with the words, 'that thoughts out of many hearts may be revealed'. Commentators are divided as to whether or not these are to be understood as exclusively bad thoughts or both good and bad. It is important to note that not only does *dialogismos* refer to bad or hostile thoughts everywhere else in the New Testament but, even more significantly, that Luke uses it elsewhere exclusively of thoughts either opposed to Jesus or at least raising doubts about him.[58] The later chapters of Isaiah often speak of the evil thoughts and counsels of the wicked (*e.g.* 59:7; 65:2; 66:18) and the fact that human ways and thoughts stand in contrast to those of God (55:7). It is true that within the Old Testament this kind of theme is not peculiar to the book of Isaiah. It is worth noting, however, that Luke does not always follow LXX closely, even in his first two chapters in which his language is strongly influenced by the vocabulary and style of LXX. In view of this we should note

[57] He uses them in Lk. 10:34; 20:12; Acts 19:16.   [58] Lk. 5:22; 6:8; 9:46f.; 24:38.

that Isaiah 65:2, which contains the Hebrew *macheshaba*, normally translated *dialogismos* in LXX, does not include the relevant phrase ('following their own devices') in LXX. Instead, it reads *all' opisō tōn hamartiōn autōn* ('but after their sins'). It does, however, contain the verb *antilegein* ('to speak against'), which we found earlier in Simeon's second oracle – in fact in the previous clause, if the parenthesis be excepted. 'Out of many hearts' would be appropriate, for the passage in Isaiah is concerned with the reaction not of a few individuals, but of the nation as a whole, and Paul employed this passage in Romans 10:21 in his discussion of Jewish rejection of the gospel. The use of this verse by Paul gives some support to what otherwise would be a rather slenderly attested allusion.

The messianic programme in Isaiah

Our study of Luke 2:25–35 has revealed that the passage is saturated with allusions to the book of the prophet Isaiah. We do not doubt that other Old Testament books have affected the thought of the passage, but Isaiah's influence is paramount. Moreover, we have discovered that the language of Luke suggests comparisons, not just with the 'stone' and 'light' verses of Isaiah 8:14f.; 42:6 and 49:6, but with many different passages in that Old Testament book.

The Spirit of God, whose anointing is seen in Isaiah, and who rests on the king, the servant and the prophet in the ministry of instruction and consolation, controls and moves Simeon. He stands in the line of Old Testament prophecy, but on the very threshold of fulfilment. Indeed, as he holds the child in his arms he has crossed that threshold. His words may include predictions, but these simply develop the implications for the future of the eschatological fulfilment which has come with the child. It seems fitting that he should declare, in the temple, the fulfilment of visions given to the prophet whose call came in the temple. In chapter 6 of his book, Isaiah saw the exalted Lord and began his prophetic ministry. Simeon held in his arms the Lord's Christ whose coming as a child was intimated in the next chapter of the same book.

Simeon recalls the long centuries of divine preparation for this event, but especially the Gentile context in which the messianic prophecies were given, and which has such a place of prominence in Isaiah. What others had eagerly anticipated, he was now privileged to see. One might study with profit the story of Anna which immediately follows that of Simeon in Luke's record. The fact that she, too, was a prophetess and came up 'at that very hour' links the two stories very closely, and we are told that she 'spoke of him to all who were looking for the redemption of Jerusalem'.[59] This language, too, has an Isaianic

---

[59] Lk. 2:36–38.

ring, as the prominence of Jerusalem/Zion in the book shows. When the prophet proclaims the consolation of God's people, it is to Jerusalem he speaks (Is. 41:14; 43:1; 44:22–24, *etc.*). Others were, like Simeon and Anna, looking for the consolation of Israel, the redemption of Jerusalem, the Lord's Christ; but it was the privilege of Simeon and Anna now to see.

Simeon sees the Lord's Christ as a child. It is not surprising therefore that his language echoes the chapters in Isaiah where the coming king is presented as a child. Nor is it out of place that his language should take in the 'stone' prophecy set in the midst of those chapters. The attitude of unbelief and disobedience shown by Ahaz and his refusal of a divine sign is representative of the outlook of the people, to whom the Lord of hosts becomes a stone of offence over which they stumble and fall. Nevertheless, the child is really the expression of God's salvation, for God is the king who saves (Is. 33:22; *cf.* v.17). People may fall and be broken, but this is not the end, for there is hope of a spiritual resurrection, presumably associated with repentance and the birth of faith.

All this keeps within the first thirty-nine chapters of the book, except that the salvation language runs right through it. 'The consolation of Israel', which is also a general Isaianic theme, takes us more particularly to chapter 40. This consolation is personalized, so that for Simeon the Lord's Christ, the divine salvation and the consolation of Israel are all one. Indeed, for him, all the ideas he has gathered from Isaiah find their focus in a person, the child in his arms. The Servant of the Lord comes into view, clearly identified with the messianic child, and we are reminded of his ministry which will bring light to the Gentiles and glory to Israel. The reversal of the normal order could be due to his understanding of Isaiah 19, to his recognition of the significance of the 'stumbling-stone' prophecy and other prophetic indications of the rebelliousness of the people, to his awareness of unresponsiveness in the Jews of his own day, or even to all three. The people show their antagonism and misunderstanding in their rejection of the servant, who is pierced through in the pursuance of his vocation. Many for whom he has given himself in sacrificial love will be completely changed in their attitude to him. He alone can suffer vicariously for the sins of others, but his people, too, are called to involvement in suffering.

Our study has shown us, therefore, that this passage in the Gospel of Luke reveals a profound understanding of the teaching of one great Old Testament prophetic book. The teaching of that book is not remote from the interests or needs of people in the first Christian century. Simeon's ministry recognizes its relevance to the messianic child, and involves a particular understanding of the nature of that child, of the vocation to which he was called, of the blessed results of that vocation, and of the importance of a right attitude to him. All this seems to have been based, not simply, if at all, on some direct revelation from heaven, but on a deep Spirit-guided study of Isaiah's prophecies. Those prophecies presented one who was a royal child and suffering Servant, Lord of hosts and God's anointed, salvation, light and glory, sanctuary and stumbling-stone, at once the epitome of divine consolation and the object of man's scornful rejection, with divine significance both for the Gentiles and for Israel.

THE SPIRIT OF CHRIST
AND CHRISTOLOGY

M. M. B. Turner

R. T. France's essay in this volume has rightly pointed out that a theology of incarnation does not depend purely on an exegesis of passages where Jesus may actually be called God, nor on a study of the well-worn, and much-disputed, Christological sections such as John 1:1–18; Philippians 2:6-11; Colossians 1:15–20 and Hebrews 1:1–4. Of as much, if not more importance than these, is the whole substratum of material which evinces an attitude which treats Jesus as divine and 'worships' him as such. The issue involved has been sharply stated by R. J. Bauckham:

> In the last resort . . . Jewish monotheism could not tolerate a mere spectrum between God and man; somewhere a firm line had to be drawn between God and creatures, and in religious *practice* it was worship which signalled the distinction between God and every creature, however exalted. God must be worshipped; no creature may be worshipped. For Jewish monotheism, this insistence on the one God's exclusive right to religious worship was far more important than metaphysical notions of the unity of the divine nature. Since the early church remained – or at least professed to remain – faithful to Jewish monotheism, the acknowledgement of Jesus as worthy of worship is a remarkable development. Either it should have been rejected as idolatry – and a halt called to the upward trend of christological development – or else its acceptance may be seen with hindsight to have set the church already on the road to Nicene theology.[1]

---

[1] R. J. Bauckham, 'The Worship of Jesus in Apocalyptic Christianity', *NTS* 27, 1981, p.322.

As Bauckham goes on to point out, one could attempt to blunt the force of this observation by insisting either that the worship of Jesus arose in a less rigidly monotheistic Judaism than that to which the rabbis bear witness, or even that it first grew and flourished in *Gentile* Christian soil. But neither assertion appears to correspond with the evidence.[2] It would seem that worship of Jesus must be traced to the earliest community; and the only real question is how to explain this striking innovation. Once again I should wish to agree with R. T. France (and others) that the explanation lies in Jesus himself, and in the impact he made on his followers, rather than in some of the currently proposed 'evolutionary' hypotheses;[3] for the phenomenon we are talking about — the worship of Jesus — is too widespread too early to be otherwise accounted for.[4] But this answer still leaves room for us to inquire more precisely what it was about Jesus which led to the conviction that to worship him as God was appropriate. What was there in his life, death or resurrection-exaltation to convince monotheistic Jews that Jesus should be honoured as something approximating to God the Son?

Professor Moule, referring to the occasions in Matthew's Gospel where *proskynēsis* ('worship') is offered to Jesus, suggests that already in his ministry Jesus had a 'numinous' presence which was occasionally recognized.[5] But (as Professor Moule would be the first to point out) this itself does not provide a very firm bridge towards the post-Easter worship of Jesus. *Proskynein* merely denotes an abject gesture of obeisance. So, while to fall on one's face (or knees) before a man, and thus to 'worship' him, was a signal recognition of the power and authority of the one so revered — a veneration of which only God, not any creature, was considered *truly* worthy (*cf.* Lk. 4:7f.//; Acts 10:26; Rev. 19:10

---

[2] *Ibid.*, pp.322-341. Bauckham's case is built on a consideration of two texts in which Christian faith is expressed in terms drawn from the tradition of Jewish apocalyptic and Merkabah mysticism (therefore not Gentile in origin) and which combine the invitation to worship Jesus with a prohibition of the worship of angels (thus evincing an awareness of the danger of infringing monotheism with the worship of creatures). The texts concerned are the Apocalypse of John and the Ascension of Isaiah.

[3] Amongst the most nuanced representatives of the 'evolutionary' hypothesis are F. Hahn, *The Titles of Jesus in Christology* (Lutterworth, 1959); R. H. Fuller, *The Foundations of New Testament Christology* (Lutterworth, 1965) and, in important respects, J. D. G. Dunn, *Christology in the Making* (SCM, 1980). At a popular level (and occasionally in speculative vein) the position is maintained by the authors of *The Myth of God Incarnate*, ed. J. Hick (SCM, 1977). Against such an interpretation of the rise of NT Christology see, *inter alios*, M. Hengel, *The Son of God* (SCM, 1976); I. H. Marshall, *The Origins of New Testament Christology* (IVP, 1976) and C. F. D. Moule, *The Origin of Christology* (CUP, 1977).

[4] For details see the chapter by R. T. France in this volume.

[5] C. F. D. Moule, *op. cit.*, p.176.

and 22:9) – such acts of self-abasement and reverence certainly do not necessarily indicate that the one so honoured was conceived to be divine (*cf.* Mt. 18:26; Rev. 3:9). The instances Mark (5:6) and Matthew (2:2, 8, 11; 8:2; 9:18; 14:33; 15:25; 20:20) provide of *proskynēsis* offered to Jesus, before the cross, belong to the pattern of Near-Eastern response to a revered or powerful figure; they need not imply more. Whilst disciples (and others) occasionally felt a 'numinous' presence in association with Jesus (*cf.* Mk. 4:35–51; 6:45–52, *etc.*), it is improbable that these experiences led them to recognize him as God; at least not before the resurrection-exaltation events – though possibly such occasions were viewed as indications of his divine nature retrospectively, and they may thus have helped to confirm the early church belief that Jesus was worthy of worship offered to God. In short, the 'worship' of Jesus during his ministry was theologically ambiguous.

Perhaps a stronger basis for the early church's worship of Jesus lies in his own explicit and implicit claims about himself. However, it must immediately be admitted that while Jesus' teaching implies a very high Christology,[6] it did not actually contain unambiguous statements to the effect that he was ontologically divine.[7] No evidence of this nature was forthcoming at his trial before the Jewish council (Mk. 14:53–64 and parallels) or on other occasions on which Jesus is charged with arrogating to himself divine prerogatives.

For example, at Mark 2:5 (and parallels) Jesus pronounces the paralytic's sins to be forgiven.[8] The reaction of the scribes present is recorded to have been, 'He

[6] See I. H. Marshall, *op. cit.,* especially ch. 3, and J. D. G. Dunn, *Jesus and the Spirit* (SCM, 1975), part 1 – who offers what I would take as a minimal claim. For a suggested correction to Dunn's position, leading to a more exalted Christology, see my article 'Jesus and the Spirit in Lucan Perspective', *TB* 32, 1981, pp.3-42, with the literature cited. Compare also R. J. Bauckham, 'The Sonship of the Historical Jesus in Christology', *SJT* 31, 1978, pp.245-260.

[7] We are not here discussing *implicit* claims to divinity such as have often been noted. For example, P. B. Payne points out that the Synoptic parables frequently apply imagery to Jesus that in the OT was primarily, if not exclusively, used by God. Such instances, he argues, were implicit claims to divinity: see his *Metaphor as a Model for Interpretation of the Parables of Jesus with Special Reference to the Parable of the Sower* (doctoral thesis, Cambridge, 1975), pp.231-234, and 'The Authenticity of the Parables of Jesus' in *Gospel Perspectives* 2 (ed. R. T. France and D. Wenham, JSOT Press, 1981), especially pp.334, 338-341. But implicit claims such as these would not themselves generate the belief that Jesus was God incarnate; they could only confirm such a belief when it had been arrived at on other grounds.

[8] The unity of the pronouncement of forgiveness with the healing miracle in this pericope has been challenged since Wrede's day. Against Wrede, and those who followed him, see especially R. T. Mead, 'The Healing of the Paralytic – A Unit?', *JBL* 80, 1961, pp.348-354. For a defence of the historicity of Jesus' proclamation of forgiveness see J. Jeremias, *New Testament Theology* 1 (SCM, 1971), pp.113-118, and *cf.* L. Goppelt, *Theologie des Neuen Testaments* 1 (Vandenhoeck & Ruprecht, 1975), pp.177-188.

blasphemes: who but God alone can forgive sins?' (Mk. 2:7 and parallels). But it is likely that the scribes understood Jesus' words not so much as a claim to *be* God, as to be able to pronounce forgiveness on his behalf.[9] This they would regard as 'blasphemy',[10] for it would represent a direct claim to prophetic office, coming at a time when most of the religious authorities believed its function to have been withdrawn from Israel (by God) with the demise of the last canonical prophets.[11] In the context, the significance which Jesus attaches to his pronouncement of forgiveness and the corroborating miracle, is not that he shares the divine essence but rather that he already has the authority of the Son of man to execute God's judgment (Mk. 2:10).[12]

Similarly, John 8:58 attributes to Jesus the affirmation 'Before Abraham was, I am',[13] and the response of the Jewish hearers is preparedness to stone him. Here a claim to pre-existence is to be discerned, but not necessarily one to divinity: for the absolute use of *egō eimi* ('I am') is not *distinctively* divine, and other beings than God were thought by the Judaism of the day to pre-exist Abraham.[14] In John 10:22–39, Jesus' profession 'I and the Father are one' (10:30) leads once again to an attempt to stone him for blasphemy. The ground given by his hearers for the intention to kill him is that 'you, a mere man, claim to be God' (10:33). But it must be questioned whether this does not amount to

---

[9] Jeremias, *op. cit.*, p.114, observes that both Mk. 2:5 and Lk. 7: 47f. involve a periphrasis for the divine action: *God* is the one who forgives. Jesus announces that forgiveness with a divine passive. For proposed Jewish parallels see G. Vermes, *Jesus the Jew* (Collins, 1973), pp.67f.

[10] According to the Mishnah (Sanhedrin, 7:5) a man is not guilty of blasphemy unless he explicitly pronounces the name of God. But in the NT period the term 'blasphemy' could apply to any 'violation of the power and majesty of God' (*TDNT* 1, p.622; *cf. ibid.*, pp.621-625; also *SB* 1, pp.1008-1019).

[11] On the Jewish doctrine that the Spirit has been withdrawn from Israel since the last prophets see W. Foerster, 'Der Heilige Geist im Spätjudentum', *NTS* 8, 1961/62, pp.117-134; R. Leivestad, 'Das Dogma der Prophetenlosen Zeit', *NTS* 19, 1972/73, pp.288-300; and P. Schäfer, *Die Vorstellung vom Heiligen Geist in der Rabbinischen Literatur* (Kösel Vlg., 1972), pp.89-114.

[12] For a judicious discussion of the critical issues involved in this use of 'Son of man' language see I. H. Marshall, *The Gospel of Luke* (Paternoster, 1978), pp.214-216 with the literature cited there.

[13] Most scholars would maintain the view that the burden of proof lies with those who wish to hold the authenticity of such pronouncements of Jesus in the Fourth Gospel. For a different general approach to the whole question see S. C. Goetz and C. L. Blomberg, 'The Burden of Proof', *JSNT* 11, 1981, pp.39-63.

[14] The commentaries by R. E. Brown, L. Morris and R. Schnackenburg take the *egō eimi* to be a reference to God's self-revelation in Ex. 3:14 and thus as tantamount to a claim to divinity. But this interpretation, while consistent with John's theology, is improbable; for it deprives the phrase of its verbal force (see the commentaries by R. Bultmann, B. Lindars and C. K. Barrett

171

a malicious misrepresentation by Jesus' hostile audience of what he intended to communicate.[15] In context, Jesus' words assert the unity of the Father and the Son in the leading and protection of the sheep, and do not directly pertain to the question of *essence* – as Jesus' response (10:34–39) indicates.[16]

At Jesus' trial before the Council (Mk. 14:53–64 and parallels),[17] and in reply to the direct question of the court, 'Are you the Messiah, the Son of the Blessed?' (Mk. 14:61),[18] Jesus gives an affirmation qualified in terms of his future disclosure as the Son of man in glory (14:62).[19] As has often enough been observed, the use of 'Son of the Blessed' (or 'Son of God', as in Matthew's parallel; 26:63) is simply messianic,[20] not an indication of divine essence; and the blasphemy in this instance may well have been thought to inhere in the anticipation of *God's* declaration of the Messiah by *Jesus'* public affirmation of

which appear to have the stronger argument on this issue). That the absolute use of 'I am' *need* not have connotations of divinity is clear from its usage by the man born blind at Jn. 9:9. Jesus' words, then, were not an unambiguous asseveration of divinity; merely of pre-existence.

[15] John would expect his readers to see the dramatic irony in the accusation; for he knows 'that Jesus, being God, has humbly accepted the form of a man' (C. K. Barrett, *op. cit.*, p.384).

[16] See especially the commentary by R. Schnackenburg.

[17] For a discussion and a defence of the historicity of the Synoptic tradition on the trial of Jesus before the Council see D. R. Catchpole, 'The Problem of the Historicity of the Sanhedrin Trial' in *The Trial of Jesus*, ed. E. Bammel (SCM, 1970), pp.47–65, and J. Blinzler, *Der Prozess Jesu* (Pustet, [4]1969).

[18] D. R. Catchpole, *op. cit.*, pp. 64f., understands Luke's account, which has two separate questions for Mark's one, as the more original, on the ground that it represents an early stage in Christological development before the titles 'Messiah', 'Son of God' and 'Son of man' were assimilated. But this will not do: 'Son of God' was probably a predicate applicable to the *Davidic* Messiah even in pre-Christian Judaism: see below.

[19] In view of Jesus' crucifixion as a messianic pretender, and the mocking of him as 'the king of the Jews' (Mk. 15:16–20, 26, 32; and parallels), it remains historically convincing that Jesus thought of himself as the Davidic Messiah, and allowed followers to interpret his ministry accordingly (Mk. 11:1–10 and parallels), even if he distanced himself from some aspects of Jewish expectation concerning that figure (so C. F. D. Moule, *op. cit.*, p.34).

[20] Ps. 2:7 had enjoyed a long history of messianic interpretation by the time of Jesus (see M. A. Chevallier, *L'Esprit et le Messie dans le bas-Judaïsme et le Nouveau Testament* [Presses Universitaires de France, 1958]), and now recent findings at Qumran have clearly demonstrated that Davidic messiahship and 'sonship' were intrinsically linked: *cf.* 4Q Florilegium 1, 11f. which identifies the 'son' to whom God will be 'Father' (according to 2 Sa. 7:14) with the *ṣmḥ dwid* ('the scion of David'). On this see R. N. Longenecker, *The Christology of Early Jewish Christianity* (SCM, 1970), p.95; E. Lohse, *TDNT* 8, pp.360-362, and M. Hengel, *op. cit.*, p.44.

It would appear that the titles 'Son of God' and 'Son of the Most High' were merely stylistic alternatives with a common denotation: the Davidic Messiah – *cf.* Lk. 1:32–35 and 4QpsDan A[a] Col. 2, 1:1 (on which see J. A. Fitzmyer in *NTS* 20, 1973/74, p.391).

messiahship before the messianic task was completed.[21]

The evidence of the Gospel tradition points clearly to Jesus' revelation of himself as someone with a unique relationship of sonship to God,[22] but not necessarily and unambiguously as God the Son. What he is reported to say is not inconsistent with the latter view – and once he had been recognized as such there would have been no difficulty in reading Jesus' statements about the relationship of the Son and the Father in this light – but we still require some clear bridge to lead us from a messianic interpretation of Jesus' words (such as would naturally be inferred from his use of the title 'Son [of God]') to the deeper one, witnessed in the early church worship of Jesus which reflects something approaching the consciousness of him as God the Son.

No doubt some stimulus was afforded to the development of a higher Christology by the resurrection appearances to the disciples.[23] Whilst there is no logical reason why the resurrection of Jesus itself should have pushed Christology from purely messianic categories towards divine ones, it is nevertheless historically convincing that the appearances were experienced as dramatic disclosure situations which thrust the Christological question of the true identity of the Risen One firmly into the forefront of the minds of his followers. In this situation it is not in the least improbable that the resurrection event served, for some, to illuminate what retrospectively seemed to have been hitherto veiled and implicit claims to divinity in the teaching of Jesus, and thus to bring about the confession of him as Lord and God (*cf.* Jn. 20:28). Nor is it implausible in such circumstances that some might have begun to feel it appropriate to offer Jesus worship – as Matthew 28:17 states – though the same verse of Matthew reminds us that others present demurred.

Thus, even the resurrection appearances do not of themselves fully explain

---

G. Schneider, *Das Evangelium nach Lukas* (Mohn, 1977), p.52, seems to think that 1QSa. 2:11 refers to a begetting of the Messiah by God – but see M. Smith in *NTS* 5, 1958/59, pp.218-224.

[21] See D. Flusser, 'Two notes on the Midrash on 2 Sam. vii', *Israel Exploration Journal* 9, 1959, pp.99ff.; R. N. Longenecker, *op. cit.*, pp.71-74; J. C. O'Neill, 'The Silence of Jesus', *NTS* 15, 1969, pp.165-167, and, by the same writer, 'The Charge of Blasphemy at Jesus' Trial before the Sanhedrin' in *The Trial of Jesus,* as at n.17, pp.72-77.

[22] *Cf.* R. J. Bauckham's essay, as at n.6.

[23] A discussion of the nature of these appearances is beyond the scope of this paper: see especially the studies by J. D. G. Dunn (as at n.6, pp.18, 21f.); G. E. Ladd, *I Believe in the Resurrection of Jesus* (Hodder, 1975), and C. F. D. Moule, *The Phenomenon of the New Testament* (SCM, 1967), pp.10-14, and his introduction to *The Significance of the Message of the Resurrection for Faith in Jesus Christ* by W. Marxsen *et al.* (SCM, 1968), pp.1–13. The fullest recent tradition-historical account of the appearances is *The Post-Resurrection Appearance Stories* by J. E. Alsup (Calwer Vlg., 1975) by much of which, however, I remain unconvinced.

the enthusiastic and committed worship of Jesus in the earliest church, though they opened the path toward it. Donald Guthrie has rightly observed that there is a sense in which the astonishing development of an exalted view of Christ can be traced back to the impetus of the resurrection.[24] Yet, as he goes on to remark, the resurrection without the ascension would be incomplete; demonstrating the conquest of death, but not exaltation.[25] Is it then possible that this latter aspect of the resurrection-exaltation complex – the ascension of Jesus – can have provided the decisive impetus to the worship of Jesus that the resurrection appearances alone leave unexplained? When we turn to the account of the significance of the ascension in Peter's speech in Acts 2 we appear to be offered an affirmative answer to this question. We shall first examine, then, the claim made by the Pentecost speech with respect to the ascension; and subsequently we shall have to enquire whether what Luke attributes to Peter can plausibly be defended as representative of the early church's view of the import of the exaltation of Jesus.

The significance of the ascension for Christology in the light of Peter's Pentecost preaching: Acts 2:14–39

Luke commences the account of the substance of Peter's speech with a *pesher* of Joel 3:1–5, derived substantially from the LXX.[26] M. Rese correctly observes that there is more to the use of the Joel citation than an explanation of the pentecostal phenomena which provide the occasion for the speech: were it otherwise, the sheer length of the quotation would be problematic.[27] Luke has incorporated this extensive section because it finishes with the statement that 'all who call on the name of the Lord shall be saved' (Acts 2:21), which he interprets Christologically. Peter is to argue that Jesus has been made the 'Lord' (2:36), and the following reference to baptism 'in the "name" of Jesus Christ' (2:38) further identifies the 'Lord' upon whose name one should call for salvation (*cf.* Joel 3:5a).[28]

The point of Peter's speech is to provide a theological undergirding for his application of Joel 3, on the one hand to Jesus as Lord, and on the other to the hearers who are to call upon his name. Peter's 'proof' depends on three points: (i) the Joel citation has already found a measure of eschatological fulfilment in the 'signs' which attended Jesus' ministry (the word 'signs' having been introduced to the Joel quotation to bring out the significance of what Peter will

---

[24] D. Guthrie, *New Testament Theology* (IVP, 1981), p.375.   [25] *Ibid.*, p.391.
[26] See M. Rese, *Alttestamentliche Motive in der Christologie des Lukas* (Mohn, 1969), pp.45ff.
[27] *Ibid.*, pp.45-55.
[28] See particularly E. Haenchen, *The Acts of the Apostles* (Blackwell, 1971), p.186.

later say about Jesus [*cf.* 2:19 and 2:22]) and the 'wonders' which mark his death;[29] (ii) Jesus is raised, and must therefore be the eschatological son of David of whom David spoke in Psalm 16 (*cf.* Acts 2:30f.); (iii) as Jesus has been exalted, it is clear that the one to whom David refers as 'my Lord', and who in turn is addressed by the Lord (God) and given dominion (in accordance with Ps. 110:1), is none other than Jesus (Acts 2:35). Jesus has been made Lord and Christ (2:36), and hence is the redeemer upon whom men must call.

The first stage of this argument need not concern us further: the point is that if the 'last days'[30] have already broken in with Jesus' ministry and crucifixion, Peter has gained a foothold for his Christological use of the Joel passage. The second stage of Peter's argument is readily understandable, though it should be noted that the appeal to Psalm 16 does not prove any more than that Jesus' resurrection was foretold by David, and that Jesus' identity is now established as the one who is heir to the throne of David. The claim that Jesus is *already* exalted to God's right hand, and *even now* vice-regent (2:34–36), while connected with the resurrection, nevertheless goes beyond it.[31] *What is it, for Luke, that demonstrates the exaltation to the right hand of God, the rule in glory, and even justifies the transfer of the title and functions of God described by Joel, lock-stock-and-barrel to Jesus?* The answer lies in 2:32f. which links the citation concerned with Jesus' resurrection to that of his exaltation. It is to this linking argument that we now turn in more detail.

Peter's case for Jesus' exaltation and reign is built on two foundations: the first is that Jesus' resurrection is part of his ascent into the heavens and to glory (*cf.* Lk. 9:51; 24:26)[32] to obtain a promised gift; the second concerns the gift

---

[29] See M. Rese, *op. cit.,* p.54; *cf.* G. N. Stanton, *Jesus of Nazareth in New Testament Preaching* (CUP, 1974), pp.81f.; J. Kremer, *Pfingstbericht und Pfingstgeschehen* (KBW, 1973), pp.173f. and M. M. B. Turner, *Luke and the Spirit: Studies in the Significance of Receiving the Spirit in Luke-Acts* (doctoral thesis, Cambridge, 1980), pp.119f.

[30] Hence the appropriateness of *en tais eschatais hēmerais* in 2:17. Against Haenchen's support of the alternative reading *meta tauta* (with B sa *al*), see Conzelmann (commentary, *ad loc.*). Against Conzelmann's non-eschatological interpretation of the usual reading see M. Rese, *op. cit.,* p.52, and R. H. Zehnle, *Peter's Pentecost Discourse* (Abingdon, 1971), pp.29f.

[31] A local meaning of *tē dexia* (rather than an instrumental one) is demanded by the context: see G. Lohfink, *Die Himmelfahrt Jesu* (Kösel, 1971), pp.226f.; D. M. Hay, *Glory at the Right Hand: Psalm 110 in Early Christianity* (Abingdon, 1973), pp.70-73. In formal terms, Pss. 16 and 110 are joined by the exegetical device of *gezerah shawah* (the bringing together of two passages with a common phrase; in this instance the mention of the 'right hand' of God at Ps. 16:11 and Ps. 110:1); but a firm theological basis is required by Peter to justify his claim that Jesus, having been preserved from the pangs of death, is *already* exalted at God's right hand and reigning.

[32] For Luke, Jesus' ascension is pivotal (*cf.* E. Franklin, *Christ the Lord* [SPCK, 1975], *passim*): he gives two accounts of it (including the longer reading at Lk. 24:53: on which see B. M.

itself and the implications of saying that Jesus 'received' it. We shall examine these separately.

The ascent of Jesus into heaven

As long ago as 1902 F. H. Chase noted by way of conjecture that Psalm 67:19 (LXX) had been adduced by Peter 'to express, or to confirm, his witness to the Lord's Ascension'.[33] The apparently independent works of W. L. Knox, G. Kretschmar and B. Lindars, and finally the survey and careful comments of J. Dupont, have all pointed to the fundamental importance of Psalm 68, and the traditions associated with it, for an understanding of Acts 2:33.[34]

When the words *tēn epangelian tou pneumatos tou hagiou* ('the promise of the Holy Spirit') and *execheen touto ho* ('he has poured out this which . . .') are seen to be modifications brought to the psalm citation by the context, and when *tē dexia tou theou* ('to the right hand of God') is recognized as preparing the way for Psalm 110:1 (Acts 2:35), then what remains of Acts 2:33 – *hypsōtheis . . . labōn para tou patros* ('being exalted (on high) . . . having received from the Father') – taken in conjunction with the assertion in 2:34 that David did *not* ascend on high, points to a framework of thought derived from Psalm 68:19.[35] The

Metzger, *Historical and Literary Studies* [Brill, 1968], pp.77f.; *A Textual Commentary on the Greek New Testament* [UBS, 1971], pp.190f.; P. van Stempvoort, *NTS* 5, 1958/59, p.36, and G. Lohfink, *op. cit.,* pp.26f.), at the turning-point of his literary work, and in highly redactional language (with Lohfink, *op. cit.,* pp. 163-209 [*contra* P. Menoud]). But, *contra* Lohfink, *ibid.,* *passim,* Luke is not the only writer to join glorification primarily with ascension rather than with resurrection (see *Vox Evangelica* 10, 1977, pp.28ff.); nor (*contra* Lohfink) does Luke actually drive a wedge *between* resurrection and ascension (*cf.* the *oun* of 2:33). For Luke (as for the Fourth Gospel) the resurrection is *part* of Jesus' ascension (*cf.* Lk 9:51: *tas hēmeras tēs analēmpseōs autou,* on which see M. Miyoshi, *Der Anfang des Reiserberichts* [PBI, Rome, 1974], ch.1, and J. Dupont, *NTS* 8, 1961/62, pp.154-158), and thus part of his entry into glory (Lk. 24:26 – as Lohfink, *op. cit.,* pp.237f. is forced to admit). For this reason Luke can portray the ascension in 24:50-53 in a way that assimilates it to the resurrection appearances to which it forms a climax (so P. Schubert, 'The Structure and Significance of Luke 24' in *Neutestamentliche Studien für Rudolf Bultmann* [Töpelmann, 1957], pp.165-186; *cf.* the revealing admission by Lohfink [*op, cit.,* p.115] that for Luke 'gehört die Himmelfahrt am Ende des Evangeliums "sachlich" . . . mit der Auferstehung aufs engste zusammen').

[33] F. H. Chase, *The Credibility of the Book of the Acts of the Apostles* (Macmillan, 1902), p.151.
[34] W. L. Knox, *The Acts of the Apostles* (CUP, 1948), pp.80ff.; G. Kretschmar, 'Himmelfahrt und Pfingsten', *ZKG* 66, 1954-55, pp.216, 218; B. Lindars, *New Testament Apologetic* (SCM, 1961), pp.51-59 and J. Dupont, 'Ascension du Christ et don de l'Esprit d'après Actes 2.33' in *Christ and Spirit in the New Testament,* ed. B. Lindars and S. S. Smalley (CUP, 1973), pp.219-228.
[35] So also at Acts 5:31f.; *cf.* B. Lindars, *op. cit.,* p.54.

similarity between the use here and that of the same verse in Ephesians 4:8ff.[36] is striking; particularly as both have moved away from the original sense in the same way. We are bound to search for a common milieu to explain how a psalm, which once spoke metaphorically of the victorious ascent of Yahweh to Zion, receiving tribute from the vanquished, has come to be interpreted as the ascent of a *different* person (Jesus) to *heaven* to receive gifts *which he then gives to men*.[37] Judaism readily provides such a milieu in its widespread speculation about ascents of Moses.[38] Such concepts are even reflected in the Targum to the very psalm with which we are concerned. While later than Luke's material, the Targum nevertheless embodies an earlier interpretative tradition which paraphrases Psalm 68:19 (*MT*): 'You have ascended to heaven, that is Moses the prophet. You have taken captivity captive, you have learned the words of the Torah, you have given them as gifts to men . . . '.[39] The author of Ephesians 4:8ff. appears to have known this tradition, and to have used it as the basis for a new-Moses typology.[40] There is evidence that Luke witnesses to a similar exegetical tradition in the words of Peter in Acts 2:33. Four lines of argument suggest that Luke understood Peter to have chosen to describe Jesus' ascension in such a way as to rival claims made within Judaism on behalf of Moses.

1. There are a number of *implicit* Jesus/Moses parallels within the speech.[41]

2. The very mention that the Spirit descended *at Pentecost* is probably pregnant with meaning in view of the growing association between this festival and Jewish celebration of the giving of the Law by Moses at Sinai (a celebration whose liturgy included the reading of Psalm 68).[42]

---

[36] On which see A. T. Lincoln, *The Heavenly Dimension: Studies in the Role of Heaven in Paul's Thought with Special Reference to His Eschatology* (doctoral thesis, Cambridge, 1974), pp.253-267; M. Barth, *Ephesians* (Doubleday, 1974), *ad loc.* and pp.472-477; J. Cambier in *NTS* 9, 1963/64, pp.262-275, and G. B. Caird, *Studia Evangelica II,* ed. F. L. Cross (Berlin: Ak. Vlg., 1964), pp.535-545.

[37] In Acts and Eph. there is the further agreement in changing from second to third person singular, and in both cases the gift given is the Spirit and consequent charismata.

[38] Cf. W. Meeks, *The Prophet King: Moses Traditions and the Johannine Christology* (Brill, 1967), pp.122ff. and 205ff.

[39] So *SB* 3, pp.596f.

[40] Cf. B. J. Roberts, *The Old Testament Text and Versions* (University of Wales, 1951), p.198. The contacts between Eph. 4 and the Targum to Ps. 68 are particularly close; see A. T. Lincoln, *op. cit.,* pp.253-257.

[41] See M. M. B. Turner, as at n.29, pp.122f.

[42] E. Lohse, *TDNT* 6, pp.48f., argues for a complete lack of contact between Moses/Sinai traditions and Pentecost before the fall of Jerusalem. *Per contra,* however, see Kretschmar (*op. cit.,* pp. 223-229), and especially B. Noack, 'The Day of Pentecost in Jubilees, Qumran and Acts', *Annual of the Swedish Theological Institute* 1, 1962, pp.73-95, who demonstrates strong links

3. When we turn to the phenomena in Acts 2:1–13 which the speech of Peter interprets, we discover the kind of allusions to Jewish Moses/Sinai speculation which, on the one hand, forbid any strictly *literary* dependence between Luke and such traditions and, on the other hand, strongly suggest that Luke's account was selected and shaped in a milieu which had contacts with such Jewish traditions, and in which the Pentecost account (in the form we have it) would have been especially striking.[43]

4. Luke's language in 2:33 (*tēn . . . epangelian . . . labōn para tou patros*) and 2:38 (*lēmpsesthe tēn dōrean tou hagiou pneumatos:* 'you shall receive *the gift* of the Holy Spirit') is parallel to Josephus' description (*Ant.* iii. 77f.) of Sinai, which states that the people rejoiced at the thought that Moses would soon return *meta tēs epangelias tōn agathōn . . . para tou theou*; for God was to give Moses a gift (*Mousei dounai dōrean*), for which they prayed.

The evidence is sufficient to warrant the conclusion that Acts 2:33 is an example of the Christological development of Psalm 68 in parallel with Jewish hagiographic tradition about Moses. This helps us to understand how Peter progresses from Psalm 16 (which he referred to Jesus' resurrection) to Psalm 110:1 which he refers to Jesus' present reign at God's right hand. If Moses attained a new level of veneration in Israel through his ascent to God at Mt Sinai, and consequent mediation of the Law,[44] it would follow *a minore ad maius* that Jesus, making a more notable ascent to heaven,[45] would provide greater gifts and attain a higher glory (*cf.* Lk. 24:46). The one whom God had anointed with his Spirit as the Mosaic Prophet to overcome the 'strong one' and despoil his booty (Lk. 11: 21f.) – to liberate men from Satan's captivity (Lk. 4:18–21; *cf.* Acts 10:38)[46] – now enters his heritage as messianic ruler under whose feet God will subjugate all his enemies (Acts 2:34–36).[47] The point of Peter's

---

between the Pentecost feast and thanksgiving for the Law/Covenant in Jubilees and in Qumran writings. Most recently the massive work by J. Potin (*La Fête Juive de la Pentecôte,* Cerf, 1971) comes to similar conclusions to those of Noack. For further detail and bibliography see M. M. B. Turner, *op. cit.,* p.123.

[43] See J. Kremer, as at n.29, pp.238-252, 259. For individual points of comparison see Kremer, *op. cit.,* pp. 87-166; J. Potin, *op. cit.,* ch. 5; J. Dupont, *Études sur les Actes des Apôtres* (Cerf, 1967), pp.481-502, and M. M. B. Turner, 'The Sabbath, the Law and Sunday in Luke-Acts' in *From Sabbath to Lord's Day,* ed. D. A. Carson (Zondervan, 1982), n.175.

[44] *Cf.* W. Meeks, *op. cit.,* pp.110f.; 117; 156ff.; 205ff.

[45] An ascension which includes and transcends resurrection goes beyond the Jewish parallels concerning Moses: *cf.* also n.32 above on relationship between resurrection and ascension in Luke-Acts.

[46] For detail of this redactionally important material see M. M. B. Turner, as at n.6, pp.14-34.

[47] *Cf.* the missing words from the citation of Ps. 68:19: 'having led captivity captive'.

speech on this occasion (contrast 3:22–25) is not primarily to identify Jesus as the Prophet-like-Moses.[48] He is affirming, rather, that Jesus is the Davidic Messiah:[49] but the parallels between Moses and Jesus in this event serve as a backcloth against which the more vividly to portray the singular importance of Jesus' ascension, and of the gift it secures.

Part of Peter's argument that Jesus is exalted to God's right hand is thus established by his allusion to traditions of Moses' ascent to God contained in his affirmation of Jesus' resurrection-ascension.[50] This parallel with Moses' ascent prepares quite adequately for a statement that Jesus has been glorified in the heavenly places, and, in some Jewish apocalyptic circles, could quite naturally lead to the thought of reigning at God's right hand.[51] It is, however, the *nature of the gift* received by Jesus, in consequence of that ascent, which clinches Peter's argument, and which breaks new Christological ground. It is to this that we now turn.

Jesus receives the gift of the Spirit promised by Joel

According to Acts 2:33, when Jesus was exalted on high he received from the Father the promised Holy Spirit. Before we can properly assess the significance of this statement for Christology we must briefly ascertain what is meant by 'the promised Holy Spirit' (*tēn epangelian tou pneumatos tou hagiou*), and also what is signified by 'receiving' it.[52]

The context establishes beyond doubt that the referent of the phrase 'the promised Holy Spirit' is Joel's prophesied gift.[53] What Joel promised amounts to a fulfilment of Moses' wistful desire expressed in Numbers 11:29: 'I wish that all the LORD's people were prophets and that the LORD would put his Spirit on them!' In the future, according to Joel, the Spirit of prophecy – the organ of

---

[48] For the importance of this figure for Luke's redactional endeavour see Turner, as at n.6, pp.26-28.

[49] Though Luke would not consider such a mixing of Christology incongruous (*cf.* G. W. H. Lampe, *NTS* 2, 1955/56, p.160: 'Luke does not follow any *one* line of interpretation to the exclusion of all others; on the contrary he prefers to make a synthesis . . . to hold a large number of threads in his hand at once'). He has already identified David as a prophet at Acts 2:30, and for him there would be no reason why the messianic Prophet should not be 'like' Moses and 'like' David simultaneously.

[50] For the legitimacy of this term see n.32 above, and compare L. Goppelt, *Apostolic and Post-Apostolic Times* (Black, 1970), p.18.

[51] *Cf.* especially in Ezekiel's 'The Exodus' (Eusebius, *Praep. Ev.*, 9:29) and see W. Meeks, *op. cit.*, pp. 147f.

[52] The arguments in this section are presented in much greater detail in M. M. B. Turner, as at n.29.

[53] See M. M. B. Turner, as at n.29, chs. 4 and 5.

179

revelation to a man, communicating to him God's word, or direction, or wisdom (either directly, or in a dream, or vision) – would not be confined to the prophets and leaders of Israel: it would be given to all. The twin aspects of Joel's promise, that it refers to the Spirit acting as the organ of communication between God and men, and that the scope of the promise is universal (for the people of God), are clearly to be perceived in his wording and formed the basis of widespread hope in Judaism.[54] Peter's words could not have been understood except as a declaration of the fulfilment of these hopes, and when he goes on (Acts 2:38f.) to say that this *epangelia* (*cf.* Lk. 24:49; Acts 2:33) is offered 'to you . . . and to your children (*cf.* 2:17c) and to all (*cf.* 2:17b) who are afar off, whoever calls on the name of the Lord', *etc.* (*cf.* Joel 3:5b), he clearly draws on the words of Joel's prophecy both for the basis of the universality spoken of, and consequently, for the nature of the promised gift.[55]

But what can it mean to say that Jesus, being exalted on high, has 'received' this gift from the Father? The language is undoubtedly metaphorical (as are all references to 'giving' and 'receiving' the Spirit)[56] but, as usual with such language, there is a real referent. The phrase 'to receive (the gift of) the Holy Spirit' denotes the beginning in a man's life or activity of some new nexus of functions of the Spirit: that is, the inception of a new set of activities of the Spirit in or through a man's life is 'pictured' by this metaphorical language as a 'gift' 'given' to the individual, and 'received' by him.[57] In Acts 2:33, the new nexus of activities related to Jesus are those described by Joel. Peter, of course, is *not* saying that Jesus has 'received' Joel's promise as the means of communication between the Father and himself. Rather, he is affirming that with the ascension Jesus has 'received' Joel's promise of the Spirit in the sense that he now has the *power to administer the operation of the Spirit as the Spirit of prophecy.*

Jesus, then, has received the Spirit in the heavenly places in the sense that he now has lordship over the gift of the Spirit given to the church. The Spirit of prophecy, promised through Joel, has become the Spirit of Jesus (Acts 16:7) and, as a consequence, he is now able to distribute its individual and varied charismata (2:33). Through this means he will direct and empower the church's mission to outsiders (*e.g.,* Acts 2:4, 33; 4:8, 31; 8:29; 10:11–21; 11:12; 13:2, 4, 9; 16:6f.; *etc.*), and he will give charismatic wisdom and revelation where it is needed either for the defence and propagation of the gospel (*cf.* Acts 6:3, 5, 10 and Lk. 21:25) or for the direction, sanctification and

---

[54] See M. M. B. Turner, as at n.29, pp.66f., 130f., 219-223.
[55] See M. M. B. Turner, as at nn.53 and 54 (especially pp.130-134); also 'The Spirit at Pentecost in Lucan Perspective' (forthcoming).
[56] See M. M. B. Turner, 'Spirit-Endowment in Luke-Acts: Some Linguistic Considerations', *Vox Evangelica* 12, 1981, pp.55-60.   [57] *Ibid.*

upbuilding of the church (*cf.* Acts 5:1–11; 9:10ff., 31; 11:28; 13:52; 15:28; *etc.*). This gift is no *donum superadditum:* it is the link between Jesus in heaven and his disciples on earth; it is the means by which Jesus continues to announce his message of messianic release (*cf.* Lk. 4:18f.); it is the very life of the church.[58]

Clearly Peter's affirmation of Jesus' ascension, and of his reception of the Spirit in the heavenly places, implies a considerable degree of exaltation. It provides a bridge between his claim (based on Ps. 16) concerning Jesus' resurrection and his subsequent asseveration of Jesus' reign at God's right hand (*cf.* Ps. 110:1 in Acts 2:35). Indeed, as far as the writer of Acts is concerned, Jesus' reception of the Spirit in the sense outlined explains the *means* of his heavenly reign.[59] We are now in a position to examine in more detail the Christological implications of Peter's affirmation.

The Christological implications of Jesus' reception of the Spirit at his exaltation
It is questionable whether the author of the declaration in Acts 2:33 can be regarded as remaining within purely messianic categories in his description of Jesus. What he says significantly transcends all that messianic Judaism was prepared to state with respect to the relationship between the Messiah and the Spirit.[60] The Old Testament and pre-Christian Judaism are perfectly acquainted with a messianic figure who will receive divine revelation and wisdom through the Spirit, and similarly a Messiah empowered by the Spirit would be familiar to them (*cf.* Is. 11:1f.; 1QSb 5:25; 11Q Melchizedek; Ps. Sol. 17:37; 18:7; Targum Isa. 11:2; 42:1–4; 1 Enoch 49:3; 66:2; *etc.*).[61] Such a relationship to the Spirit merely represents an extrapolation from previous experiences of the Spirit of God working through the prophet, the wise judge and the powerful monarch: in the Messiah of Jewish expectation the traditional modes of activity of God's Spirit with an individual will attain their ideal. But Peter speaks of something entirely unparalleled: a Messiah who *directs* the activity of the Spirit in such a way that he can be described as *giving* the Spirit and as the *author* of specific charismata amongst the people of God *by* the Spirit (as when the apostle says Jesus has 'poured out this which you both see and hear': 2:33).

The nearest parallels in Judaism only betray the distance between the Jewish

[58] The substance of the last paragraph is a quotation from my article in *TB* 32, 1981, p.39. It is defended in my thesis (as at n.29, chs. 4 and 5) in detail. I am grateful to the editor of *TB*, Dr R. T. France, for permission to re-use the material.

[59] For an exploration of this perspective see the essay by G. Stählin in *Christ and Spirit in the New Testament*, as at n.34, pp.229-252; *cf.* also M. M. B. Turner, as at n.29, ch.4.

[60] For the Spirit and the Messiah in Judaism see the brief account in *TDNT* 6, pp.383-386, or, more fully, M.-A. Chevallier, *Souffle de Dieu* (Beauchesne, 1978), pp.21-76. The only detailed account of the relationships is that of R. Penna, *Lo Spirito di Christo* (Paideia, Brescia, 1976), pp.25-156.   [61] See R. Penna, *op. cit.*, for a full discussion.

conceptions and this one. J. D. G. Dunn has tentatively argued for the view that at Qumran there was already a relatively close parallel to the Christian claim in that the Messiah was regarded as a bearer of the Spirit, and would bestow God's Spirit in virtue of his own anointing.[62] But this reconstruction seems entirely conjectural. The case rests mainly on the observation that 1Q Isa. 52:15 ('he shall sprinkle (*yzh*) many nations because of himself') uses the same verb as 1QS 4:21, where the medium with which God sprinkles men, thereby cleansing them, is the Spirit. Dunn goes on to suggest that while CD 2:12 (God 'made known to them [the remnant] by the hand of his anointed ones his holy spirit . . .') refers primarily to the Old Testament prophets; 'yet if this is the correct translation, it would seem to confirm that the idea of the Holy Spirit being somehow passed on by messiah(s) was not far off.'[63] But, in the first place, there is no indication that the use of *yazah* in 1Q Isa. 52 envisages a purifying sprinkling of the *Spirit* performed *by* the Messiah: the verb 'to sprinkle' is used here as a metaphor to denote the act of cleansing salvation performed by him, without any indication of *how* that act would be performed – whether through the purging influence of the revelation given to and through him, or by virtue of his righteous rule conducted under the influence of the Holy Spirit (*cf.* Is. 11:1–9; 42:1–7), or, perhaps, by his atoning suffering (*cf.* Is. 53), or whatever. 1Q Isa. 52:15 is not to be conflated, without further ado, with 1QS 4:21 where God is the author of a cleansing act (hence the metaphor *yzh* again) performed by the Spirit of Truth. No doubt this latter act might include the work of a Spirit-anointed Messiah, but there is no reason to read into the texts a *giving* of the Spirit *by* the Messiah. Secondly, while CD 2:12 probably claims that throughout Israel's history the faithful have been able to hear the Spirit in the voice of the prophets,[64] it is precisely the Spirit with and in the anointed figure(s) that is 'made known' – an endowment of the faithful *by* such anointed figures is nowhere in view. Even the exalted being depicted in 11Q Melchizedek does not totally transcend this relationship to the Spirit. A single reference in the Testament of Judah 24:3 ('He [the Messiah] will pour out the Spirit of Grace upon you') speaks of a bestowal of the Spirit by the Messiah, but it is hard to escape de Jonge's conclusion that this is part of an extensive network of Christian interpolations into, and redaction of, that work.[65] There are therefore no known pre-Christian references to the Messiah

---

[62] J. D. G. Dunn, 'Spirit-and-Fire Baptism', *NovT* 14, 1972, pp.89-91: following Brownlee, but with less confidence.   [63] *Ibid.*, pp.90f.

[64] See T. M. Crone, *Early Christian Prophecy* (St Mary's University, Baltimore, 1973), pp.100, 325: *cf. TDNT* 9, p.517 n.134.

[65] M. de Jonge, *The Testaments of the Twelve Patriarchs* (Van Gorcum, 1953), pp.80-90; also *NovT* 4, 1960, pp.199-218.

bestowing the Spirit: even John the Baptist's promise gives no hint of such, but speaks, rather, of the inauguration of judgment and redemption by the Messiah under the image of an overwhelming deluge of Spirit-and-fire (Lk. 3:16f. and parallels).[66]

Pre-Christian Judaism speaks of a Messiah-of-the-Spirit, not of the Spirit of Christ,[67] and it is at this point that the vital distinction must be made. The closest analogy in the Old Testament and Judaism to Jesus' relationship to the Spirit (as specified by Peter at Pentecost) is not that of men anointed with God's Spirit, but the Old Testament picture of God's relationship to the Spirit. Just as God is envisaged there as encompassing the activity of particular men with his own *ruaḥ*, and so making them his instruments, revealing his will to them, and empowering them for specific tasks, so now Jesus begins to do the same in the lives of his disciples on the day of Pentecost.[68] As the Spirit had mediated God's activity, and thus his presence, amongst his people, so, according to the perspective of Acts 2:33, the Spirit has now become the means of Jesus' presence and activity too.

Once this claim is made, it is hard to see how those who affirmed it could avoid a divine Christology. If their pneumatology still remained within pre-Christian Jewish lines they would regard the Spirit not as a second divine person but as a way of speaking of God himself;[69] his own vitality, self-expression, and the extension of his personality[70] — as a man's 'spirit' is his own 'life' and vitality.[71] To speak of Jesus directing God's Spirit (understood in this sense) would surely be tantamount to calling him God (*cf.* the gently mocking enquiry of Is. 40:13). The same, I think, applies if Acts 2:33 be read in the context of a Christian understanding of the Spirit as a divine person: could Jesus be less than God if he is Lord of the Spirit? Either way, once Christians ever begin to speak of the Spirit mediating the activity and presence of Jesus, they

---

[66] On this see M. M. B. Turner, as at n.56, section 4 and the literature cited there.

[67] So R. Penna, *op. cit., passim.*

[68] This is also how the author of Acts understood the reference. Against those who, with H. Conzelmann, speak of Luke's absentee Christology see M. M. B. Turner, as at n.29, pp.128-147.

[69] The touchiness manifest in Judaism in the face of any suggestion of there being 'two powers in heaven' all but rules out the possibility that (*e.g.*) rabbinic personification of the Spirit should be understood as anything more than literary licence in describing Yahweh's immanence: *cf.* A. F. Segal, *Two Powers in Heaven* (Brill, 1977), and M. M. B. Turner, as at n.29, pp.197f. (nn.77f.).

[70] See, *inter alios*, A. R. Johnson, *The Vitality of the Individual in Ancient Israel* (University of Wales, 1964), pp.26-39; *idem, The One and the Many in the Israelite Conception of God* (University of Wales, 1961), pp.15ff.; G. W. H. Lampe, *God as Spirit* (Clarendon, 1977), chs. 2 and 8.

[71] *TDNT* 6, pp.360-362, *etc.*

would be drawn irresistibly towards a divine Christology. The Acts account of the Pentecost speech suggests that this move had already been taken by Peter. If, for him, Jesus' functions have become so aligned with Yahweh's that both can be said to pour out the Spirit (*cf.* 2:17, 33) then there is nothing to prevent the Christological application of the Joel citation being carried through at every point. Jesus can barely be other than the one denoted by Joel's expression *to onoma kyriou* ('the name of the Lord': *i.e.* the Lord himself) upon whom all men are to call for salvation (compare 2:36, 38f. with 2:21, 33); so he is to be acknowledged as 'Lord', and that in its transcendent sense.[72] If we have understood the Pentecost speech correctly, it is far from being a piece of opportunistic preaching seizing on Joel as a proof-text; it represents a careful exposition of the Christological implications of saying that the exalted Jesus has 'received' and 'poured out' the gift of the Spirit of prophecy.

Peter's speech and early Christianity

The 'Pentecost speech' in Acts 2:14–39 gives the impression that the primitive church had already taken the step of proclaiming a divine Christology. If Jesus were understood at an early stage to be Lord of the Spirit, as Acts implies, then we do not need to wait until the second half of the first century for the expression of a firm basis for incarnational theology.[73] But will Luke's evidence stand the light of scrutiny? We certainly cannot provide a historical proof that the words derive from Peter on the day of Pentecost, but I would suggest that there are a number of indications that the burden of proof should fall on the shoulders of those who dispute the early Jewish-Christian origin of the substance of the speech.[74]

Firstly, there are general considerations which support the historicity of

---

[72] J. C. O'Neill wrote of the Pentecost sermon that 'Jesus was preached as the Lord whom the Jews worshipped', *SJT* 8, 1955, p. 162. More recently he has denied that such a view could have been held by the earliest Aramaic-speaking community, on the ground that they could not have failed to distinguish the two 'lords' in Ps. 110:1: the first was *Yahweh,* the second *'ᵃdōnay: The Theology of Acts in its Historical Setting* (SPCK, ²1961), p. 131. What O'Neill says is of course true for any attempt to derive Christology from Ps. 110:1; but it is not clear that *'ᵃdōnay need* necessarily mean less than Yahweh, and if the earliest community had other reasons for using God-talk of Jesus, as we have suggested to be the case, it would have read the two titles as equivalents.

[73] The possibility that the 'Lordship' of Jesus over the Spirit might have been considered by the church as a revelation of his divine nature seems generally to have been ignored by those seeking the origins of NT Christology. For Dunn's more nuanced sidestepping of this possibility see below.

[74] The purport of the essay by S. C. Goetz and C. L. Blomberg (as at n. 13) should be borne in mind in attempting to assess where the burden of proof lies.

Luke's speech material. The relationship between tradition and redaction in the speeches is fiercely difficult to solve, but neither extensive verbatim use of written sources[75] nor yet creation *ex nihilo* can be demonstrated. E. Plümacher undoubtedly takes the sceptical view of M. Dibelius, U. Wilckens and E. Haenchen too far when he attempts to argue that all the 'traditional' material in the speeches is essentially hellenistic mimesis, and that all alleged semiticisms are really created septuagintalisms.[76] The form of the argument within the speeches is too realistically 'Jewish' especially where it depends on *pesher* interpretation and other midrashic techniques.[77] We should be wise to assume that Luke did indeed attempt to follow the example of such historians as Thucydides and Polybius (though not in the sense Dibelius imagines),[78] and that it involved him in a search for traditions which was at least in part successful.[79] Luke's handling of the words of Jesus in Mark and Q suggests that he tried to keep substantially to the meaning of the speakers he reports, and offers little comfort to those who search for evidence of a propensity to extensive free creation.[80]

Secondly, there are considerations which pertain specifically to the Pentecost speech. The brevity of the speech, the very concise nature of its argument, and

[75] So J. Dupont, *The Sources of Acts* (Darton, Longman and Todd, 1964), *passim.*

[76] E. Plümacher, *Lukas als hellenistischer Schriftsteller* (Vandenhoeck & Ruprecht, 1972), pp.38-77.

[77] Plümacher unfortunately does not discuss the important works by J. W. Bowker (*NTS* 14, 1967/68, pp.96-110); J. Doeve, *Jewish Hermeneutics in the Synoptic Gospels and Acts* (Van Gorcum, 1954); J. Dupont (as at n.43, pp.245-390); E. E. Ellis ('Midrashic Features in the Speeches of Acts' in *Mélanges Bibliques*, ed. A. Descamps and A. de Halleux (Ducolot, 1970), pp.303-312, and finally, B. Lindars (as at n.34, ch. 2 *etc.*). For a well-balanced introduction see M. Wilcox in *Christianity, Judaism and Other Greco-Roman Cults, Part 1*, ed. J. Neusner (Brill, 1975), pp.207-225.

[78] M. Dibelius, *Studies in the Acts of the Apostles* (SCM, 1956), ch. 9, interprets Thucydides to mean that the author freely composed his speeches: but Thucydides actually insists that even when he was not able to be present at the giving of a speech what he wrote adhered 'as closely as possible to the general sense of what was actually spoken' (*Peloponnesian War* 1, 22). *Cf.* T. F. Glasson, 'The Speeches of Acts and Thucydides', *ExpT* 76, 1965, p.165; W. W. Gasque, *A History of the Criticism of the Acts of the Apostles* (Mohr, Tübingen, 1975), pp.225ff. For the debate on Luke as a historian see the long bibliographical note in M. M. B. Turner, as at n.43, n.2, to which add M. Hengel, *Acts and the History of Earliest Christianity* (SCM, 1979), pp.1-68.

[79] *Cf.* J. Jervell, *Luke and the People of God* (Augsburg, 1972), pp.19-39; F. F. Bruce, 'The Speeches in Acts – Thirty Years After' in *Reconciliation and Hope*, ed. R. J. Banks (Paternoster, 1974), pp.53-68.

[80] Commenting on Lk. 21 as an example of Luke's use of sources, F. C. Burkitt (*BC* 2, p.115) remarked 'What concerns us here is not that Luke has changed so much, but that he has invented so little'. The comment is as apt today, in the redaction-critical era, as it was then before it: *cf.* M. M. B. Turner, as at n.78.

its lack of polished style, tell against the view that it is a free composition,[81] as does its Jewish-Christian character. This 'sermon' makes considerable use of Jewish exegetical devices: for example, *gezerah shawah* formally unites Psalm 16 and Psalm 110:1 on the basis of the common phrase 'at my right hand', and all three Old Testament quotations in the speech are (in differing degrees) 'peshered'.[82] In addition, the reference to David as a prophet (2:30),[83] the particular form of the allusion to Psalm 68:19 in connection with Jesus' ascension and reception of the Spirit, the implicit (rather than explicit) Moses Christology, and the emphasis on the Spirit as the Spirit of prophecy of Jewish expectation,[84] all point away from the view that the speech was a late and free composition by a Gentile.[85] Nor need we believe that with the passing years no-one would be able to remember the essential thrust of such a sermon, for the content of a like speech would have been of such crucial apologetic and kerygmatic significance within the Jewish-Christian mission to the Jews that its memorable argument would probably quite frequently have been rehearsed.

Thirdly, I wish to point to some evidence outside Luke-Acts; not, of course, in support of the authenticity of the *form* of the argument in the speech, but at least to sketch the sort of evidence that might establish the early provenance of the *kind of conclusions* which Peter is alleged to have reached. The evidence to

---

[81] Contrast the rhetorical and literary grace evinced by Josephus in even his briefest created speeches: *e.g. Ant.* I, 228-231.

[82] *Cf.* R. N. Longenecker, *The Expositor's Bible Commentary* 9 (Zondervan, 1981), pp.274-281; *idem, Biblical Exegesis in the Apostolic Period* (Eerdmans, 1975), pp.96-103 and *passim*; M. Rese, as at n.26.

[83] See J. A. Fitzmyer, *CBQ* 34, 1972, pp.332-339.

[84] Against the many who have followed H. Leisengang's view that the Spirit of prophecy in Acts belongs to the world of Greek 'enthusiasm' see M. M. B. Turner, as at n.29, pp.5-7; 189f. and chs. 4 and 5.

[85] Haenchen (commentary, *ad loc.*) considers the use of the LXX for the OT citations to be evidence of Luke's creation of the speech; but it is almost inevitable that in translating speeches from Aramaic that involved OT citations Luke would refer to, and use, the LXX: *cf.* Rese, as at n.26. R. H. Zehnle (as at n.30, pp.26-36; 61-70; 95-130) denies the traditional origin of the Pentecost speech mainly on the ground that it is too similar to what Luke says elsewhere, and replete with redactional interests. Zehnle has an unfortunate tendency to assume that Luke created everything that conforms with his theological perspectives; and to infer sources only where material in Acts allegedly runs counter to Luke's concerns. But the more one stresses Luke's creativity, the harder it is to believe he included much with which he *disagreed* – and surely he must have found *some* sources with which he agreed entirely, and which expressed his interests! The baptismal narrative in Lk. 3:21f., for example, should provide a warning against the sort of simplistic approach adopted by Zehnle: it is full of redactional language and of theological motifs of great importance to Luke, but Luke, nevertheless, certainly depends on traditional material for its content.

which I allude is the almost universal understanding, witnessed in the New Testament, that the Spirit is the Spirit *of Christ*.

Admittedly New Testament genitives are notoriously ambiguous, and recently G. W. H. Lampe has defended the thesis that the only way we can meaningfully speak of the action of the 'Spirit of Christ' is to take this language as a way of saying that God as Spirit acts in Christians in the manner in which he acted supremely in Christ: creating sonship.[86] For Lampe, Jesus *himself* cannot be considered to be at work *through* the Spirit, for that implies a literal resurrection of Jesus and the acceptance of the whole cosmology and soteriology with which 'resurrection' belongs. But at just this point he (wittingly) departs from the outlook of the New Testament writers. While undoubtedly its authors regarded the Spirit as fashioning Christ-likeness in men – and nowhere is that more clearly said than in 2 Corinthians 3:18 – nevertheless for the most part they go beyond that affirmation to assert that the risen Lord himself plays an active role in this transforming process, through the Spirit.[87]

The exposition of this theme of Jesus' sharing with the Father in the work of the Spirit in disciples finds its most luminous expression in the Paraclete discourses of the Fourth Gospel which announce the coming of the Son and the Father to live in the disciple (14:23), and to direct him in the truth (16:13), through the gift of the Spirit given jointly by the Father and the Son (14:26; 15:26; 16:7).[88] A similar phenomenon is to be discerned behind parts of the vivid symbolism of the Apocalypse: Jesus has 'the seven spirits of God sent out into all the earth' (5:6)[89] and he gives his word (*e.g.*, 2:1) to the churches through the Spirit of prophecy (*e.g.*, 2:7a; *cf.* 19:10).[90] Paul speaks in like vein. While he does not identify Jesus and the Spirit ontologically (as Deissmann supposed), he tends to do so functionally – to the point where N. Q. Hamilton can aptly sum up much of Paul's pneumatology: 'The Spirit so effectively performs His office of communicating to men the benefits of the risen Christ that for all intents and purposes of faith the Lord Himself is present bestowing grace on His own. The Spirit portrays the Lord so well that we lose sight of the

---

[86] G. W. H. Lampe, as at n.70, *passim*.

[87] Appeal is often made to 2 Cor. 3:17-18b to justify this latter assertion. But such appeal is exegetically disallowed by J. D. G. Dunn, *JTS* 21, 1968, pp. 309-320; C. F. D. Moule on 2 Cor. 3:18b in *Neues Testament und Geschichte*, ed. H. Baltensweiler and B. Reicke (Mohr, Tübingen, 1972), pp.231ff.

[88] For details see M. M. B. Turner, *Vox Evangelica* 10, 1977, pp.26-28 and the literature cited.

[89] See the commentaries by Beckwith and Beasley-Murray; also F. F. Bruce, 'The Spirit in the Apocalypse' in *Christ and Spirit in the New Testament* (as at n.34), pp.333-336.

[90] F. F. Bruce, *op. cit.*, pp.340-342 and 337-340.

Spirit and are conscious of the Lord only'.[91] The way that the apostle writes suggests that Paul expected his congregations to understand the Spirit as an ambassador acting on behalf of both God and Christ, and thus as the power of Christ exercising his lordship in the church.[92] The fact that this is not something Paul feels he has to explain is telling evidence that the idea had a wide currency in the earliest period.

What is more, the way the Spirit is depicted as related to the risen Christ, throughout the New Testament documents, suggests that such phrases as 'the Spirit of Jesus' (Acts 16:7), 'the Spirit of Jesus Christ' (Phil. 1:19), 'the Spirit of Christ' (Rom. 8:9) and 'the Spirit of his Son' (Gal. 4:6) arose by analogy with the expressions 'the Spirit of God' and 'the Spirit of the Lord', and were used to express the belief that the Spirit acted on behalf of God and of Christ, and under the sovereignty of both. In other words, the evidence outside Acts would appear to confirm that Jesus was acknowledged as 'Lord of the Spirit' (in some sense) very soon after the resurrection-exaltation.

The objection may be raised, against this view, that the earlier material – Paul's – requires a more nuanced treatment. Thus according to Dunn, Paul never states that Jesus gives the Spirit (only God is said so to do), and so he would not describe Jesus as 'Lord of the Spirit'.[93] For Paul, such expressions as 'the Spirit of Christ' would denote not Jesus' sovereignty over the Spirit but the stamping of the character of the earthly Jesus and the risen Christ on the Spirit and his activity.[94] But it is questionable whether the objection can be sustained. The argument that Jesus cannot be called 'Lord of the Spirit' because he is not said to *give* the Spirit is quite unconvincing. The language of the giving of the Spirit is a metaphor to denote the beginning of a specific new nexus of *activities* of the Spirit in a man, and Paul clearly regards Jesus as the co-author (with

[91] N. Q. Hamilton, *The Holy Spirit and Eschatology in Paul* (Oliver and Boyd, 1957), p.6. He uses these words to describe what he envisages to be Paul's meaning in 2 Cor. 3:17f. – a view we have suggested to be exegetically ill-founded (*cf.* n.87 above) – but the description is valid of Paul's pneumatology more generally, provided that not Christ alone, but God *and* Christ are spoken of as mediated by the Spirit. J. D. G. Dunn relies as heavily on 1 Cor. 15:45 to support his claim concerning the functional identity of Christ and the Spirit as others do on 2 Cor. 3:17f.; but against his understanding of the former passage see M. M. B. Turner, *Vox Evangelica* 9, 1975, pp.61-63.

[92] So C. H. Pinnock, *The Concept of the Spirit in the Epistles of Paul* (doctoral thesis, Manchester, 1963); I. Hermann, *Kyrios und Pneuma* (Kösel, 1961); M. M. B. Turner, 'The Significance of Spirit-Endowment for Paul', *Vox Evangelica* 9, 1975, pp.56-69. J. D. G. Dunn, *JTS* 24, 1973, p.59, can describe the Spirit in Paul's thought as 'the executive power of the exalted Christ'.

[93] J. D. G. Dunn, as at n.3, pp.143-147. This represents a sharpening of his thought and a distinction not always made in his earlier writing.

[94] J. D. G. Dunn, as at n.3, pp.144-146; *idem,* as at n.92, pp.40-68.

God) of charismata operating in the church *through* the Spirit (1 Cor. 12:5; Eph. 4:8–10; *etc.*).[95] In that case 'Lord of the Spirit' remains an appropriate description (however much it needs qualifying in order to give a complete account of Paul's thought),[96] and the phrase 'the Spirit of Christ' still holds its implications of divine Christology (whatever deeper resonances it *may* have had, for Paul, with the life of Jesus in the Spirit).[97]

In the light of this discussion, we have no reason seriously to doubt Luke's evidence that the risen and exalted Jesus was proclaimed from the beginning of the Christian mission as the one who had 'received' and 'poured out' the gift of the Spirit. The length of this paper does not permit us to enquire in detail as to what convinced the church that indeed not only the Father but Jesus too was involved in the dispensing of the Spirit and the administration of the charismata. The conviction probably had many roots. It would draw on the growing realization that the character of the Spirit's activity was deeply stamped with the Christ-event, and that Jesus' supra-individual life, death and resurrection were being conveyed to his disciples, and impressed on them, by the Spirit.[98] The conviction would also be fed by the Christocentric character of the charismata imparted by the Spirit.[99] But it would be based particularly in the belief that Jesus himself had spoken of his future role in relationship to the Spirit;[100] in the feeling that Jesus was continuing his proclamation in the preaching of the church empowered by the Spirit;[101] in a widespread sense of the presence of the risen Lord in and through the Spirit – the impression that he was 'with' them (*cf.* Acts 18:10),[102] and, perhaps most important, in that the charismata of the Spirit were so often experienced by the early church as a direct

---

[95] As Dunn, as at n.3, p.145 admits. *Cf.* his description as at n.92.

[96] Both in Paul and in John the Lordship of Jesus over the Spirit is under the overarching sovereignty of God (*cf.* Jn. 14:16, 26).

[97] See the important article by Dunn, as at n.92, pp.40-68: the position seems, nevertheless, to be an overstatement. In any case, such views as Dunn atrributes to Paul here can in no way be traced back behind him to the church at large, and thus serve to explain the expression 'the Spirit of Christ'.

[98] For substantiation of this description see C. F. D. Moule, as at n.3, ch.2, and Dunn's works, especially *Jesus and the Spirit,* as at n.6, part 3.

[99] *Cf.* J. D. G. Dunn, as at n.6, chs. 8, 10; M. Hengel in *Studia Biblica 1978: Part 3,* ed. E. A. Livingstone (*JSNT,* 1980), pp.173-197.

[100] John 14 – 16; *cf.* Lk. 21:15. This material is usually consigned to the limbo of 'inauthentic' sayings – but the reasons adduced why Jesus cannot have spoken this way are not convincing, and in any case the traditions embodied in John 14 – 16, with their implicit divine Christology, had a long history of use before finally being written up in the Fourth Gospel: see the commentaries, especially that by R. E. Brown.

[101] *Cf.* M. M. B. Turner, as at n.29, pp.128-147.

[102] *Ibid.*

word or vision of the risen Lord addressing them (from Acts [7:55; 9:3–6, 9–16 and *passim*] through to the Apocalypse [1:1 and *passim*]).[103] My purpose in this paper has simply been to ask what explains the widespread worship of Jesus, and to enquire how early it can be traced. And the answer which emerges is that such reverence for Jesus can be found as early as Christians experienced the risen Lord through the Spirit, and as soon as they were prepared to speak of the Spirit as the Spirit of Christ. And that appears to date from the beginnings of the church after the resurrection-ascension.

Conclusion

Jesus may not have announced himself as God the Son – certainly he did not do so unambiguously, though it is not unreasonable to hold that he said things which implied that status. But we need not accept the theory that a divine Christology only very gradually evolved in the New Testament period. Jesus was worshipped from the earliest days of the post-resurrection church, and we are in a position to offer a rationale for that worship. The church's experience of the Spirit revealed Jesus as the one who through resurrection-exaltation had 'received' the gift of the Spirit promised by Joel and now had the power to dispense its charismata. In them the church was confronted with a Jesus who was Lord of the Spirit: the Spirit of God had become the Spirit of Jesus too, and that would most probably have been understood as a revelation of Jesus' divine nature, and fitting grounds for worshipping him.

---

[103] *Ibid.*, and, once again, Dunn, as at n.6, ch. 8.

'ONE LORD'
IN PAULINE CHRISTOLOGY

D.R. de Lacey

'Jesus is Lord' is a fundamental Christian affirmation;[1] so it is perhaps not immediately striking that at an early stage Christians should acknowledge him to be their *only* Lord.[2] Yet behind the attribution to Jesus of the title 'one Lord' there may well lie a significant Christological development. It is the purpose of this essay to investigate this possibility.

Kyrios ('Lord') in the Septuagint

In our Greek Old Testament, the Septuagint (LXX), the ineffable name of God is represented by *Kyrios*;[3] but it may not always have been so. Kahle[4] has argued that in LXX texts written by Jews and for Jews the name of God was left untranslated[5] or written as *Pipi*.[6] Only under later, Christian, influence was the

---

[1] See especially Rom. 10:9; 2 Cor. 4:5; Acts 2:36. Possibly 1 Cor. 12:3 and Col. 2:6 also witness to 'an established confessional formula': C. E. B. Cranfield, *Romans (ICC)* 2 (T. & T. Clark, 1979), p.527.

[2] The earliest evidence is probably 1 Cor. 8:6, on which see below. See also Eph. 4:5. The phrase eventually found its way into the (Eastern) creeds: see J. N. D. Kelly, *Early Christian Creeds* (Longman, ³1971), pp.182ff. Note also the 'one Christ' of 1 Clement 46:5. This attitude also lies behind the consistent refusal of Christians to acknowledge Caesar as Lord.

[3] This is something of an oversimplification. The compound name *YHWH elohim* ('LORD God') is sometimes represented by *theos* ('God') alone; and in a handful of cases we find either an alternative translation (*despotēs*, 'master', Pr. 29:25); a periphrasis (*hagios Israēl*, 'the holy one of Israel', in Je. 3:16; *eusebia*, 'piety', for 'the fear of the LORD' in Is. 11:2) or a sheer mistake (Jdg. 1:22(A); 3:1(A); 1 Kgdms. 1:21; 2 Kgdms. 1:12; 3 Kgdms. 17:20). There are also several places where no name stands at all in the translation: on this see below at n.12.

[4] P. E. Kahle, *The Cairo Geniza* (OUP [for the British Academy], ²1959), pp.224ff. *Cf.* also B. J. Roberts, *The Old Testament Text and Versions* (University of Wales, 1951), pp.173f.

[5] And written either in archaic Hebrew script or in the Aramaic script which was current in the first century.

[6] Which in Greek letters resembles the Aramaic form.

word *kyrios* introduced. The evidence is as follows.

1. Manuscript evidence. Very few early manuscripts of the LXX survive. Of those two which are manifestly pre-Christian and contain the divine name, one (pFouad 266, of the second or first century BC) has the name added, in Aramaic letters and by another hand, in spaces left by the original scribe. The other, a Qumran fragment, uses the Greek letters IAŌ. An Oxyrhynchus papyrus of the third century AD has the letters ƵƵ, representing the Hebrew letters *yy,* which was a common abbreviation of the divine name. Some other manuscripts leave blanks.[7]

2. Other translations. In his Hexapla, Origen brought together several Greek translations of the Old Testament, and from surviving fragments it appears that all of these apart from the LXX used Hebrew or Aramaic characters to represent the name of God. In his own transliteration of the Hebrew text Origen also used the Aramaic letters.[8]

3. The church Fathers. Jerome states that in his day some Greek manuscripts of the Old Testament contained the divine name in archaic[9] characters, and elsewhere he comments that some people, not realizing this, read them as *Pipi.*[10] Origen also comments on 'the most accurate copies' containing the divine name in Hebrew characters, 'not the current ones, but the most archaic characters'.[11] He adds that the name was pronounced *adonai* by Jews and *kyrios* by Greeks. He does not mention the use of the pseudo-name *Pipi,* but it later occurred in Syriac versions of the Hexapla, even though the Syriac letters look nothing like the Hebrew or Aramaic. It is, however, not perfectly clear whether these comments of Jerome and Origen refer to the LXX or to the more accurate (*i.e.* literalistic) translations of Aquila and others.

4. The text of the LXX. In some places in the LXX no divine name stands at all, even where this leaves an awkward gap in the sense.[12] One obvious explanation of this phenomenon is that early in the textual tradition spaces

---

[7] Details in B. J. Roberts, *loc. cit.*; P. E. Kahle, *loc. cit.,* and H. B. Swete, *An Introduction to the Old Testament in Greek* (CUP, 1902), pp.39f.

[8] B. J. Roberts, *loc. cit.*

[9] By 'antiquis litteris' he appears to mean not the archaic Hebrew letters but the Aramaic, since he says elsewhere (see n. 10) that some people pronounced the name *Pipi,* which can only be a misunderstanding of the Aramaic forms.

[10] *Prologus Galeatus* (*MPL* 28, 594f.) and *Epistula 25 ad Marcellam* (*CSEL* 54, 219); both texts and translations conveniently in E. Würthwein, *The Text of the Old Testament* (SCM, 1980), p.178.

[11] *Comm. in Psalm 2:2* (*MPG* 12, 1104f.).

[12] See L. C. Allen, *The Greek Chronicles, Part Two* (supp. to *VT,* vol. 27, Brill, 1974), pp.58f. for details.

were originally left for another scribe to insert the Hebrew or Aramaic characters (as in pFouad 266), and that the second scribe overlooked some of these.[13]

The evidence, however, is not quite adequate to support Kahle's full thesis. A satisfactory explanation of the phenomena must also account for the following facts.

1. Despite Origen's statement about the 'most accurate copies' containing the divine name in Hebrew script, and his preserving this for his other columns of the Hexapla, the fact that in his LXX he used *Kyrios* must indicate that he felt strong reasons for making this exception.

2. As Kahle is obliged to acknowledge, no single tradition emerges from the evidence summarized above. The use of Hebrew script, Aramaic script, and various Greek equivalents (*Pipi, Iaō* and the like) witnesses to a wide variety of practice.

3. Whatever was written, it is evident that the normal practice in reading was to use the word *Kyrios*. This is evidenced by Origen,[14] by some manuscript evidence[15] and by citations by Jewish writers.[16]

4. In the Hebrew tradition, there was already a move towards replacing the ineffable name, at least in speech, with a periphrasis, and for the reading of

---

[13] So L. C. Allen, *ibid.* The statement by Roberts that Fischer has arguments against the Tetragrammaton being originally written in Hebrew letters in the LXX (*op. cit.*, p. 174) rests on a misunderstanding of Fischer's work.

[14] The evidence of Origen is somewhat unclear, but justifies the claim made in the text. Origen states that when they read the Tetragrammaton, the 'Hellenes' pronounce it *'kyrios'* and the 'Hebrews' pronounce it *'Adōnai'* (*loc. cit.*). But it is not clear what the distinction is between these two groups. There seem to be two possibilities. If the 'Hellenes' are Greek-speaking Jews, and the 'Hebrews' are Palestinian, or Hebrew-speaking, Jews, then presumably the latter read the Hebrew, and not the Greek, Scriptures. If the 'Hellenes' are Gentiles, in contrast to the 'Hebrew' Jews, then it is rather surprising that they should be reading Scripture at all, and remarkable that they should have known what to say when they met these unfamiliar letters, unless there was already a tradition of reading them as *'kyrios'* in the context of the LXX. Either way, it seems reasonable to suppose that *'kyrios'* was the normal means of representing whatever it was that was written in the LXX for the Tetragrammaton.

[15] For instance, in one place in the Aquila fragments, where there was not enough room for the four Hebrew characters, the copyist inserted the *Greek* abbreviation *k̄ȳ* (H. B. Swete, *Introduction,* p. 39 n. 4).

[16] Of the writings which remain, not many contain explicit citations of the Old Testament (barring the New Testament, whose evidence is also relevant and witnesses to the use of *kyrios*). Philo is the only author with any significant number of citations: on him, see later in the text. But no citation known to me shows any evidence of an alternative to *kyrios* for whatever stood in the LXX.

Scripture this periphrasis was universally *Adonai* ('Lord'),[17] which is most naturally translated *kyrios*.

It is therefore unlikely that the universal tradition of reading *kyrios* in the LXX as a translation for YHWH can be traced exclusively to Christians. Rather, we should probably think of a fluid tradition from the outset, perhaps originally keeping the Hebrew or Aramaic script, but with a great deal of variety including Greek transliteration and also Greek translation. And this last would be exclusively *kyrios*.

It is noteworthy that the form is commonly the anarthrous *kyrios*, 'Lord'; not the definite *ho kyrios*, 'the Lord'; though 'there is a strong element of caprice in the tradition'.[18] The effect of this is to present *kyrios* as much more a name than a title. This is of course consonant with the *name* of God which is being translated. It is also significant that, although *kyrios* is used to translate other words,[19] it is not much used in the religious sphere: it is, for instance, never used for *baal* (= 'lord', but used almost as a proper name in Canaanite religion) when this word is used of a pagan deity. If *kyrios* did not stand originally for YHWH in the LXX, then it is fortuitous that it remains primarily the name of God, and of no other deity, in the Old Testament.

Kyrios elsewhere in Jewish literature

In the pseudepigrapha we find *kyrios* used frequently of God, though normally in compounds.[20] It is perhaps not surprising that writings in conscious imitation of Scripture (*e.g.* the Psalms of Solomon) should retain the specifically scriptural name of God. Rather more surprising is the fact that in the hellenistic environment, where the simple 'Lord' would be less likely to be understood,[21] we still find it commonly occurring: those works which were

---

[17] Whether this move was related to the choice of *kyrios* in the LXX or not (see *TDNT* 3, pp.1081-3) is not relevant here. Although in the earliest stages of the tradition of avoiding the divine name the substitution *elohim* ('God') was common (witness the elohistic Psalms), the Dead Sea Scrolls witness to an already-established practice of substituting *adonai* for YHWH (B. J. Roberts, *op. cit.*. p.70).

[18] *TDNT* 3, p.1059 (Quell).

[19] Especially *adon* ('lord'), which is used in the Old Testament of both men and God.

[20] See the index in R. H. Charles, *The Apocrypha and Pseudepigrapha of the Old Testament* 2 (Clarendon, 1913), *s.v.* 'God, names of'. Charles does not clearly indicate, however, the number of places where 'Lord' stands alone.

[21] W. Foerster, *Herr ist Jesus* (Bertelsmann, Gütersloh, 1924), pp.69-98; and *idem, TDNT* 3, pp.1046-1058, points out that *kyrios* is not widespread as a title for the gods in our period. He also notes that *kyrios* is linked to words such as *theos* ('god') and *basileus* ('king') without any intermediate *kai* ('and') (p.1050), and considers that this indicates the final stage of a development

originally written in Greek use *kyrios* more frequently than *theos* ('God'), in apparent contradistinction to those works originally written in Hebrew.[22] One may observe in both strands, however, a move towards the development of other, periphrastic, ways of speaking of God: it appears that the special sanctity attaching to the Tetragrammaton also applied, albeit with less force, to the words used to represent it.

In Josephus *kyrios* as a name for God occurs in only two places. One is a citation of an Old Testament text, Isaiah 19:19; where 'to the Lord' (LXX: *tō kyriō*) is represented as *kyriō tō theō* ('to the Lord God'). The other is the prayer of Izates, a Gentile proselyte: 'If it is not in vain, O sovereign Lord (*ō despota kyrie*), that I have had a taste of Thy goodness, and that I have made it my belief that Thou art the first and only rightful Lord of all (*tōn pantōn de dikaiōs monon kai prōton . . . kyrion*), come to my aid . . .'.[23] Elsewhere, Josephus uniformly uses the word *theos*.

Much of Philo's writing concerns the interpretation of biblical texts; and the word *kyrios* is therefore quite common in his writings. He occasionally speculates on its significance as a title of God, regarding it as speaking of his power, specifically his power to harm. Hence Philo thinks that 'it is His will that the wicked man should be under His sway as his Lord . . . ; that the man of progress should be benefited by Him as God . . . ; that the perfect should be guided by Him as Lord and benefited by Him as God'.[24] This rather negative assessment of the significance of *kyrios* underlines its unsuitableness, without qualification, as a title of God in a hellenistic milieu.

Heis Kyrios: The *Shema'* in hellenistic Judaism

The monotheism which lay at the very heart of orthodox Judaism was explicitly affirmed in the twice-daily recital of the *shema'*. This is a catena of three (originally four)[25] biblical passages: Deuteronomy 6:4–9; 11:13–21

---

of older Egyptian and Syrian practices. But it is equally likely that it marks an *early* stage of development in which *kyrios* is still regarded as primarily an adjective rather than a noun.

[22] W. Foerster, *Herr ist Jesus*, pp. 118f.

[23] *Antiquities* 13:68 and 20:90; texts and translation as in the Loeb edition (Heinemann, 1969).

[24] *Mut. Nom.* 19; translation as in the Loeb edition (Heinemann, 1968). The other significant passages are *Leg. Alleg.* I.95f.; *Plant.* 86-89; *Mut. Nom.* 15; 24; *Somn.* I.163. In distinction to "Lord', 'God' ('*theos*') speaks of the power of his grace and love.

[25] The catena appears to have begun with the decalogue, but this was later omitted under pressure from the *minim* ('heretics'), who seem to have argued from the practice that only these passages were 'truly' Scripture. Even today the decalogue has no place at all in the Jewish liturgy as a result.

and Numbers 15:37–41; obligation is laid upon every male adult Israelite to recite these, and the associated blessings, twice every day.[26] The significance of the *shema'*, for the diaspora as well as for Palestinian Judaism, may be seen from the regard in which it was held. To the rabbis, its recital was a 'taking upon oneself the yoke of the kingdom of heaven'.[27] To the community of Qumran, it was entering into the covenant of God.[28] To Philo it provided 'visions of the just'.[29] To Josephus it was a grateful memorial of God's gifts after the deliverance from Egypt.[30] To Aristeas it gave opportunity for meditation upon the manifold works of God.[31] To all of Judaism it was at once a focus and foundation of their faith in God. The Mishna explicitly allows for the recital to be in any language (in contrast to other parts of the liturgy).[32] The Jerusalem Talmud comments explicitly on the use of Greek for this purpose at Caesarea.[33] In the LXX the passage runs *Akoue, Israēl; kyrios ho theos hēmōn kyrios heis estin*... ('Hear, O Israel, the Lord our God is one Lord'),[34] the form found also in Mark 12:29.

In its original context in Deuteronomy the declaration was almost certainly an answer to the implicit question, not 'Who is YHWH?' but 'Who is our God?'.[35] In Zechariah 14:9 an eschatological fulfilment of this is seen when YHWH becomes king over the whole earth: then he shall truly be 'one' and his name 'one'. At an early stage the rabbis put these two passages together, so that 'The LORD our God' referred to the present relationship between God and his people Israel, while the second part of the affirmation, 'the LORD (is) one', referred to the coming universal rule of God over all the nations. It is not impossible that Paul was aware of this treatment of the text.[36] There has thus been a shift in the application of these words. Another shift is seen in the context of Jewish martyrdom at the hands of polytheist Romans, when the creed on the lips of the martyr becomes a triumphant

[26] See most conveniently *Encyclopaedia Judaica* (Macmillan, New York, 1971), *s.v.* 'Shema, Reading of'.

[27] MBerakoth 2.2.   [28] IQS X.10.

[29] *Spec. Leg.* 4. 141.   [30] *Antiquities* 4.212.

[31] *Letter of Aristeas* 160.

[32] MSotah 7.1   [33] JSotah 21b.

[34] The Hebrew of the Massoretic text is patient of other translations. At the very least the LXX witnesses to one early interpretation, also found in the Hebrew text of the Nash Papyrus (second century BC). See S. D. McBride, 'The Yoke of the Kingdom', *Interpretation* 27, 1973, pp.273-306 (291-297), for a brief discussion of the issues. Despite his disclaimer, p.280 n.12, McBride's translation of the Greek text is, to say the least, forced. It appears to demand that *kyrios* (rather oddly 'translated' as 'Adonai') be taken as a proper name; but McBride does not elaborate on this.

[35] See S. D. McBride, *art. cit.*, pp.292f.

[36] So S. D. McBride, *ibid.*, p.278 n.10.

affirmation of monotheism and of God's exclusive sovereignty.[37] An emphasis on monotheism is, of course, not lacking in the original context of Deuteronomy.[38] It was an integral part of Jewish propaganda, though perhaps not surprisingly the *shema'* itself is not found in propagandist texts.[39] Yet it must surely be regarded as that which informs and gives urgency to this aspect of the propaganda. Hints of this same urgency are also to be found in the first Christian evangelism of Gentiles: again the *shema'* is latent rather than patent.[40]

The phrase *heis kyrios* has already therefore a prehistory when we meet it in the writings of Paul, and its reference is to God, as revealed in his uniqueness in the *shema'*.

Scripture and Christ

Before we discuss the way in which the *heis kyrios* phrase is applied to Christ, it is worth noting how Paul in other ways applies Scripture to him. There are, first, places where Paul sees him as fulfilling what Scripture had, implicitly or explicitly, prophesied; for instance, he describes Jesus as the true 'seed' of Abraham in Galatians 3:16.[41] These present no problem from our point of view. More significant are those places where Paul alludes more or less loosely to Old Testament passages and applies them to Jesus, when in the original context they referred to God. These deserve closer investigation.

In 2 Thessalonians 1:8–10 Paul alludes to a variety of Old Testament texts,[42] but the Lord of verse 9 who will punish the unbelievers is

[37] The tradition is traced back to the martyrdom of Rabbi Aqiba (AD 135), who prolonged the final word *echad* ('one') (bBerakoth 61b).

[38] This is true whether Dt. is seen in the context of polemic against Canaanite religion, as, presumably, Mosaic authorship would presuppose, or that of polemic against a multiplication of traditions and sanctuaries of Yahweh himself, as G. von Rad has argued in his commentary (SCM. 1966) and in his *Old Testament Theology* 1 (Oliver & Boyd, 1962), p.227. See S. D. McBride, *op. cit.*, pp.291-297 for a discussion.

[39] *Cf. Sibylline Oracles* 3, lines 11, 16, 571, 586-593, *etc.*; *Letter of Aristeas* 15f. (where as a sop to the Gentile audience he is identified with Zeus, but called Lord, Creator and Ruler of all; *cf.* the reference in 19 to 'the supreme God'), 37 ('the supreme God'), 132 ('he proved that there is only one God'), *etc.*

[40] Acts 17:24, 29; Rom 3:29f.; 1 Thes. 1:9; Jas. 2:19.

[41] The question of the validity of this treatment of Old Testament 'prophecy' is beyond the scope of this paper. See E. E. Ellis, *Paul's Use of the Old Testament* (Oliver & Boyd, 1957), pp.70-73.

[42] With *en pyri phlogos* (8) *cf. en phlogi pyros* (Is. 66:15); with *didontos ekdikēsin* (8) *cf. apodounai ekdikēsin* (Is. 66. 15); with *tois mē eidosin theon* (8) *cf. ta mē eidota se* (*sc.* God) (Je. 10:15); with *apo prosōpou tou kyriou kai apo tēs doxēs tēs ischuos autou* (9) *cf. apo prosōpou tou phobou kyriou kai apo tēs doxēs tēs ischuos autou* (Is. 2:10, 19, 21); with *endoxasthēnai en tois hagiois autou kai thaumasthēnai en pasin*

indisputably the Lord Jesus (in contrast to verse 5). Similarly, in 2:8, whether or not we read *Iēsous*,[43] the *kyrios* must again be Jesus, but is described in language appropriate to God from the Old Testament.[44] The most striking example of this is in Philippians 2, where the name *kyrios* which is given to Jesus[45] can only be that of YHWH himself, if we are expected to see an explicit link with Isaiah 45:23.[46]

A similar phenomenon is observed in the way in which the Old Testament concept of 'the Day of YHWH' is 'Christified' in the New Testament: the New Testament Day of the Lord is the day of *Christ's* coming, and so can also be called the day of Christ.[47] Similarly 'glory', which in the Old Testament is a divine prerogative, is commonly attributed to Christ by Paul.[48] Thus, at the very least, divine functions and attributes are seen as appropriate to the Lord Jesus Christ, now or in the future.[49]

The very fact that Jesus is called *kyrios* witnesses to the same attitude on the part of the early church. In the writings of Paul in particular, it is often difficult to decide whether *kyrios* should be taken as referring to God the Father or to Jesus.[50] This ambiguity of expression may well be indicative of a fluidity of thought.[51] He who fulfilled Scripture, and in the light of whom *all* Scripture is

---

tois pisteusasin (10) *cf. ho theos endoxazomenos en boulē hagiōn* (Ps. 88:8) and *thaumastos ho theos en tois hagiois autou* (Ps. 67:36).

[43] It is omitted in BD^{c}K *pm*.

[44] With *anelei tō pneumati tou stomatos autou cf. pataxei gēn tō logō tou stomatos autou kai en pneumati dia cheileōn anelei asebē* (Is. 11:4) and *tō pneumati tou stomatos autou* (Ps. 32:6).

[45] As still seems to me most likely, *pace* C. F. D. Moule, 'Further Reflexions on Philippians 2:5–11', in W. W. Gasque and R. P. Martin (eds.), *Apostolic History and the Gospel* (Paternoster, 1970), pp.264-276.

[46] This phenomenon is seen elsewhere in the NT as well: *cf.* 1 Pet. 3:14f. (Is. 8:12f.); Heb. 1:10 (Ps. 102:25); Rev. 17:14; 19:16 (Dt. 10:17; Dn. 2:47); Rev. 1:13-14 (Dn. 7:9). See F. F. Bruce, 'Jesus is Lord', in J. M. Richards (ed.), *Soli Deo Gloria* (John Knox, n.d.), p.33, and C. F. D. Moule, *The Origin of New Testament Christology* (CUP, 1977), pp.41-44 and the references cited there.

[47] See 1 Cor. 5:5 (?); 1 Thes. 5:2; 2 Thes. 2:2 ('day of the Lord'), and 1 Cor. 1:8: 5:5 (?); 2 Cor. 1:14; Phil. 1:6, 10; 2:16 ('day of Jesus/Christ'). *Cf.* also Acts 2:20 and 2 Pet. 3:10.

[48] On this see my 'Image and Incarnation in Pauline Christology', *TB* 30, 1979, pp.3-28.

[49] L. Cerfaux, '"Kyrios" dans les citations pauliniennes de l'Ancien Testament', *Eph. Theol. Louv.* 20, 1943, pp.5-17, notes that 'Paul transporte sur le Christ. *à l'occasion de la parousie,* cette glorification du *Nom* par excellence' (p.9); and it is important to notice that this transference of divine characteristics to Christ is primarily eschatological. But (like all of Paul's eschatology) this 'spills over' into the present age too: Christ is *now* glorified, and Christians *already* bow the knee to him and acknowledge him as Lord.

[50] See L. Cerfaux, *loc. cit..* and D. Guthrie, *New Testament Theology* (IVP, 1981), p.299.

[51] This is discussed further in my 'Image and Incarnation' (above, n.48).

now seen as prophetic,[52] fulfils also those passages which were seen in their original contexts as revelations of YHWH.

Jesus the one Lord

But Jesus was not simply 'the Lord' to the early church. He was the one, and so implicitly the only, Lord.

Cullmann has said, 'The lordship of Christ must extend over every area of creation. If there were a single area excluded from his lordship, that lordship would not be complete and Christ would no longer be the *Kyrios*.'[53] This, however, seems false logic. There were indeed 'lords many' in the world of the first century who were properly regarded as 'lords' of their respective spheres, though many other areas were excluded from their lordship. Cullmann's point holds, however, as soon as Christ is acknowledged as the *one* Lord. For if any single area is excluded from his lordship, there must be some other lord, and that the 'one Lord' formula prohibits.[54] We turn, then, to investigate 1 Corinthians 8:6, where the 'one Lord' formula explicitly occurs.

Most studies of this verse have had other purposes than an investigation of the Christological implications, and add nothing to our search.[55] In terms of its Christological content, attention has focused on the question whether the *kyrioi* ('lords') with whom the 'one Lord' is contrasted are to be regarded as human or divine; the balance of opinion is fairly evenly divided,[56] which

[52] *Cf.* Rom. 3:21, 31; 10:4, which (at least in part) refer to a prophetic aspect of the Torah; as, probably, does our Lord's statement about 'fulfilling' the Law: see R. J. Banks, *Jesus and the Law in the Synoptic Tradition* (CUP, 1975).

[53] O. Cullmann, *The Christology of the New Testament* (SCM, ²1963), p.228. Cullmann's statement which immediately follows, that *Kyrios Christos* is to be seen as 'opposed to the confession *Kyrios Kaisar*', probably needs modifying: it is unlikely that the *Kyrios Kaisar* confession is so early as part of an emperor-cult in our area (see *TDNT* 3, pp.1054-8), and the ascription of lordship to Christ began in the Palestinian church (see R. N. Longenecker, *The Christology of Early Jewish Christianity* (SCM, 1970), pp.121-124, 140).

[54] O. Cullmann, *loc. cit.*, discusses areas which are in fact at present outside the sphere of Christ's lordship: 'flesh' and 'death' (with equal validity one might add demonic powers). But as Cullmann points out, these are already in principle vanquished, and so in no way threaten the unique and total lordship of Jesus. The one real threat to the uniqueness of Christ's lordship is not discussed at all by him: see below.

[55] As well as the standard works, see J. Murphy-O'Connor, '1 Cor., VII, 6: Cosmology or Soteriology?', *RB* 85, 1978, pp.253-267, and P. H. Langkammer, 'Literarische und Theologische Einzelstücke in I Kor VII. 6', *NTS* 17, 1970-71, pp.193-197.

[56] Among those who regard them as men may be mentioned Deissmann, Schlatter and Grosheide (Weiss thinks of deified men), while Wendland, Meyer and C. H. Giblin ('Three Monotheistic Texts in Paul', *CBQ* 37, 1975, pp.527-547) think in terms of divinities. Other authorities remain non-committal.

suggests that with the evidence presently available (or lacking), such speculation is not likely to prove fruitful. The Christological implications of the phrase in and of itself do not seem to have been discussed in this context. Kramer[57] is perhaps typical when he regards the *heis kyrios* phrase as an *addition* to the *heis theos* ('one God') formula, with the implication that it was the latter which enshrined the heart of the *shema'*. But if this is not so, the verse has significant implications for our study.

The verse comes towards the beginning of an extended discussion of the use of idol-meats. Paul begins his response to the Corinthians' question about a Christian attitude to such things with the emphatic statement: 'there is no God but one' (v. 4). This in itself would be an adequate basis for the argument of verses 7ff., but Paul pauses to emphasize his point and at the same time to expand it.[58] Verse 5 paints a standard picture of Gentile attitudes of the time, and it is difficult to believe that in countering these attitudes the mind of an orthodox Jew such as Paul had been should not turn immediately to the *shema'*. The *heis theos* of verse 4 is probably already informed by it,[59] and this may well account for the expansion of the following two verses.[60] In verse 6, then, in contradistinction to the hellenistic world which he is opposing,[61] Paul presents a 'Christianizing' of the *shema'*.[62] Just as his contemporaries saw a dual *function* in the confession,[63] so Paul sees a dual *referent* in *kyrios* and *theos*, glossing the latter with *patēr* ('father') and the former with *Iēsous Christos*.[64] 'It

---

[57] W. Kramer, *Christ, Lord, Son of God* (SCM, 1966), section 22f (p.97).

[58] Those who see a liturgical formula behind v. 6 (see for instance Murphy-O'Connor, *op. cit.*) note that v. 6 gives more detail than is called for by the context, but fail to note that this is true even in v. 5.

[59] So, *inter alios*, H. Conzelmann and C. K. Barrett, *ad loc*. Barrett and Schlatter note that the linking of 'gods' and 'lords' here depends on Dt. 10:17 ('the LORD your God is God of gods and Lord of lords'); but fail to note that again Paul has radically Christified this statement by making Jesus the one Lord in contrast with the many.

[60] This seems more reasonable than to suppose, with those authors referred to in n.58, that Paul uses a formula taken from the baptismal (or other) liturgy, and applies it in a place where much of it is not really relevant.

[61] On this see N. T. Wright, *The Messiah and the People of God* (unpublished thesis presented to the University of Oxford in 1980), p.279, nn.180, 181 and 182.

[62] The word is used by F. F. Bruce in his commentary, though he does not work this idea out as here.

[63] See the discussion above.

[64] See N. T. Wright, *op. cit.*, pp.42-44 for a similar assessment of the passage. Wright notes (p.279 n.181) that he knows no-one who has interpreted 1 Cor. 8:6 in this way. Although I am much indebted to Wright's discussion, the ideas here presented had been worked out at least in general before I read his thesis.

is hard to conceive of a clearer means by which Paul could indicate *both* that he was aligning Jesus with the *kyrios* of the LXX *and* that he was doing so within a thoroughly Jewish framework of thought.'[65]

But why does Paul feel that this is the right place to express such an idea? Since he does not tell us himself, any answer must be pure speculation, but it seems not unreasonable to suggest that at least two factors may be relevant. In the context of 1 Corinthians 8 – 10, the eating of idol-meats is contrasted with the Christian meal at the table of the *Lord*, so that the status of Jesus is relevant in this whole discussion. Secondly, I would suggest that Paul's Christianizing of the *shema'* is so complete[66] that he would have needed reason to omit the reference to Jesus rather than reason to add it. To Paul the lordship of Jesus is so fundamental that there is a sense in which it challenges, or at least significantly modifies, the *heis theos* to which as a Jew he was totally committed.

This can be seen to be so from an incidental remark which Paul feels obliged to make later in the Epistle. In chapter 15 he quotes Psalm 8:6 (LXX: Ps. 8:7) as proof that Christ's lordship will ultimately extend over all things, including even the last enemy, death. He then feels obliged to add, 'but when it says, "All things are put in subjection under him," it is plain that he is excepted who put all things under him' (v. 27). So plain is this, one might have thought, that it scarcely needs a mention; yet Paul seems to underline the point, and indeed emphasizes that this is not the end of the story: the ultimate goal is the time when Jesus gives up again the universal lordship which now (at least proleptically) he possesses. Thus to Paul, Jesus' lordship can almost threaten the Father's godship;[67] conversely, the Father's status remains firmly outside the realm of the Son's lordship. This perfectly coheres with the Christianizing of the *shema'* discussed above. The Father, by bestowing lordship on the Son,[68] shares with him his status and functions; the Son, by remaining in submission to the Father and ultimately restoring to him all lordship and dominion, never usurps his position.[69]

---

[65] N. T. Wright, *op. cit.*, p.43.

[66] As can be seen by its influence on much of Paul's theology: it is this, it seems to me now, which lies behind many of the points mentioned in my 'Image and Incarnation in Pauline Christology', pp.4f., and discussed later in that essay.

[67] Barrett feels the need to posit 'a Corinthian belief (of which we have no other evidence) that at his exaltation Christ became the one supreme God' to account for verse 27b, but this seems unnecessary. Such a belief, if Paul thought it existed, would be likely to call forth more than half a verse from the apostle in response. The need for the corrective seems more reasonably to be placed within Paul's own thought than within that of his readers.

[68] Note this unusual absolute use of *huios* in v. 28; see H. Conzelmann, *ad loc.*

[69] The contrast with Adam is manifest, and this may help to account for the development of

The pair *heis kyrios . . . heis theos* occurs again at Ephesians 4:5f., but here in a list of seven unities which undergird Paul's call for complete unity in the church. The reason for the selection of these seven in particular is not obvious, nor does the suggestion of a credal formula here[70] shed much light on this problem. That Christians all worship one Lord would of course be true, even if that Lord were not thought of as being Lord of all; so this passage cannot add to our understanding of Paul's attitude to the exclusive lordship of Christ,[71] though it is worth noting that again God is implicitly denied the title 'lord'. What has been said above, however, makes excellent sense in the context of Ephesians 4; and it would certainly have been impossible for Paul to make either of the assertions *heis kyrios* and *heis theos* without the other, in the light of what we have seen.

Conclusions

We have seen no reason to doubt that to Paul the phrase *heis kyrios,* like the phrase *heis theos,* would have most naturally referred to God. By retaining the latter for God and transferring the former to Jesus, he was perhaps doing no more than systematizing what was already experienced by his Christian predecessors: that Jesus was worthy of divine honour. But the systematization which he chose is of the utmost significance. In Christ Paul found the eschatological fulfilment of Zechariah 14:9 for which his co-religionists were still waiting. In Christ he found one who was equal with God but who was not simply the totality of deity. From within the security of Jewish monotheism, therefore, Paul was able to see a duality within the Godhead well expressed in the phrase 'one God . . . and one Lord'; and by his radical re-interpretation of the creed of Israel was able to steer the church down the road towards a truly trinitarian faith.[72]

Paul's Adam-Christology. See my *The Form of God in the Likeness of Men* (unpublished thesis presented to the University of Cambridge in 1974), ch. 5.

[70] On which see the commentary of M. Barth, Comment IV. Against the possibility of the passage being a creed must surely stand the facts that the members are of very uneven length (note particularly the extensive development of the 'one God' member, while the 'one Lord' is totally undeveloped); that one member is not in the nominative (*viz.* the 'one hope') and that the list is surprisingly and oddly selective.

[71] And therefore, *pace* F. Hahn, *The Titles of Jesus in Christology* (Lutterworth, 1969), p.111, we cannot use this passage to support theories of an early entrenchment of the *heis kyrios* formula in early Christian confessions.

[72] The place of the Holy Spirit in this development is another story, which must be left to another place.

Thus the acknowledgement of Jesus as the *one* Lord may well prove to have been a significant milestone in the development of New Testament Christology.[73]

---

[73] G. Wagner, *An Exegetical Bibliography on Paul's First Letter to the Corinthians* (Rüschlikon-Zürich, Baptist Theological Seminary, 1975) refers to W. Born, 'Der eine Herr', in L. Schmidt (ed.), *Kleine Predigt-typologie III (Das Neue Testament)* (Vandenhoeck & Ruprecht, 1965), pp. 72-78; but I have not been able to consult Born's work.

PAUL, WISDOM AND CHRIST

John F. Balchin

Since the last century when the manhood of Jesus was established once and for all among theologians, generations of scholars have given themselves to the question of how the New Testament authors could bring themselves to describe this same man in divine terms. The History of Religions School has long dominated the scene with the thesis that they did so by adopting contemporary pagan mythical patterns, thereby unwittingly or deliberately bringing about his apotheosis. Because the purported sources are historically well after our period, and because the parallels proposed are not always obvious, this procedure has prompted some to look elsewhere.

Perhaps this is one of the reasons why there seems to have been a growing interest in Old Testament and hellenistic Jewish wisdom speculation as being a more likely conceptual background to the 'high' Christological statements of the New Testament.[1] In particular the pre-existence and cosmological significance of wisdom appear to be closely related to claims made for Christ.[2]

This line of argument has been taken up recently in a stimulating book by J. D. G. Dunn, but with a difference. He has suggested not only that early inspirational Christology moved in the direction of incarnation as the wisdom motif was adopted and applied to Christ by the New Testament writers, but that Paul assisted in the development almost unwittingly.[3]

---

[1] *E.g.* O. Cullmann, *The Christology of the New Testament* (SCM, 1959), pp.249-269: W. D. Davies, *Paul and Rabbinic Judaism* (SPCK, 1970), pp.151ff.; E. Schweizer, *Jesus* (SCM, 1971), pp.81-83; J. D. G. Dunn, *Christology in the Making* (SCM, 1980). It has been noted more than once that this was R. Bultmann's earlier solution to the background of the Johannine prologue. *Cf.* J. T. Sanders, *The New Testament Christological Hymns* (CUP, 1971), pp.29ff.

[2] According to the History of Religions School, of course, a Sophia myth was already fused with an Anthropos myth before our literature was written. *E.g.* U. Wilckens, *TWNT* 7, p.491.

[3] He appears to argue that the author of Hebrews was the first actually to embrace Christological

His argument derives from the fact that, for all the extravagance of the terminology employed in the Old Testament and Jewish literature, at no point was wisdom ever considered to be a contender for deity. In the Old Testament Yahwism was never threatened by its most vivid personifications.[4] For that kind of process one must turn to the thoroughgoing hypostases of pagan religion, particularly in Egypt or Babylonia.[5] Though the wise men of Israel may well have adopted 'outline myths' from their neighbours,[6] they filled them with a thoroughly monotheistic content,[7] a tradition which runs on into later Judaism.

Dunn claims that this is how Paul regards wisdom in the first instance.[8] It stands for God's self-revelation, for his saving purposes, especially as they were fulfilled as never before in Christ. The apostle's interest was primarily soteriological and eschatological. It centred in Christ's death and resurrection, and in the early Christians' experience of him as designated Son and Lord.

However, in using wisdom themes to describe Christ in this way, in the first instance in response to trouble at Corinth when he took up terms they were already using, Paul began to credit Christ with something more.[9] Hence by the time he wrote Colossians he had moved one step further away from simple inspiration, and had helped the process along towards actual incarnation and the trinitarian formulas of the fourth century.[10] Even in Colossians, Dunn is reluctant to allow Christ real, personal pre-existence and a cosmological role.[11] It is only in John's Gospel that he admits such an identification,[12] but that serves his hypothesis in that he sees in the New Testament what has become a somewhat familiar pattern of Christological development. In the earlier strata

---

pre-existence as such. However, he argues that this was due to the author's indebtedness to Platonic idealism (much in the same way that Philo treats the Logos), which resulted in an *ideal* pre-existence 'in the mind of God'. Dunn maintains that it is beyond our evidence to say that the author was expressing real personal pre-existence. *Op. cit.*, pp.54-56.

[4] *Ibid.*, p.171.

[5] *Cf.* H. Ringgren, *Word and Wisdom* (Lund, 1947), pp.9-88.

[6] O. S. Rankin, *Israel's Wisdom Literature* (T. & T. Clark, 1936), pp.223ff.; W. L. Knox, *St. Paul and the Church of the Gentiles* (CUP, 1939), p.57; R. H. Fuller, *The Foundations of New Testament Christology* (Lutterworth, 1965), p.74; H. Conzelmann, 'The Mother of Wisdom' in *The Future of our Religious Past*, ed. J. M. Robinson (SCM, 1971), pp.230-243; H.-P. Müller, *TDOT* 4, p.384, *et al.*

[7] H. Ringgren, *op. cit.*, p.192; F. B. Craddock, *The Pre-existence of Christ in the New Testament* (Abingdon, 1968), p.35; G. von Rad, *Wisdom in Israel* (SCM, 1972), p.153.

[8] J. D. G. Dunn, *op. cit.*, pp.195, 209-212. [9] *Ibid.*, pp. 176ff., 211f.

[10] *Ibid.*, p.212. [11] *Ibid.*, pp.187-194.

[12] *Ibid.*, p.239.

we are told that there is a simple inspirational Christology; in the later works, overt incarnation.[13]

Whether or not we can accept his propositions, Dunn's claims prompt us to re-examine the concept of wisdom as it would have been available to the New Testament authors, and to evaluate his own methodology.

Personal wisdom

In what sense did the authors of the Old Testament material and later Jewish works regard wisdom as *personal*? Would it be correct to understand this personification in terms of hypostasis, that is, as a personal entity distinct from God and yet in some way participating in the divine?[14] This could be regarded in a purely pagan sense as the production, creation or emanation of a lesser deity, or in later trinitarian terms. Or do we have to be content with something less?

Because of our Christian preoccupation with personalized wisdom, the fact is often overlooked that as far as the Old Testament and LXX evidence is concerned, the vast majority of references to wisdom are entirely impersonal. They refer to the spiritual understanding, intelligence, insight, knowledge or skill which God gives to men and women.[15] This is illustrated by the way in which wisdom is often combined or used in parallel with other words for knowledge or understanding.[16] At this level it may be regarded as simply one term among many.

At the same time we are persistently told that this is no ordinary knowledge. Only God is wise, and therefore all true insight must come from him. Hence there is frequent contrast between the truly wise man and the man who neglects God's wisdom, the fool, as well as repeated denigration of human understanding by itself.[17] But God's wisdom is more than just knowledge; it is what a man needs to live a godly life. Although the term is wide enough to include courtly wisdom, the artisan's skill and even scientific knowledge, the Old Testament

---

[13] *Ibid.*, pp.251-258. Dunn makes two assumptions in his thesis. On the one hand, he believes that we can date the writings of our New Testament and lay them out in chronological order. On the other he assumes that Christology needed to develop from simpler to more complex, from lower to higher forms. There is little hard evidence for either assumption.

[14] *Cf.* H. Ringgren, *op. cit.*, p.8 (citing Oesterley and Box): 'a quasi-personification of certain attributes proper to God occupying an intermediary position between personalities and abstract things.'

[15] *E.g.* Ex. 35:30–35; 1 Ki. 4:29–34; Pss. 51:6; 90:12; Pr. 2:5f.; Dn. 1:17; 1 Esdras 4:59f.; Ecclus. 1:1.

[16] *E.g.* Ex. 31:3; 1 Ki. 4:29; 1 Ch. 22:12; Jb. 12:13; Ps. 49:3; Pr. 1:2–7; 2:1–6; Ec. 1:16.

[17] Jb. 12:2; Pr. 3:5, 7; Is. 29:14; Je. 8:9; 9:23; Baruch 3:23; *etc.*

saints were not interested in wisdom simply for its own sake. The wisdom of God was the preoccupation of the godly, that they might live better. Hence we are persistently reminded that the fear of the Lord is the beginning of wisdom.[18] In this respect, although the actual identification of a personalized wisdom with the Law may be late,[19] wisdom and God's commandments are closely related early on.[20]

The conclusion to which this leads us is that the concern of the authors in question was not so much theological as devotional. They sought after, prayed for, meditated upon and loved the wisdom of God, because they loved God and were concerned for his will in their lives.[21]

It is in this context that, along with the mass of references to wisdom, we have to deal with the comparatively few passages which actually personify wisdom, even though it must be admitted that it is striking when they do.[22] When we read of wisdom appealing in person, or contrasting her charms with those of a loose woman (or pagan goddess), or being personally involved in the creation of the world, it is easy to forget that the writers' concern was primarily devotional. But we must remember that they were equally ready to describe wisdom in a series of non-personal metaphors as well.[23]

All this taken together seems to indicate that 'hypostasis' is much too strong a word for the phenomenon. There is nothing to indicate that wisdom became a lesser or secondary god (or goddess) to Yahweh. That would have been inconceivable in the monotheistic setting of the Old Testament and Judaism. It would certainly be a misuse of the sources to read back into them the church's later trinitarian debates. Whatever the dogmatic use of this theme historically, or however the New Testament authors were to take it up, in its original setting it can be no more than poetic personification.[24]

---

[18] Jb. 28:28; Ps. 111:10; Pr. 1:7; 9:10; 15:33; Ecclus. 1:14, 27.

[19] Ecclus. 24.

[20] *E.g.* Dt. 4:4f.; Ps. 37:30f.

[21] Wisdom had an international character even when the earliest biblical Wisdom literature was produced, and probably owed a great deal to an interchange at courtly level, but the motivation behind the OT use of the category does not seem to be apologetic. Later on this seems to have been the case as in Wisdom, Ecclus, and Philo. *Cf.* F. B. Craddock, *op. cit.,* pp.34f. With the growing stress on divine transcendence in the intertestamental period, it may well also have proved to be a useful intermediary.

[22] *E.g.* Pr. 1:20ff.; 7:4f.; 8:1ff.; 9:1ff.; Wisdom 6:12ff.; 7:22ff.; 8:17ff.; 10:1ff.

[23] *E.g.* Pr. 16:16; 24:13f.; Ec. 2:13; 7:11f.; Ecclus. 1:20; 20:30; Baruch 3:12.

[24] *Cf.* G. F. Moore, *Judaism in the First Centuries of the Christian Era* 1 (OUP, 1927), p.415; H.-P. Müller, *op. cit.,* p.383; R. N. Whybray, *The Book of Proverbs* (CUP, 1972), pp.19, 49f.; R. B. Y. Scott *VT* 10, 1960, p.223. F. B. Craddock, *op. cit.,* p.32, extends this definition: 'a personification of God's mind and will, at times a principle, at other times hypostatically

However, to ask what they were actually personifying in this way is another issue. Categories like 'the meaning implanted by God in creation'[25] seem to be a little too abstract for the texts in question. Again, to say that wisdom represents God's wise purposes in the world and among men,[26] although true, describes where we see wisdom rather than wisdom itself.

The wisdom they were describing was the wisdom of God. It is one of his many attributes. God is wise, and we can see that both in what he has made and in his dealings with mankind. Personalized wisdom, therefore, is the personification of an attribute, and it was not the only attribute they personified.[27] Wisdom derived what personality it had from God. It is God's mind and intelligence. That is why it can speak on his behalf and make claims which only properly pertain to the divine. That is also why coming to know wisdom necessarily involves an attitude of humble submission towards God, for it is coming to know God.

Having said all this, we are still left with a conceptual residue which the Jews could take no further, but which proved to be very fertile ground for Christians.[28] Wisdom originates with God,[29] shares his throne,[30] and was with him from the beginning.[31] Wisdom is the agent of creation,[32] and providence,[33] as well as revelation.[34] Wisdom both comes[35] and is sent into the world,[36] and even returns to heaven again.[37] Wisdom has a soteriological function in the world.[38] Wisdom seeks out men and women and makes personal claims and promises.[39] Wisdom is associated with the Spirit.[40] Wisdom is even the agent of judgment.[41] All this would fuse together in a new pattern when a real person eventually did emerge whose status and origin could only be described in terms

---

conceived' (in language very similar to that of 4th-century trinitarian formulas), but this goes beyond the evidence.

[25] G. von Rad, *op. cit.,* p.148; R. G. Hamerton-Kelly, *Pre-existence, Wisdom and the Son of Man* (CUP, 1973), p.279: 'the essence of creation, its inherent form'.

[26] J. D. G. Dunn, *op. cit.,* p.174: 'simply ways of describing Yahweh's wise creation and function'.

[27] H. Ringgren, *op. cit.,* pp.149ff.; W. L. Knox, *op. cit.,* p.58; J. D. G. Dunn, *op. cit.,* pp.174f. This would help to explain the ambivalence between wisdom as a person and wisdom as a principle (*e.g.* Pr. 3:19ff.; *cf.* 8:22ff.), and also the parallel between God's word and wisdom (*e.g.* Ps. 33:6; *cf.* Ps. 104:24; Wisdom 9:1).

[28] *Cf.* Philo's use of the motif. [29] Wisdom 7:25f.; Ecclus. 1:1; 24:9.

[30] Wisdom 9:4; *cf.* 1 Enoch 84:3. [31] Jb. 28:25–27; Wisdom 9:9; Ecclus 1:4.

[32] Pr. 2:22–31; *cf.* 3:19f.; Wisdom 8:4–6. [33] Wisdom 1:7; 8:1, 4.

[34] Wisdom 7:26f.; 11:1. [35] Baruch 3:37. [36] Wisdom 9:10–17; Ecclus. 24:8.

[37] *E.g.* 1 Enoch 42:1–2. [38] *E.g.* Wisdom 10:1ff. [39] Pr. 1:20–33; 8:1–21; 9:4ff.

[40] Ex. 31:3; Wisdom 1:6; 7:7, 22; 9:17; Ecclus. 39:6; *cf.* Is. 11:2.

[41] Wisdom 1:8.

like these, and who may even have laid claim to them himself. For although there is no one book where all these characteristics occur together, the New Testament authors were heir to them all through the LXX.

Pre-existence and wisdom

If we are to assess the degree to which the Old Testament and LXX writers thought of wisdom as being pre-existent, we will need to define what we mean by that term. Dunn makes a great deal of the distinction between 'ideal' and 'real' pre-existence. Ideal pre-existence can be understood as what always existed 'in the mind of God' from the beginning. Real pre-existence implies that the entity had actual existence prior to its manifestation on earth, or in cosmological terms, prior to creation. In the proposed development of the concept in the New Testament, Dunn maintains that what began as ideal pre-existence crossed the line into real pre-existence, and thus incarnation was inevitably the outcome.[42]

But is it correct to make this distinction? When it comes to examining ideal pre-existence, there seems to be little difference between this and what we traditionally know as foreknowledge or predestination. If something exists because it is in the mind of God, everything could be described as pre-existent.[43] Surely what we ought to signify by this term is that the entity in question really did exist, that it was not just an idea (even a divine idea), but that it was actually 'there' before creation or manifestation. Ideal pre-existence is really a misnomer. It is not really pre-existence at all, but predestination couched in terms of pre-existence.[44]

---

[42] *Op. cit.*, pp. 54–56, 59f., 211f. *Cf.* R. G. Hamerton-Kelly, *op. cit.*, p.11, who defines pre-existence as 'a mythological term which signifies an entity had a real existence before its manifestation on earth either in the mind of God or in heaven.' He says that entities would be 'real' because they are in the mind of God and not in the mind of man (*op. cit.*, p.32). He distinguishes between pre-existence and predestination in that the latter refers to events that happen, while the former to entities that exist (*op. cit.*, p.3). Although Dunn heavily criticizes Hamerton-Kelly's monograph, he appears to accept his idea of pre-existence.

[43] *Cf.* W. Meeks, *JBL* 93, 1974, p.619.

[44] J. D. G. Dunn, *op. cit.*, pp.230-239, says as much. F. B. Craddock, *op. cit.*, pp.79-81, argues for different categories of pre-existence directly related to the intensity of the felt problem of man's relation to the world in which he lives. If he feels 'at home', he has no need of the concept; if the sense of discontinuity is strong, the idea of pre-existence will be strong also. But this hardly answers to the idea of pre-existence found in a book like Proverbs, where the writers seem to be perfectly at home in the world. *Cf.* R. Bultmann, *Theology of the New Testament* 1 (SCM, 1952), pp.304f. and H. Conzelmann, *An Outline of the Theology of the New Testament* (SCM, 1969), pp.201ff., who understand pre-existence in existential terms although it may be expressed mythologically. As such it becomes an expression of a man's personal transcendence, a definition which does not take the biblical language seriously enough.

209

By this definition, of course, only God is absolutely pre-existent. Other spiritual creatures like angels are excluded in that they are regarded biblically as part of creation. The question in hand is whether or not Christ was thought of as being originally pre-existent in this sense (when, for example, he is described as being involved in creation), or only in the sense of being the focus of God's plans for the redemption of the world. Do the categories of the Wisdom literature in the Old Testament and LXX help us in any way to determine this?

If we do understand wisdom in these writings as a divine attribute poetically personified, even though this is expressed in God's creative or redemptive activity, we see that it was not really an issue for the authors, even though it might appear to be one to us. By definition God's wisdom, being integral with God's person, is as eternal, and therefore as pre-existent, as God himself. There never was a time when God was without his wisdom, and there is no indication that the ordinary monotheistic Jew ever thought otherwise.[45]

If this is the case, we have to accommodate those references in these writings which speak about wisdom being created. Both Proverbs and later works like Ecclesiasticus and Baruch give the impression that wisdom was brought into being by God as his first work, and that wisdom's agency in the rest of creation followed.[46] As far as the cosmos was concerned, even in these terms, wisdom could still be described as pre-existent. At the same time, as far as God was concerned, she was created and derivative.

We need to ask ourselves just how seriously we have to take these assertions. Was this doctrine or poetry? The picture of God 'acquiring' wisdom or 'searching out' wisdom is surely part and parcel with the anthropomorphism of the Old Testament. We humans have to acquire wisdom and learn knowledge, but we are told quite clearly elsewhere that God needs no mentor. He knows all things, and his omniscience was an aspect of Israel's basic understanding of who God was,[47] even though they had to be reminded of it at times.

The picture of a personal, pre-existent wisdom, working alongside God in the creation of the world, is a highly poetic representation of the fact that, not only is creation the product of the divine intelligence, but something of God's mind can be seen in what he has made. This was emphasized in later writers when they came under the influence of Platonic and particularly Stoic ways of thinking about reality, but it was no new thought. In the Old Testament figure

---

[45] Ps. 104:24; Pr. 3:19f.; Jb. 9:4; 12:13; 28:1ff.; Ec. 1:1, 8; 15:18; *etc.*

[46] Pr. 8:22; Ecclus. 1:4, 9; 24:9; Baruch 3:32, 36; G. von Rad, *op. cit.*, p.151. In Job wisdom is present at creation but not distinctly personal. In the Book of Wisdom the idea of created wisdom is nowhere to be found. *Cf.* G. von Rad, *op. cit.*, p.170. W. L. Knox, *op. cit.*, pp.70f., suggests that this may have been due to Stoic influence.

[47] *E.g.* Pss. 33:13–15; 139:1–6; Is. 40:13f.; Ecclus. 42:21.

of wisdom the hellenistic Jews of the intertestamental period had a ready-made apologetic tool. The reason inherent in the world was nothing less than the wisdom of their God. All intelligent men should recognize this as they contemplated the created world, and also as they came to terms with Israel and the Law.[48] It was a concept which tied together the general and the particular, cosmos and historical revelation.

But although there was something in common between the Old Testament understanding and hellenistic philosophic categories (enough for a Jew like Philo to try and synthesize them), there were also fundamental differences.[49] Philo's pre-existent Logos is something more than just a development of the Old Testament and LXX motifs. There is a rich admixture of Platonic dualism which makes his idea of pre-existence different again, even though his motive was apologetic.[50]

For the later rabbis, pre-existence had its own meaning. Their seven pre-existent entities[51] express the idea of predestination or veneration,[52] rather than what we have defined as real pre-existence. Whereas it is useful to compare the ways in which Philo and the rabbis have employed the theme with the work of the New Testament authors, we must recognize that the latter could have used the motif in rather different ways. Though our examination of the evidence so far supports Dunn's thesis, this is not the entire story.

The search for precedent

The search for sources for New Testament themes, and in particular Christological motifs, has been popular and correct. It is only right from the point of view of historical criticism that we set the New Testament in its proper context, and that means establishing, as far as we are able, where they quarried their materials as well as how they built the house. In this respect the evidence for Old Testament and Jewish wisdom speculation has been laid out and discussed more than once. Apart from the fact, often overlooked, that the usefulness of some of the 'sources' can only ever be corroborative,[53] and may

[48] F. B. Craddock, *op. cit.*, pp.34f.

[49] *Ibid.*, pp.36f. Craddock sums up the situation by saying that in the Wisdom literature the universal was subservient to the concrete, while for Philo the opposite was true. Because of Philo's stress on divine transcendence and the consequent need for mystical experience, the Logos/Sophia motif conveniently filled the gap.

[50] This in part may explain his preference for the masculine Logos to the feminine Sophia, although as Knox has pointed out (*op. cit.*, p.84) the latter element did survive in Philo in terms of 'goddess' motifs.

[51] G. F. Moore, *op. cit.* 3, p.526.

[52] F. B. Craddock *op. cit.*, p.48: 'more doxological than didactic'.

[53] *Ibid.*, pp.27–30. Craddock, who criticizes the 'definition by source' approach to the NT,

sometimes illustrate the New Testament discussion by contrast rather than by comparison,[54] this is a necessary procedure. With regard to wisdom, we would like to be able to read the New Testament references in the same way that the average first-century reader would have done.

It would be poor scholarship, however, which stopped there, and which explained the phenomenon of the New Testament message simply in terms of its precedents. If we are to take the claims of the authors seriously, precedents, though useful by way of illustration, must always be inadequate for complete explanation. Something had happened which had never happened before, even though the whole conceptual history of the Jewish people might have prepared for it. The Christ event was a new thing, different not simply in degree from what had gone before, but also in kind. The Christian gospel was not just an extension of Judaism, for all its acknowledged roots in the Old Testament. It was the fulfilment in that it was the final manifestation, the *mystērion* long hidden but now revealed, and in a manner unguessed by generations who had gone before. Because of this, all the themes and images taken up by the New Testament authors were inadequate in themselves. In spite of their lengthy history they had to be reinterpreted in the light of the creative impulse of the resurrection and the outpouring of the eschatological Spirit. This included the concept of wisdom.

The Old Testament and Jewish personification of wisdom, as we have seen, may well be described as poetry, the objectification of what was, after all, an abstract idea at that time. We have only to examine how it was taken to its ultimate and somewhat florid expression in Philo's work to realize that. For all his permutations of the Logos/Sophia theme, he is employing it only to express abstract religio-philosophical concepts.

But there was nothing abstract about the Lord Jesus Christ. He was a living, real and historic person. He not only fulfilled God's purposes in the sense that, for example, Moses might have done. God's purposes became *personal* in him. When Paul tells us that 'in him all things were created', he is not thinking of an abstract idea, any more than he conceives of the cross as abstract. It is no argument to have recourse to the Old Testament and LXX description of wisdom, saying that its personification is no more than poetic. Christ has both fulfilled it and *gone beyond it*.[55]

---

says that we should not ask 'what is the source?', but 'what is the function?....' Hence he prefers to talk about 'background materials' rather than sources. Sources imply a direct connection with the NT. Some have and some have not.

[54] Some of the rabbinic material might be a direct response to Christian claims.

[55] The fact that they were prepared to utilize the cosmogenic function of Wisdom while

All the Old Testament themes which the New Testament writers used were partial anticipations. For them the real thing was bigger than them all put together. The fact that there is no direct precedent for incarnation is not surprising. It had never happened before!

It is possible, of course, to regard the fulfilment theme in the New Testament as referring primarily to Christ's foreordained role in salvation.[56] We are told there that God had a deep-laid plan for the salvation of men and women from the beginning, which he worked out in the earthly ministry of Jesus, his death and resurrection. But it would be wrong to say that this was the only way in which Christ fulfilled the Old Testament anticipations. Paul's use of that term *mystērion*, for example, that secret long hidden but now revealed, can most certainly refer to the gospel,[57] but it can equally refer to Christ himself.[58] What is more, the apostle does this in a context where he has just made the fullest statements about Christ's pre-existence and cosmological functions.[59] The fact that God would use a man's death to save is certainly strikingly novel, but the unexpectedness and hiddenness of God's plan goes even further. God was prepared for his Son to *become* a man in order to save. The heart of the *mystērion* is that no-one could ever have conceived that.

Dunn admits that the 'revelation-schema' might introduce us to the idea of pre-existence.[60] What was originally described as the outworking of God's purposes by means of Christ could possibly lead on to pre-existence. Hence he sees this sort of language in the process of accruing 'a developing christological significance', leaving us 'somewhere between Christ understood as the word preached and Christ understood as the Word incarnate'. We must not overlook the fact that Paul, once again in that letter where he makes explicit claims for Christ's pre-existence, not only uses manifestation terminology with respect to the gospel message; he also employs the same word to describe Christ's second coming.[61] If his final manifestation requires his existence prior to the event, it is not unreasonable to suppose that, in the same context, the apostle understood his first manifestation as being subsequent to his pre-existence.[62]

Had the New Testament writers been content with Jewish precedent, they

---

ignoring the gender, which forms no insignificant part of the OT/LXX presentation, and the fact that they were able to relate the Spirit to Christ without identifying the two, as had happened in the Wisdom literature, is evidence of a discriminating creativity.

[56] J. D. G. Dunn, *op. cit.*, pp.234ff.

[57] *E.g.* Rom. 16:25f.   [58] Col. 1:27; 2:2.

[59] Col. 1:15–17. Statements about God's predetermined purpose in Christ (*e.g.* 1 Cor. 2:7) make even better sense when read in the light of those which speak about his pre-existence.

[60] *Op. cit.*, p.238.   [61] Col. 1:26; 3:4 (*phaneroō*).

[62] *Cf.* the implication of Heb. 9:26–28.

would surely have avoided some of the scandal attaching to their message among their own people. We have no record of Philo ever being persecuted by his contemporaries in the same way that Christians were from the beginning. On the whole he seems to have lived a comfortable and respected life in spite of the extreme statements in his writings. No doubt this was because, for all his talk about an intermediary Logos or Sophia figure, he never breached the confines of Jewish monotheism. When it came to the idea of an intermediary between God and man, Christians *did* go much further than any of their contemporaries in Palestinian or hellenistic Judaism.[63] This was part of the reason why they were accused of heresy and hounded for their beliefs. From a Jewish point of view, if there was no incarnation, the New Testament statements are heresy.

In spite of such disincentives, the New Testament authors were prepared to ransack the Old Testament as well as the intertestamental writings for themes, titles, promises and prophecies which might anticipate the unique event they were presenting to the world. It is quite understandable that their presentation would be adapted to the particular audience that they were addressing. To home-born Jews, Son of man, Son of David, Messiah and the like may well have been adequate expressions, although their cumulative impact is staggering.[64] Faced with a cosmological heresy at Colossae, Paul was prepared to exploit wisdom terminology to establish the supremacy of Christ, although it would be going far beyond the evidence of a collection of occasional writings like the New Testament to say that this had never been done before. But then this was no new thing. Our evidence suggests that Paul had been addressing Jesus in divine terms since his encounter with him on the Damascus Road.[65]

How early is early?

It does seem most reasonable to understand the conceptual background of the statements in Colossians 1:15-17 as being the Jewish wisdom motif, whether we regard these verses as part of a pre-Pauline hymn, or as being Paul's own composition.[66] Paul used it quite deliberately to meet the threat of an error

[63] G. F. Moore, *op. cit.* 1, p.417, tells us that there is no evidence of an intermediary in the Palestinian schools.

[64] Not only did the NT writers draw a variety of OT and Jewish themes into a new synthesis, some had been previously unrelated and, in terms of the OT, some were contradictory.

[65] C. F. D. Moule, *The Origin of Christology* (CUP, 1977), pp.43f., admitting the possibility of a Christology derived from Wisdom speculation, wonders 'whether a more proximate cause may not have been the discovery, simply, of his absolute aliveness beyond death'. Paul was not unintentionally crediting Christ with real personal pre-existence. What he attributed to him was only an aspect of the regard with which he held him already.

[66] C. F. D. Moule, *The Epistles to the Colossians and Philemon* (CUP, 1957), p.59; E. Schweizer,

which had cosmic dimensions. Moreover the text clearly identifies Christ as the agent of creation, revelation and providence, for although Paul is using wisdom language here, he is not talking about an abstract principle as his forbears were. He is describing the person who had become reconciler and Lord. Even so, in Dunn's opinion, he was not describing Christ in terms of real, personal pre-existence, and he might not have been aware of the momentous step that he was taking. We are told that we need to go to John for full incarnation, in that he, rather than Paul, makes the wisdom idea into full and explicit incarnational Christology.[67]

Dunn maintains that we must understand the passage in the sense that Christ became the embodiment of God's purpose and power, the same power and intelligence that we see in creation. Because of this we can now understand creation in the light of Christ's redemptive work. Accordingly this is not to be read as a statement about Christ's real pre-existence and activity in creation; rather it is 'the writer's way of saying that Christ now reveals the power behind the world'.[68]

This simply does not do justice to the text. As the vast majority of scholars have recognized, even though they may have explained it in diverse ways, the plain meaning here is that Christ pre-existed the creation of the world, was involved in its formation, and is even regarded as the cohesive force which holds it all together. It is because all other creatures owe their origin to his agency in this way that he is supreme, possessing a pre-eminence which was endorsed by the resurrection. Paul's readers would have needed extremely subtle minds to have understood these statements otherwise. The dangerous implications would have been obvious to Paul's monotheistic countrymen. He had explicitly identified Christ with pre-existent wisdom in a way that no ordinary Jew would ever have dared.

What is more, there is no hint that Paul did not realize what he was doing when he made this identification. Although he was prepared to use a variety of tools in his task, he was not a careless or slipshod workman. He knew what he was about. He was applying the categories of pre-existence and more to one who had been his contemporary in a studied and deliberate manner which is

---

Lordship and Discipleship (SCM, 1960), p.102; E. Lohse, *Colossians and Philemon* (Fortress, 1971), p.46. *Cf.* C. F. Burney, *JTS* 27, 1925-26, pp.160 *et al.* Other suggested backgrounds have been Jewish views about Adam, a Stoic world-view and the gnostic Redeemer myth. *Cf.* R. P. Martin, *Colossians* (Paternoster, 1972), pp.40-44; J. L. Houlden, *Paul's Letters from Prison* (Penguin, 1970), pp.155-173.

[67] J. D. G. Dunn, *op. cit.*, pp.190, 193.

[68] *Ibid.*

only a little less explicit than John in his prologue. And he was doing this because of the creative incentive of his experience of the resurrection, something which his non-Christian Jewish former friends refused to accept.

However, we have evidence that this may not have been the first time Paul had described Christ in cosmological terms. Many scholars have seen an anticipation of Colossians 1:15-17 in 1 Corinthians 8:6.[69] Once again Dunn has urged that cosmogony is excluded here. According to him, this statement has to do with Christ's present rule over creation and the church, and demonstrates that Christ's lordship is the 'continuation and fullest expression of God's own creative power'.[70]

With all the debate about the original form and purpose of this statement,[71] most are agreed that the terminology here gives Christ a cosmogonic role even if it also has soteriological implications: *ta panta* was a regular expression for the created universe;[72] *dia* was a regular preposition of agency. Philo also fused this kind of formulation with the wisdom motif in the sense of cosmogony.[73] What he lacked was the living person with whom Paul identified it. The evidence as we have it once again leads us to the most reasonable conclusion that Paul was using cosmological wisdom terminology here implying Christ's pre-existence and agency in creation.

All of which leaves us with a very early reference to Christ's involvement in creation. Perhaps it is too slender a piece of evidence from which to argue that Paul had fully worked out all that this might mean at this stage in his ministry, but even this need not be the whole story. What if Colossians was not written at the end of Paul's career, but considerably earlier? What if it emanates from an Ephesian rather than from a Roman imprisonment?[74] Such a dating is as reasonable as the more traditional, later date on the evidence as we have it. If that was the case, it would mean that Paul had a developed wisdom Christology by the early fifties. Colossians would be roughly contemporaneous with the Corinthian correspondence, which would illuminate Paul's statements about Christ in the latter. To argue that because there seems to be a higher Christology in Colossians than 1 and 2 Corinthians we must place the Colossian material

---

[69] A. Feuillet, *Le Christ sagesse de Dieu d'après les épîtres pauliniennes* (Paris, 1966); B. Reicke, *TWNT* 5, p.893; E. Lohse, *op. cit.*, p.50.

[70] J. D. G. Dunn, *op. cit.*, pp. 179-183. *Cf.* J. Murphy O'Connor, *RB* 85, 1978, pp.253-259.

[71] *Cf.* H. Conzelmann, *1 Corinthians* (Fortress, 1975), pp.144f.; R. A. Horsley, *ZNW* 69, 1978, pp.130-135. Many have detected a Stoic formulation here.

[72] E. Lohse, *op. cit.*, p.51; B. Reicke, *op. cit.*, p.892.

[73] *De Cherub.* 125.

[74] G. S. Duncan, *St. Paul's Ephesian Ministry* (Hodder & Stoughton, 1929).

much later, is no argument at all. Rather we must ask if the situations addressed by Paul demanded a full exposition of Christ's cosmological function.

But then, what if Paul was not simply composing or even quoting a Corinthian assertion[75] in 1 Corinthians 8:6, but referring to his own teaching?[76] He may have been reminding them of his basic *didachē* in Gentile churches. One can certainly appreciate that, for those with a pagan background, some sort of primary theology would have been necessary when they came to faith in Christ.

According to many, however, Paul may have been quoting an even older tradition at this point.[77] He may have been reminding them of a principle which he had not only taught in the Gentile mission, but which went back to 'those in Christ before him'.[78] If that is the case, the identification of Christ with the wisdom motif took place very early indeed.

There is also further evidence for us to consider. The fact is that Paul was not the only New Testament author who applied the wisdom theme to Christ.[79] We certainly find it again both in Hebrews and John, writings which, in spite of their individual formulations of the gospel, agree when it comes to crediting Christ with pre-existent cosmological functions, and which do so because of their common dependence on wisdom. It is highly unlikely that the authors used Paul's writings or that he used theirs, so was it simply coincidence that three major yet dissimilar authors independently came to the same conclusion? Surely some sort of common source would be a more reasonable suggestion.

It is at this point that we need to re-open the case for the identification originating with Jesus himself. It has been admitted that his interpreter, Matthew, certainly understood him in these terms,[80] but why the hesitancy to ascribe to Christ the *implicit* claim that he was the wisdom of God of which the Old Testament and intertestamental literature spoke? We would not necessarily expect an *explicit* claim.[81]

---

[75] F. W. Grosheide, *Commentary on the First Epistle to the Corinthians* (Marshall, Morgan & Scott, 1955), p.192.

[76] A. Feuillet, *op. cit.*, ch. 3.

[77] *Cf.* O. Cullmann, *op. cit.*, pp.1f., 247, who says that it is erroneous to believe that in early Christianity the work of Christ was related to salvation and not creation: 'Actually the oldest formulas connect Christ with creation'. *E.g.* 1 Cor. 8:6; *cf.* H. Conzelmann, *op. cit.*, p.144.

[78] J. G. Gibbs, *Creation and Redemption* (Brill, 1971), p.74.

[79] R. H. Fuller, *op. cit.*, p.246, points out that the widespread appearance of pre-existence as applied to Christ suggests that it was not a Pauline innovation.

[80] M. J. Suggs, *Wisdom, Christology and Law in Matthew's Gospel* (Harvard, 1970), pp.55-61; J. D. G. Dunn, *op. cit.*, p.206.

[81] The suggestion that in Lk. 11:49 Jesus is speaking on his own behalf in the 3rd person is excluded by the aorist *eipan*. M. J. Suggs, *op. cit.*, p.18.

Some have suggested that it is sufficient to say that Christ understood himself as the bearer or messenger of wisdom, rather than wisdom itself,[82] but that is somewhat less than what Christ actually claimed for himself. One of the most curious features of the Old Testament formulation of the motif, which von Rad has called 'puzzling',[83] is the way in which wisdom, as a created entity, can speak in absolute, personal, revelatory terms. wisdom does not call men to God, but to herself. wisdom does not simply claim to reveal God's truth; she *is* God's truth. Had the writers not employed the idea of her created and secondary status, even though this was understood as being prior to the rest of creation, they would have been open to the charge of ditheism.

When we come to the Gospels, we find Jesus making just this sort of claim for himself in his own teaching. The demanding, inviting 'I' of his ministry echoes the first person of the wisdom appeals.[84] Moreover this is found in a particularly marked manner where Christ sets his ministry in the context of the old dispensation, enshrined in the Torah.[85] We have remarked on the way in which Jewish thinkers eventually identified wisdom with Torah.[86] If Davies is correct, Christ's claims *vis-à-vis* the Law are also an implicit claim on his behalf to be the New Torah, the wisdom of God.[87]

Dunn's thesis does emphasize what is essentially correct and we must be grateful to him for restating it: that God's saving purposes worked out through the history of the world find their complete and ultimate expression in Christ. In that sense he *was* God's wisdom, and his ministry was the outworking of God's mind and plan. But he is more than that. As we have said, as much could be said in different degree about Moses or Elijah or any of the crucial figures of biblical history.[88] In Christ's case, however, we have people talking about a man in a way that they would never have done with reference to Old Testament predecessors: in terms which properly pertain only to deity. Wisdom was only one such category.

At this level there is an ambivalence about the way in which we use language. For example, God is loving in his actions, but God can also be described as love in himself. He is the source, the absolute, the ultimate, because he is God. In a similar way, Christ is not only the one who expresses or imparts God's wisdom, although he does both of these things. He *is* God's

---

[82] J. D. G. Dunn, *op. cit.*, p.206.   [83] G. von Rad, *op. cit.*, p.163.

[84] M. J. Suggs, *op. cit.*, p.96.   [85] *E.g.* Mt. 5:17–48.

[86] Ecclus. 24; G. F. Moore, *op. cit.* 1, pp.256-269. G. von Rad, *op. cit.*, p.166, maintains that it was not a case of the Torah taking over Wisdom, but Wisdom taking over the Torah. F. B. Craddock, *op. cit.*, p.36, goes as far as to say that Wisdom became incarnate in Law.

[87] W. D. Davies, *op. cit.*, chs. 6, 7.

[88] *E.g.* Paul's sense of personal commission, Rom. 15:14ff., *etc.*

wisdom.[89] This is what Paul and the others said about him, and when they did it they were attributing, possibly against every inbred instinct to the contrary, the prerogative of deity to a man who had been their contemporary. With all its apparent self-contradiction, this was the only way in which they were able to describe what was without precedent, however well anticipated, the unique Christ event.

[89] Hence Paul can use *sophia* in both senses, *e.g.* Col. 1:9; 2:2f.; *cf.* the use of terms like truth, light and life in John's Gospel.

PSALM 45:7–8 (6–7)
IN OLD AND NEW TESTAMENT
SETTINGS

Leslie C. Allen

It gives me great pleasure to contribute an essay to this Festschrift in honour of Donald Guthrie. Its presence is meant as a personal tribute to his wisdom and friendship enjoyed over the past twenty years. Written in the year of the royal wedding and at a time when my colleague is concluding a commentary on the Letter to the Hebrews, the subject-matter of this essay may be regarded as doubly appropriate.

The more conservative student of the Scriptures feels constrained to harmonize exactly Old Testament texts and New Testament quotations. Yet Psalm 45:7[1] cannot be rendered 'Your throne, O God, is everlasting...' or the like on dogmatic grounds, merely because Hebrews 1:8 is held to be its exact echo. The principle of exact quotation can create problems for those who are concerned with the history and religion of Israel. Isaiah 7:14, rendered in accord with Matthew 1:23 'A virgin shall conceive...', could imply belief in an eighth-century BC virgin birth in the light of Isaiah 7:16. Similarly insistence on a claim to deity in both Hebrews 1:8 and the underlying Psalm 45:7 may become a trap for the unwary. It can signify agreement with scholars who find in Israel divine kingship modelled on ancient Near Eastern prototypes.[2] K. A. Kitchen was alert to this danger in refusing to accept that the Israelite king was ever regarded as a divinity or a demi-god, 'the crux of Ps.

---

[1] Usually the Hebrew verse numbering will be followed.

[2] It is possible to overcome this problem by regarding Ps. 45 as directly messianic, as O. T. Allis did in *PTR* 21, 1923, p.260. J. B. Payne, *The Theology of the Older Testament* (Zondervan, 1962), p.262, related vv. 2–6, 8–18 to a royal wedding ('presumably' Solomon's) and treated only v. 7 as a messianic prediction. For the present writer it is axiomatic that v. 7 was relevant for an ancient royal setting. *Cf.* R. Rendall, *EQ* 27, 1955, p.215: 'Interpretation of the psalm as messianic does not exclude an original historical circumstance which led to its being composed... The psalm clearly bears the marks of some specific occasion.' Comparable with Allis' interpretation

45:6 notwithstanding'.[3] The present writer has no axe to grind in investigating the significance of Psalm 45:7. Not seldom one must reckon with the fact that a straight line cannot be drawn between Old Testament text and New Testament quotation. Within the parameters of a canonical whole there often lie development and re-interpretation of texts which had their own earlier levels of meaning.

Psalm 45:7

So significant was the publication of J. S. M. Mulder's doctoral thesis[4] in 1972 that scholarly study of Psalm 45 may be divided into pre-Mulder and post-Mulder eras. He has marshalled evidence and weighed arguments in an impressively judicious manner. As one of his chief conclusions he urged that the first colon of Psalm 45:7 be translated 'Your throne is God's for ever and ever'. His arguments have a threefold basis: the psalm's poetic structure, Hebrew syntax and the royal ideological background. Accordingly these will be the guidelines to be followed here.

Structure

In order to put Mulder's scheme into perspective and to evaluate it, it is necessary to mention first some other structural analyses. C. Schedl divided this royal wedding song into an introduction (verse 2) and a conclusion (verses 17-18) framing two main units, verses 3–10 addressed to the king and verses 11–16 addressed to the bride.[5] A. A. Anderson adopted this analysis in his commentary.[6] J. Schildenberger, whose earlier work on structure in the Psalter[7] has been of great value, analysed the psalm into the following units: verses 2–3, 4–9a, 9b–16, 17–18.[8] His concern with Psalm 45 was to achieve a

---

is that of R. Tournay, who, characteristically taking the psalm to be post-exilic, has understood it as an allegory of the royal messiah and his union with Israel ('Les affinités du Ps. xlv avec le Cantique des Cantiques et leur interprétation messianique', *Congress Volume Bonn 1962, VT Supp* 9 [Brill, 1963], pp. 168-212).

[3] *Ancient Orient and Old Testament* (Tyndale Press, 1966), p. 106 n. 76.

[4] *Studies on Psalm 45* (Witsiers).

[5] 'Neue Vorschläge zu Text und Deutung des Psalmes xlv', *VT* 14, 1964, pp. 310-318, esp. pp. 310f., 314f.

[6] *The Book of Psalms* (Oliphants, 1972), pp. 347-354.

[7] 'Bemerkungen zum Strophenbau der Psalmen', *Estudios Eclesiásticos* 34, 1960, pp. 673-687.

[8] 'Einige beachtliche Septuaginta-Lesarten in den Psalmen', *Wort, Lied und Gottesspruch. Beiträge zur Septuaginta. Festschrift für J. Ziegler*, ed. J. Schreiner (Echter Verlag, 1972), pp. 145-159, esp. pp. 150-154. The article is a refinement of 'Zur Textkritik von Ps. 45 (44)', *BZ* n. f. 3, 1959, pp. 31-43. A popular form of Schildenberger's conclusions has appeared, 'Der

structural end via text-critical means. Verses 12–16 appear notoriously deficient in metrical form, surprisingly in view of the regular metre of verses 2–11 and 17–18. Schildenberger endeavoured to reconstruct the five verses on the same metrical pattern. His commendable procedure was to test the variant readings of the Massoretic Text and the ancient versions by tracing those readings which explained the development of variants. As a text-critical exercise his work is impressive, but whether the psalm ever existed in this hypothetical, drastically pruned and 'pure' form cannot be proved. In terms of structure he found two strophes, verses 4–9a, 9b–16, each of four tricola of triple four beats (4+4+4).[9] It is probably better to accept with T. H. Gaster[10] that the psalm is metrically mixed.

N. H. Ridderbos did not venture into text criticism in establishing his analysis,[11] which was later to inspire Mulder's own structural conclusions. In verses 2, 18 the psalmist speaks of himself and his poem. Ridderbos claimed, however, that these verses cannot be separated from adjacent verses, although he did not thereafter explore their structural relationship to their contexts. Verse 3 is a *preludium* focusing upon the king, and verse 17 a *postludium*. The core of the poem falls into two units, verses 4–10 and 11–16. The first unit subdivides into three parts, verses 4–6 being concerned with the king as warrior and verses 9–10 with his wedding, while verses 7–8 have a linking role, concluding the portrait of the king in verse 7a and introducing the wedding in verse 8bc. The second unit has two parts, an address to the bride in verses 11–13 and a description of the wedding procession in verses 14–16. Both units develop similarly. The address to the king in verses 4–6 corresponds to that of the bride in verses 11 – 13 and anticipated results are included in verses 6,13. The glory of the king in verses 7–10 is parallel to the splendour of the bride in verses 14–16. Each unit reaches a culminating peak, the mention of the bride in verse 10 and that of procreation in verse 17.

Ridderbos' work was to become a formative influence upon Mulder, as the latter himself implied.[12] Mulder made comparatively little attempt to

---

Königspalm 45', *Erbe und Auftrag* 56, 1980, pp.128–133. *Cf.* E. Beaucamp's analysis as vv.2, 3–9a, 9b–17; v.18 is regarded as a gloss ('Agencement strophique du Psaume 45', *Laval Théologique et Philosophique* 23, 1967, pp.169-174.

[9] Schildenberger commended H. Bardke's layout of vv. 12–16 in BHS, but was critical of his textual apparatus (*Erbe und Auftrag* 56, p.132 n.6).

[10] *JBL* 74, 1955, p.248.

[11] 'The Psalms: Style-Figures and Structures. Certain Considerations, with Special Reference to Pss. 22, 25 and 45', *OTS* 13, 1963, pp.43-76.

[12] *Studies on Psalm 45*, p.9 n.18.

harmonize verses 12–16 metrically with the rest of the psalm. In his scheme[13] verse 2, a preface which states the poet's task, corresponds to verse 18, an epilogue stating the poet's aim. Verse 3, which has an analogue in verse 17, provides an introduction alluding to the two secondary themes of the psalm, the king's wedding by reference to his beauty (*cf.* the bride's beauty in v. 12) and the king's justice by reference to his speech. Both these themes are based upon the central theme, God's everlasting blessing upon the king. The body of the psalm falls into three units, not two. Verses 4–8a are the first unit, concerning the king's justice. It subdivides into three parts: concrete tasks to achieve justice in verses 4–5a, the consequences in verses 5b–6 and his justice in relation to its God-given basis in verses 7–8a. Verses 8bc–10 form a transitional unit: verses 8bc–9a conclude the first main unit and hint at the joyful festivities of the second one, while verses 9b–10 introduce the second unit and also hint at the first in that the king is still addressed.[14] The second main unit is verses 11–16. It treats the king's wedding in a pattern similar to that of the first: verses 11–12 specify concrete tasks to achieve, verse 13 their consequences and verses 14–15 the suitability of the bride for the marriage. There is, however, a further part, verse 16, in which the action slows down by means of lengthy repetition. It forms an inclusion (*i.e.* matching beginning and ending) with verse 9a by its reiteration of rejoicing (*śmḥ*) and the palace (*hykl*). Mulder explains this difference from the first unit by stating that there its end has to move on to the second unit, while here the poem slows down, now that it is reaching its goal. Verse 17 corresponds to verse 3: it fits the subsidiary theme of marriage into the main theme of the everlastingness of the king's reign *qua* dynasty.

There are a number of finer points in Mulder's analysis, but this summary is sufficient for present purposes. Of special importance is the corollary which he has drawn from this structuring. He speaks of the framework of the poem as a fourfold series of parallel statements:[15]

---

[13] Structure is discussed in *op. cit.*, pp.9-29.

[14] Mulder, like Schedl before him, judges the basic metre of vv. 2–10 to be 2+2. Consequently he calls these parts three strophes, although occasionally he uses the term tristichon (= tricolon). More commonly the metre is taken to be 4+4+4 (*cf.* H. Gunkel, *Die Psalmen* [Vandenhoeck & Ruprecht, 1926], p.193: H.-J. Kraus, *Psalmen* [Neukirchener Verlag, ⁵1978], p.488), in which case vv. 4–8a are three triple four-beat lines or tricola. There is little material difference, except that in v. 5c *n'wr'wt* has awkwardly to span the caesura in Mulder's metrical scheme. Accordingly a four-beat metre is more likely.

[15] *E.g. op. cit.*, p.12.

verse 3c	'*l-kn*	*brkk*	'*lhym* *l'wlm*
verse 7a		*ks'k*	'*lhym* '*wlm w'd*
verse 8b	'*l-kn*	*mšḫk*	'*lhym*
verse 18b	'*l-kn* '*mym yhwdk*		*l'lm w'd*

How in structural terms may these four statements be regarded as a frame? Verse 3 stands out as an introduction to the first main unit, verse 8b as the close of that unit and verse 18b as the end of the entire poem. Mulder has some difficulty in aligning verse 7a. Several times he admits that it 'does not form part of the frame'.[16] Elsewhere, however, he speaks of verses 7–8a as 'the central strophe of the first section'; verse 7a is 'the kernel of the whole psalm', while verses 7b–8a are also 'the heart of the first section'.[17] It is difficult to match these definitions to Mulder's actual analysis, in which verses 7–8a or even verses 4–9a form the first main unit. He appears to envisage at this point a larger entity, verses 3–10, which is certainly a constituent part of Schedl's structural scheme, but hardly of Mulder's. It carries little conviction to affirm that 'the line v. 7a must be an important link in the poem because by its position it does not belong to the frame and nevertheless it is very much parallel with the key-verses 3b [=3c], 8b and 18b.[18] Surely verse 7a ought then to be a structural landmark in its own right.

The importance of Mulder's highlighting the four similarly formed statements is that he deduces the meaning of the second, verse 7a, from the first and third, verses 3c and 8b, where God as supreme being is the subject. In verse 3c God's blessing of everlasting kingship is mentioned, while Mulder interprets verse 7a primarily in terms of the king's enthronement and only secondarily of his wedding. Accordingly verse 7a too should state the divine basis of the king's rule, and '*lhym* 'God' should be used in the same sense as in verses 3c, 8b. The framework points to an interpretation such as 'Your throne is God's (throne) for ever and ever', which matches the purport of verses 3c and 8b.[19]

It is necessary to re-examine the structure of Psalm 45, on which Mulder leaned heavily. There are good grounds for siding with Schildenberger in postulating an initial unit of verses 2–3, two tricola, and a closing one of verses 17–18, two bicola. As even Ridderbos affirmed at one point, verses 2 and 18

---

[16] *Op. cit.*, p.44; *cf.* pp.28, 33.   [17] *Op. cit.*, p.24.   [18] *Op. cit.*, p.28.

[19] *Op. cit.*, pp.43f., 73f., 80. Mulder allowed that M. Dahood's repointing of *ks'k* as a denominative piel verb with suffix, 'God has enthroned you' (*Psalms 1:1–50* [Doubleday, 1966], p.273) also matched the first and third parallels, but he required clear confirmation of such a verb before preferring it (*op. cit.*, pp.70–72, 80). It is probable that the innovation goes back to D. N. Freedman in view of Gaster's mention of a private suggestion to this effect made by Freedman (*JBL* 74, p.244 n.20).

cannot be isolated from what follows or precedes.[20] Verses 17 and 18 are interwoven in that verse 18 deals not only with the poet but also with the king and his everlasting fame, which complements the motif of progeny in verse 17. The double subject-matter of poet and king is also the concern of verses 2–3. The incorporation of verse 3 is indicated by its parallels with verses 17–18. Universality is the keynote of verses 3a, 17b,[21] 18b, and everlastingness that of verses 3c, 18b (*cf.* 18a). The motif of blessing in verse 3c is developed in the reference to progeny in verse 17a, since in the Old Testament blessing has a primary sense of fertility. Also the two second singular suffixes referring to the king in verse 3 are resumed and doubled by way of climax in the fourfold occurrence of verses 17–18.

A new unit begins in verse 4: its imperative addressed to the king matches that directed to the bride in verse 11, as Mulder maintained. Ridderbos' subdivision of the second main unit into verses 11–13 and 14–16 also appears to be correct, as an address to the bride and a description of the wedding procession. Although Ridderbos primarily analysed the first unit into three sub-units, his subsequent paralleling of verses 4–6 with verses 11–13 (address to the king/bride and consequences) and of verses 7–10 with verses 14–16 (description of the king's/bride's splendour) is significant, despite vague labelling of the second halves. One of Mulder's objections to finding a vocative in verse 7a was a structural one: none is expected at this point. 'The vocatives . . . are exactly where they should be: at the start of the two addresses, in v. 4 and v. 11.'[22] Supposing that *'lhym* is a vocative in verse 7a, has it a parallel in the next unit? Strictly no, since second person reference to the bride ceases at verse 13. Yet verse 14a does refer explicitly to her as *bt mlk* 'princess'. Apart from the appellation *bt* 'daughter' in verse 11a, this is most probably the only place in the second main unit where she is specified.[23] Is this double reference matched in the first unit at verse 4a (*gbwr* 'warrior') and verse 7a (*'lhym* 'divine one')? The personal nouns in verses 7a, 14a may be used to mark the beginnings of the second halves of their units. In verses 4–6 and 7–10 there appears to be a

[20] M. Dahood, *op. cit.*, p.272, although he isolates v. 2, mentions the inclusion of vv. 2–3 and vv. 17–18.

[21] Heb. *'rs* can mean 'land' or 'earth'. 'The reference to subject and allied peoples (vv. 5, 17) makes it probable that *in all the earth* is right' (A. F. Kirkpatrick, *The Book of Psalms* [CUP, 1902], p.252).

[22] *Op. cit.*, p.46.

[23] In v. 13 *bt sr* is to be taken as a communal personification, 'daughter Tyre' like *bt bbl* 'daughter Babylon', *etc.*, as the parallelism indicates. *Cf.* A. A. Anderson, *op. cit.*, p.353. However, A. Fitzgerald, '*BTWLT* and *BT* as Titles for Capital Cities', *CBQ* 37, 1975, pp.167-183, esp. p.182, noting the tendency of OT prophets to limit these titles to a context of disaster, refers the reader to Dahood's interpretation of *bt sr* as 'a Tyrian robe' (*Psalms* I, p.274).

deliberate antithesis in the king's location and instruments, which is enhanced by the repetition of *ṣdq* 'righteousness' in verses 5, 8 and of *ymynk* 'your right hand' in verses 5, 10.[24] Verses 4–6 focus upon the king engaged in a just war, wielding sword and bow in his right hand; verses 7–10 envisage him on his throne wielding his royal sceptre, symbol of justice, and in his palace precincts in festive garb with his new consort at his right hand.

It is possible to use a metrical argument to pinpoint the structural symmetry of verses 7a, 14a: each colon is apparently the seventh colon of its unit.[25] The difficult nature of the prosody of the second unit diminishes its worth, but it carries a little weight as a cumulative argument. A more significant procedure is to analyse the mutual relationship of the four similar statements of verses 3c, 7a, 8b and 18b. Mulder focused his attention on the first three, but tended to ignore the fourth. The first and third seem to be closely alike. The parallels are fourfold: (i) the initial *'l-kn* 'therefore', (ii) a third singular verb, (iii) a second singular verbal suffix, and (iv) *'lhym* 'God'. The second and fourth statements have three parallels: (i) a second singular suffix, (ii) and (iii) *(l)'(w)lm w'd* 'for ever and ever'. If *'lhym* refers to the king in verse 7, a fourth parallel suggests itself. The phrase *hzkyr šm* 'proclaim the name/fame', used in verse 18a, is mostly used with reference to God,[26] while the verb *hwdh* with a second singular suffix in verse 18b is of course very often employed of God in the Psalter. Was it because of these divine associations that the two expressions were used?

Thus there is affinity between verses 3c and 8b, and between verses 7a and 18b. The structural importance of verse 7a is not only that it evidently begins the second half of the first main unit: from another structural aspect two criss-crossing arcs link the four related statements, tying the main part of the psalm to its frame. Mulder stressed the relation of the second to the first and

---

[24] *Cf.* too the evident parallelism of the cluster of three nouns in v. 5b with those of v. 9a. In both groups abnormally only the first and second nouns are linked with the conjunction *waw*. The parallelism suggests that MT is correct in v. 5b. Heb. *'nwh* is to be rendered 'clemency' with A. Weiser, *The Psalms* (SCM, 1962), p.360: *cf.* the connotation 'kind(ness)' in post-biblical Hebrew for nouns and adjectives derived from *'nh* (*cf.* M. Jastrow, *A Dictionary of the Targumim* [Trübner, 1903], pp.1092, 1094). With regard to the proposed emendation *y'n h(ṣdq)* cited in BHS and adopted by RSV see the strictures of Schildenberger, *BZ* 3, pp.34f.

[25] Vv. 4–10 consist of fifteen cola divided into five tricola. For v. 6b see J. S. M. Mulder, *op. cit.*, p.18; for v. 10ab see Mulder, *op. cit.*, pp.19-20, who, dividing v. 10 after *nṣbh*, takes the verb as an archaic third feminine plural form, as does Dahood, *Psalms I*, p.274. Vv. 11-16 may be divided into eleven cola which comprise five lines: vv. 11, 12, 13 are bicola, vv. 14–15a are a tricolon and vv. 15bc–16 a bicolon. There is no consistent metre, but for the use of bicola *cf.* vv. 17–18.

[26] J. S. M. Mulder, *op. cit.*, p.139.

third; but the closer relationship of the second to the fourth may support a divine reference of some kind to the king in verse 7a.

Syntax

This section will to a large extent be devoted to an account, with comment, of Mulder's careful investigation of this area. A vocative reference in verse 7a is attested by all the ancient versions. However, Mulder has queried whether the king was necessarily addressed. Certainly the Targum by specific use of the abbreviated form of the Tetragrammaton does not relate the vocative to the king but to God as supreme being. Thus it is quite possible that all the Jewish Greek versions, the Septuagint and those of Aquila, Theodotion and Symmachus, reflect the same atomistic tradition, which is of course exegetically untenable. Only the two versions of Jerome and the Peshitta are left, all of which doubtless reflect a Christological viewpoint derived from Hebrews 1:8f.[27] Accordingly the ancient evidence may give much less support to a royal vocative than might be supposed. Mulder dismisses as not absolute the ruling that vocative *'lhym* would have had the definite article.[28] More pertinent in his view is the phenomenon that elsewhere *'wlm* when used predicatively always has a preceding preposition, whether the clause is verbless, as here, or includes the verb *hyh,* 'to exist, last'. He admits that this argument is relatively weak since other temporal expressions are used as the sole predicate in verbless clauses, including *nṣḥ,* a semantic equivalent of *'wlm,* in Jeremiah 15:18.[29] Mulder uses as his main objection a contextual one, comparison with verses 3c and 8b, discussed earlier.[30] He also appeals to the work of F. I. Andersen on verbless clauses in the Pentateuch, noting that a sequence 'predicate-subject' would be expected when the predicate is indefinite, as here; but he grants that strictly this rule is valid only for pentateuchal verbless clauses.[31]

The supposition that *ks'k 'lhym* represents the subject, with *'lhym* as a genitive, 'your throne of God', 'your divine throne', Mulder discounts doubtless rightly as an improbable solution and a very unusual construction in the Old Testament; for him it incurs too the objections levelled against a predicative use of *'wlm.* But he does state that such an interpretation is not to be excluded absolutely.[32] Mulder deals next with two interpretations of *'lhym* as part of the predicate, the rest of which is to be understood. The first is the rendering 'your throne is (like) God ('s throne)', for which G. R. Driver and more recently J. A. Emerton[33] have argued. Emerton pointed to examples of ellipsis of the

---

[27] *Op. cit.,* pp. 48f. But see n.73 below.   [28] *Op. cit.,* pp.39f.   [29] *Op. cit.,* pp.40-43.
[30] *Op. cit.,* pp.43f., 46f.   [31] *Op. cit.,* pp.47f.   [32] *Op. cit.,* pp.51-54.
[33] 'The Syntactical Problem of Psalm xlv. 7', *JSS* 13, 1968, pp.58-63.

pregenitive noun and he also urged that the preposition *kaph* 'like' can be omitted.[34] Mulder granted that in some circumstances metaphor and simile have a similar meaning, but he maintained that in this case a comparison would give the wrong meaning. Verses 3c, 8b require a direct relationship and a straightforward identification, as in verse 7b, rather than a simile or metaphor. 'It is the king's dependence on God that forms the fundament of the king's justice and thus of the permanence of the king's reign.'[35] Accordingly Mulder urged that verse 7a be rendered 'Your throne is God's throne . . .'. There are in the Old Testament parallels where the predicate indicates a material or quality, but not where the predicate is a concrete person or thing: 'We have to admit that from the syntactical point of view there are no good parallels to this way of expressing oneself in the Old Testament.' However, Mulder pointed for contextual support to verse 7b, where the construct chain is expressed fully. He judged that in his opinion his understanding was a better solution than any other proposal.[36]

It is clear that syntax gives an uncertain sound and cannot of itself settle the exegetical issue. Presuppositions derived from the material content of this royal psalm and also from its ideological background, together with formal analysis, must provide the weight needed to tip the scales one way or another.

Ideology

Attempts have been made to claim as relevant the use of *'lhym* to refer to a supernatural being, such as an angel or even the shade of Samuel (1 Sa. 28:13), and to argue that since David is compared with an angel (1 Sa. 29:2; 2 Sa. 14:17; 19:28) *'lhym* can here be applied to the king.[37] Emerton has correctly observed with regard to the latter group of texts that comparison does not necessarily imply identity, and that since the comparison in 1 Samuel 29:9 relates to a period when David was not yet king, the king of Gath would hardly have regarded him as a divine ruler.[38] Appeal to the apparent use of *'lhym* for human judges is exegetically unfounded.[39] Mulder admits that *'l gbwr* 'Warrior

---

[34] Emerton suggested that Ps. 80:11b has a parallel sense, rendered as in the Revised Psalter 'The boughs thereof were like the boughs of cedars of God' (*art. cit.,* pp.60-62). In Pss. 45:7; 80:11 the NEB adopted this construction. In Ps. 80:11 the text, rendered as in RSV, may be interpreted of territorial dominion in the light of v. 12, with reference to the central Palestinian uplands and to Lebanon respectively.

[35] *Op. cit.,* pp.55-58, esp. p.58.   [36] *Op. cit.,* pp.58-65.

[37] *E.g.* J. R. Porter, 'Psalm xlv. 7', *JTS* 12, 1961, pp.51-53, esp. p.51.

[38] *JSS* 13, p.58.

[39] In Ex. 21:6; 22:7, 8 *'l/'d 'lhym* means 'to the sanctuary' (B. S. Childs, *Exodus* [SCM, 1974], pp.469, 475). In Ps. 82:6 the reference is not to men but to gods, 'the heavenly beings, each of which controls the destiny of a nation (see Deut. 32:8)' (J. W. Rogerson and J. W. McKay,

God'[40] in Isaiah 9:5 would be the best parallel to *'lhym* in Psalm 45:7, but he objects that no question of real divinity is indicated there.[41] This parallel is worthy of closer study. There is a redactional relationship between *'l gbwr* in Isaiah 9:5 and the same title used of God as supreme being in Isaiah 10:21.[42] H. Wildberger has related the title to the use of *gbwr* and *'lhym* in Psalm 45:4,7 respectively.[43] This twofold parallel is of special interest in that, if the structural conclusions reached earlier are correct, the titles feature prominently as vocatives at the beginning of two halves of a unit. Is the breaking up of a stereotyped phrase employed in Psalm 45:4, 7, except that for *'l* the longer *'lhym* is used? The prophet may have been applying to a future ideal king a motif already in use for the Davidic king. O. Kaiser seems to make this assumption when he explains the title in Isaiah 9:5 in terms of the relationship of the Davidic monarch to Yahweh as adoptive son (*cf.* 2 Sa. 7:14; Ps. 2:7) and thus legitimate representative of God upon earth.[44]

In the case of Psalm 45:7 Kraus is among the commentators who similarly see in verses 3c, 7a, 17 the influence of the conception of the Davidic dynasty as set out in 2 Samuel 7; with reservations he renders *'lhym* 'Göttlicher'.[45] A comparative application of a divine epithet occurs in Psalm 89:28 (27), where *'lywn* 'most high' is used of the king. The epithet functions as an echo of Yahweh's role as head of the heavenly council, described in verses 6–9 (5–8): elsewhere *'lywn* is employed for this divine role. 'The king's dominion on earth (is made to) appear as the reflexion of God's cosmic supremacy . . . The king does on earth what God does in heaven.'[46] The Davidic king was neither a mere secular leader nor a deified monarch but a theocratic vicegerent. A comment made by B. S. Childs concerning the royal Psalm 72 is applicable both to Isaiah 9:5 and to Psalm 45:7: 'The extravagant language is possible in Israel because

---

Psalms 51–100 [CUP, 1977], p.164). For the supposed use of *'lhy'* with reference to a king in a fifth-century BC Aramaic letter (A. A. Macintosh, *Trivium* 1, 1966, pp. 182f., followed by B. Couroyer, *RB* 78, 1971, p.240), Mulder's adverse observations are significant (*op. cit.*, p.45 n.59).

[40] H. Wildberger takes *gbwr* as adjectival, comparing 1 Sa. 14:52 (*Jesaja* [Neukirchener Verlag, 1972], p.382). R. E. Clements regards it as substantival, 'Divine Warrior' (*Isaiah 1-39* [Marshall, Morgan & Scott, 1980], p.108).

[41] *Op. cit.*, p.38.

[42] A. R. Johnson urged that in both cases the title may mean no more than 'mighty warrior' (*Sacral Kingship in Ancient Israel* [University of Wales, ²1967], p.30 n.1). The recurrence of the title in Dt. 10:17; Je. 32:18 suggests that in the case of Is. 9:5 'a divine epithet has been applied here to the king' (T. N. D. Mettinger, *King and Messiah* [Gleerup, 1976], p.273).

[43] *TZ* 16, 1960, pp.322f.; *op. cit.*, p.383.   [44] *Isaiah 1-12* (SCM, 1972), p.129.

[45] *Psalmen*, pp.489, 491, 494.   [46] T. N. D. Mettinger, *op. cit.*, p.263.

the rule of God is the ultimate object being praised.'[47] There are two safeguards in Psalm 45 against misunderstanding metaphorical language descriptive of theological function: its background in an event taking place at the royal court, rather than in any cultic activity, and the denial of identity with Yahweh in verse 8, where God is unmistakably differentiated from the king.[48]

In this connection the content of verses 7–8 is significant. The divine anointing of verse 8bc is the consequence of verses 7b–8a, while verse 7bc appears to be the ground of verse 7a.[49] Thus the two divinely orientated statements of verses 7a, 8bc form an artistic cluster around descriptions of the moral emphasis of the king's rule in verses 7b–8a. The king's permanent rule as God's viceroy (in a dynastic sense, as in v. 17?)[50] is dependent upon the justice of his administration, while in turn the wedding festivities[51] are a divine recompense for the king's just rule.[52] The latter corollary invites comparison with the royal Psalm 18:21–25 (20–24),[53] and the former one is reminiscent of 1 Kings 3:6; 8:25 and the royal Psalm 132:12.[54]

Mulder's case for understanding verse 7a 'Your throne is God's for ever and ever' has as its main planks structural considerations and the semantic difficulty of applying '*lhym* to the king, and as a supporting argument a syntactical contention that his rendering is the least improbable, although incapable of actual proof. Mettinger has described, and accepted, this rendering as one which 'Mulder has made probable'.[55] An attempt has been made here to show that Mulder's conclusions concerning the structure of the psalm are not necessarily correct, and that the boundaries of his study of possible human applications of

---

[47] *Introduction to the Old Testament as Scripture* (SCM, 1979), p.517.

[48] K.-H. Bernhardt, *Das Problem der altorientalischen Königsideologie im Alten Testament*, VT *Supp* 8 (Brill, 1961), p.263. He relates the psalm to the monarchy of the northern kingdom; for a southern provenance see Kraus, *op. cit.*, p.489.

[49] *Cf.* A. B. Rhodes, *Psalms* (SCM, 1960), pp.78f.: 'The king's dynasty will continue since he seeks to rule in equity and righteousness.'

[50] *Cf.* the discussion and affirmative conclusion of J. S. M. Mulder, *op. cit.*, pp.74-76.

[51] As observed above, Mulder relates the anointing of v. 8b to the king's accession and secondarily to the festive event of the wedding (*op. cit.*, pp.24, 28). Since v. 8c immediately follows v. 8b in the same clause, it is probably preferable to reverse the references.

[52] *Cf.* the Mesopotamian parallels adduced by J. S. M. Mulder, *op. cit.*, p.120.

[53] *Cf.* Ps. 101, which is probably to be understood as a lament in which negative confession is used as the basis of a plea for divine intervention in time of trouble.

[54] For the conditionality *cf.* the hypothesis of M. Weinfeld, *JAOS* 90, 1970, p.196, that the conception of a conditional promise concerning the Davidic dynasty developed especially after the division of the kingdom; it existed alongside that of an unconditional promise and was eventually taken up by the Deuteronomists.

[55] *Op. cit.*, p.273.

the term *'lhym* were too narrow in that no room was allowed for theological sophistication. A vocative understanding may not be ruled out of court as an impossible or improbable option.[56]

Hebrews 1:8–9

Psalm 45:7–8 is cited from the Septuagint in the first chapter of the letter to the Hebrews as part of a catena of Old Testament quotations. Its presence in this hellenistic Christian milieu raises a number of questions as to its text, context and relevance.

Text

There are a number of variations between the Septuagint (Ps. 44:7–8) and the text of Hebrews. K. J. Thomas in an analysis of the relationship between the two texts has discussed the three main variants: the addition of *kai* 'and' between the two clauses of 1:8, the transference of the article *hē* from the second *rhabdos* 'sceptre' to the first, and a reading *autou* 'his' instead of *sou* 'your' at the end of verse 8.[57] In the last case Thomas considers original the reading *autou* of P[46] Aleph B. He also explored the relationship of the Hebrews text with LXX codices A and B, and concluded that it represented a primitive form of the LXX text, in its reading with A *ton aiōna tou aiōnos* 'the age of the age' instead of B's anarthrous *aiōna aiōnos* (v. 8), and its reading with B *anomian* 'lawlessness' instead of A's *adikian* 'unrighteousness' (v. 9), a more literal antithesis to *dikaiosynēn* 'righteousness'. Accordingly the author of Hebrews used a LXX text in a comparatively pure form before it had undergone diverse revision in A and B respectively.

The second of the variants mentioned above, the transference of the article, reverses subject and predicate: 'the sceptre of uprightness is (the) sceptre . . . '. The stylistic effect is to achieve a symmetrical order between the two clauses of verse 8. A. Vanhoye has suggested that semantically the difference is that the new subject refers to the divine sceptre; he notes that *euthytēs* 'uprightness' is not infrequently used of God in the Greek Psalter.[58] The addition of *kai* may have been simply to heighten the balance of the clauses. However, the author's practice of linking separate quotations with *kai* (1:10 and perhaps 10:37) or *kai palin* 'and again' (1:5; 2:13; 10:30) suggests that he divided the quotation into

---

[56] Mulder at one point seems to imply that if a plausible meaning could be given to a vocative *'lhym* 'grammatical objections should not be considered insuperable' (*op. cit.*, p.48).

[57] 'The Old Testament Citations in Hebrews', *NTS* 11, 1964/65, pp.301-325, esp. pp.305, 321-323.

[58] *Situation du Christ* (Les Éditions du Cerf, 1969), p.185.

two, verse 8a and verses 8b–9.[59] The third variant is more controversial. Most manuscripts read *sou* 'your (kingdom)', which has been judged to be an easier reading, conforming to the second singular references of the context and also to the LXX. Accordingly *autou* is preferable as a harder reading and also as having early and strong attestation.[60] The issue has a syntactical and theological corollary. The reading *autou* requires *ho theos* in verse 8a to be its antecedent, which must then function as predicate (or subject): 'Your (= the Son's) throne is God (the Father) for ever and ever, and the sceptre of uprightness (the Son's) is the sceptre of his (the Father's) kingdom.'[61] Kistemaker has argued that, in view of the separation of clauses by *kai*, a change from a second person address of the Son to a third person reference is plausible.[62] B. M. Metzger, however, is surely right in considering that this explanation only slightly removes the strangeness of a shift in persons.[63] Similarly Vanhoye has objected that this construing of the clauses creates an illogicality: if God is identified with the throne, how can the sceptre be attributed to him?[64] Others have objected that an odd and extremely unlikely meaning is imposed upon the first clause.[65] Metzger, expressing the decision of a majority of scholars responsible for the United Bible Societies' third edition of the *Greek New Testament*, has justified *sou* on the grounds of this internal difficulty and the weight and variety of external evidence for *sou*.[66] The contextually unsuitable reading *hymōn* 'your' for *hēmōn* 'our' attested by the same group P^{46} Aleph B in 2 Corinthians 6:11 'is a reminder that antiquity of attestation is not always a pointer to the true reading'.[67]

---

[59] B. F. Westcott, *The Epistle to the Hebrews* (Macmillan, 1892), p.26; S. Kistemaker, *The Psalm Citations in the Epistle to the Hebrews* (van Soest, 1961), p.25; A. Vanhoye, *La structure littéraire de l'Épître aux Hébreux* (Desclée de Brouwer, [2]1976), pp.71f.; J. C. McCullough, 'The Old Testament Quotations in Hebrews', *NTS* 26, 1980, pp.363-379, esp. p.369.

[60] *Cf.* K. J. Thomas, *art. cit.,* p.305; C. Spicq, *L'Épître aux Hébreux* 1 (Gabalda, 1952), p.418; G. Zuntz, *The Text of the Epistles* (OUP, 1953), pp.63f.

[61] K. J. Thomas, *loc. cit.*; *cf.* Westcott, *op. cit.*, pp.24–26, who argued that exegetically a divine address to the Son does not suit the context. It is of interest to note that Wycliffe and Tyndale translated similarly.

[62] *Op. cit.,* p.25; *cf.* NEB.

[63] *A Textual Commentary on the Greek New Testament* (UBS, 1971), pp.662f.

[64] *Situation,* pp.184f.

[65] F. F. Bruce, *Commentary on the Epistle to the Hebrews* (Marshall, Morgan & Scott, 1964), p.19; N. Turner, *Grammatical Insights into the New Testament* (T. & T. Clark, 1965), p.15.

[66] *Op. cit.,* p.663. A. Souter, *Novum Testamentum Graece* (Clarendon, [2]1947), *ad loc.,* also reads *sou*. See further n.80 below.

[67] F. F. Bruce, *1 and 2 Corinthians* (Marshall, Morgan & Scott, 1971), p.213.

Messianic background

Psalm 45 belongs to a group of royal psalms. These psalms, including Psalms 2, 72, 110 among others, are conspicuously scattered throughout the Psalter. C. Westermann has made the plausible suggestions that once they all belonged to a single collection and that, since the final form of the Psalter is a post-exilic work, their distribution presupposes an understanding of them as eschatological and messianic in non-monarchical Judaism after the exile.[68] The LXX rendering of (*šyr*) *ydydt* 'love (song)' in the psalm heading as *hyper tou agapētou* 'for the beloved' accords with a messianic perspective. Such an interpretation features too in later Jewish texts. In the *Testaments of the Twelve Patriarchs* messianic use of Psalm 45 appears in the *Testament of Judah* 24:1 (verse 5) and possibly of verse 3 in 24:3 and verse 7 in 24:5–6.[69] Rabbi Eliezer (end of first and beginning of second century AD) in a discussion whether there would be weapons in the messianic age answered on the basis of Psalm 45:4 that weapons would have an ornamental use.[70] The Midrash cites Psalm 45:7 in connection with the Judah oracle, Genesis 49:10–12.[71] In turn the Psalms Targum refers in Psalm 45:3 explicitly to *mlk' mšyḥ* 'the King Messiah'.[72] Messianic usage, apart from the Hebrew Psalter, seems to be attested sufficiently widely for a Jewish background to be postulated behind the Christological application in Hebrews 1:8–9.[73]

Context

Hebrews 1:8–9 is part of a series of Old Testament quotations intended to confirm that as the Son of God Christ has a name superior to that of angels. The overall purpose was evidently to demonstrate that God's ancient word, the law once revealed through angels, is inferior to that now given through the Son (Heb. 1:2; 2:2).[74] The inferiority of angels *vis-à-vis* the Son implies the superiority of the Christ-mediated revelation. G. Hughes is doubtless correct in evaluating the perspective of the quotations related to Christ: they do not

---

[68] *Theologia Viatorum* 8, 1961/62, p.284.

[69] *Cf.* R. H. Charles, *The Apocrypha and Pseudepigrapha of the Old Testament in English* 2 (Clarendon, 1913), pp.323f. Mention should be made of M. de Jonge's claim that the work is a Christian production of the end of the second or beginning of the third century AD, using Jewish materials (*The Testaments of the Twelve Patriarchs* [van Gorcum, 1953]).

[70] Talmud *Shab.* 63a.   [71] *Gen. Rabbah* 99:8.

[72] *Cf. SB* 3, pp.679f.; A. Vanhoye, *op. cit.,* p.177.

[73] If in the LXX the address referred to God as supreme being (see n.27 above), it is here transferred to Christ, like that of Ps. 102:26-28 in vv. 10-12. However, this understanding of Ps. 45:8 is unlikely; essentially the LXX is much less atomistic than the Targum.

[74] *Cf.* J. W. Thompson, 'The Structure and Purpose of the Catena in Hebrews 1:5–13', *CBQ* 38, 1976, pp.352-363, esp. p.363; G. Hughes, *Hebrews and Hermeneutics* (CUP, 1979), pp.7f.

function as Christological *proofs,* but work back from the accepted truths set out in the confessional elements of the prologue (1:1–4), and they serve as *illustrations* of this high standing.[75] In fact 1:5–14 appear to be part of a larger section 1:5 – 2:18, in which Christ is compared with angels. In 1:5–14 stress is laid upon his divine nature, with side glances at his humanity, while after the exhortation in 2:1–4 his humanity is emphasized in 2:5–18, not without reference to his heavenly roles.[76]

Hebrews 1:5–14 subdivides into three parts: verses 5–6 in which two quotations refer to the Son and a third to angels, verses 7–12 in which the first quotation relates to angels and two to the Son, and verses 13–14 where one relates to the Son before a contrast is drawn with angels.[77] The framework of 1:5–14 consists of Psalm 2:7, cited in verse 5, and Psalm 110:1, used in verse 13. Psalm 2 has a wider influence upon the text than verse 5: in the LXX Psalm 2:8 speaks of the Son as destined to possess the nations as an 'inheritance' (*klēronomian*). A. Snell rightly affirms that 'the reader is expected, as often in the New Testament, to bear in mind the words which follow those explicitly quoted and refer to his dominion'.[78] A *klēronom-* word-group appears in verses 2, 4 and 14. The vocabulary of a messianic psalm is used to describe both the work of Christ and its representative nature as applicable to the church. The use of Psalm 110 (LXX 109) in the concluding part of the framework is significant: at 5:5–6, Psalm 110:4 is cited alongside Psalm 2:7, while already in the prologue (at verse 3) oblique reference has been made to Psalm 110:1 as well as to Psalm 2. The link between the psalms for the author is that both refer Christologically to the Son's exaltation. The association is not unexpected since the two psalms relate primarily to the enthronement of the Davidic king, and use similarly structured performative formulations in which God bestows upon him kingship (Ps. 2:7) and royal priesthood (Ps. 110:4). Was the association encouraged too by the rendering *exegennēsa se* 'I begot you' in 109: 3 LXX, which would recall *gegennēsa se* 'I have begotten you' in 2:7? Be that as it may,

---

[75] *Op. cit.,* pp.60f. *Cf.* G. B. Caird, 'The Exegetical Methods of Hebrews', *Canadian Journal of Theology* 5, 1959, pp.44-51, esp. p.51: 'He starts from Christ and from the Christian experience of salvation which he shares with his readers. He goes back to the Old Testament with his ears already attuned to the voice of him who has spoken from heaven. But the Old Testament enables him to make his experience articulate, coherent and reasonable.'

[76] The disagreement between J. Swetnam, *Bib* 54, 1972, pp.372-375, and A. Vanhoye, *Bib* 55, 1974, p.371, may be resolved partially at least in this way.

[77] *Cf.* J. W. Thompson, *CBQ* 38, p.354. Vanhoye had drawn attention to the AB/BA/ AB... alternation of Son-related and angels-related material, which continues as far as 2:3 (*Situation,* p.121).

[78] *An Explanation of the Epistle to the Hebrews* (Faith Press, 1959), p.59.

Hebrews 1 exhibits a network of closely related Old Testament material.[79] It may be asked whether and how Psalm 45 fits into this literary skein. Kistemaker has suggested that it was used because of the association of its content with that of 2 Samuel 7:13. The next verse, 2 Samuel 7:14, features at 1:5 together with Psalm 2:7. 2 Samuel 7:13 is a divine promise relating to David's offspring; 'I shall establish the *throne* of his *kingdom for ever.*'[80] In addition, was the presence of the royal *rhabdos* 'sceptre' in Psalms 2:9; 44:7; 109:2 LXX a contributory factor? More obviously, in view of the dominant role of Psalm 110 in chapter 1, the phrase *eis ton aiōna* 'for ever' in Psalm 109:4 LXX (which is not actually cited until 5:6, but from then on plays a most important role in the Epistle)[81] must have forged a latent link with the longer phrase in Psalm 44:7 LXX, which Hebrews 1:8 cites. A similar conclusion doubtless applies to the motif of everlastingness in Psalm 101:27–28 LXX, quoted in Hebrews 1:11–12.[82] Another possible contextual link is *christon* 'anointed one' (Ps. 2:2) with *echrisen* 'he anointed' (Ps. 44:8 LXX), quoted in Hebrews 1:9.

Meaning

The Old Testament quotations related to Christ as the Son of God in Hebrews 1 have been shown to be tied together closely in wording and/or motifs. The content of verses 8–9 may now be examined in greater detail. Vanhoye has noted the device of inclusion employed in these verses: the two linked by the author with the conjunction *kai* begin and almost end with *ho theos*.[83] Since a similar phenomenon occurs in verse 5 with *huios/huion* 'Son' as the inclusive element and the device is there used to highlight a key term, it is likely that the double *ho theos* has a similar importance, and so is to be rendered in both cases as a vocative referring to Christ.[84] The Son is unmistakably aligned with God as divine king over against the angels, who function in a subordinate role as messengers and ministers. The divine claim, which serves to illustrate the relationship of verse 3a, is controlled and qualified not only by the distinction of the text itself in verse 9b, but also by contextual association with Psalm 110:1. The latter verse was used by the early church to affirm supreme

---

[79] The network continues into ch.2. For the NT association of Ps. 110 and Ps. 8, which appears in ch. 2, see B. Lindars, *New Testament Apologetic* (SCM, 1961), pp.50f.

[80] *Op. cit.*, p.78. S. Kistemaker, *loc. cit.*, plausibly links the variant *autou* in Heb. 1:8 with 2 Sa. 7:13.

[81] Heb. 6:20; 7:17, 21, 24, 28. *Cf. dienekes* 7:3; 10:12, 14.

[82] M. R. D'Angelo, *Moses in the Letter to the Hebrews* (Scholars Press, 1979), p.166.

[83] *Structure,* p.71.

[84] For the vocative usage Vanhoye has compared the quotation in 10:5–7, where it indubitably occurs, albeit concerning the Father (*Situation,* pp.176f.).

exaltation without calling into question the glory of God the Father. It permitted Christians to confess faith in the lordship of Christ before they had resolved such problems as ditheism or subordinationism. 'This image (of session at God's right hand) intrinsically affirmed a continuing relationship between the exalted Christ and God, precluding any possibility of conceiving Christ as a new deity dethroning an older one.'[85]

A further contrast between verses 8–9 and verse 7 is the immutability of the Son. Angels may be changed into creaturely winds and flames, but the Son is far above this transient world, as verses 10–12 are to elaborate, and he is enthroned for ever.[86] Thompson has drawn attention to the spatial distinction between the earthly and the heavenly which underlies chapter 1, especially verses 7–9 (*cf.* 7:26).[87] Whereas Jewish traditions conceived of an earthly king reigning for ever and metaphorically sitting beside God as his plenipotentiary, Greek metaphysical thinking has been brought to the text so that Christ was understood to be above the created order and eternally in the heavenly presence of God in an ironically literal manner.[88]

Significant features of Psalm 44:8 LXX, which is cited in Hebrews 1:9, are the triple use of past tenses and the idea of an ordered, logical sequence. The aorist tenses of the first two verbs are a literalistic rendering of the Hebrew perfects which connote a present attitude of mind. For the author approaching the text from a Christological perspective the verbs describe past activities of the Son, which lead causally to God's own action. I. de la Potterie has observed that the anointing constitutes a recompense for the work of justice accomplished by the Son in his earthly life, and refers to the accolade of celestial royalty granted at the time of his exaltation.[89] Spicq has compared *dia touto* 'therefore' with *dio* in Philippians 2:9, which is a hinge between Christ's earthly humiliation and obedience on the one hand and his exaltation by God on the other.[90] One does not need to go outside the context to find a pattern of passion and glorification: Vanhoye has called attention to 1:3b and noted that the pattern is a recurring feature of the Epistle (*cf.* 2:9; 4:7–10; 7:27 – 8:1; 10:12).[91] The author evidently equated the honour of sitting at God's right hand with anointing, for which Acts 2:34–36 may be compared. Comparison of 1:9 with

---

[85] D. M. Hay, *Glory at the Right Hand: Psalm 110 in Early Christianity* (Abingdon, 1973), p.160.

[86] *Cf.* J. Schneider, *The Letter to the Hebrews* (Eerdmans, 1957), pp.14f.

[87] *CBQ* 38, p.359; *cf. NovT* 19, 1977, pp.214f.

[88] *Cf.* O. Linton, *NTS* 7, 1971, pp.260f.

[89] 'L'onction du Christ', *Nouvelle Revue Théologique* 80, 1958, pp.225-252, esp. p.249.

[90] *L'Épître aux Hébreux* 2 (Gabalda, 1953), p.19.   [91] *Situation*, pp.187f.

Acts 2:36; 4:26–27 suggests that *echrisen* 'anointed' was intended to evoke the term *christos*. The gladness associated with the anointing would connote for the author the joy associated with his exaltation to God's right hand (*cf.* 12:2).

Anticipations

Subsequent content of the Epistle suggests that with Christian eyes the author glimpsed other insights in Psalm 45:7–8. Reference to the 'companions' (*metochous*) of the Son in 1:9 has met with diverse explanations. Some scholars interpret in terms of the angels, noting that the preposition *para* 'in comparison with' has already been used of them in 1:4.[92] Others look ahead into the Epistle and explain with reference to Christians, as in 3:14.[93] Both explanations are tantalizingly plausible. Vanhoye has resolved the impasse by seeing a double reference, to angels in the immediate context and also in open-ended fashion to Christians, whom the Son calls to share his heavenly glory (*cf.* 2:10, 14; 12:22–23).[94] They are *metochoi* of a 'heavenly calling' from the 'Apostle' (3:1). According to 3:14, steadfast Christians are *metochoi* of 'the Christ': significantly two motifs of 1:9 are blended. They are also *metochoi* of 'the Holy Spirit' (6:4). Was there an underlying association of the 'oil of gladness' of Psalm 45:8 with that of Isaiah 61:3? The Hebrew is the same (*šmn śśwn*); the LXX uses different vocabulary. It is of note that both Psalm 45:8 and Isaiah 61:1 speak of anointing (LXX *echrisen* in both), while Isaiah 61:1 mentions the Spirit. In Hebrews 12:8 *metochoi* is used with *paideias,* 'partaking in chastisement'; the phrase is set in a context of Christian sonship.

More recent commentators tend to affirm that the term 'Christ' in Hebrews lacks any messianic connotation or reference to the basic meaning 'anointed'.[95] Westcott distinguished between *ho christos,* which 'appears always to retain more or less the idea of the office as the crown of the old covenant', and the anarthrous form which he judged to be simply a proper noun.[96] A test as to whether any etymological force survives in the term may be applied by checking its contextual associations in each case. Vanhoye has noted that in 3:6 *christos* is linked with 'Son', the key word of chapter 1.[97] Hebrews 3:14 has been discussed above. In 5:5 *ho christos* is set in a context echoing that of the first chapter. Psalm 2:7 and Psalm 110 (verse 4) are quoted: an authorial link with Psalm 45:8 may be discerned. Perhaps in 9:11, where the anarthrous *christos* is

---

[92] E.g. J. Héring, *The Epistle to the Hebrews* (Epworth, 1970), p.10.
[93] F. F. Bruce, *op. cit.,* p.21.
[94] *Situation,* p.193.
[95] E.g. F. L. Filson, *Yesterday* (SCM, 1967), p.36.
[96] *Op. cit.,* pp.33f.   [97] *Situation,* p.192.

associated with the high priesthood, its scriptural basis in Psalm 110:4 suggests the same conclusion.[98]

It is a truism to refer to the importance of Psalm 110 for the theology of Hebrews. 'It is not too much to say that the entire christology of the Epistle stems from a study of this psalm,' concluded Lindars.[99] More precisely, 'all that [the author] says about the eternity of Christ and His work is connected with what he has read in Ps. 110 about "a priest for ever".'[100] Dunn has observed that most of the references to Jesus as Son revolve around 'the Melchizedek motif of the priest-king'. The three quotations in 1:5, 8 refer to the king, and five of the remaining references to the Son (4:14; 5:5, 8–10; 7:3, 28) speak of him as high priest.[101] G. Theissen has asked whether any traces of the priestly dignity of Jesus are to be seen in Hebrews 1, in the light of Philo, *Fuga* 108–110, 118, where the high priestly and royal Logos has God as father, is anointed with oil (*cf.* Heb. 1:9) and clothed with the world (*cf.* 1:11–12).[102] All this highlighting of the Melchizedek theme prompts a closer look at 1:8–9. It has already been noted that the motif of eternity (*eis ton aiōna*) connects with the same element in Psalm 110:4. The author evidently bracketed verses 8b–9 by prefacing with *kai* to form a separate quotation. Was his reason a desire to draw his readers' attention to *basileias* 'kingdom' and *dikaiosynēn* 'righteousness'? Students of Hebrews sometimes wonder why the citation of Psalm 45 was continued after verse 8a or after verse 8b.[103] The author may well have intended an anticipation of Melchizedek, whose priesthood was perennial and whose name by popular etymology means *basileus dikaiosynēs* 'king of righteousness' (7:2).[104] While the high-priestly motif is treated in detail in and after chapter 7, the author seems gradually to edge towards it. Its exposure to view at 2:17 and 3:1 seems to pick up earlier material, 1:3 and also 1:9 (*metochoi*). For the author

---

[98] Underlying 11:26 are definite messianic roots, but the origin is Ps. 89 (LXX 88): 51f.: *cf. inter alios* J. D. G. Dunn, *Christology in the Making* (SCM, 1980), n.215 on pp.288f.

[99] *Op. cit.*, p.51.

[100] R. Williamson, *Philo and the Epistle to the Hebrews* (Brill, 1970), p.447.

[101] *Op. cit.*, p.55.

[102] *Untersuchungen zum Hebräerbrief* (G. Mohn, 1969), pp.42f.

[103] *E.g.* J. van der Ploeg, 'L'exégèse de l'Ancien Testament dans l'Épître aux Hébreux', *RB* 54, 1947, pp.187-228, esp. p.206.

[104] *Cf.* Philo, *Leg. All.* iii. 79, and Josephus, *Ant.* i. 10. 2; *Wars* vi. 10, who similarly translated the name, but in better Greek, *basileus dikaios*. In Targum *Pseudo-Jonathan* in place of the name is the rendering *mlk' ṣdyq'* 'righteous king' (*cf. Neofiti I mlk' ṣdq*). *Cf.* J. A. Fitzmyer, 'Now This Melchizedek... (Heb. 7:1)', *Essays on the Semitic Background of the New Testament* (Geoffrey Chapman, 1971), pp.221-245, esp. pp.229-231; A. Rodríguez Carmona, 'La figura de Melquisedec en la literatura targúmica', *Estudios Bíblicos* 37, 1978, pp.79-102, esp. pp.81-85, 101.

the royal, righteous and eternal Son of Hebrews 1:8–9 would hardly have failed to suggest the Melchizedek-type priesthood.

A number of commentators have remarked upon the ways in which the end of the Epistle echoes its beginning. Angels feature outside chapters 1–2 only at 12:22; 13:2. The work of Christ is applied representatively to the church as the Epistle draws to a close. The firstborn Son (1:6) shares his attribute with his people (12:23). They receive from him a kingdom (1:8; 12:28) which is unshakeable, unlike the earth and heavens (1:10; 12:28). Jesus is 'the same' (1:12; 13:8) 'for ever' (*eis tous aiōnas*, 13:8; *cf. eis ton aiōna*, 1:8). Slightly earlier, in 12:8–11, there is a noteworthy cluster of vocabulary: *metochoi, huioi, eirēnikon* 'peaceful', *dikaiosynēs* and the motif of joy (*charas*). The second echoes chapter 1 in general, including 1:8, the first, fourth and fifth echo 1:9, while the third and fifth are modelled on 7:2.[105]

At this point a fresh look at *ho theos* in 1:8–9 may be ventured. Fragments of a Qumran scroll, 11Q Melchizedek, dating from the first half of the first century AD or earlier, appear to refer to Melchizedek as an angel-warrior, calling him *'lwhym* 'god, heavenly being'.[106] The significance of this Qumran tradition for Hebrews is disputed. M. de Jonge and A. S. van der Woude have claimed with regard to chapters 1 – 2 that it 'helps us to understand certain ways of thinking in the Judaism of the first century AD which form the background against which the argumentation of Heb. i–ii can be understood'.[107] As for chapter 7, Melchizedek is understood to be 'an (arch-)angel who appeared to Abraham long ago' (*cf.* 7:15–16), whose priesthood lasts for ever, but who is inferior to the Son.[108] R. N. Longenecker, taking into account Philo's treatment of Melchizedek as a representative of the eternal Logos, has similarly proposed that on the basis of 7:3 'in agreement with his addressees [the author of Hebrews] acknowledges the legitimacy of considering Melchizedek a heavenly figure of continuing priestly significance', but as a prototype of the greater high priesthood of Christ.[109] The issue is a difficult one; to a large extent it turns on the interpretation of 7:3, whether its language was meant to be interpreted literally or as literary rhetoric grounded in rabbinic hermeneutics. A factor to be taken into account is that 11QMelch makes no reference to Genesis 14 or to Psalm 110, in its present state at least, nor does it represent Melchizedek as a priest. There are points of contact between the Christ of Hebrews and the figure

---

[105] The content of 7:2 appears to be more important than Hughes grants: 'The etymological explanations of the names of Melchizedek are passed over without further mention.' 'The royal qualities of Melchizedek . . . are all but passed over in silence' (*op. cit.*, pp. 14, 29).

[106] See the excursus below.   [107] *NTS* 12, 1965/66, p. 318.   [108] *Art. cit.*, p. 321.

[109] 'The Melchizedek Argument of Hebrews', *Unity and Diversity in New Testament Theology. Essays in Honor of G. E. Ladd,* ed. by R. A. Guelich (Eerdmans, 1978), pp. 161-185.

of 11QMelch.[110] Horton, however, has judged that 'there is no need for the additional hypothesis that . . . exegesis [of Gn. 14] was augmented by concepts similar to those in 11Q Melchizedek' and affirms that 'Hebrews should not be reckoned with the literature in which Melchizedek is considered a divine or heavenly figure'.[111] Hughes may well be correct in maintaining that chapter 7 would have been formulated differently: it would have included an explicit statement that Christ is superior to the heavenly Melchizedek.[112] B. Demarest has found in Hebrews negative polemic: the author's 'extraordinary emphasis upon the humanity of Jesus, who subsequently was exalted to heavenly priesthood, suggests that the writer may have consciously striven to *refute* all such mystical speculation'.[113]

The issue does not affect Hebrews 1 directly except insofar as 'the possibility of a figure other than Yahweh being addressed as *theos* is enhanced by the precedent of 11Q Melchizedek', as Horton states.[114] He adds the caution that other evidence is required before the usage can with complete certainty be regarded as forming a background for the Christian practice of calling Christ *theos*, whether in the New Testament or later.[115] If the present writer is correct in finding in Hebrews 1:8–9 three links with the Melchizedek material presented in 7:2 and in the citation of Psalm 110:4, the use of *ho theos* for Christ may well point to a fourth point of contact and so specifically to the author's knowledge of the angelic Melchizedek being so designated and to his (polemical?) Christological re-use of the tradition.[116]

In this essay an endeavour has been made to investigate the Old Testament significance of Psalm 45:7 and to demonstrate the use to which verses 7–8 were put in the Epistle to the Hebrews. In the latter context the passage reflects a different thought-world; its usage is based upon conviction that the exalted Jesus is the Christ for whom the psalm waited through centuries of Jewish devotions. The author's enquiring faith taught him the lesson that the psalm might be used to encapsulate the sequence of humiliation and exaltation to

---

[110] F. L. Horton, *The Melchizedek Tradition* (CUP, 1976), p.167, has listed five: both are eschatological redemptive figures, are exalted in the heavens, make atonement for sin, overcome the forces opposed to God and bring the promise of a new age.

[111] *Op. cit.*, pp. 164, 167.

[112] *Op. cit.*, n.218 on p.289.

[113] *A History of Interpretation of Hebrews 7:1–10 from the Reformation to the Present Day* (J. C. B. Mohr, 1976), p.129 n.2.

[114] *Op. cit.*, p.168.

[115] *Ibid.*

[116] *Cf.* F. F. Bruce's judgment that the recipients of the Epistle were Jewish Christians whose background was the 'nonconformist' Judaism of which the Qumran tradition is one but not the only representative (*ExpT* 80, 1968/69, p.263).

which he referred in 1:3b. In his hands the psalm looks forward to the heart of the Epistle as much as it looks back to its prologue. It prepares the way for the author's distinctive teaching of the representative, high-priestly work of 'our Lord Jesus'.

Excursus: The Qumran Melchizedek

Basic studies have been produced by M. de Jonge and A. S. van der Woude,[117] and by J. A. Fitzmyer.[118] They maintained that in 11QMelch *'lwhym* is used of Melchizedek, and once of other angels:[119] God is called *'l*, once in replacement of MT *yhwh* (1. 11), while *'ly* is used once of heavenly beings. J. Carmignac has dissented from this interpretation and claimed that *'lwhym* refers to God himself and that 'Melchizedek' was a human figure associated with the Qumran community and was so called because he was regarded as an antitype of the biblical Melchizedek.[120] In his opinion 11QMelch uses *'l* for God and *'lym* for other heavenly beings, but when the Bible is quoted, biblical usage is followed (*'l* or *'lwhym*), except that *yhwh* becomes *'l*. Both interpretations appear to be possible. However, de Jonge and van der Woude have found it significant that in lines 15-16 the document cites Isaiah 52:7, concluding with *mlk 'lwhyk* 'your *'lwhym* is king'; the passage is expounded in lines 17-26. In line 25 (*cf*. line 24) *'lwhyk* is repeated prior to the comment, of which unfortunately only one word, *bly'l* 'Belial', survives. De Jonge and van der Woude have argued with reason that 'if the author had meant to refer to God, an explanation of this expression would hardly have been necessary . . . it seems certain that *'lwhyk* . . . was explained as referring to the heavenly Melchizedek, the antagonist of Belial (line 13 and line 26)'.[121]

J. A. Emerton has suggested that in the light of the quotation of Psalm 82:1–2 in lines 10-11, *nhlt mlky ṣdq* 'the inheritance of Melchizedek' in line 5 is a reference to Psalm 82:8.[122] De Jonge and van der Woude concurred. They urged that *šbwyym* 'captives' in line 5 referred to exiles whom God was to bring back to the land of Israel; they compared the use of the jubilee motif in line 7 with that in Jeremiah 29:10 and Daniel 9:24–27 to refer to the end of the exile.[123] M. Delcor has similarly interpreted in terms of returning exiles.[124] If

[117] '11Q Melchizedek and the New Testament', *NTS* 12, 1965/66, pp.301-326.

[118] 'Further Light on Melchizedek from Qumran Cave 11', *op. cit.*, pp.245-267.

[119] It is the second instance in line 10, which cites Ps. 82:1, where the Hebrew originally used *'lhym* of a pantheon of gods presided over by Yahweh.

[120] 'Le document de Qumran sur Melchizedek', *RQ* 7, 1970, pp.343-378.

[121] *Art. cit.*, p.304.   [122] *JTS* 17, 1966, p.401 n.2.   [123] *Art. cit.*, pp.303f.

[124] 'Melchizedek from Genesis to the Qumran Texts and the Epistle to the Hebrews', *Journal for the Study of Judaism* 2, 1971, pp.115-135, esp. pp.124, 134.

this interpretation is correct, it is noteworthy that Psalm 82:8 is addressed to *'lhym,* who is to inherit *(tnḥl)* 'among all the nations'. A reference to 'all the nations' might then be the unmentioned or perhaps unpreserved link between exiles and 'inheritance': Isaiah 52:7, cited in lines 15–16, has in its context mention of 'all the nations' (v. 9). Then line 5 implies an identification of Melchizedek and *'lwhym.*

However, Fitzmyer has impressively argued that *šbwyym* applies to the Qumran community itself, in conformity with the tenor of its biblical exegesis, and is a quotation from Isaiah 61:1, other parts of which are cited in line 9 and — if [*m*]*šwḥ ḥrw*[*ḥ*] is read with Y. Yadin — in line 18.[125] J. A. Sanders has also interpreted *šbwyym* in this way.[126] Then *nḥlt*[127] refers to a priestly inheritance (*cf.* Jos. 13:33; 18:7).[128]

Milik has referred to two Qumran texts, 4Q 'Amram [b] 2. 3 and 4Q280 2. 2, which employ the name *mlky rš'* 'king of wickedness' as one of the names of Satan.[129] By its formation it appears to relate to one who is the spiritual adversary of *mlky ṣdq.* The inference to be drawn is that Melchizedek was a heavenly figure, *contra* Carmignac.

---

[125] *Art. cit.,* p.257.

[126] 'The Old Testament in 11Q Melchizedek', *Journal of the Ancient Near Eastern Society of Columbia University* 5, 1973, pp.373-382, esp. p.375; *cf.* 'From Isaiah 61 to Luke 4', *Christianity, Judaism and Other Greco-Roman Cults,* ed. by J. Neusner, *Part 1 New Testament* (Brill, 1975), pp.75-106, esp. pp.92, 97.

[127] The reading, disputed by Carmignac, has been confirmed by J. T. Milik, '*Milkî-ṣedeq* et *Milkî-rešaʿ* dans les anciens écrits juifs et chrétiens', *JJS* 23, 1972, pp.95-114, esp. p.103.

[128] Fitzmyer, *op. cit.,* p.258; Milik, *art. cit.,* pp.124f.

[129] *Art. cit.* in n.127.

WORTHY IS THE LAMB:
THE HYMNS IN REVELATION

David R. Carnegie

A glance at a hymnbook shows the extent to which the content and setting of the hymns in Revelation have influenced so many of the great Christian hymns. It is therefore surprising that despite considerable interest in hymns in the New Testament, these should have, until recently, remained unexplored. Undoubtedly one of the most important contributions has been the study of their structure and function by Klaus-Peter Jörns.[1]

The Revelation hymns are less directly Christological than those found in the Pauline Epistles, focusing rather on the acts of God and Christ, and in this they are akin to the Lucan canticles.[2] However, they presuppose a high Christology, and our object will be to consider this. We shall discuss first of all the contention that the author has incorporated quotations or adaptations of early Christian hymns into his work. On the conclusion that the hymns are rather his own composition, we shall suggest ways in which they form an inseparable and indispensable part of his portrayal of the Lamb and his triumph.

The hymns and early Christian worship

It has been widely assumed that the Revelation hymns, like those in other parts of the New Testament, originated in worship and were taken over and modified by the author. Some have seen in the series of hymns a clue to a liturgical sequence. In particular it has been claimed that the language of some of the

---

[1] Klaus-Peter Jörns, *Das hymnische Evangelium. Untersuchungen zu Aufbau, Funktion und Herkunft der hymnischen Stücke in der Johannesoffenbarung* (Gütersloher Verlagshaus Gerd Mohn, 1971). By 'hymns' are meant the following passages, Rev. 1:5b f.; 4:9-11; 5:9b f.; 5:11-14; 7:9-12; 11:15-18; 12:10-12; 13:4; 14:1f.; 15:3f.; 16:5-7; 18:20; 19:1-8.

[2] See, however, below.

David R. Carnegie

hymns indicates that they originated in a eucharistic setting.[3] If this is so, then the hymns could provide a valuable insight into the development of Christology and of Christian worship generally during the obscure period between Paul and Ignatius. This, however, can be proved only if terminology can be found in the hymns and their setting which cannot be other than eucharistic.

Such is the claim made for the hymns in Revelation 4:8b and 11:17f. In the case of the former, the use of the trisagion has an interesting parallel in 1 Clement 34:6. It is maintained that the latter affords evidence for the early use of the *Sanctus* in the eucharist. If this is correct, we have an almost contemporary source (*c*.95) for a eucharistic use of the *Sanctus*, and the possibility that Revelation 4:8b is to be similarly understood.[4] But if the arguments for a eucharistic understanding of 1 Clement 34:6 are undermined,[5] the case for Revelation 4:8b automatically collapses, as there is no other support either in the hymn or its setting for such an interpretation.

The second possibility of eucharistic terminology lies in the expression *eucharistoumen soi hoti* (we give thanks to thee that) in Revelation 11:17a. This exact form does not occur elsewhere in the New Testament, but it can be paralleled in Didache 10:4; *cf*. 9:2f.; 10:2. To those who maintain an early date for the Didache, a connection in setting seems most attractive. Jörns[6] regards this (together with Rev. 22:20) as the sole instance where the hymns offer a decisive link with primitive Christian liturgy.

There are, however, several features that would suggest caution. In the first place, the terms *eucharistia* and *eucharistein* in the Didache give the impression of being used in a technical sense. This is decidedly the impact of Didache 9:1, *peri de tēs eucharistias houtōs eucharistēsate*, corresponding to later use.[7] This impression is strengthened when we contrast the above with the New Testament, where it is clear that the precise meaning must be determined from the context. Whilst a eucharistic setting may be inferred from 1 Corinthians 14:16, this is clearly not the case with *eucharistia* in 1 Timothy 2:1; 4:4 or with *eucharistein* in 2 Corinthians 1:11; 9:12 or 1 Thessalonians 5:18.

Secondly, in the Didache, whether or not the setting is eucharistic, the term does have reference to eucharistic food.[8] However, in Revelation 11:17f. there

---

[3] D. M. Stanley, 'Carmenque Christo quasi deo dicere....' *CBQ* 20, 1958, pp.182 f.
[4] J. H. Srawley, *The Early History of the Liturgy* (CUP, 1913), pp.29 f.
[5] W. C. van Unnik, '1 Clement 34 and the Sanctus', *Vigiliae Christianae* 5, 1951, pp.204 f.
[6] K. -P. Jörns, *op.cit.*, p.99.
[7] Ignatius, *Eph.* 13:1; *Sm.* 7:1; *cf.* Justin, *Apol.* 1:65-67.
[8] The question revolves around the disputed relationship of Didache 9 and 10 - 14. Some have challenged the view that all three chapters describe the eucharist, and have maintained that 9 and 10 describe the agape and 14 the eucharist, or that the former section depicts a private, and the

is nothing apart from the phrase in question that would point to a eucharistic setting.[9]

An ingenious attempt has been made by S. Läuchli[10] to show that the Revelation hymns follow the order of an Ephesian eucharist. Having extracted the hymns, Läuchli compares their sequence with accounts of early Christian liturgies. Most of his material is drawn from Justin's account of the baptismal eucharist[11] and Sunday eucharist,[12] but since not all features can be matched, he supplements these by reference to the Didache. Remaining differences are accounted for on the grounds that the supposed Asia Minor liturgy would, like the Egyptian and Roman forms, have its own distinctive features. Läuchli concludes that the Revelation hymns are evidence of an ancient liturgical tradition from Asia Minor, older than all documents from Egypt and Rome, which throws light on Pliny's *'carmen Christo quasi deo'*.

The main objection to Läuchli's theory is that the mid-second-century data to which he appeals cannot provide a convincing background, even when supplemented by the Didache. The assumption of a tradition localized in Asia Minor is, of course, speculative. The great merit of such a work is, however, to demonstrate the indisputable unity of the hymns, and their relationship with one another. It is a reminder that any satisfactory theory must treat them as a unity.

The more closely it is examined, the less tenable becomes the case for a eucharistic origin for the hymns, either separately, or as a sequence. Vincent Taylor,[13] who allows for the possibility that the hymns reflect early worship, nevertheless draws attention to the lack of eucharistic teaching in any of them. Certainly if the hymns took shape in such a setting, one would expect a more positive indication of this. Under the circumstances one accepts the conclusion of C. F. D. Moule on the Revelation hymns that 'there is nothing to prove them eucharistic'.[14]

---

latter a public eucharist. Some who argue for an early date for the Didache contend that all three chapters envisage a situation where agape and eucharist are still undivided.

[9] G. Schille, 'Das Leiden des Herrn', *ZTK* 52, 1955, pp. 174 f., sees a eucharistic tone in Rev. 11:15-18 on the strength of allusion to Ps. 2, which from Acts 4:25f. he assumes to have had eucharistic significance. However, not only is Acts 4:25f. not explicitly eucharistic, but the use of Ps. 2 elsewhere in Rev. in situations which can hardly be termed eucharistic, *e.g.* 2:26; 19:15, suggests that the psalm itself was important to the writer, and it is in this sense of relevance to the whole work that its presence here is to be understood.

[10] S. Läuchli, 'Eine Gottesdienststruktur in der Johannesoffenbarung', *TZ* 16, 1960, pp. 359-378.   [11] Justin, *Apol.* 1:65f.   [12] Justin, *Apol.* 1:67.

[13] Vincent Taylor, *The Atonement in New Testament Teaching* (Epworth, 1954), pp. 34-43.

[14] C. F. D. Moule, *Worship in the New Testament* (Lutterworth, 1961), p. 64.

The hymns are composed by the author

We need, therefore, to consider more closely the alternative that the author has composed the hymns rather than taken them over. This may be affirmed on two main grounds.

The first is that of vocabulary. One feature that indicates the presence of earlier material is the use of terms which are either *hapax legomena* or rare for the writer himself. The opposite is the case with the Revelation hymns. Not only does the same vocabulary recur in different hymns, but as Charles[15] in his chapter-by-chapter analysis has shown, the vocabulary and style are the same as that for the rest of the book.

This feature may be seen in the recurrence of the same formula such as *axios* (worthy) + *eimi* (are) + *labein* (to take) in several hymns, 4:11; 5:9; 5:12. The same applies to the repeated use of connected terms both within and outside the hymns, *e.g. alēthinos kai dikaios* (true and just) in 15:3; 16:7; 19:2, and *mikroi kai megaloi* (small and great) in 11:18; 13:16; 19:5,18; 20:12. To this may be added the use of the divine names both within and outside the hymns: *kyrios ho theos ho pantokratōr* (the Lord God the Almighty) in 1:8; 4:8; 11:17; 15:3; 16:7; 19:6; 21:22, and *ho ōn kai ho ēn kai ho erchomenos* (who is and who was and who is to come) 1:4,8; 4:8, and in 11:17 and 16:5 where the omission of *ho erchomenos* indicates that the hymns in which they occur are part of an overall pattern. As a final example we may take the use made by the author of the term *dynamis* (power). The frequent use of this term in hymns not only unites them (4:11; 7:12; 11:17; 12:10; 19:1) but also suggests that *dynamis* plays a key role both in the hymns and their context. Thus in 13:4, the key to the worship of the beast lies in the fact that the dragon has given him *dynamis* (13:2). This forms a striking and intentional contrast to the heavenly attribution of *dynamis* to God and the Lamb in 4:11 and 5:12.

The second main ground for seeing these hymns as the author's composition is their close relationship with their immediate context. Unlike other New Testament hymns which show signs of being interpolated, those in Revelation are intimately connected with their context. They can therefore hardly have had independent standing or have ever been sung in Christian worship. Herein lies one of the differences between the Revelation hymns and the Lucan canticles; the *Benedictus, Magnificat* and *Nunc Dimittis* possess an independent standing that could not be the case with such hymns as Revelation 5:9b f.; 11:15,17f.; 12:10-12; 16:5-7; 19:1-8.

Revelation 1:5b f., however, suggests an interesting exception. Unlike the other hymns, the abrupt introduction is striking, as is the sudden transition to

15 R. H. Charles, *Revelation* (T. & T. Clark, 1920).

the dative. The ideas of redemption issuing from the love of Christ rather than God and of loosing from sin are unusual. The setting of the 'Amen' between verses 6 and 7 is striking, and is suggestive of a liturgical fragment. P. von der Osten-Sacken[16] has examined these verses and concludes that they do represent earlier material, which he believes originated in a baptismal situation.

To conclude that the hymns are the author's composition does not, however, imply that they throw no light on Christian worship and its content. The presence of such terms as 'amen', the use of doxologies and the antiphonal relationship of the hymns[17] all reflect Jewish, and almost certainly early Christian, practice. A further connection, and the most important one for an enquiry into Christology, is in the spirit of worship reflected in the hymns. Particularly helpful here is the analysis of J. Marty[18] which shows that the hymns under consideration contain adoration, enumeration of blessings and an expression of eschatological hope couched in Old Testament language.

The picture thus recreated is one where praise played an important role, and where doxologies and antiphonal singing were involved. Doctrinally, worship was permeated by a strong eschatological hope, and Christ was worshipped on terms equal with God. As H. B. Swete notes, the hymnic section of Revelation 5 'is highly suggestive of the devotional attitude of the Asiatic Church in the time of Domitian towards the Person of Christ'.[19] Thus although the hymns are not taken over from Christian worship, they do bear witness to it, giving an impression which is confirmed by the later glimpse provided by Pliny.

The place of the hymns in the author's portrayal of Christ

If the hymns are the author's own composition, how do they contribute to his picture of Christ? We suggest three main approaches to this question.

In the first place, we shall consider how, as a connecting link between the visions, the hymns throw important light on the relationship of the visions one to another, and in particular enable the author to develop his picture of Christ. Secondly, we shall see how these hymns have clear points of contact with the eschatological songs of praise to be found in Isaiah 40 – 55. It will be noted as

[16] P. von der Osten-Sacken, 'Christologie, Taufe, Homologie – Ein Beitrag zu Apc. Joh. 1:5ff.', *ZNW* 58, 1967, pp.255-266.

[17] A significant result of Jörns' investigation is to show the way in which the Rev. hymns stand in antiphonal relationship to one another. This feature is to be seen in the relationship of Rev. 4:9 to 4:11; 5:9b f. to 5:12; 7:10b to 7:12; 11:15b to 11:17f.; 16:5b f. to 16:7 and throughout the whole section 19:1b-8a.

[18] J. Marty, 'Étude des textes cultuels de prière contenus dans le Nouveau Testament', *RHPR* 9, 1929, pp.236 ff.

[19] H. B. Swete, *The Apocalypse of John* (Macmillan, 1906), p.83.

important that the writer applies hymns of this type, in their original setting referring to Yahweh alone, to Christ. Allied to this, we shall see how the hymns represent a widening circle of praise of which the Lamb is the worthy recipient. Thirdly, we shall consider the extent to which the author's presentation of Christ in the hymns and their setting represents a reaction against the Imperial cult.

The hymns as a connecting link

With the exception of the hymn in 1:5b f., all the hymns occur within Revelation 4 – 19. R. Deichgräber[20] observes that they are so placed that each of the vision sections has at least one hymn. This gives a pointer to their purpose as ancillary to the visions.

G. Delling has drawn attention to the function of the hymns in interpreting the visions[21] and he has also pointed out that they serve as a connecting thread, linking the visions with each other. Such a connection is important, as it enables the author to develop his theme as the visions proceed.

A clear example of this is provided by Revelation 11:15-17, where the phrase *eilēphas tēn dynamin* (thou hast taken power) (11:17b) clearly recalls *axios ei labein tēn dynamin* (worthy art thou to take power) in the hymn in 4:11. The effect of this is to show that the power ascribed to God in the first vision in chapter 4 is the eschatological power exercised in the visions depicting judgment. However, this same hymn also provides a connecting link with what is to come, as the phrase *kai basileusei eis tous aiōnas tōn aiōnōn* (and he shall reign for ever and ever) (11:15b) clearly anticipates the situation in 22:5, *basileusousin eis tous aiōnas tōn aiōnōn* (and they shall reign for ever and ever). Thus by means of the hymns the situation reached is linked up with what has passed and what is yet to come.

The author uses the hymns in this way to develop his picture of Christ. Two examples will make this clear. The first is found in a comparison between the wording of the hymns in chapters 4 and 5.

Revelation 4		Revelation 5	
4:11	*axios ei labein*	5:12	*axios estin to arnion labein*
	tēn dynamin		*tēn dynamin*
	hoti ektisas	5:10	*hoti epoiēsas*

[20] R. Deichgräber, *Gotteshymnus und Christushymnus: Untersuchungen zu Form, Sprache und Stil der frühchristlichen Hymnen* (Göttingen, 1967), p.45, cf. p.47.

[21] G. Delling, 'Zum gottesdienstlichen Stil der Johannesapokalypse', *Nov T* 3, 1957, p.136.

The effect of this is to align God's initial act of creation with the creative work of the Lamb in redemption. Furthermore, the proleptic hymn in 5:13f. looks forward to the culmination of this creative work in the new creation set forth in chapters 21 and 22. Taken together the above also shows that worthiness ascribed to the Lamb is an honour given to God. The interaction of these hymns, therefore, shows that, in sharing the activity of God and in receiving the honour ascribed to God, the Lamb is appropriately worshipped on equal terms with God.

The second example concerns the way that the author has developed the hymn in 1:5b f., which, as we have already noted, is the one instance where a hymn appears to have been taken over from existing worship.

The clearest link is that between this hymn and that in 5:9b f. This has been investigated by E. Fiorenza, who accepts the view that 1:5b f. was taken over by the author. Since he was seeking to combat a gnostic tendency according to which salvation is completed at baptism, the author altered the outlook of the hymn, replacing it with a stress on the corporate and futurist aspects of salvation.[22]

Apart from the fact that the book as a whole does not bear out such a sharp distinction between the present and future aspects of salvation,[23] the theory requires one to assume that the author began his work with a statement with which he disagreed, and systematically set out to correct it. For a writer to give such prominence to a statement he regarded as misleading is unparalleled in the New Testament. It is also important to observe that this theory is not able to account for such features as the paschal emphasis on the Lamb's work which appears in the author's development in 5:9b f. This suggests that the most important aspect of the link is Christological, which Fiorenza has not touched.

It is possible that a clue to the relationship between these two hymns may be found in the Isaac theme. Jubilees 16:17b f. provides confirmation of a connection between the Isaac theme and Exodus 19:6; and the idea of a people of God great in number, expressed in Revelation 5:9b, is not out of keeping with Genesis 15:1-6.

Moving on to much more speculative ground, it might be possible to see references to ideas associated with Isaac in the two unusual expressions in Revelation 1:5b f.

The idea of redemption issuing from the love of Christ rather than God is too

---

[22] E. Fiorenza, 'Redemption as Liberation', *CBQ* 36, 1974, pp.220-237.

[23] The difference between the two hymns is the authentic New Testament, 'even now, not yet', a principle which T. Holtz, *Die Christologie der Apokalypse des Johannes* (Berlin, 1962), p.214, regards as essential for a correct interpretation of Rev.

David R. Carnegie

easily passed unnoticed, and the expression *lyein ek tōn hamartiōn* (to loose from
sins) is readily assigned to Pauline theology. However, not only is the phrase
non-Pauline, it is not found elsewhere in the New Testament.

It is interesting to find that in the Targum of Genesis 22 there is, in the first
place, a stress on the active role of Isaac in the sacrifice, rather than on the role of
Abraham. Secondly, Isaac is identified with the lamb to be offered, explicitly in
Neofiti 1. Thirdly, the prayer of Abraham contains the request that the merits
of the sacrifice may bring deliverance to future generations. It is worth noting
that the Tgl TJII and 110 versions actually read '*loose* and forgive their *sins*'.
This at least raises the possibility of a type of exegesis in which the elements
found in Revelation 1:5b f. not only cohere, but lend themselves to the kind of
development found in 5:9b f., whereby Jesus is the perfect Passover lamb,
redeeming a new people of God, no longer restricted by race.

The hymns as eschatological songs of praise
A second way in which the hymns in Revelation contribute to the author's
picture of Christ is in their function as eschatological songs of praise, showing
definite affinities with such songs in Isaiah chapters 40 – 55.

C. Westermann[24] has drawn attention to the presence of these songs in Isaiah
40 – 55. A feature of these songs is that in several instances they serve to round
off main sections of the book. Although not all these songs serve that function,
one may note as particularly striking Isaiah 48:20f., which rounds off the first
main section of this part of Isaiah. The second main section is rounded off by
Isaiah 52:9. E.J. Kissane[25] has also drawn attention to rounding-off passages in
this section of Isaiah, but he shows how, as well as expressing thanksgiving,
some of these songs serve to summarize the theme of the whole passage.

Several features encourage a comparison between these Isaianic songs and the
hymns in Revelation. Whilst it is true that doxologies are used to round off the
main sections of Psalms, it is noteworthy that the author of Revelation is at
several points influenced by the Isaianic reinterpretation of Psalms[26] and there
are numerous occasions where the vocabulary and thought of the Revelation
hymns reflect Isaiah 40 – 55 and in some instances Isaiah 56 – 66.[27]

---

[24] C. Westermann, 'Sprache und Struktur der Prophetie Deuterojesajas' in *Forschung am Alten
Testament. Gesammelte Studien* (Theologische Bücherei 24) (Chr. Kaiser Verlag, Munich, 1964),
pp.151-163.
[25] E. J. Kissane, *The Book of Isaiah* 2 (Browne & Nolan, Dublin, 1943), pp.xxiii-xxx.
[26] *E.g.* Rev. 7:10; 11:17; *cf.* 19:6b.
[27] A. Gangemi, 'L'utilazzione del Deutero Isaiah nell' Apocalisse di Giovanni', *Euntes Docet*
27, 1974, pp.109-144 and 311-339. As well as showing the way in which the main themes are

One feature of the Isaianic songs is their call for praise for events which as yet show no sign of fulfilment. This suggests a comparison with those Revelation hymns which are proleptic, like points of light in a sombre setting.

Revelation 4:1 – 19:8, the area in which the hymns occur, may be divided into five main sections. The subject has been investigated by Bornkamm,[28] according to whom Revelation 6:1 – 22:15 consists of three main sections standing in close relationship to one another, hence the description 'recapitulation' theory. Clearly Revelation 4 – 5 must be included in any structural scheme.[29] Furthermore there is a division between Revelation 4 and 5. The main ground for this assertion is the omission of all reference to the Lamb in Revelation 4, despite identity of setting. Kiddle[30] explains the difference on the supposition that Revelation 4 depicts a vision of God as seen by the prophets, remote from men, whereas Revelation 5 transcends the Old Testament. Whether or not his assessment of the writer's purpose is altogether correct, Kiddle is undoubtedly right in noting the difference in atmosphere, which justifies our seeing a distinct break between the chapters.

If we accept Jörns' modifications of Bornkamm's sections, we have five: 4:1-11; 5:1-14; 6:1 – 7:17; 8:1 – 11:18; 11:19 – 19:8. The third of these sections is proleptic, and within the final section 12:1 – 14:20 is a parenthesis. Having noted these sections, we shall now see that each one is concluded by a hymn.

1. *Revelation 4:11.* In this case the hymn rounds off the chapter by way of summary, which, as we have seen from Kissane's study, may be paralleled in Isaiah. As Kiddle says, 'This hymn sums up what has been implicit in all the imagery of chapter 4.'[31]

2. *Revelation 5:13f.* This hymnic doxology rounds off the vision. The linking of the worship of God (the theme of ch. 4) and the worship of the Lamb (the theme of 5:1-12) emphasizes its character as a finale. The final 'Amen!' has both a closing as well as a responsive function.[32] Jörns[33] characterizes this as an eschatological song of praise.

3. *Revelation 7:9-12.* This does not occur at the very end of the section, but is followed by a further passage, Revelation 7:13-17. The latter serves to explain

---

drawn from Is., he also points to a similarity of purpose. Is. is addressed to a captive people, Rev. to a persecuted church.

[28] G. Bornkamm, 'Die Komposition der apokalyptischen Visionen in der Offenbarung Johannis', *ZNW* 36, 1937, pp.132-149.

[29] K. -P. Jörns, *op.cit.*, pp.177 f.

[30] M. Kiddle, *The Revelation of St. John* (Hodder & Stoughton, 1940), p.74.

[31] *Ibid.*, p.93.   [32] K. -P. Jörns, *op.cit.*, p.55.   [33] *Ibid.*, p.76.

the hymn, and so does not invalidate the contention that the section itself is rounded off by a hymn. This is confirmed by the content. The word 'Amen' occurs twice in 7:12. In 12a its function is responsive, whereas in 12b, attached as it is to a doxology, its function is to conclude.[34] Jörns classifies this too as an eschatological song of praise.[35]

4. *Revelation 11:15-18.* The rounding-off function of these hymns is less clear, and it must be admitted that there is widespread disagreement whether they close the fourth section or open the fifth. However, the hymns anticipate later events, and as it is the author's practice to close a section with ideas he intends to develop in the next section, we may endorse the conclusion of Jörns that these hymns belong to the end of this section.[36]

5. *Revelation 19:1-8.* This series of hymns unquestionably rounds off the fifth section. Deichgräber describes it as *'ein abschliessender Höhepunkt'.*[37] Their function is obvious from the broad structure of the passage. Thus 19:1b-4 marks the end of the heavenly worship, followed by a call in 19:5 which has a response in 19:6-8 from the earthly community. Their inclusion at this point also marks the character of this passage as a finale. Despite this, there is here too a proleptic element: 19:6b-8 leads on to chapters 21 and 22, and the whole passage has important links with 19:11ff., for the overthrow of Babylon and the singing together of heaven and earth is the prelude to the events depicted in the latter part of chapter 19.

We thus see that all the main sections of visions in Revelation 4 – 19 are rounded off by songs of praise, each including an element of anticipation of what God will do.[38]

The conclusion is, therefore, that the author of Revelation, influenced in so many ways by Isaiah 40 – 55, has also been inspired by the songs found there. The significance for Christology is obvious when one bears in mind that the Isaianic songs, like the book in which they are set, proclaim the incomparability of Yahweh. Such is the author of Revelation's estimate of Christ, that these songs can form a fitting background to praise now jointly addressed to God and Christ. 'Salvation belongs to God . . . and to the Lamb' (7:10)

Not only do the hymns in Revelation show the Lamb as the worthy recipient of homage due to God, but they also show how this homage is forthcoming from every quarter; for a study of the setting of the hymns, particularly the

---

[34] *Ibid.,* pp.85-88. [35] *Ibid.,* p.88. [36] *Ibid.,* p.176.
[37] R. Deichgräber, *op.cit.,* p.45.
[38] Note should also be taken of the hymn in Rev. 18:20. Although not occurring at the end of a main section, it is nevertheless used to round off a proleptic proclamation, and also shows a remarkable identity in structure to the Isaianic songs.

introductory wording, shows how the hymns represent an expanding circle of praise to God and Christ. The situation is complicated by the presence of the proleptic hymns in 5:12-14; 7:10-12; 14:1f.; 15:3f.; but four stages may be found.

The first stage is in 4:6b-11 and 5:8-12 where worship is offered to God and the Lamb by heavenly beings.[39]

The second stage is reached in Revelation 11:15. The *phōnai megalai* (loud voices) are not identified, and the question is investigated in detail by Jörns.[40] He draws attention to similar expressions used in connection with hymns in 12:10 and 19:1, and he concludes that the same meaning applies in all three cases. This means that behind all three lies the full description found in Revelation 19:1, *hōs phōnēn megalēn ochlou pollou* (like the loud voice of a great multitude). From the uses of *ochlos* (multitude) elsewhere, Jörns concludes that it refers to the redeemed. He also observes that in all three cases the same description *en tō ouranō* (in heaven) is used, and he maintains that this describes a situation where God or Christ are addressed, whereas *ek* or *apo tou ouranou* (from heaven) describes a situation where others are addressed. Thus, according to Jörns, the hymn in 11:15 is offered to Christ and God by the redeemed in heaven. In 7:9-12 the whole company of the redeemed appear[41] but since that situation is wholly proleptic and has not at this point been fulfilled, then those who sing here and in Revelation 12:10 and 19:1 must be those who have already died or been killed.

Jörns' contention receives decisive confirmation if we take account of the close affinity between this passage and Wisdom of Solomon 3. There the subject is the reward of the righteous who have been persecuted (Wisdom 3:1-9) and the punishment of the ungodly (Wisdom 3:10-19). The righteous are particularly those who have died (Wisdom 3:1-5) and who are considered by their persecutors to have received their just punishment. The writer then develops the theme that at God's visitation[42] the situation will be reversed, they will be rewarded and the Lord will be their king for ever and ever.

It is against this background that those who have suffered death now rejoice that God reigns. The hymn which follows in Revelation 11:17f. sees this reign in terms of reward and punishment, which is entirely in accord with the spirit of the Wisdom passage. We thus accept that the second stage of worship to

[39] R. H. Charles, *op.cit.* 1, pp.129 f., argues convincingly against regarding the elders as glorified men.

[40] K. -P. Jörns, *op.cit.*, p.91.

[41] The great multitude are to be identified with the church as a whole, not with the martyrs. See the comments of G. R. Beasley-Murray, *The Book of Revelation* (Oliphants, 1974), p.145.

[42] If this is the sense of the disputed *episkopē*.

God and Christ is that of the redeemed who have died, particularly as martyrs. The third stage is reached in Revelation 19:5. Following the argument of Jörns, we note that the hymn in this verse is introduced by a voice *apo tou thronou* (from the throne). The preposition denotes that what follows is directed to those other than God and Christ, in this case the earthly community whose response to the summons is the hymn of 19:6-8. That earthly singers are meant is confirmed by the absence of reference to a heavenly setting.

The fourth and final stage is reached in 21:26. There the picture is of the new Jerusalem whose temple is the Lord God and the Lamb. To this will be brought *hē doxa kai hē timē* (the glory and the honour) which was first offered by heavenly beings in 4:9. This represents the ultimate in worship, offered as it is by the nations. Such a situation is clearly envisaged in several Old Testament passages, notably Isaiah 60 and others such as Zechariah 8:22f.[43]

The Christology of the hymns and the Imperial cult
This situation where the Lamb is accorded universal homage on terms equal to God stands in sharp contrast to the historical situation of the readers, and this leads directly to the third and final aspect of the picture of Christ presented by the Revelation hymns.

There is an obvious and intended contrast between the heavenly worship of God and the Lamb in Revelation 4 and 5, and the earthly worship of the beast in Revelation 13. It is particularly noteworthy that the worship of the beast is set in the form of a hymn[44] (Revelation 13:4b) corresponding to the hymns of praise offered to God and the Lamb. We must therefore enquire whether, in presenting Christ, the author of Revelation reacts against the titles and terminology current in the Imperial cult, and perhaps by his very use of hymns intends to counter songs used in the cult.[45]

---

[43] See also the exposition of Rev. 21 and 22 by J. Comblin, 'La Liturgie de la Nouvelle Jérusalem', *Ephemerides Theologicae Lovaniensis* 29, 1953, pp.5-40.

[44] K. -P. Jörns, *op.cit.*, p.121.

[45] The term *ho theologos* traditionally associated with the author of Revelation was also used of the dignitaries of the Imperial cult. C. J. Hemer, *A Study of the Letters to the Seven Churches of Asia with special reference to their local background* (Manchester University Thesis, 1969), p.190, sets out evidence of their activities from Pergamum, Smyrna and Ephesus. As the true *theologos*, the author of Revelation opposes their teaching. It is also most interesting to note that the term *hymnodos* denoted those connected with the Imperial cult who sang and composed hymns. T. Reinach, 'Hymnodes,' *Dictionnaire des Antiquités Grèques et Romaines d'après les textes et les monuments*, ed. Daremberg et Saglio (Paris, 1900) 3, pp.40ff., gives much relevant information, mentioning that the centre of their activity was Asia Minor. No example of their compositions is available, but it is reasonable to suppose that just as the author is the true *theologos*, so he is the true *hymnodos* countering the blasphemous claims of the Imperial cult.

A clear example of polemic is to be found in the expression *ho kyrios kai ho theos hēmōn* (our Lord and God) (4:11a) which is almost certainly directed against Domitian's arrogation of the title *Dominus et Deus noster*.[46] A similar purpose is possible in the participial title of God, *ho kathēmenos epi tou thronou* (the one sitting on the throne) (4:9b), which is used in the LXX of earthly rulers. It is possible that this has motivated the author to make a contrast with the Imperial cult, in which case its present setting would not be without significance. E. Stauffer[47] refers to Domitian's desire to be considered as Jupiter's son and the earthly manifestation of the king of heaven, calling his throne a seat of the gods which he adorned with the emblems of Jupiter's throne. The connection of the term with specific acts of obeisance in Revelation 4:9; 7:10 and 19:4 is striking, and if the intention behind the term is polemic, then the conjunction of *ho kathēmenos epi tou thronou* with the Lamb in the hymnic finale to Revelation 5 would constitute the Christian answer to Domitian's claim to be the representative of Jupiter. Thus the Lamb, not the Emperor, is worthy of praise and worship.

Some writers have claimed far-reaching polemic parallelism in Revelation, including the hymns. Thus E. Peterson[48] maintains that the author's use of *axios* (worthy) reflects an acclamation used in the Imperial cult. Such a view if accepted would certainly influence our understanding of the way the hymns present Christ, and to some of those who see Revelation 5 as an enthronement scene, Peterson's theory is attractive.[49] However Peterson is unable to offer any evidence contemporary with Revelation for such a use of *axios*. In fact no example of *axios* or any equivalent term in any form corresponding to an Imperial acclamation is to be found prior to the third century.[50] Similar is the approach of R. Schütz, who endeavours to show that much of the terminology used in the hymns has reference to the Imperial cult. In particular Schütz draws up an impressive array of links between titles given to

[46] Suetonius *Domit.* 13. See also K. Scott, *The Imperial Cult under the Flavians* (r.p. Arno Press, New York, 1975), pp. 102 ff. The comparison is emphasized by the use of the nominative.

[47] E. Stauffer, *Christ and the Caesars* (SCM, 1951), p. 151. C. J. Hemer, *op. cit.*, p. 184, regards *thronos tou Satana* in the Pergamum letter as a likely reference to the Imperial cult.

[48] E. Peterson, *Heis theos: Epigraphische, formgeschichtliche und religionsgeschichtliche Untersuchungen* (Göttingen, 1926), pp. 176-179.

[49] For a critical assessment of the enthronement view, see W. C. van Unnik, '"Worthy is the Lamb": The Background of Apc. 5', *Mélanges Bibliques en hommage au R. P. Beda Rigaux* (Gembloux, 1970), pp. 445-451.

[50] K. -P. Jörns, *op. cit.*, pp. 56-73, investigates the whole question of *axios* and concludes that the formula *axios* + *eimi* + *labein* cannot be attributed to any existing cultic formula and is the writer's own composition.

255

Christ in the hymns and those found in adulations of Domitian.[51] It must, however, be stressed that terms such as *dynamis, exousia, sōtēria* (power, authority, salvation)[52] were widely diffused throughout the pagan East, and it is precarious to draw a straight line from the occurrence of similar terminology in Martial and Statius to the Revelation hymns. It must also be remembered that such terms as these are also biblical. To one such as the author who is steeped in the Old Testament the appropriation of them by any other than God would be blasphemous, and in this sense a polemic intention is to be seen.

The conclusion of our study is that the hymns in Revelation are an essential part of the structure of a book whose message is that all events past, present and future revolve around the Lamb, the historical Jesus who died and is alive for evermore. Fittingly the Lamb is worshipped on terms equal to God, with language reserved for God. The hymns give expression to the highest devotion to the person of the Lord Jesus Christ, and as such have enriched Christian worship down the ages.

---

[51] R. Schütz, *Die Offenbarung des Johannes und Kaiser Domitian* (Göttingen, 1933), p.35.

[52] See the claim of Peterson, *op.cit.,* p.313, for a cultic setting for *sōtēria.*

CHRISTOLOGY BEYOND CHALCEDON

A. N. S. Lane

Christology has been in the forefront of theological debate in recent years. There has been a spate of literature, mostly critical of the traditional Christian doctrine of the incarnation. The *Definition of Faith* of the Council of Chalcedon (AD 451), the major statement of patristic orthodoxy, has come under heavy fire. How should the evangelical, committed to the final normative role of Scripture, react to this situation? Should he rush to the defence of the Chalcedonian Definition? This is the approach of Dr Gerald Bray, in a recent article. He argues not just that the Definition is true in what it affirms about Christ but that it is 'a comprehensive analysis of biblical teaching' in the sense that 'it is inclusive of every factor necessary to do justice to the New Testament picture of Christ'.[1] He does not content himself with merely defending Chalcedon as an accurate expression of biblical truth in the thought forms of the ancient world but maintains that 'the Definition presents us with a thought-world which claims eternal validity and relevance'.[2]

The Chalcedonian Definition, however ancient, venerable and authoritative, is not part of the canon of Scripture and is therefore always open to correction in the light of Scripture, the final norm. This is not to say that it can simply be ignored or treated with disrespect.

> In the Church and hence in theology the commandment, 'Honour thy father and thy mother', is valid, and this commandment remains binding on the children even when they have left their parents' house.[3]

---

[1] G. E. Bray, 'Can we dispense with Chalcedon?', *Themelios* NS 3.2, January 1978, p.3. A similar claim is found in B. B. Warfield, *Christology and Criticism* (OUP, 1929), p.263.

[2] G. E. Bray, *art. cit.,* p.9. In this and the previous quotation Dr Bray is stating what Chalcedon claims for itself but the article as a whole makes it clear that he accepts these claims.

[3] K. Barth, *The Humanity of God* (Collins, 1967), p.10. *Cf. Church Dogmatics,* 1/2 (T. & T. Clark, 1956), pp.585f.

We are not to follow the arrogance of those who cannot see beyond their own contemporary biblical studies as if they were the first generation to study the Bible. 'In the Reformed church, we somewhat pride ourselves on cutting away the tangle of tradition, forgetting both that tradition may be a genuine medium of interpretative insight and that by now we have created our own rather rigid traditions which have a greater rigidity for all our pretending that they do not exist.'[4] We cannot afford to despise or ignore the lessons of the past since those who are ignorant of history are condemned to repeat it. Groups who have sought to go back to the Bible and bypass tradition have often illustrated this point by themselves repeating some of the early heresies.[5] But to respect the past is not to be in slavish bondage to it. To respect Chalcedon is not necessarily to affirm its perfection. To be committed to the biblical doctrine of the incarnation is not necessarily to be totally committed to the Chalcedonian exposition of it. Simply to identify the two is to confuse text with commentary. This allows the opponents of the incarnation to discredit the biblical doctrine simply by exposing the inadequacies of Chalcedon. It will be the thesis of this essay that, valuable though the Chalcedonian Definition may be, it is neither necessary nor desirable nor possible to accept it unreservedly.

The Chalcedonian Definition

The Chalcedonian Definition followed nearly a century of Christological debate.[6] The affirmation of the full deity of Christ, in response to Arianism, thrust the Christological issue to the forefront: how could this Christ be both God and man? Three major attempts at an answer to this were deemed to be heretical. Apollinaris[7] believed firmly in the full deity of Christ and his incarnation, but held these at the expense of his full humanity. He established the unity of the incarnate Christ by teaching that the divine Logos replaced the highest part of humanity in Christ: the mind or rational soul. If we are mind, soul and body, Christ was Logos, soul and body. The presence of the divine Logos rendered the human mind superfluous. This teaching was rejected by the Western church at Rome in AD 377 and 382 and by the Eastern church at the Council of Constantinople in AD 381. On the basis of the ancient maxim that what is not assumed is not healed, it was held that a Christ with a truncated human nature

[4] J. McIntyre, *The Shape of Christology* (SCM, 1966), pp.26f.
[5] *E.g.* the sixteenth-century Anabaptists and the early Brethren. For the latter, *cf.* F. F. Bruce, 'The Humanity of Jesus Christ', *Journal of the Christian Brethren Research Fellowship* 24, 1973, pp.5-10.
[6] *Cf.* A. Grillmeier, *Christ in Christian Tradition* (Mowbrays, [2]1975).
[7] *Cf.* R. A. Norris, *Manhood and Christ* (OUP, 1963), pp.81-122.

could not save the whole man. 'The Good Shepherd came to seek and to save that which was lost, and carried home on His shoulders not the fleece only, but the entire sheep.'[8]

Apollinaris, in his denial of a human mind to Christ, was following in the Alexandrian tradition but he presented this traditional teaching in a particularly exaggerated form, and what had been acceptable in the third and early fourth centuries was no longer held to be acceptable as the issue was further explored. Nestorius suffered a similar fate in that he followed the traditional, though less popular, Antiochene teaching, especially as found in Theodore of Mopsuestia.[9] He held firmly to the full deity of the divine Logos and the full humanity of the man Jesus. But despite his attempt to weld these together into one Christ he never fully escaped from what has been called the 'pantomime horse' theory of the incarnation in which Christ appears to be one but at the deepest level remains two.[10] His teaching was vigorously opposed by Cyril of Alexandria, who was motivated as much by theological as by political considerations,[11] and condemned at the Council of Ephesus in AD 431. This led to a breach between Cyril's Alexandrian party and the Antiochene party, who supported Nestorius. This breach was resolved in AD 433 when Cyril, in a letter to John of Antioch, accepted the moderate Antiochene *Formula of Reunion* and the Antiochenes agreed to accept the condemnation of Nestorius.

The third heretic was Eutyches. He was accused of heresy at Constantinople in AD 448 and tried by the Home Synod under the archbishop, Flavian. His teaching appears to have been as much confused as unsound, but the error for which he was eventually condemned was that of confusing or blurring together the two natures of Christ (his deity and humanity). This meant that Christ was neither truly God nor truly man but a third entity (*tertium quid*) arising from the blending of divinity and humanity – much as green paint comes from the blending of blue and yellow, or a mule comes from the mating of a horse and a donkey. Eutyches refused to acknowledge two natures in Christ during the incarnation and was equivocal over whether or not Christ is of one substance with us (*homoousios hēmin*). He was condemned, but Dioscorus of Alexandria, Cyril's nephew and successor, persuaded the emperor to call a council, which

[8] Gregory of Nyssa, cited by G. L. Prestige, *Fathers and Heretics* (SPCK, 1940), p. 113.

[9] *Cf.* R. A. Norris, *op. cit.*, pp. 125-262.

[10] Not all would accept this account of Nestorius. *Cf.* C. E. Braaten, 'Modern Interpretations of Nestorius', *Church History* 32, 1963, pp. 251-267.

[11] H. Chadwick, 'Eucharist and Christology in the Nestorian Controversy', *JTS* NS 2, 1951, pp. 145-164. For an account of events from Ephesus to Chalcedon, *cf.* R. V. Sellers, *The Council of Chalcedon* (SPCK, 1953), pp. 3-129.

met at Ephesus in AD 449.[12] Here Eutyches was vindicated and the Antiochene party all deposed. Leo of Rome had written a *Tome* for the occasion, attacking Eutyches,[13] but this was not read at the council, which Leo rejected as a 'Robber Synod' (*Latrocinium*). Leo was unable to alter the situation in the East but in July 450 the emperor died in a riding accident and his successor, Marcian, was less favourably inclined to the Alexandrian party. He called another council which eventually opened at Chalcedon, near Constantinople, in October 451. Those deposed in 449 were reinstated and the Ephesine council was renounced. Eutyches and Dioscorus were deposed and the *Formula of Reunion* and Leo's *Tome* were accepted, in addition to Cyril's letters. The bishops wished to stop there, but the emperor was determined to have a unifying statement of faith. And so the Chalcedonian Definition was born.

The Definition reaffirms the creeds of Nicea and Constantinople, which are quoted in full. This should have sufficed for orthodoxy but unfortunately 'those who attempt to set aside the preaching of the truth have produced foolish utterances through their own heresies'.[14] To refute such error the Definition accepts Cyril's second letter to Nestorius and his letter to John of Antioch, as a refutation of Nestorius, and Leo's *Tome*, as a refutation of Eutyches.

The main section of the Definition consists of a collection of anathemas and a positive statement.[15] The former rejects the four heresies:

> For [the Synod] opposes those who would rend the mystery of the dispensation into a duad of Sons;[16] and it banishes from the assembly of priests those who dare to say that the Godhead of the Only-begotten is passible;[17] and it resists those who imagine a mixture or confusion of the two natures of Christ;[18] and it drives away those who fancy that the form of a servant taken by him of us is of a heavenly or any other 'ousia';[19] and it

---

[12] For an account of these events from an Alexandrian, non-Chalcedonian perspective, *cf.* V. C. Samuel, 'Proceedings of the Council of Chalcedon and its Historical Problems', *Ecumenical Review* 22, 1970, pp.321-347.

[13] For a theological analysis of the *Tome*, *cf.* R. V. Sellers, *op. cit.*, pp.228-253.

[14] For the full text of the Definition, *cf.* T. H. Bindley (ed.), *The Oecumenical Documents of the Faith* (Methuen, ⁴1950), pp.191-193 (Greek); 232-235 (English). For a detailed analysis of the Definition, *cf.* R. V. Sellers, *op. cit.*, pp.207-228.

[15] The translation of the main section is taken from R. V. Sellers, *op. cit.*, pp.223f., 210f.

[16] Nestorianism.

[17] Arianism. To call Christ's Godhead passible was to deny his true deity, since God was held to be impassible. *Cf.* further the section below, *Immutability*.

[18] Eutychianism.

[19] Apollinarianism. Apollinaris himself clearly denied that he held this.

anathematizes those who, first idly talk of the natures of the Lord as 'two before the union', and then conceive but one 'after the union'.[20]

The positive statement blends together four traditions: the Alexandrian, drawn from Cyril; the Antiochene, from the *Formula of Reunion;* the Constantinopolitan, from Flavian; and the Western, from Leo's *Tome.*

> Following, then, the holy Fathers, we all with one voice teach that it should be confessed that our Lord Jesus Christ is one and the same Son, the Same perfect in Godhead, the Same perfect in manhood, truly God and truly man, the Same [consisting] of a rational soul and a body; *homoousios* with the Father as to his Godhead, and the Same *homoousios* with us as to his manhood; in all things like unto us, sin only excepted; begotten of the Father before ages as to his Godhead, and in the last days, the Same, for us and for our salvation, of Mary the Virgin *Theotokos* as to his manhood;
>
> One and the same Christ, Son, Lord, Only-begotten, made known in two natures [which exist] without confusion, without change, without division, without separation; the difference of the natures having been in no wise taken away by reason of the union, but rather the properties of each being preserved, and [both] concurring into one Person (*prosopon*) and one *hypostasis* – not parted or divided into two Persons (*prosopa*), but one and the same Son and Only-begotten, the divine Logos, the Lord Jesus Christ; even as the prophets from of old [have spoken] concerning him, and as the Lord Jesus Christ himself has taught us, and as the Symbol of the Fathers has delivered to us.

This reduces to four basic statements against the four heresies: Christ is fully God (against Arius) and fully man (against Apollinaris), indivisibly one (against Nestorius) yet without confusion (against Eutyches).

The emperor intended this document to cement unity in the Eastern church. Rarely has such an attempt so disastrously backfired.[21] Whole areas of the Eastern church, such as Egypt, never accepted the Definition. The West held unswervingly to it and the imperial government at Constantinople had to decide

---

[20] A second condemnation of Eutyches, this time drawn from Leo's *Tome* and probably added at the insistence of the Roman delegates (R. V. Sellers, *op. cit.,* p.226).

[21] For the post-Chalcedonian period in the East, *cf.* R. V. Sellers, *op. cit.,* pp.254-350; J. Pelikan, *The Spirit of Eastern Christendom (600-1700)* (University of Chicago, 1974), pp.37-90; J. Meyendorff, *Christ in Eastern Christian Thought* (St. Vladimir's Seminary, 1975).

between unity with Rome at the cost of intense division in the East or a united East (by dropping the Definition) at the cost of breach with Rome. Imperial policy wavered between these alternatives and two further councils met at Constantinople in 553 and 680-1 to seek to resolve the issue. In the end the controversy was concluded not by agreement but through the removal of the dissenting areas from the Empire by the Muslim invasions.

While in the East the Definition was and remains the major cause of church disunity, in the West it was fully accepted.[22] There was dissent among heretical groups both in the Middle Ages and at the Reformation, but Chalcedon was unchallenged in Roman Catholic and mainstream Protestant theology. This situation first began to change at the beginning of the last century. It was with Schleiermacher who, in this matter also, founded not a school but an era, that the Definition came first to be questioned within mainstream Protestantism.[23] Since then it has come increasingly under fire.

Objections to Chalcedon

This section is concerned with modern objections to the Chalcedonian Definition from the perspective of a biblical doctrine of incarnation.[24] It is not concerned with objections to the biblical doctrine of the incarnation. Nor is it concerned with the objections of the Eastern dissenters in the ancient world, except inasmuch as these might be echoed today.

Hellenization

The first class of objection falls under the general heading of hellenization. Chalcedon is deemed to be unfaithful to Scripture because it has polluted it with Greek philosophy. This is a common charge. It can be considered under three different headings.

1. *Cultural form.* It is futile to seek to deny that the Chalcedonian Definition is an expression of the doctrine of the incarnation in terms of ancient Greek thought. Terms such as hypostasis, nature, substance and person cannot be understood correctly except against that background. But this is not necessarily

---

[22] *Cf.* A. Grillmeier, 'The Reception of Chalcedon in the Roman Catholic Church', *Ecumenical Review* 22, 1970, pp.383-411.

[23] F. Schleiermacher, *The Christian Faith* (T. & T. Clark, 1928), pp.391-413. Schleiermacher attacked the Chalcedonian formulas as they are found in later confessions. He did not mention Chalcedon by name.

[24] This assumes that the incarnation is a biblical doctrine. Most of the leading opponents of the doctrine today do not deny this.

to criticize Chalcedon. Recent studies in the field of contextualization have shown that the gospel needs to be expressed in relation to each culture.[25] The Word must repeatedly become flesh in the proclamation of the church. To say that Chalcedon expressed the doctrine of the incarnation in fifth-century Greek terms is simply to say that the Chalcedonian fathers were (albeit unconsciously) being faithful to their calling to contextualize. Of course, the supplementary question then arises concerning their fidelity to the biblical message in the process of contextualizing it. But to convict them of being unfaithful it is necessary to show that they compromised the biblical message in some way: it is not sufficient merely to show that they hellenized it.

The impression is sometimes given that to show that the concepts of patristic Christology arose from the Greek environment is to prove it false. But this is to fall into the genetic fallacy, the idea that to show the origin of an idea is to falsify it. While not all Greek thought is correct, it does not follow that to brand an idea as Greek is to falsify it. Furthermore, while the Fathers used Greek concepts, their resulting Christology was profoundly un-Greek.[26]

To acknowledge that Chalcedon is a hellenized version of New Testament Christology is not yet to prove its error. But it is to admit that it may need to be translated into contemporary terms.[27] There cannot be any valid objection to this demand since even the text of Scripture needs to be translated in this way. The problem with many so-called modern 'translations' of Chalcedon is not that they seek to express it in today's terms, but that the Christology expressed is not that of Chalcedon but one of the heresies there condemned, usually Nestorianism.[28]

2. Functional versus ontological. Chalcedon is often accused of being unfaithful to New Testament Christology on the grounds that the New Testament picture of Christ is functional (what he does) while Chalcedon is ontological (who he is). God's servant and Messiah has become one person in two natures. This criticism depends for its force on the assumption that New Testament Chris-

---

[25] *E.g.* D. von Allmen, 'The Birth of Theology', *International Review of Mission* 64, 1975, pp.37-52; C. H. Kraft, *Christianity in Culture* (Orbis, 1979); B. J. Nicholls, *Contextualization: A Theology of Gospel and Culture* (Paternoster, 1979).

[26] *Cf.* below, 3. *True versus false.* It has often been noted that while the Fathers used Greek philosophical terms they gave them a distinctively Christian meaning.

[27] *Cf.* below, 3. *Impersonal humanity*, for the need to translate the term 'person'.

[28] E. L. Mascall, *Theology and the Gospel of Christ* (SPCK, 1977), p.121, charges Pittenger with expounding 'what to everyone but himself is plainly an adoptionist doctrine, though he has persuaded himself that it is what Chalcedon was really trying to say'. This fault is not confined to Pittenger.

tology is *purely* functional and not at all ontological. But this is not so.[29] If it be conceded that New Testament Christology is at least in part ontological, Chalcedon cannot be criticized for being ontological. It can freely be admitted that whereas the New Testament is predominantly (but not exclusively) functional, Chalcedon is overwhelmingly ontological in its approach.[30] This admission militates against any claim that Chalcedon presents an all-embracing, totally sufficient Christology, but this it did not set out to do. Its essential task was to protect Christology against heresy, in four particular forms, and to expound the essential points which those heresies undermined.[31] With such a limited, albeit important, aim there is no need to represent the full range of New Testament teaching about Christ.

3. *True versus false.* While hellenization is in principle valid and while an ontological emphasis is not necessarily incorrect, it does not follow that the Chalcedonian Definition actually succeeded in presenting New Testament Christology in those terms without distortion or error. Expression of the gospel in terms of a new culture is valid and indeed essential, but that does not imply licence to adopt any and every idea from the culture irrespective of its truth. The gospel challenges culture as well as incarnating itself into culture. The early Fathers were not unaware of this. The very fact that they were prepared to formulate a doctrine of the incarnation shows that they were prepared to challenge Greek culture at a fundamental point. As Peter Brown puts it, for a late fourth-century Roman 'to accept the Incarnation would have been like a modern European denying the evolution of the species: he would have had to abandon not only the most advanced, rationally based knowledge available to him, but, by implication, the whole culture permeated by such achievements'.[32] If the Chalcedonian Fathers did err, it should be recognized that their error was minor in comparison with their achievement in upholding the biblical doctrine of the incarnation in an essentially alien environment.

It is sometimes implied that the doctrine of the incarnation was easy and congenial in the early church but that today it has become difficult and unintelligible.[33] 'Modern man' can no longer hold to it. But it was harder for

---

[29] *Cf.*, *e.g.*, R. H. Fuller, *The Foundations of New Testament Christology* (Lutterworth, 1965), pp.247-250.

[30] In fairness to the Fathers it should be noted that the dominant concern underlying their Christology was soteriological (and therefore functional).

[31] *Pace* R. V. Sellers, *op. cit.*, pp.207-228, where the Definition is seen primarily as a positive exposition of the faith.

[32] P. Brown, *Augustine of Hippo* (Faber & Faber, 1967), p.302.

[33] *E.g.* by M. F. Wiles & F. Young in J. Hick (ed.), *The Myth of God Incarnate* (SCM, 1977),

'modern man' in the ancient world to accept the incarnation than it is today. The early Fathers held to the incarnation despite 'modern thought', not because of it. If they had followed the modern maxim of 'I don't understand therefore I won't believe' they too would soon have ditched the concept of incarnation. But the early Fathers believed that they were handling the revelation of Almighty God and that the correct response to intellectual difficulty was not 'I don't understand therefore it cannot be true' but 'I believe in order that I might understand'.

Immutability

Greek thought posited a fundamental distinction between the world of becoming (changing and impermanent) and the world of being (eternal and unchanging). The former is inferior, if not evil. To the Greek mind it was inconceivable that God could but belong to the world of being. It therefore followed that he was immutable or incapable of any sort of change. This could be proved by a simple argument:

> If he change at all he can only change for the worse, for we cannot suppose him to be deficient either in virtue or beauty . . . It is impossible that God should ever be willing to change, being, as is supposed, the fairest and best that is conceivable.[34]

The argument already assumes its conclusion in the concept of perfection presupposed. But to the Greek mind, *i.e.* to the Fathers of the third to fifth centuries, it was self-evident. The Greek concept of God meant that he was essentially unchanging and static. He was impassible in that he could not be subject to any suffering or emotion.

This is not the place to enter fully into the debate concerning immutability and impassibility, but suffice it to say that the present author concurs with the majority of modern theologians in believing both concepts to be alien and inimical to the biblical concept of God. The changelessness of God in Scripture refers primarily to his moral constancy and to his unchanging purposes. While it is true that God could not change in a fundamental way, *e.g.* by ceasing to be God, the Bible is far removed from the essentially static and immobile Greek picture of God. Furthermore, the God of the Bible is not cold and emotionless.

---

pp.4, 87-121. Wiles responds to criticism on this point in M. Goulder (ed.), *Incarnation and Myth* (SCM, 1979), p.11.

[34] Plato, *Dialogues,* cited by R. B. Edwards, 'The Pagan Dogma of the Absolute Unchangeableness of God', *Religious Studies* 14, 1978, p.309.

'My heart recoils within me, my compassion grows warm and tender' (Ho. 11:8). 'Serve the Lord with fear . . . for his wrath is quickly kindled' (Ps. 2:11). It can freely be acknowledged that all such language is anthropomorphic and is therefore to be seen as analogical rather than literal. But it should not therefore be imagined that while scriptural revelation is merely anthropomorphic and analogical, (Greek) philosophy can leave such weakness behind and present a truer and more literal picture of God. If revelation leaves us with analogy and anthropomorphism it is because this is the most that the human mind can grasp, not because the readers of the Bible are deemed to be too stupid to understand the truths of Greek philosophy. The biblical picture of God may be imperfect (in the sense of 1 Cor. 13:12) but this does not mean that philosophy can transcend such human limitations.

The doctrine of impassibility has led traditional theologians to statements like the following:

> thou art compassionate in terms of our experience, and not compassionate in terms of thy being . . . thou art both compassionate, because thou dost save the wretched, and spare those who sin against thee; and not compassionate, because thou art affected by no sympathy for wretchedness.[35]

Professor Mascall seeks to escape from such conclusions by arguing that God does have compassion on us but that 'this is infinitely surpassed by the beatitude which God enjoys in the interior fullness of his own divine life, which it therefore can neither augment nor diminish'.[36] This, he maintains, reconciles the compassion and impassibility of God. It is an ingenious argument but if it does protect God's impassibility it does so only by arguing that we are infinitely irrelevant to God. Professor Moltmann has a better approach, distinguishing between three different types of change or suffering: 'If God is not passively changeable by other things like other creatures, this does not mean that he is not free to change himself, or even free to allow himself to be changed by others of his own free will.' 'There are other forms of suffering between unwilling suffering as a result of an alien cause and being essentially unable to suffer, namely active suffering, the suffering of love, in which one voluntarily opens himself to the possibility of being affected by another.' 'The one who is capable of love is also capable of suffering, for he also opens himself to the

---

[35] Anselm, *Proslogion* 8 (Anselm, *Basic Writings* [Open Court, ²1962], pp. 13f.).

[36] E. L. Mascall, *He Who Is* (Darton, Longman & Todd, ²1966), p. 111. *Cf. Whatever Happened to the Human Mind?* (SPCK, 1980), pp. 64-96.

suffering which is involved in love, and yet remains superior to it by virtue of his love.'[37] While the traditional arguments may establish that God is not subject to coerced change or suffering, they do not prove his absolute immutability and impassibility.

The Chalcedonian Definition presupposes God's immutability and impassibility. At the trivial level this is seen in the rejection of 'those who dare to say that the Godhead of the Only-begotten is passible'. More fundamentally, the Definition is the outcome of a long process of patristic Christology which was based solidly on the conviction that God is immutable and impassible.

Dualism

If God cannot change or suffer, it is hard to see how he could become man and suffer for us. The classical Antiochene response to this dilemma was to avoid the idea of incarnation, to think of God *producing* a perfect man rather than God actually *becoming* man. Their concern was as much to preserve God's impassibility as to maintain Christ's full humanity.[38] The Alexandrians, on the other hand, affirmed the incarnation in the teeth of their doctrine of God's impassibility. Cyril did not shrink from the paradoxical affirmation that the Logos impassibly made his own the sufferings of his own flesh.[39] Clearly the very concept of incarnation involves mystery and paradox, but this does not entitle us to add further paradoxes of our own. The paradox of impassible passion arises not from the Christian revelation itself but from its conflict with Greek philosophy.

If God cannot change, it follows that the Word must have become flesh without undergoing any change. The incarnation involved no change in the Logos who, as Cyril put it, 'ever abides what He is and has not been changed, neither, indeed, could He ever be changed or be capable of variation'.[40] While the Fathers spoke of his kenosis or self-emptying, this was interpreted as his condescension in adding humanity to an unaltered deity.[41]

The absolute immutability of the Logos means that while he was incarnate

---

[37] J. Moltmann, *The Crucified God* (SCM, 1974), pp.227-230.

[38] The motivation behind Eustathius' switch from an Alexandrian to an Antiochene Christology would be one illustration of this (A. Grillmeier, *Christ in Christian Tradition*, pp.296-301). The Antiochenes are much praised by their modern disciples for their concern to maintain Christ's full humanity.

[39] T. H. Bindley (ed.), *The Oecumenical Documents of the Faith*, p.215, cf. pp.210, 222f. The patristic citations in this section are taken from the works of Cyril and Leo which were formally accepted at Chalcedon, together with Cyril's *Third Letter to Nestorius*, which sometimes expresses the same point as the others more succinctly.

[40] *Ibid.*, p.222, cf. pp.210, 214 and, for Leo, 227.

[41] *Ibid.*, pp.214, 222 (both Cyril) and 226 (Leo).

on earth he was still seated at the right hand of the Father and upholding the universe. The Fathers did not shrink from this conclusion:

> While visible as a babe in swaddling clothes, and yet in the bosom of the Virgin who bare Him, He was filling all creation as God, and was enthroned with Him who begat Him.[42]

> So, then, the Son of God enters upon this lower world, descending from His heavenly seat without retiring from the Father's glory.[43]

The Chalcedonian picture of Christ is unashamedly dualist.[44] The historical Jesus has a dual existence, as God and as man.[45] He acted sometimes as God, sometimes as man:

> Each nature performs what is proper to itself in communion with the other; the Word, that is, performing what is proper to the Word, and the flesh carrying out what is proper to the flesh. The one of these is brilliant with miracles, the other succumbs to injuries.... To feel hunger, thirst, and weariness, and to sleep, is evidently human; but to satisfy thousands of men with five loaves, and to bestow living water on the Samaritan woman... to walk on the surface of the sea with feet which did not sink, and to allay the 'rising billows' by rebuking the tempest, is without doubt Divine.[46]

This dualism is foreign to the New Testament portrait of Christ.

Docetism

If the immutability and impassibility of God inevitably led Chalcedon to a dualistic portrait of Christ the most serious consequence of this dualism is the

---

[42] *Ibid.*, p.214 (Cyril).   [43] *Ibid.*, p.226 (Leo).

[44] J. McIntyre, *The Shape of Christology*, pp.83f., notes this dualism. Later (p.93) he emphasizes the Chalcedonian concern for the unity of Christ. But, as W. R. Matthews, *The Problem of Christ in the Twentieth Century* (OUP, 1950), p.30, puts it, 'the fact is that, in spite of the genuine anxiety of the Fathers to preserve the unity of the Person, they did not succeed in evolving a doctrine which secured this necessary affirmation'.

[45] E. L. Mascall, *Christ, the Christian and the Church* (Longmans, Green & Co., 1946), pp.20-22, shows clearly that for Chalcedon the duality applies to the historical Christ.

[46] T. H. Bindley (ed.), *op. cit.*, p.227 (Leo). The first part of this quotation was suspected of Nestorianism at Chalcedon but a similar statement was found in Cyril (R. V. Sellers, *The Council of Chalcedon*, pp.247f.).

undermining of his true humanity.[47] Theoretically Chalcedon affirms that Christ is 'perfect in manhood . . . truly man . . . [consisting] of a rational soul and a body . . . *homoousios* with us as to his manhood: in all things like unto us, sin only excepted'. The Definition can be praised for holding fast to the true humanity of Christ in opposition to those who undermined it by blurring it into his deity.[48] But Chalcedon has not succeeded in maintaining a practical belief in Christ as fully human; this can be seen, for instance, by the history of mariology. Theoretical acknowledgement of Christ's full humanity has repeatedly gone hand in hand with a *de facto* docetism, *i.e.* a neglect or belittling of New Testament teaching on the full humanity of Christ. Christ was 'made like his brethren in every respect' (Heb. 2:17) and we have no warrant for making him different from us except where Scripture itself states such differences – *e.g.* in the claim that he was 'without sin' (Heb. 4:15). But it is not docetic to affirm such biblical doctrines as the virgin birth and Christ's pre-existence.[49] 'According to New Testament writers, the humanity of Jesus is both continuous with and discontinuous from that of the rest of mankind.'[50] To call this docetic is to give the term a radically new meaning.

Why has the church repeatedly neglected Christ's true humanity? A number of factors can be blamed. One would be ignorance of and failure to appropriate the teaching of Chalcedon, which has not always filtered down from the theological study to the pew. Another would be the misinterpretation of Chalcedon. In the present writer's experience, the great majority of evangelicals who think that they hold to the Chalcedonian 'one person in two natures' in fact hold to an Apollinarian or Eutychian position.[51] But to some extent the fault

---

[47] *Cf.* D. Guthrie, *New Testament Theology* (IVP, 1981), pp.220-228, for a summary of New Testament teaching on the humanity of Christ.

[48] Especially Eutyches. *Cf.* the teaching of Gregory of Nyssa that Christ's humanity is 'mingled in the Godhead like a drop of vinegar in a vast sea' (A. Grillmeier, *op. cit.*, p.376).

[49] *Contra* the charge made by, among others, J. A. T. Robinson, *The Human Face of God* (SCM, 1973), pp.36-66, 143-179.

[50] C. F. D. Moule, 'The Manhood of Jesus in the New Testament' in S. W. Sykes & J. P. Clayton (eds.), *Christ, Faith and History* (CUP, 1972), p.102, *cf.* pp.102-7. *Cf.* S. W. Sykes, 'The Theology of the Humanity of Christ', in S. W. Sykes & J. P. Clayton, *op. cit.*, p.66: 'Any account which does not distinguish [Christ] from the rest of humanity is not credible as christology'.

[51] Asked whether Christ has one or two wills (or 'psychologies'), the majority opt for one will which is divine (Apollinarianism) or, more popularly, divine/human (Eutychianism). *Cf.* W. R. Matthews, *op. cit.*, p.29: 'I have noticed that those who, while anxious to be orthodox and priding themselves on it, have not perhaps taken much pains to discover what orthodoxy is, tend, when this question is put to them, to embrace the Monothelite heresy.' D. M. Baillie was extremely premature in declaring that 'Eutyches . . . is dead, and he is not likely to be as fortunate as Eutychus in finding an apostle to revive him!' (*God was in Christ* [Faber & Faber, 1948], p.20).

lies not simply in ignorance of or misinterpretation of the Chalcedonian Definition but in the Definition itself.

1. *Human limitations.* If Christ was truly 'made like his brethren in every respect' it is essential that he shared in human limitations. Referring to the limitation of real manhood, Donald Guthrie writes that 'all that Jesus did during his earthly ministry was governed by that limitation'.[52] Professor Quick was perhaps guilty of pardonable exaggeration when he wrote that the principle 'that the eternal Son or Word in his incarnation by a voluntary act limited himself to a historical human consciousness and human faculties of knowledge and action, has, I believe, proved itself to be the most important fresh contribution to Christology which has been made since the time of Irenaeus'.[53]

While the Chalcedonian Definition may allow a theoretical acknowledgement of human limitations in Christ, in practice it denies them. As man he may have been limited, but the same one person at that very instant was unlimited as God. The early Fathers may have debated whether or not Christ (as man) knew all things, but the debate is futile since they maintained that the historical Jesus did know all things as God. They might have spoken of his weakness as man, but as God he was omnipotent. This is like my claiming that I am experiencing both poverty and wealth because there is no money in my left pocket while in my right pocket I have a million pounds. Wealth eliminates poverty. Omniscience and ignorance, omnipotence and impotence cannot coexist. The former swamps the latter. A cup cannot become empty while remaining full.

These criticisms are not to be construed as a rationalistic attack on paradox. The problem with Chalcedon is not that it affirms the biblical paradox of God accepting human limitations but that it effectively denies these limitations. The affirmation that the historical Jesus was omniscient and omnipotent, which undermines his participation in human weakness and limitations, is not one half of a biblical paradox but an alien intrusion foreign to the New Testament.

2. *Knowledge.* The issue of human limitation is felt most acutely in the area of Christ's knowledge.[54] Did he know everything? The Fathers held that he did know everything as God, while his human knowledge may have been limited.

---

[52] D. Guthrie, *op. cit.,* p.226.

[53] O. C. Quick, *Doctrines of the Creed* (Nisbet, 1938), pp.132f.

[54] It is because we think today in psychological terms that the question of Christ's knowledge has become so acute. *Cf.* J. McIntyre, *op. cit.,* pp.129f.

His learning was often interpreted as the gradual infusion of knowledge from the divine to the human mind. It was often taught that he deliberately pretended not to know things.[55]

The New Testament picture of Christ is strikingly different. 'Jesus increased in wisdom' (Lk. 2:52). This 'suggests a development under normal laws of human growth. There is nothing to suggest any fantastic developments.'[56] During his ministry Jesus asked many questions, though it is true that in at least some instances these were not prompted by ignorance (*e.g.* Jn. 6:5f.). But it is hard to see how expressions of surprise can be reconciled with omniscience, short of postulating conscious deceit on the part of Christ.[57] Furthermore, he himself explicitly denied his omniscience (Mt. 24:36 = Mk. 13:32) but even the clear words of Christ have not sufficed to counter the pull of docetism. It is true that the Christ of the Gospels taught with a supreme authority and manifested supernatural knowledge. But neither of these can be equated with omniscience. The affirmation of the omniscience of the historical Jesus has no biblical basis and indeed runs counter to the clear teaching of the Gospels.

The question of omniscience is far from being merely academic. The affirmation of Jesus' omniscience is not simply contrary to specific teaching about him in the Gospels. It has serious theological implications in that it undermines his true humanity as taught in Scripture. It is hard to see how an omniscient man could be genuinely tempted to do something that he *knew* that he would not do (since omniscience must include a full knowledge of his own life history). It is hard to see how omniscience could be reconciled with the struggles of Gethsemane and Calvary. Yet to undermine these is to strike at the heart of New Testament Christology. To refuse to accept the omniscience of the historical Christ is not to deny a biblical paradox but to defend the biblical doctrine of the true humanity of Christ against an unbiblical intrusion.

Unfortunately the issue of Christ's omniscience has been clouded by its association with the reliability of his teaching. Many have felt it necessary to assert the former in order to defend the latter. But the New Testament nowhere bases the authority and reliability of Jesus' teaching on his omniscience. Indeed the contrary is affirmed in that Jesus' teaching is not his own but his Father's.[58] It is strange how often those who have sought to defend the authority of Jesus' teaching have done so by invoking a doctrine which he himself explicitly denied.

[55] C. Gore, *Dissertations on Subjects Connected with the Incarnation* (John Murray, 1895), pp.130-138.   [56] D. Guthrie, *op. cit.*, p.221.

[57] *E.g.* Mk. 6:6; Lk. 7:9. *Cf.* C. Gore, *op. cit.*, pp.77-88. For a very thorough discussion, *cf.* J. S. Lawton, *Conflict in Christology* (SPCK, 1947), pp.44-110.

[58] Jn. 7:16f.; 8:26-28; 12:49f.; 17:8.

Most contemporary defenders of Chalcedon recognize that to defend the omniscience of Jesus' human mind is undesirable.

> There are obvious difficulties in supposing that, in the plain and obvious sense of the words, the human mind of the Babe of Bethlehem was thinking, as he lay in the manger, of the Procession of the Holy Ghost, the theorems of hydrodynamics, the novels of Jane Austen and the Battle of Hastings.[59]

But alongside the human ignorance they assert the simultaneous divine omniscience. Both of these are, on the Chalcedonian model, attributed to the historical Jesus Christ. It does not make sense to speak of the same one person being simultaneously ignorant and omniscient.[60] This is not a biblical paradox but a docetic undermining of the biblical teaching on the true humanity of Christ.

3. *Impersonal humanity.* Chalcedon has been accused of attributing to Christ an 'impersonal humanity'. Christ has two natures, divine and human. But he is only one person or hypostasis, and that one person is God the Logos. This seems to imply that Christ's humanity is without a hypostasis (*anhypostatic*), which in the ancient world met with the objection that no nature can exist without a hypostasis. This philosophical maxim was used by Nestorians to argue that Christ's two natures must make him two persons and by Monophysites to argue that the unity of person allows only one nature. The force of this logic was met on the Chalcedonian side by the doctrine of *enhypostasia*: the human nature of Christ is not merely *anhypostatic* (without a hypostasis) but *enhypostatic* in the Logos – *i.e.* the hypostasis of Christ's human nature is that of God the Logos.

To say today that Christ's humanity was 'impersonal' sounds blatantly docetic. 'Human nature which is not personal is not human nature.'[61] But this is to misunderstand the meaning of 'person' in the ancient world.[62] For us

---

[59] E. L. Mascall, *Christ, the Christian and the Church*, p.53. But in the subsequent discussion he is not unequivocal about Christ's human ignorance, claiming 'at least to have shown the possibility of the reconciliation of a real omniscience in our Lord's *human* nature with an equally real growth and development' (p.65, my emphasis).

[60] Comparisons with us simultaneously knowing and not knowing something (*e.g. ibid.*, pp.58f.) are not valid because we are here dealing with omniscience (J. McIntyre, *op. cit.*, pp.137f.).

[61] R. C. Moberley, cited in D. M. Baillie, *op. cit.*, p.86.

[62] For a most helpful clarification of this, *cf.* R. Williams, '"Person" and "Personality" in Christology', *Downside Review* 94, 1976, pp.53-58.

today the word 'person' has strong psychological overtones. This was not so in the patristic period. The term was essentially ontological. The denial of a human person in Christ was not a psychological statement but a denial of Adoptionism. It meant that the sole subject of the human experiences of Christ was God the Logos. To affirm the existence of a human person alongside the person of the Logos would mean that Jesus was not in fact the incarnate Word but simply a man who was especially friendly with the Word, *i.e.* Adoptionism.[63] The human psychology falls into the category of nature rather than person. To affirm that Christ had a human nature is to imply the completeness of his human psychology. The only difference between him and us in this respect is that while we are mere human beings he was the divine Logos incarnate: *i.e.* his hypostasis was the Logos, who was the subject of his human experiences. To deny this is to deny the very doctrine of the incarnation. To call this docetic is simply to state that *any* doctrine of the incarnation is docetic. This is precisely what is maintained by many of the modern successors of Nestorius. Such criticism of Chalcedon should be stated explicitly as an Adoptionist critique and not smuggled undeclared into debates about *enhypostasia.*

The debate about impersonal humanity illustrates a point that has already been made: the need to translate Chalcedon into contemporary terms. To state today that Christ is one person, without a detailed explanation, will inevitably cause the great majority of people to seek to locate Christ's unity at the psychological level. 'Person' will be taken in the modern psychological sense and not in the purely ontological sense of the Fathers. The result is that the majority who accept the Chalcedonian wording will in fact hold to some form of Apollinarianism or Eutychianism through locating Christ's unity in his psychology.

Beyond Chalcedon

Is Chalcedon of permanent value? A number of serious criticisms have been levelled against the Definition and it cannot be accepted without reservation. But that does not mean that it has no abiding value. This may be considered at three different levels.

First, and most important, the achievement of Chalcedon is negative.[64] First and foremost the Definition is a rejection of heresy: Arianism, Apollinarianism,

---

[63] For a lucid summary of the value of *anhypostasia* and *enhypostasia, cf.* K. Barth, *Church Dogmatics,* IV/2 (T. & T. Clark, 1958), pp.49f. The term 'Adoptionism' is used here for the belief that Jesus was a man who at some stage acquired some sort of divine status, without necessarily denying that the initiative was wholly God's.

[64] For this paragraph, *cf.* n. 31, above.

Nestorianism, Eutychianism. At this level its achievement is permanent. These heresies were wrong in their own day and they will always be wrong. There will never come a time when any of them will become right, whether in their original form or in a modern guise. The primary aim of Chalcedon was the elimination of heresy and the Definition successfully excludes the four ancient heresies.[65]

Secondly, Chalcedon proclaims a positive Christology against these heresies. This Christology is not flawless, due to the intrusion of the unbiblical belief in an immutable and impassible God. It is, therefore, open to correction and improvement. But such improvement is likely to come through a modification of Chalcedon, building on the achievement of Chalcedon, rather than an attempt to start again from scratch.

Thirdly, Chalcedon is a document of the fifth century. As such it is, like all documents, including the Bible, culturally relative inasmuch as it is expressed in the language and concepts of a particular age. Like the Bible, it needs to be translated into contemporary terms if it is not to be misunderstood.

The doctrine of the Trinity

The early Fathers moved from the deity of Christ to the doctrine of the Trinity. Arius thrust the issue of Christ's full deity to the forefront. In the 360s the debate became explicitly trinitarian with the denial of the deity of the Holy Spirit by the Egyptian Tropici. Thus far the Fathers followed the New Testament order. The New Testament explicitly teaches the deity of Christ but contains only hints which point in the direction of a doctrine of the Trinity and lay the foundations for it rather than propound a formal trinitarian doctrine.[66] Thus in the New Testament as in the Fathers, the doctrine of the Trinity arises out of the deity of Christ.

Unfortunately, serious Christological debate among the Fathers did not begin until the doctrine of the Trinity was all but resolved, in the time of Apollinaris. This meant that the Fathers started with a clearly defined belief in God the Son, the immutable and impassible second person of the Trinity, and then asked how this divine person could become man.[67] Their debates therefore centred on the relationship between the Logos and the humanity of Jesus. This approach differs significantly from the New Testament. The problem lies not in the affirmation of Christ's deity but in the way that his deity is affirmed. For the Fathers it is the

---

[65] While the two following councils at Constantinople were deemed necessary to complete the task, these may legitimately be considered to spell out more fully the implications of Chalcedon.

[66] D. Guthrie, *op. cit.,* pp. 113f.

[67] There was, of course, Christological debate before Apollinaris, and this followed broadly the same approach as here described.

deity of the eternal Logos which is affirmed and the problem is how to relate him to the human Jesus. The New Testament writers did not start with belief in the pre-existent divine Son and then identify this being with Christ.[68] It was only after they came to believe in the deity of Christ that they started to think in terms of an eternal Trinity. They did not work from the doctrine of the Trinity to Christology.

To work from the doctrine of the Trinity to the person of Christ is to work from the unknown to the known. Christ came to show us the Father, to reveal to us what God is like. While it is excessive to claim that God is known *only* in Christ, any doctrine of God established independently of Christ will clearly be defective. Yet to start with a precisely formulated doctrine of the Trinity before resolving one's Christology is to fall into that trap. This can have serious consequences for Christology. The doctrine of the Trinity is often invoked against this or that Christological theory.[69] But this procedure is dangerous:

> Theologically speaking, we might almost say that it was in order to make intelligible the experience of the incarnation and the atonement that the doctrine of the Trinity was formulated. Therefore we ought to test the truth and significance of our doctrine of the Trinity by our apprehension of the truth and significance of the incarnation, and not to limit the significance of the incarnation by the supposed demands of the doctrine of the Trinity.[70]

This is all the more desirable when we remember that God cannot be fully grasped by human reason. This being so, to work out a neat philosophical doctrine of God and then to use this to control the formulation of Christology is an unwise procedure. Better to start with what is (relatively) clearly revealed and then to move on to the doctrine of God.

In the New Testament the economic Trinity is primary. God is known to be three because of his action for our salvation as Father, Son and Holy Spirit. The immanent Trinity (God's eternal being) follows from this on the ground that God's revelation of himself is true to his real being. If we know the second person of the Trinity as the 'Son' it is because Jesus as man enjoyed the relation of Son to the Father. If the Holy Spirit is thought to proceed eternally from the

---

[68] John's Gospel begins with the pre-existent Logos, but after the prologue (1:1-18) the person of Christ is not expressed in terms of his relation to the Logos.

[69] *E.g.* by D. M. Baillie, *op. cit.*, p.96, in his criticism of kenoticism.

[70] O. C. Quick, *Doctrines of the Creed*, p.139. It is not, of course, being suggested that Christology be done as if there were *no* doctrine of the Trinity. It is the use of a *precise* doctrine of the Trinity to control Christology that is wrong.

Father (and the Son) it is because this relationship is seen in his being sent to us (Jn. 15:26). It is dangerous to argue in the reverse order. To use philosophy or speculative theology to build a doctrine of the immanent Trinity and then to use this doctrine to control our understanding of the economic Trinity is to argue from the unknown to the known. This is what has happened in the application of the doctrine of the Trinity to Christology.

Christ's ignorance presents a problem to those who start by thinking of the eternal Son as omniscient God. How could this divine person lose his omniscience? But if we start with the incarnate Son we see that his special knowledge arises out of his relation of dependence on the Father.[71] It is therefore reasonable to suppose that in the eternal relationship between Father and Son the Son's knowledge is derived from the Father. This same relationship would continue in the incarnation, but with a different outworking adjusted to the conditions of Christ's manhood.

The historical Christ

The starting-point for Christology should be the historical Christ, as portrayed in the New Testament, not the eternal Trinity. The Chalcedonian portrait of Christ is of one person in two natures whose acts are sometimes human, sometimes divine.[72] It was as man that he wept over his friend Lazarus, as God that he raised him from the dead. This approach theoretically allows human limitation but in practice smothers it. This can be seen from the difficulty that the Chalcedonian tradition has had in handling Jesus' own confession of ignorance.[73] It can also be seen by the neglect of Jesus' moral life in the same tradition. He experienced temptation like us (Heb. 2:17f.; 4:15f.). Obedience was something that he *learned* (Heb. 5:8). It is not that he was ever disobedient (Heb. 4:15); but obedience is a positive concept which embraces more than the mere absence of disobedience, and this human obedience Jesus learned. Of the ancient Christological traditions, only the Antiochenes did justice to this aspect of Jesus' humanity – and they were able to do this only by virtue of their crypto-Adoptionism, in that the subject of this moral life was Jesus the man rather than the incarnate Logos.

While the New Testament ascribes deity to Christ, it does not encourage the view that some of his acts were human while others were performed in his divine nature. Traditionally, his miracles have been seen as being performed in his divine nature and therefore as evidences of his deity in that they could be performed only by God. This interpretation runs into a number of difficulties.

---

[71] *Cf.* n. 58, above.   [72] *Cf.* above, *Dualism.*

[73] *Cf.* above, *Knowledge,* especially n. 59.

Most, if not all, of Jesus' miracles can be paralleled in other biblical characters. Jesus expected his disciples to perform similar miracles (Jn. 14:12) and the Acts of the Apostles implies that they did. Jesus himself said that it was by the Holy Spirit/finger of God that he cast out demons (Mt. 12:28; Lk. 11:20). He said that his deeds were done in dependence upon his Father (Jn. 5:19f.; 10:18). Therefore he prayed before performing miracles (Mk. 7:33f.; 9:29; Jn. 11:41f.).[74] Jesus' ministry was preceded by the reception of the Holy Spirit in his baptism and it would appear that his miracles were performed as man, in dependence upon the Father, through the Holy Spirit, rather than by his own divine nature.[75] In the same way, his supernatural knowledge is evidence not of his own personal omniscience but of his perfect relationship to his Father.

This is not to deny Christ's true deity or to reduce him to a perfect man in a perfect relationship to God. But it is to claim that in the incarnation God revealed himself not by the direct unmediated display of deity but through the medium of a human life. This does not detract from Christ's glory: it is the marvel of God's grace that he condescends to speak to us in our language, in terms that we can understand. The transfiguration may have served to show the disciples *who* Jesus was, but it is not there that we see the significant disclosure of God's character. The supreme revelation of God is seen on the cross, where Jesus is at his weakest and 'most human'.[76] For John, Jesus' exaltation lies in his being 'lifted up' upon the cross. The New Testament portrait of Christ is of God revealing himself through the medium of a human life, not by the alternation of merely human life with direct divine revelation.

Jesus and the eternal Trinity

How is this picture of the historical Christ to be related to the eternal Trinity? A strictly Chalcedonian Christology will not suffice as it undermines the reality of Christ's human limitations. A number of incarnational variations of the Chalcedonian model have been tried, with varying success. Space permits no more than a brief summary of and comment on three main approaches.

The most radical is the *kenōsis* approach, as found mainly in nineteenth-century German writers. This approach held that the Logos became incarnate by, in some sense, emptying himself of his deity. The thoroughgoing approach

---

[74] Jn. 11:42 could be taken as a public acknowledgement that his miracles were done in dependence upon the Father.

[75] *Cf.* C. Gore, *Dissertations on Subjects Connected with the Incarnation*, pp. 140, 165f.

[76] The docetic tendency of traditional Christology is seen in the popular idea that Jesus could at any moment have left the cross. The nearest that the New Testament comes to this is Jesus' statement that he could appeal to his Father who would at once send angels to the rescue, which is significantly different (Mt. 26:53).

of W. F. Gess[77] involved the extinction of the divine life of the Logos such that he to all intents ceased to be God. This came to be called incarnation by divine suicide and it was said that it required a 'kenosis of understanding' before one could accept it. A more moderate approach was adopted by G. Thomasius,[78] who held that the Logos emptied himself of the 'relative' divine attributes of omnipotence, omniscience and omnipresence (the three 'o's), while retaining the essential moral attributes.

These kenosis theories have been subjected to intense criticism.[79] While by no means all of the objections were well founded, the general consensus is that such kenosis theories are untenable. But this does not mean that the idea of kenosis has nothing to offer. The basic principle of the kenosis approach – the genuine self-limitation of the divine Logos in the incarnation – has influenced Christology far beyond the limits of those who would be willing to associate themselves with kenoticism.

Bishop Gore is often credited with introducing the kenosis approach into Britain, but in fact he held to a distinctly different approach, originally proposed by the Danish bishop H. L. Martensen, which may be called *the double life of the Logos.*[80] This approach maintains that the incarnate Logos lives a purely human life with a human consciousness (as with kenoticism) but that he continues to live his divine life separately and without interruption. Thus the divine Logos simultaneously but separately lives his divine life with his divine consciousness and a human life with a human consciousness. The divine consciousness is aware of the human but the human consciousness has no direct access to the divine. Thus, as God he was seated at the right hand of the Father, omniscient and upholding the universe, while at the same time he was as man subject to human limitations.

This approach is consistent with the picture of the historical Christ presented in the last section, while maintaining the Chalcedonian one person in two natures. But it achieves the former only by drastically separating the two natures in a way that is contrary to Chalcedonian Christology (*e.g.* Leo) and

[77] *Cf.* A. B. Bruce, *The Humiliation of Christ* (T. & T. Clark, ²1881), pp. 144-152.

[78] *Ibid.*, pp. 138-144; D. G. Dawe, *The Form of a Servant* (Westminster, 1963), pp. 92-100. Chronologically, Thomasius precedes Gess.

[79] *E.g.* D. M. Baillie, *God Was in Christ*, pp. 94-98; E. R. Fairweather, 'The "Kenotic" Christology', in F. W. Beare, *A Commentary on the Epistle to the Philippians* (A. & C. Black, 1959), pp. 159-174; E. L. Mascall, *Christ, the Christian and the Church*, pp. 23-26.

[80] C. Gore, *op. cit.*, pp. 71-225, developing his *The Incarnation of the Son of God* (John Murray, 1891). *Cf.* J. S. Lawton, *Conflict in Christology*, pp. 143-156. For Martensen, *cf.* A. B. Bruce, *op. cit.*, pp. 159-163.

explicitly rejected by Chalcedon ('without division, without separation').[81] This has led to the charge of Nestorianism, but that is not warranted as the Logos remains the sole subject of the two natures.

As this approach offers consistency with the picture of the historical Christ presented in the last section with the minimum of departure from Chalcedon, many have found it an attractive option.[82] But it avoids the dualistic Chalcedonian picture of the historical Christ only by shifting this dualism 'upstairs' on to the eternal Logos. This dualism leads to anomalies, *e.g.* that on the cross the (incarnate) Logos was forsaken by himself (disincarnate). As with Chalcedon, the relation between the human Jesus and the divine Logos becomes central, rather than the relation of Jesus to his Father. Furthermore, it seems to make the entire doctrine of the Trinity superfluous since a unitarian God could as easily have become incarnate while retaining his unaltered divine life. This turns the Trinity into an esoteric doctrine only accidentally related to the incarnation.

The third approach is often inaccurately called kenosis but is better called one of *self-restraint*. This approach was popular in Britain earlier this century, its leading exponents being P. T. Forsyth, H. R. Mackintosh and Vincent Taylor.[83] They recognized that the Logos could not cease to be God nor actually lose any of his attributes. They modified the kenosis approach by teaching that the Logos did not literally empty himself but rather limited himself during the incarnation. Attributes like omniscience were not renounced but rather became latent or potential. By this means the Logos restrained himself to live within the self-imposed limitations of humanity. During the incarnation the Logos was confined to the historical Christ, not existing independently outside of Christ in a divine realm.

This approach avoids the grosser faults of the German kenosis and escapes from the dualism of the double life of the Logos. But in its escape from dualism it falls into the danger of Eutychianism in that it can easily present a picture of the incarnate Logos as no longer fully God and not quite become a true man.

---

[81] Gore, in *Dissertations on Subjects Connected with the Incarnation*, pp.210-213, claims that his view is consistent with Chalcedon.

[82] *E.g.* J. N. D. Anderson, *The Mystery of the Incarnation* (Hodder & Stoughton, 1978), pp.144-157. For a very lucid account of this position by a fellow-contributor to the present volume, *cf.* R. L. Sturch, 'The Metaphysics of the Incarnation', *Vox Evangelica* 10, 1977, pp.65-76.

[83] P. T. Forsyth, *The Person and Place of Jesus Christ* (Independent Press, 1909), pp.291-320; H. R. Mackintosh, *The Doctrine of the Person of Jesus Christ* (T. & T. Clark, 1912), pp.463-486; V. Taylor, *The Person of Christ in New Testament Preaching* (Macmillan, 1958), pp.260-276, 286-304. *Cf.* D. G. Dawe, *op. cit.*, pp.131-141. For criticisms of this approach, *cf.* n. 79, above.

All of these approaches seem to start from a common presupposition: they all seem to approach the pre-incarnate Logos as if he were an independent divine being with his 'own' omniscience and omnipotence. How can this omniscient, omnipotent God accept human limitations? Again, criticisms of the kenosis and self-restraint approaches treat them as if they were describing the incarnation of God *tout simple* rather than of one person of the Trinity. The most blatant example of this is the charge of cosmic chaos, which implies that the universe would fall to pieces during the Son's 'absence' on earth. If the doctrine of the Trinity is reassessed in the light of the incarnation, and the Son's knowledge and power are seen to flow from his relationship to the Father, rather than being an independent possession of his own, some of the problems may be less acute. While this implies a subordination of relationship between Father and Son, it does not imply a subordination of being.[84]

Conclusion

Three modifications of Chalcedon have been outlined in the previous section. Which of these is the biblical approach? There is a sense in which none of them is biblical and another sense in which they can all claim to be biblical. They are none of them biblical in the sense that few today would claim that any of these theories is explicitly formulated in Scripture. You will not find the formula of one person in two natures in the New Testament. It cannot be maintained that Paul was thinking of a full-blown kenosis theory when he wrote Philippians 2:5-11.

In what sense then can the theories claim to be biblical? The New Testament gives us a certain amount of material about Jesus but no systematic formulation of this. The theories come in at this level. They are not themselves biblical but they are models which purport to interpret the biblical material.[85] The New Testament provides the data, the theories seek to organize and interpret it. Thus while they do not set out to add to Scripture in the sense of providing more material, they do go beyond Scripture in the sense of offering a framework within which the biblical material can be understood. They are different models, each seeking to do justice to the biblical material. They are to be judged by their success or otherwise in interpreting the biblical data – much as a pair of shoes is judged by its ability to fit comfortably round our feet. Which model fits the most comfortably? They are only models and it must be freely admitted that none of them is a perfect fit – each shoe pinches somewhere. They are each more or less satisfactory attempts to do something which may

---

[84] *Cf.* J. N. D. Anderson, *op. cit.,* pp.153-157.
[85] For the idea of models, *cf.* J. McIntyre, *The Shape of Christology.*

ultimately be impossible for the human mind to achieve perfectly. But to admit that no model is perfect is not to say that they are all equally imperfect or that there is nothing to choose between them.

In practical terms, the important point about any Christology is the picture of the historical Christ that it offers us. All of the Christologies outlined in the last section agree broadly in their understanding of the historical Jesus. The significant differences between them concern the relation between this Jesus Christ and the eternal Trinity, especially the question of how the eternal Logos could genuinely embrace human limitations. None of the theories is wholly adequate in answering this question, but this is *relatively* of secondary importance. They agree on the *what* of the incarnation: that God the Logos became man and lived a truly human life, with human limitations. Where they differ concerns the *how* of the incarnation: how he achieved his incarnation and in particular how his human limitations are to be reconciled with his deity. This is a legitimate question to ask and the New Testament is not totally silent on this point. But it is perhaps being over-optimistic to expect to be able to resolve so great a mystery.

THE CHRISTOLOGY OF ISLAM

F. P. Cotterell

The name '*Īsā*, 'Jesus', occurs in eleven of the 114 Suras of the *Qur'ān*[1] and it would not be difficult to construct a rudimentary Life of Christ from these and other references. It would begin with a reasonably detailed account of the conception and birth of Jesus from (the virgin?) Mary. It would include reference to specific miracles performed by him in his childhood and more general reference to miracles attributed to him in adulthood. It would be noted that he had disciples. There would be reference to his crucifixion, or at least to attempts made to have Jesus crucified, and to his translation to a place of refuge in heaven, or in one of the heavens. And finally there might be reference to his eschatological role as an indicator of the imminence of the final judgment through his return to earth (although this return to earth would culminate not in his coronation, as in Christian eschatology, but in his death).

Evidently there is a considerable amount of material common to the Christian Gospels and the *Qur'ān* and although similarities are evident there are fundamental differences between them. Of course within Islam the question of source criticism as applied to the text of the *Qur'ān* does not arise, since the *Qur'ān* is understood to be a revelation to Muhammad ben Abd-Allāh from the Preserved Tablet[2] and owes nothing at all either to Muhammad's own knowledge of Christianity or his interpretation of such knowledge. It is, however, important to note that some of the information contained in the *Qur'ān* is paralleled in other

---

[1] There are other references to Jesus which do not specifically use his name. The relevant passages are: 2:81, 130, 254; 3:40, 45, 48, 52, 78; 4:156, 161, 169, (170); 5:(19), 50, (76), (79), 82, 109, 112, 114, 116; 6:85; 9:(30), (31); 19:35; 21: (91); 23:(52); 33:7; 42:11; 43:(57), 63; 57:27; 61:6, 14.

[2] *al-Lawḥ al-Maḥfūz*, one of several designations of the Writing, *al-kitāb*, from which the Jewish, Christian and Muslim scriptures are supposed to derive.

writings: the Gospels (both canonical and apocryphal)[3] and works such as the *Book of James.*[4]

Of course there is no suggestion here that these parallel passages are *quoted* in the *Qur'ān*. The plausible Muslim tradition that Muhammad was illiterate (a tradition based in part on Sura 7:158, but see the interesting discussion of the understanding of the verse in the Ahmadi edition of the *Qur'ān*, edited by Malik Ghulām Farīd, Rabwah, 1969) militates against direct quotation and in any event is unlikely that an Arabic translation of the Gospels was available to Muhammad (*cf.* footnote 3). Clear verbal parallels would, in any event, be difficult to demonstrate unless source and quotation were both in the same language. In the case of the apocryphal *Gospel of the Infancy of Jesus* quotation becomes a possibility since it does exist in Arabic, but it cannot be shown conclusively that the *Gospel* ante-dates Islam.[5] It is more likely that it is later than the *Qur'ān* which it echoes.

Whatever might be the source or sources of the incidents in the *Qur'ān* which relate to Jesus, the incidents themselves represent a *selection* of the extant material, and it is precisely this selection which is determinative of Muslim Christology today.

The designations of Jesus
Any of the standard works on Islam will yield an impressive list of titles accorded

---

[3] Canonical Luke appears to lie at the root of the two accounts of the annunciation and the birth of Christ, although it is no longer possible to trace the links between the root and the fruit, between Gospel and *Qur'ān*. Quite apart from the traditional illiteracy of Muhammad referred to, there is considerable doubt whether an Arabic translation of the NT would have been available to him. Muhammad was born in 570 and died in 632. There is a tradition that a Monophysite Christian produced a translation into Arabic in the very decade of Muhammad's death, but if it ever existed no part of it has survived. Fragments of an Arabic translation from the ninth century do exist; whether these come from an original which included the entire NT cannot now be determined. Ahmad ibn-Abdullah ibn-Salam is supposed to have produced such a translation in the first half of the ninth century, *cf.* B. Metzger, *The Early Versions of the New Testament* (OUP, 1977), chapter 6.

[4] Origen used this title. The work is more generally known as the *Protevangelium of James*. It is primarily an account of the birth of Mary, of the annunciation and of the birth of Christ. Some of the pious assumptions of the early Christians are here 'legitimized'. Joseph is declared to be a widower, entrusted with the care of Mary, thus protecting her eternal virginity and explaining Jesus' 'brothers'. The work was, apparently, highly valued by the Syrian churches, *cf.* E. Hennecke, *New Testament Apocrypha* 1 (Lutterworth, 1962), pp.370-388.

[5] The Arabic *Infancy Gospel* is potentially important since only there (five times) and in the Syriac *Gospel of the Infancy* is the title 'Son of Mary' found in the whole mass of apocryphal works. But the significance disappears if it is, in fact, post-*Qur'ān*.

to Jesus.[6] He is Messiah, the *'abd*-servant of God, a *nabī*-prophet, a Messenger of Allah (*rasūl*). He is a sign from God, a word from God and the blessed of God (*mubarak*). But two designations demand individual consideration: the name *'Īsā* itself and the designation of Jesus as Son of Mary.

'Īsā[7]

The English name *Jesus* is a rendering of Greek *Iēsous*, itself descending from Aramaic and Hebrew *Yeshua*, 'he saves'. The Arabic *'Īsā* may well have come from Syriac *Yeshū'* (which would be in accord with the general observation that Muhammad's knowledge of Christianity stemmed from Syrian *Jews*), but the rationale for the transition is not linguistically convincing. The alternative suggestion that the Jews referred contemptuously to Jesus as *'Īsā* because of the obvious near-homophony with Esau (Hebrew *'Esā*), the despised brother of Jacob, could well be correct, despite Parrinder's objection[8] that Jesus is honoured, not despised, in Muslim literature. Nöldeke suggests that Muhammad adopted the name in good faith, unaware of the pejorative overtones.[9]

But even if this latter explanation of the origin of the name *'Īsā* is correct, it cannot be unimportant for Muslim Christology that the Arabic rendering of the name of Jesus as *'Īsā* severs from the name its soteriological significance, 'The Lord saves'.[10] This is important in that Islam does not admit the need for *salvation* and thinks in terms of *revelation* and *enlightenment* rather than *redemption*.[11] While Islam recognizes a prophetic role for Jesus there is no place for him as Saviour, his central role in Christianity.

Son of Mary

The title 'Son of Mary', *'ibn-Maryam*, is found in the *Qur'ān* twenty-three

---

[6] E.g. Geoffrey Parrinder, *Jesus in the Qur'ān* (Sheldon Press, 1965), chs. 2–4.

[7] A useful and concise examination of the origin, significance and usage of this name is given in the revised *Shorter Encyclopaedia of Islam*, ed. H. A. R. Gibb and J. H. Kramers (Brill, 1974).

[8] *Jesus in the Qur'ān*, p.17.

[9] *ZDMG*, 45, 352. Note also the concise explanation offered by al-Baidawi in his commentary on Sura 3, *Chrestomathia Baidawiana*, ed. D. S. Margoliouth (Luzac, 1894), p.35: '*'Īsā* is an arabized form of *Īshū'*. The derivation of... *'Īsā* from *'ayasun* which means white with a shade of red [is] of no value.' Margoliouth takes this to mean that Baidawi does not accept the link with Esau (in his footnote 197).   [10] Mt. 1:21.

[11] 'Islam does not normally use the word "salvation", still less "regeneration"' (abd al-Tafahum, *Religion in the Middle East* 2, p.401). The main lines of OT history are recognized in Islam but there is no *development* apparent, no unfolding of salvation history. Moses and Joseph have no soteriological role to play.

times. This may be set against the contrasting New Testament title for Jesus, 'Son of God' which appears there forty-five times.[12] The designation 'Son of Mary', on the other hand, occurs in the New Testament only once, at Mark 6:3, and then precisely in the context of the assertion of Christ's mere humanity.

Here again it is difficult to estimate the significance of the use of the title 'Son of Mary' in the *Qur'ān*. It is certainly contrary to Arab patronymics, but the *'ibn-Yūsuf* (Lk. 4:22; Jn. 6:42) would be even less acceptable as a designation for Jesus. Moreover the metronymic is not unknown to Arab culture, particularly where, as in the case of Mary, the mother is for some reason more honoured or simply better known than the father.

The suggestion that the title 'Son of Mary' originated in Abyssinia, and indicated a high view of *Mary* rather than a low view of *Jesus*, fails at two points. Firstly it is supposed that the title was brought back from Abyssinia by returning Muslim refugees, after the first *hijra*. However, the title occurs in Meccan Suras, decisively in Sura 19 which, according to tradition, was recited *to* the Abyssinian *Nagash* (Eth. *negūs*, 'king') by the refugees.[13] Secondly there is no evidence that the title 'Son of Mary' was used by the Abyssinian church: it does not appear in the Ethiopic *Qiddase*.[14] In any event the use of the title by the Abyssinian church is highly unlikely since its strong monophysite position ensured that the deity of Christ all but eclipsed his humanity.

The fact that Jesus is five times designated 'Son of Mary' in the *Gospel of the Infancy of Jesus* is important not as providing the *source* of the title as it appears in the *Qur'ān* but as indicating that the title was current in the seventh century and so available to Muhammad. We do not, therefore, need to assume that Muhammad was the creator of the (pejorative?) title 'Son of Mary', but that he elected to employ this title as a proper indication of Jesus' status.

[12] See Vincent Taylor, *The Person of Christ in New Testament Teaching* (Macmillan, 1959), p.147.

[13] J. M. Rodwell (ed.), *The Koran* (Dent, 1909 and onwards), footnote on p.117. See also Pickthall's introduction to Sura 19 in his *The Glorious Koran*, where he quotes ibn Ishaq's original record of the interview between the refugees, the *Negūs* and the messengers from Mecca.

[14] It is true that the Ethiopic liturgy exalts Mary, but this it accomplishes rather by emphasizing the deity of her Son than by exalting her at his expense. I have been unable to trace any appearance of the title 'Son of Mary' in the Ethiopic liturgies. See, for example, the *Maṣihafe-Qiddase*, published by the Ethiopian Orthodox Church in Asmara in 1965, a well printed Ge'ez and Amharic compendium of three *Qiddases* including one attributed to Dioscorus, Patriarch of Alexandria from 444. It is interesting to note in these liturgies the forthright designation of Jesus as *amlakina*, 'our God' (*cf.* p.66 *etc.*).

A Qur'ānic 'Life of Christ'

We turn next to a consideration of the central features of a life of Christ as it might be constructed from the *Qur'ān*.

The annunciation (S. 3:33–47; S. 19:1–22)

The comparatively brief account of the annunciation given in the early Meccan Sura 19 is generally reconcilable with the corresponding New Testament data.[15] The later Medinan Sura 3, 'The family of Imran', raises a number of questions bearing on the source or sources of the account and their factual reliability. There is certainly a *prima facie* case to be answered with respect to an apparent confusion between Amram and his family in the period of the Exodus, Hannah and the period of the Judges, and Mary in the New Testament period. The wife of Imran (3:35) becomes the mother of Mary and, echoing 1 Samuel 1:11 and the *Protevangelium of James,* dedicates her child to the service of God.

If Imran is to be equated with the Old Testament Amram, then we have a simple example of confusion arising out of the use of oral sources and the understandable identification of Old Testament Miriam with New Testament Maryam. But *is* Imran to be identified with Amram? Muslim commentators certainly identify two individuals, with Imran distinguished from Amram. The text itself does not help us. In Sura 3:33 there is a chronological sequence of which Imran is, unfortunately, the last; Adam, Noah, Abraham and Imran. If David had been listed after the family of Imran it would have set the identity of Imran beyond reasonable doubt. As it is, the possibility of leaping forward into the New Testament period from Abraham, and identifying Imran as the father of Mary becomes just tolerable.

The details of the annunciation in Sura 3 may be related to two written sources, the New Testament and the *Protevangelium of James*. It is the *Book of James* which supplies the story of Mary being assigned to the guardianship of Zechariah through casting lots, and again the *Book of James* which gives the story of Mary being miraculously fed as a child in the Temple. Of course the Gospel of Luke makes reference to a three-month visit paid by Mary to the home of Zechariah (1:39–56) and it is possible that this is the basis for the *James* elaboration.[16] The Lucan account of the annunciation makes the doctrine of a

---

[15] Although there are some discrepancies; Zechariah is dumb for three days (19:10), where in Lk. 1 he is dumb for the entire period between the revelation to him and the naming of the child (1:20–64).

[16] Again it must be emphasized that there is no suggestion here that Muhammad used written sources. The two *Qur'ān* accounts are precisely what one would expect of an orally circulating tradition which mixed fact with legend.

virgin birth explicit through the use of the Greek *parthenos* (1:27) which then explicates Mary's remonstrance 'I have no husband' in 1:34. Here we cannot avoid the observation that behind Greek *ginōskein*, 'to know', lies the Hebrew idiom for sexual intercourse, so that Mary's response clearly asserts her virginity. This assertion is confirmed by the Matthaean reference to the prophecy of Isaiah (Mt. 1:22f.). The teaching of the New Testament on the issue of Mary's virginity is, therefore, quite clear.

The same, however, is not the case with the *Qur'ān*. The text here does not *require* a virgin birth although it does not exclude a virgin birth. In this respect the contrast with the *Protevangelium of James,* where the virginity of Mary is very plainly asserted, [17] is apparent. In the *Qur'ān* Mary's response to the annunciation, 'How can I have a child when no man has touched me?', parallels Luke 1:34, but there is no parallel to Matthew 1:18–23 to confirm the virginity of Mary.

But while the text of the *Qur'ān* does not require us to understand it as asserting a virgin birth, it is certainly the most reasonable understanding of the text. The fact is that amongst Muslims there has been general agreement that the text does teach the virgin birth of Christ [18] and only in comparatively recent times have alternative interpretations been suggested.

Thus at the beginning of a Muslim Christology there would stand a birth-sign, most reasonably understood as a virgin birth, a sign that would explain the advent of the Word of God in terms of the spoken word of God:

[17] The *Protevangelium* is, in fact, more concerned with providing a formal basis for popular beliefs about Mary than with augmenting orthodox teaching about Jesus.

[18] Both orthodox and unorthodox writers have generally agreed that the *Qur'ān* teaches a virgin birth. In his commentary, al-Baidawi remarks that a fresh topic is introduced at 3:43 'to ease her mind and to banish fears of censure that may have troubled her when she knew that she should bear *without a husband*' (*Chrestomathia Baidawiana,* p.36). The Ahmadi editor of the *Qur'ān,* Malik Ghulām Farīd, comments: 'The news of a son, however happy, in ordinary circumstances, must have greatly perplexed Mary who was not only still unmarried but was also meant to remain so for life. The verse reflects her justified perplexity. It also shows that Jesus had no father, as hinted in Mary's words, *no man has touched me*' (p.139, n. 419).

Attempts by commentators on NT or *Qur'ān* to deny the presence of passages which must be understood as teaching the doctrine of a virgin birth owe more to modern scepticism than to honest dealing with the text. As Caird says of such exposition of the Bible text, 'There is no harm in such conceits as long as they are recognised for what they are, sheer fiction. But anyone who takes them seriously is more credulous than the most naïve believer in the biblical text' (*The Language and Imagery of the Bible* [Duckworth, 1980], p.60). It is, of course, true, as Parrinder points out (*Jesus in the Qur'ān,* p.73), that the *Qur'ān* repeatedly insists that God does not engage in sexual intercourse; but this is no argument in support of the thesis that the *Qur'ān* cannot teach a virgin birth for Jesus. The *Qur'ān* itself indicates the manner of the conception: through the Word of God (S. 3:47).

She said: My Lord! How can I have a child when no mortal hath touched me? He said: So (it will be). Allah createth what He will. If He decreeth a thing, He saith unto it only: Be! and it is (S.3:47).

It must be made clear, however, that even if the *Qur'ān* does allow for the doctrine of the virgin birth of Christ, this would not permit us to draw any conclusions regarding the uniqueness or sinlessness of Christ. 'Jesus is as Adam' (S. 3:59) according to the *Qur'ān*, in the sense that neither had a human father, but Jesus is seen as *less* than Adam in that Adam had neither human father nor human mother. As with so much else in Islam, the identification of parallels turns out on inspection to mean less than a superficial appraisal suggested.

The life of Christ (S. 3:48–53; S. 5:110–115; S. 57:27)

The *Qur'ān* evinces little interest in the events of Jesus' life. The thirty years are passed over as an essentially uncharted region between the two well-documented regions of his birth and death.

The absence of information is not total, although there is again a mixture of sources for such information as does appear. The story of the child Jesus forming clay birds and then breathing life into them (S. 3:49 and S. 5:110) appears also in the second chapter of the apocryphal *Gospel of Thomas*. (It also appears in the Arabic *Gospel of the Infancy*, but, as we have already seen, this is most probably post-Muhammad and echoes the *Qur'ān* rather than being echoed by it; see footnote 5.)

In the same two places there are references to miracles performed by Jesus: he heals the sick, the blind and the leper and he raises the dead to life, although no details of individual miracles are offered.

In several places in the *Qur'ān* reference is made to Jesus having disciples.[19] In Sura 5:112–114 these disciples ask:

> O Jesus, son of Mary! Is thy Lord able to send down for us a table spread with food from heaven? . . . We wish to eat thereof, that we may satisfy our hearts and know that thou hast spoken truth to us, and that thereof we may be witnesses.

In response to their request Jesus prays for a table 'spread with food from heaven' (S. 5:112–114). Rodwell, in a footnote, refers to 1 Corinthians

[19] S. 61:14; S. 3:52. The word used for disciples, *al-hawariyīn,* is Ethiopic, from the verb *hora*, 'to go' (and not from *hur*, 'white'. *Cf.* Rodwell's footnote on p.499 of his edition of the *Qur'ān*).

11:27ff., and comments 'Muhammad obviously refers to the Eucharist'.[20] In a lengthy footnote Sale records Muslim tradition that following Jesus' prayer a red table was at once sent down from heaven with food on it, large numbers of people were fed from the food (1,300, not the 5,000 of the New Testament miracle), leaving the food intact at the end, those who ate were all healed of whatever diseases they had, and the miracle was repeated daily for forty days.[21] Helmut Gätje helpfully reproduces at-Tabari's comments on the conflicting Muslim interpretations of the passage.[22] At-Tabari concluded that exegesis required that a table should actually descend, that food should be on it and that the food should be consumed, but that the event should be seen as establishing a continual celebration because of the use of the technical term *id*, 'feast', and because of the reference to 'the first of us and the last of us', the latter phrase being taken to mean future generations of the followers of Jesus.

It does appear that the *Qur'ān* pericope represents a conflation of the imperfectly perceived accounts of the miracle of the feeding of the five thousand and of the institution of the Eucharist, but interpreted by the Muslim community and their commentators in the light of their further, but still imperfect, knowledge of each event. Christologically the passage is interesting in that it contains neither the Johannine sequel (the discourse on the bread of life) nor the eucharistic identification of the bread as representing the body of Christ. It *is* a sign, in the Johannine sense, leading to faith on the part of those who witness it, but the sign establishes only the common relationship between *nabī* and God, and not the unique relationship between the Servant-Son and the Father.

The death of Christ (S. 3:54f.; S. 4:157–159)

According to the *Qur'ān* Jesus did not die on the cross. There are two interpretations of the relevant passages of the *Qur'ān*. The first, orthodox, view is that Jesus was not crucified but was translated to heaven, leaving someone else to be crucified in his place; the second, the Ahmadi view, is that Jesus was crucified but did not die on the cross. According to the Ahmadi view Jesus recovered in the tomb and eventually made his way to Kashmir, where he died.

Concerning Jesus, Sura 4:157 states that the Jews

> slew him not nor crucified him, but it appeared so unto them; and lo! those who disagree concerning it are in doubt thereof; they have no

[20] *The Koran*, p.499, n. 3. Bell agrees: 'This section... is apparently based, not on any knowledge of the New Testament, but on some hearsay information about the Christian sacrament' (*The Qur'ān translated* 1, p.111).

[21] See Sale, *The Koran*, pp.87f.

[22] *The Qur'ān and its Exegesis* (Routledge & Kegan Paul, 1976), pp. 123–125.

knowledge thereof save pursuit of a conjecture; they slew him not for certain, but Allah took him up unto Himself. Allah was ever Mighty, Wise.

The Ahmadi translation of this passage differs significantly:

they slew him not, nor did they bring about his death on the cross, but he was made to appear to them like *one crucified*; and those who differ therein are certainly in a state of doubt about it.[23]

In a footnote, the translator, Malik Ghulām Farīd, comments: 'The verse does not deny the fact of Jesus's being nailed to the cross but denies his having died on it.'[24]

Whichever of these two versions is accepted, it remains a fact that the *Qur'ān* is taken to teach that Jesus did not die on the cross. The important phrase *shubbiha la-hum* is taken to mean either 'it seemed to them that he died on the cross' or 'the one who was crucified seemed to them to be Jesus'.

This aspect of Muslim Christology is vital for two reasons. Firstly, if the *Qur'ān* does, indeed, teach that Christ was not crucified, then the *Qur'ān* flies in the face of all scholarship. As Parrinder rightly comments:

No serious modern historian doubts that Jesus was a historical figure and that he was crucified, whatever he may think of the faith in the resurrection.[25]

That is to say, modern historians of all shades of belief or unbelief accept the historicity of the crucifixion. The *Qur'ān*, apparently, denies it.

Secondly, this aspect of Muslim Christology is vital since it strikes knowingly (in the case of the Ahmadis) or possibly unwittingly (in the case of the original composition of the *Qur'ān*) at the heart of the Christian faith.[26] The

---

[23] Malik Ghulām Farīd (ed.), *The Holy Qur'ān with English Translation and Commentary* (Oriental and Religious Publishing Corporation, Rabwah, Pakistan, 1969), p.232. The verse numbering in this translation differs from Pickthall's because the *bi-smillāh* at the beginning of the Suras is included in the verse numbering.

[24] *Ibid.*, n. 697. [25] *Jesus in the Qur'ān*, p.116.

[26] Ahmadi literature is notable for its strongly anti-Christian polemic and its high but unwarranted claims for scholarship. See, for example, the book by the founder of the Ahmadi movement, Hazrat Mirza Ghulan Ahmad, *Jesus in India,* reissued in 1978 by the London Mosque, and the more recent work noted below (n. 27), *Deliverance from the Cross.* So sympathetic a writer as Kenneth Cragg comments on Ahmadi writing: 'It is by character highly provocative

distinguished Ahmadi writer Muhammad Zafrulla Khan writes:

> Once it is established that Jesus did not die on the cross, there was no accursed death, no bearing of the sins of mankind, no resurrection, no ascension and no atonement. The entire structure of church theology is thereby demolished. [27]

There can be little doubt that the Ahmadi interpretation of Sura 4:157 is to be rejected. It can best be understood as an attempt to rid Islam of a Christ of embarrassing eschatological importance, still awaited from heaven by those Muslims who accept the traditional interpretation of the event as a miraculous deliverance from crucifixion followed by translation to heaven.

Why and how did the central historical event of Christianity come to be denied by Muhammad?

The problem for Islam arises first of all from its general failure to come to terms in any serious way with the Christian doctrine of the Trinity. This leads inevitably to the identification of Jesus as a man: a prophet, it is true, but no more than a man. As a mere man Jesus *cannot* atone for the sins of the world.

On the question of the Christian Trinity, Mohamed al-Nowaihi, Professor of Arabic Languages and Literature and Director of the Center for Arabic Studies in the American University, Cairo, has admitted:

> It is true that many Muslims have mistakenly believed that Christians worship three Gods, and have not paid sufficient attention to the latter's

---

and yet purports to be the vanguard of the religion of peace. It makes bold with an exhaustive erudition and yet perpetrates deep and serious lapses from objectivity in scholarship.' In the same place, in a footnote, Cragg refers to *Jesus in Heaven on Earth,* by the Ahmadi writer Khwaja Nazir Ahmad, published in Lahore and Woking in 1952. The book, according to Cragg full of misquotations and distortions, was banned by the Pakistan Government, and the author's petition to have the ban lifted was dismissed. The court declared that 'its Biblical quotations had been pulled out of context against the sense of the text and that it could not but breed "an intense feeling of hatred" towards its unscrupulous authorship on the part of other communities' (K. Cragg, *Islamic Surveys 3, Counsels in Contemporary Islam* [Edinburgh UP, 1965], pp.165, 213f., n. 13).

So far as more orthodox Islam is concerned, reference may be made to Muhammad 'Ata ur-Rahim, *Jesus, a Prophet of Islam* [MWH, London, 1977], which is, again, littered with inaccuracies and quite unjustified innuendoes (*e.g.* the absurd suggestion on p.42 that Ragg's translation of the *Gospel of Barnabas* 'abruptly and mysteriously disappeared from the market' and that only two copies are known to exist; true enough, the book is out of print, but it can readily be obtained through any lending library).

[27] *Deliverance from the Cross* (The London Mosque, 1978), p.89.

protestation that their belief in the Trinity does not imply a multiplicity of Gods, that God is still one with them.[28]

But, of course, the misunderstanding takes us beyond the mere accusation of polytheism to the fundamental issue of the person of Christ. If Islam's rigid monotheism identifies Jesus as simply human, then the normal concepts of divine justice must be applied to his case. Professor al-Nowaihi continues:

> Islam rejects the idea that God would allow Jesus to be killed, which fate would have been a violation of divine justice and would have constituted an act of treachery.[29]

Al-Nowaihi goes so far as to commit himself to the view that Jesus 'was indeed placed on the cross'[30] but does not commit himself to a particular view of how he was delivered. A very full explanation is supplied by Malik Ghulām Farīd in an extended footnote in his edition of the *Qur'ān*, and begins with the flat assertion:

> Being a Divine Prophet Jesus could not have died on the cross because according to the Bible 'he that is hanged is accursed of God' (Deut. 21:23).

Death on the cross would have been 'a violation of divine justice', on the one hand because Jesus was a prophet and on the other hand because being a prophet his prayer for deliverance (Mk. 14:36) *must* have been answered.

That Jesus was a prophet would not necessarily imply for the Muslim that he could not suffer wrongfully. Immediately before the passage under consideration we find a plain statement concerning the 'People of the Scripture . . . and their slaying of the prophets wrongfully' (S. 4:155). The case of Jesus is unique, because of the generally 'high' Christology of Islam, a high regard for his moral purity, and more importantly, because of his prayer for deliverance. In referring to this prayer, Zafrulla Khan comments that Jesus ' . . . had full confidence that his prayer would be accepted'[31] and

> Jesus supplicated most earnestly to be delivered from death upon the cross and was reassured in answer to his supplications that God would deliver him from such a death.[32]

[28] 'The Religion of Islam', *IRM* 65, 258, April 1976, p.216.
[29] *Ibid.*, p.217. [30] *Loc. cit.* [31] *Deliverance from the Cross*, p.26. [32] *Ibid.*, p.27.

The manner in which this deliverance is supposed to have come about must now be considered. According to the Ahmadi writers, Pilate conspired with Joseph of Arimathea to deliver Jesus. Delaying judgment until three hours before sunset ensured that Jesus would survive crucifixion until the time at which the bodies would have to be removed from the crosses because of the onset of the Sabbath. Nicodemus (who becomes 'an expert physician'[33]) is then supposed to have assisted Joseph in taking the body to a nearby 'spacious room hewn in the side of a rock'[34] where Jesus was revived with the aid of the mysterious *marham 'Īsā*, 'ointment of Jesus'.[35]

The more orthodox interpretation of the deliverance of Jesus from the cross is that he was not crucified at all; his place was taken by someone else. This view is explained in great detail in the so-called *Gospel of Barnabas* (which must be carefully distinguished from the early second-century *Epistle of Barnabas*). Translated from an Italian manuscript by Lonsdale and Laura Ragg and published by Oxford University Press in 1907, it has been re-issued in Pakistan[36] and circulates in this form rather extensively in the Western world. It is a curious compilation, which makes mention of Muhammad by name[37] and, surprisingly, has Jesus sailing to Nazareth.[38] According to *Barnabas*,

---

[33] *Ibid.*, p.33.   [34] Malik Ghulām Farīd's translation of the *Qur'ān*, p.233, n. 699.

[35] *Ibid.* See also *Jesus in India*, ch. 3, which is entirely devoted to the question of the magic ointment.

[36] Begum Aisha Bawany Wakf (Karachi, Pakistan, 1973).

[37] Ch. 136. On the background to the *Gospel of Barnabas* see my brief summary in *Vox Evangelica* 10, 1977, pp.43-47; Ragg's 'The Mohammedan "Gospel of Barnabas"', *JTS* 6, 1904-5; and the notes in Sale's invaluable 'Preliminary Discourse' to his *Koran*, especially section iv. It is generally agreed that the *Gospel of Barnabas* as published by Ragg has no connection with a work of the same name mentioned in the *Decretum Gelasianum* but otherwise unknown. It was apparently written in the thirteenth or fourteenth centuries in Italian, by a convert to Islam, and was at some point translated into Spanish. It is not a translation from Arabic or Greek, and no Arabic, still less Greek, original has so far been offered.

It is interesting to note that Sale's confident assertion, 'The Mohammedans have also a Gospel in Arabic, attributed to St. Barnabas' (*op. cit.*, p.58), when subjected to investigation by Ragg, turns out to be without foundation. In his introduction to the text of the *Gospel of Barnabas*, Ragg comments, 'And so we find the external authority for an Arabic original melts away into the conjecture of Cramer', with neither Sale nor Toland actually having any first-hand acquaintance with an Arabic version of *Barnabas*. It is salutary to observe the process of clarification from William Axon's article in *JTS* 3, 1901-2, to Ragg's *JTS* article in 1904-5 (before he had seen the Italian text of *Barnabas*), to Ragg's published translation of *Barnabas* in 1907. The early confident statements about an Arabic *Barnabas* wither away under Ragg's scrutiny (see Ragg's *Barnabas*, pp.xvf.).

[38] Ch. 20: 'Jesus went to the sea of Galilee, and having embarked in a ship sailed to his city of Nazareth. . . . Having arrived at the city of Nazareth the seamen spread through the city all that Jesus had wrought. . . .'.

Jesus was translated to heaven by three angels prior to the arrest. Judas was made to appear like Jesus and was arrested and crucified in the place of Jesus.[39] Jesus himself was removed to the 'third heaven' where he remains, 'blessing God for evermore'.

At least two problems are left apparently unresolved by this version of the crucifixion: the empty tomb and the post-resurrection appearances of Christ. In *Barnabas* the empty tomb is explained by reiterating the accusation of the tomb guards that some of Jesus' disciples came in the night and stole the body (Mt. 28:13).[40] The resurrection appearances are dealt with by having the three angels escort Jesus from the third heaven back to Jerusalem in order to comfort Mary and the disciples.[41]

There is, of course, a further problem raised by the *Barnabas* version of the crucifixion, that Jesus is in the third heaven without having passed through death. *Barnabas* explains that God has reserved Jesus 'till near the end of the world' (ch. 220), in general agreement with Sura 43:61 which appears to make Jesus a 'sign' of the end time.[42] The expectation, then, is that Jesus will eventually return to earth as a sign of the imminence of the end, will live a human life, correct the present 'aberrant' Christianity, die and be buried, to be raised at the last judgment like all others.

What is certainly striking about the Muslim understanding of the crucifixion is its precarious base in the *Qur'ān*. The critical passage, Sura 4:157, is open to numerous interpretations. It may be taken to mean that Jesus was not crucified, *or* that he was crucified but did not die on the cross, *or* that he was crucified and did die on the cross but that this was a divine act and not a human act.[43] It is remarkable that, granted the slenderness of the textual evidence requiring such an interpretation, Islam has, nonetheless, rather uniformly developed the theme that Jesus did not die on the cross.

Summary

Although the *Qur'ān* presents us with an outline life of Christ which *could* be interpreted in a way generally conformable to the New Testament, with birth

---

[39] Chs. 215f.   [40] Ch. 218.   [41] Ch. 219.

[42] S. 43:61, although there is disagreement about the meaning of the verse. Pickthall renders it: 'And lo! verily there is knowledge of the hour', over against Rodwell's 'He [Jesus] shall be a sign of the hour'. The pronoun most naturally has Jesus as its antecedent. In a similar context in 4:175 the Ahmadi commentator Malik Ghulām Farīd suggests that the reference is either to Muhammad or to the *Qur'ān* and no consideration is given to the possibility of Jesus being the referent.

[43] It is just possible to interpret the passage as teaching that Jesus *did* die on the cross but that the Jews did not kill him; his death was a divine act. See Parrinder's discussion of this alternative interpretation (first offered by E. E. Elder) in *Jesus in the Qur'ān*, pp. 119-121.

from a virgin at one pole and crucifixion at the other, in fact this has not been the traditional Muslim Christology.

Specifically, the question mark set by the *Qur'ān* itself, and more particularly by the interpreters of the *Qur'ān*, against the crucifixion and death of Christ, cannot adequately be disposed of by the common dialogue procedures. It is striking to observe that in the papers published by the World Council of Churches which cover ten years of dialogue between Christians and Muslims[44] there is no attempt to deal with this central issue. Much is said in the papers about the mutual search for community (ch. I, 5), and there is adequate consideration of the problems posed sociologically by the conflicting demands of Muslim *da'wah,* 'calling', and Christian mission. But the historical crux which focuses on the passion is passed over.

Of course this is not to suggest that there is no mention in the papers of the crucifixion, death and resurrection of Christ and of his role as Saviour, from the Christian side. But the issue is not taken up in discussion, presumably because there is really no base from which discussion might take place. Either Christ was crucified, died on the cross and rose from death to be the sole Saviour of men and the New Testament is right, or else he did not and the New Testament is wrong. The historicity of events is not a matter for dialogue.

Nor is the conflict resolved by the mere recognition by some Muslims that the New Testament doctrine of redemption cannot simply be dismissed. Redemption corresponds to a real need of man, and the absence of redemptive self-giving in Islam constitutes an identifiable *lacuna* in Muslim theology. To quote al-Nowaihi again:

> among the intelligentsia of contemporary Muslims, there has been a growing awareness of the sheer beauty and nobility of the idea of redemption, not, indeed, as a literal fact or an article of creed, but as a symbol, a magnificent and uplifting symbol of what some self-abnegating men, in their tremendous love for their fellow-men and their chagrined concern over their ignorance, folly and crime, have to undergo for the sake of humanity's salvation.... This new development is prominent in the poetry of a new school of Arabic poets, which started in the late 1940s, and whose frequent use of the symbol of the cross and the figure of the Redeemer has caused much consternation among their traditional readers.[45]

---

[44] *Christians meeting Muslims* (WCC, Geneva, 1977).
[45] *IRM* 65, 258, April 1976, p.218.

But of course a symbol cannot redeem. The question must still be faced of the historicity of the passion. The Christology of Islam, hampered by its failure to come to terms with the doctrine of the Trinity, offers only a human Christ who cannot redeem.

The overt Christology of the Qur'ān

We turn finally to a brief consideration of those passages which make the Christology of the *Qur'ān* overt. Sura 4 presents, perhaps, the clearest statement, echoed in Sura 5. In a passage directed at Christians ('O people of the Scripture!', 4:171) we are told:

> The Messiah, Jesus son of Mary, was only a messenger of Allah, and his word which He conveyed unto Mary, and a spirit from Him. So believe in Allah and His messengers, and say not "Three" – Cease! (it is) better for you! Allah is only One God. Far is it removed from His transcendent Majesty that He should have a son.

The reference to Christian confession of 'Three' indicates Muhammad's rejection of trinitarian theology. The actual identity of the Three is indicated in Sura 5:116f.:

> And when Allah saith: O Jesus, son of Mary! Didst thou say unto mankind: Take me and my mother for two gods beside Allah? he saith: Be glorified! It was not mine to utter that to which I had no right. If I used to say it, then Thou knewest it. Thou knowest what is in my mind. . . . I spake unto them only that which Thou commandest me, (saying): Worship Allah, my Lord and your Lord.

Clearly Muhammad understood trinitarianism as requiring a belief in three gods and he identified these three gods as Allah (Father?), Mary (Mother?) and Jesus (Son). Just how he acquired this piece of misinformation is unclear. Although Ameer Ali deals with early Christological questions in the church and with incipient tritheism in some detail,[46] he does not deal with the particular problem raised by Muhammad's heretical Trinity. The Muslim commentator Zamakhsharī, writing on Sura 4, says:

> According to the evidence of the *Qur'ān*, the Christians maintain that God, Christ and Mary are three gods and that Christ is the child of God by Mary . . . [47]

[46] *The Spirit of Islam* (Chatto & Windus, ³1922), pp.xlv-liv.
[47] In Helmut Gätje, *The Qur'ān and its Exegesis,* p.126.

That is indeed the evidence of the *Qur'ān*. It is *not* the teaching of the New Testament.

Precisely where this particular identification of the Trinity originated it is now impossible to say. It is certainly a logical trinity, a nuclear family. It is also an understandable trinity, one that might be expected to commend itself to the theologically uninitiated. It is just possible that it echoes the Collyridian heresy of the fourth and fifth centuries.[48] The Collyridians were a sect of women, originating in Thrace but moving into Arabia, possibly under the pressure of persecution. The Collyridians (from Greek *kollyris*, 'a cake') apparently offered a cake to Mary, the Queen of Heaven, on appropriate days, and offered her worship. Epiphanius certainly knew of them[49] and it is possible that, if not the sect itself, its teachings lingered on in Arabia to provide Muhammad with his information.

In overtly rejecting the deity of Christ the *Qur'ān* raises the problem of the incorrect identification of the Trinity. Malik Ghulām Farīd makes the best of a bad job by accepting the manifest error as though it were essentially correct:

> The verse refers to the practice of the Christian Church to ascribe Divine powers to Mary... Church Fathers in the past have regarded her as Divine,

although he adds the observation that Protestants denounce such doctrines as Mariolatry.[50]

Conclusion
Muslim Christology is here briefly presented as seen through two significant designations used for Jesus, through the content of the life of Christ which might be constructed from the material contained in the *Qur'ān* and through two overt indications of Muhammad's insistence on the mere humanity of Jesus. The study is not offered in any sense of hostility toward the Muslim peoples, but with the hope that we can clear away the confusing mists created by dialogue which has always carefully avoided the crucial issue: the person of Christ.

The two Christologies, Christian and Muslim, are not reconcilable. The Muslim position is reached partly as a consequence of the doctrine of undif-

---

[48] See *The New Schaff-Herzog Encyclopedia of Religious Knowledge* (Funk & Wagnalls, New York and London, 1911), article 'Collyridians'.

[49] Epiphanius, *Haereses,* lxxvii-lxxix. Perhaps it is more important for our purposes to note that Epiphanius knew of the Collyridians as *heretics*.

[50] In his edition of *The Holy Qur'ān*, p.276, n. 811.

ferentiated monotheism, partly because of an initial lack of acquaintance with the Scriptures, but most of all as a consequence of failing to know Jesus. The result has been a religion without redemption. By contrast, redemption is the very heart of Christianity. It is not altogether surprising, then, if to the Christian the omission of redemption from Islam is the clearest indication that, whatever insights it may contain, Islam does not issue from divine revelation.

KARL BARTH'S CHRISTOLOGY

Klaas Runia

In his introduction to Barth's theology Herbert Hartwell naturally includes a chapter on Jesus Christ. He gives it the following heading: 'Jesus Christ, the key to the understanding of God, the Universe and Man'.[1] This is certainly no exaggeration. For Barth, Jesus Christ is the point of departure for every theological proposition. Dealing with the 'mystery' of revelation Barth writes: 'A church dogmatics must, of course, be christologically determined as a whole and in all its parts as surely as the revealed Word of God, attested by Holy Scripture and proclaimed by the Church, is its one and only criterion, and as surely as this revealed Word is identical with Jesus Christ. If dogmatics cannot regard itself and cause itself to be regarded as fundamentally Christology, it has assuredly succumbed to some alien sway and is already on the verge of losing its character as church dogmatics.'[2]

According to Barth, Jesus Christ is the beginning of all God's ways and works. In this respect Barth's supralapsarianism is a purified one,[3] but his whole approach is clearly recognizable as being of a supralapsarian nature. Everything starts with God's eternal election of the God-man Jesus Christ. Barth starts his doctrine of election with these words: 'The election of grace is the eternal beginning of all the ways and works of God in Jesus Christ. In Jesus Christ God in His free grace determines Himself for sinful man and sinful man for Himself. He therefore takes upon Himself the rejection of man with all its consequences, and elects man to participation in His own glory.'[4] Hence

---

[1] Herbert Hartwell, *The Theology of Karl Barth: an Introduction* (Duckworth, 1964), p.16.

[2] *Church Dogmatics (CD)* I, 2, p.123. Cf. *Dogmatics in Outline* (SCM, 1949), pp.39, 65ff. On p.66 Barth says that Christology is the touchstone of all knowledge of God in the Christian sense, the touchstone of all theology. 'Tell me how it stands with your Christology, and I shall tell you who you are.'

[3] Cf. *CD* II, 2, pp.140ff.　　　[4] *CD* II, 2, p.94.

everything else must be seen in the light of Jesus Christ. This is true of the doctrine of creation (*Church Dogmatics* III, 1), of anthropology (III, 2), of providence (III, 3), of election (II, 2) and also of the doctrine of God himself (II, 1). It is therefore not surprising that at times Barth has been accused of 'Christomonism'. His whole eleven-volume *Church Dogmatics* is one long explanation and unfolding of this one name: Jesus Christ.

The person of Jesus Christ

Who is Jesus Christ for Barth? When we first deal with this question under the heading 'The Person of Christ', we seem to go straight against his own views, for in the introduction of his doctrine of reconciliation he has explicitly stated that the person and work of Christ can never be separated. 'In the New Testament are many christological statements both direct and indirect. But where do we find a special Christology? – a Christ in Himself, abstracted from what He is amongst the men of Israel and His disciples and the world, from what He is on their behalf? Does He ever exist except in this relationship?'[5] I believe that Barth is fully right here. The person and the work of Christ are essentially inseparable.[6] Yet, for practical purposes we may distinguish them as two different aspects of the same 'reality'. In a way Barth himself has done the same when in *Church Dogmatics* I, 2 he deals at length with the question who Jesus, the Word of God, is (although, admittedly, even then he never separates the person of Jesus from being the revelation of God).

As to the view of the person of Jesus, Barth stays within the framework of orthodox theology. Without any hesitation he accepts the Christology of the early church. 'The central statement of the Christology of the Early Church is that God becomes one with man: Jesus Christ "very God and very man".'[7] The last words are from the famous statement of the Council of Chalcedon (AD 451) about the two natures of Christ. Barth fully accepts this statement and rejects the charge of intellectualism that has been brought against it by such scholars as Herder and Harnack. 'In speaking of the two natures, of the *vere Deus* and the *vere homo*, in the one Person of Jesus Christ, the Council did not intend to solve the mystery of revelation, but rather it perceived and respected this mystery.'[8]

Barth then goes on to give his own view in a profound and penetrating exegesis of John 1:14 – '*Ho Logos sarx egeneto*' – 'The Word became flesh'.

1. First of all this phrase says that Jesus is *very God*. 'Ho Logos, the "Word", spoken of in John 1:14, is the divine, creative, reconciling, redeeming word

---

[5] *CD* IV, 1, p.124.
[6] *Cf.* also G. C. Berkouwer, *The Person of Christ* (Eerdmans, 1954), ch. 1.
[7] *CD* I, 2, p.125.　　[8] *Ibid.*, p.129.

which participates without restriction in the divine nature and existence, the eternal Son of God.'[9] In his further exposition of the phrase Barth points to the following elements. (a) The Word is the *subject* of the becoming; nothing befalls him, but the incarnation is *his own* act. (b) This becoming took place in the divine *freedom* of the Word; it does not rest upon any necessity in the divine nature, but God did it in sovereign freedom. (c) Even in the state of becoming or of having become, the Word is *still* the free and sovereign Word of God. On the basis of these three statements Barth defends the title *'theotokos'* (Mother of God), given to Mary by the Council of Ephesus (431) and reaffirmed by Chalcedon (451). This has nothing to do with Roman Catholic Mariology and the elevation of Mary in this theology, but it is a Christological statement. 'The New Testament, like the Councils of Ephesus and Chalcedon, takes a christological and only a christological interest in Mary.'[10]

2. Jesus is *very man*. Very God is not the only thing to be said here (although it is the primary thing). We have to add immediately: 'very man', for the Word became *'flesh'*, *i.e.*, truly man. 'He became man, true and real man, participating in the same human essence and existence, the same human nature and form, the same historicity that we have.'[11] But at the same time we must add: 'without sin'. Being the Word of God in the flesh excludes sin. 'In it God Himself is the Subject. How can God sin, deny Himself to Himself, be against Himself as God, want to be a god and so fall away from Himself in the way in which our sin is against Him, in which it happens from the very first and continually in the event of our existence?'[12] However, we have to understand this sinlessness properly. It is not a static state of affairs, a static idea of human excellencies of character, virtue or good works, but rather it is a dynamic relationship to God. 'Unlike Adam, this second Adam does not wish to be as God.'[13] He is obedient, even to the extent that he is willing to be the second Adam. 'In Adam's nature He acknowledges before God an Adamic being, the state and position of fallen man, and bears the wrath of God which must fall upon this man, not as a fate but as a righteous necessary wrath. He does not avoid the burden of this state and position but takes the conditions and consequences upon Himself.'[14]

3. 'The Word *became* flesh.' In the third place we must stress the word 'became'. This does *not* mean that the Logos *changes* into a man and ceases to be what he is in himself. Neither does it mean a third kind of being, midway between God and man. No, he takes a human nature upon himself *in addition to* a divine nature. Barth even defends such abstract terms as *'anhypostatos'* and

<hr>

[9] *Ibid.*, p.132.   [10] *Ibid.*, p.139.   [11] *Ibid.*, p.147.
[12] *Ibid.*, p.155.   [13] *Ibid.*, p.157.   [14] *Ibid.*, p.157.

'enhypostatos'.[15] There can be no doubt that in all this Barth is fully in agreement with the Christology of the early church. In fact, thanks to Barth there arose a revival of interest in and acceptance of ancient Christology in many circles which for a long time had been very critical or even negative. (In passing I must add that unfortunately in the years since World War II this interest has disappeared and in many circles a liberal or semi-liberal Christology has taken over again.)

In accordance with this is also Barth's defence of the *virgin birth*. All of the older liberals had rejected this doctrine as a myth that had been added to the nativity stories to embellish them. Also some more conservative scholars, who did accept the Christology of Chalcedon, nevertheless rejected the virgin birth. I am thinking here, for instance, of Emil Brunner. Barth, however, defends it. Why? The reason is *not* that it is mentioned in the Bible. Since Barth also accepts the critical approach to Scripture, he could, at least in theory, have gone along with Brunner. The reason why Barth accepts it is that in his opinion it is in conformity with the whole New Testament's view of the incarnation. Barth himself finds it *the* sign, the supreme sign of the mystery of the incarnation. On purpose he uses the word 'sign' and emphatically adds that the meaning of the virgin birth is *noetic* and not *ontic*. The miracle of the virgin birth does not 'explain' or make the incarnation 'possible'. In that case it would belong to the very *essence* of the incarnation. Its meaning is *noetic*, it is in the nature of a sign that teaches us two things in particular. First, it makes evident that the mystery of the incarnation, namely, the *vere Deus* and the *vere homo* in one person, cannot be understood intellectually but only spiritually. Second, it makes evident that God alone is the author of the new creation of the God-man Jesus Christ.[16] There is no place for any form of synergism here, for the active factor in every birth (the male partner) is excluded.

Even though we are grateful for Barth's defence of the virgin birth, we believe that the contrast *noetic/ontic* is incorrect. According to the New Testament there definitely is an *ontic* aspect to the virgin birth, for this birth was the *way* in which God's Son was born as a sinless man. *I do not say that this was the only way*. This we do not know. We have no right to limit God's possibilities. But the New Testament makes it quite clear that this was the way in which God has done it and that there is an inseparable connection between this

---

[15] *Ibid.*, p.163. Both terms belong together. The *'anhypostatos'* stresses the negative aspect. The human nature has no separate *'hypostasis'* (person) in the abstract. The *'enhypostatos'* emphasizes the positive aspect: from its very beginning the human nature has its *'hypostasis'* in the *'hypostasis'* of the Logos.

[16] Hartwell, *op. cit.*, p.80.

miraculous birth and Jesus' sinlessness. The angel Gabriel says to Mary: 'The Holy Spirit will come upon you, and the power of the Most High will overshadow you; therefore the child to be born will be called holy, the Son of God' (Lk. 1:35). Very significant is the word 'therefore', indicating an inferential, if not instrumental connection.

The work of Christ

When we now turn to the work of Christ, we are not really dealing with a *different* subject-matter. Barth is, of course, right when he says that the person and the work of Christ cannot be separated. *This* person does *this* work; conversely, *this* work is done by *this* person. Therefore every time Barth deals with the person of Jesus Christ he also deals with his work.

When one reads the *Church Dogmatics,* one discovers that Barth actually deals twice with the work of Christ. In *CD* I he deals with it under the heading of revelation. In *CD* IV he discusses it under the heading of reconciliation. For Barth, however, there is no contrast between the two different sides of the one coin. He writes: 'The work of the Son or Word is the presence and manifestation of God, which we can only designate *revelation*. The word *reconciliation* is another word for the same thing. So far as God's revelation as such achieves, what only God can achieve, namely, the restoration of man's communion with God . . . so far as, in the fact of revelation, God's enemies are already his friends, revelation itself is reconciliation. Just as on the contrary reconciliation, the restoration of that communion, the mercy of God triumphant in wrath over wrath, can only take the form of the mystery, which we actually designate revelation.'[17] In the remainder of this essay we shall concentrate on the latter aspect, the work of reconciliation.

Barth's doctrine of *reconciliation* is rather difficult. The reason lies not only in the fact that time and again he takes a new road, but it is also due to the fact that his doctrine of reconciliation comprises nearly all the other chapters of dogmatics (the exceptions being the doctrines of creation and eschatology). Thus it includes the Christology, the hamartiology (the doctrine of sin), the soteriology (the work of the Spirit in the renewal of man) and the ecclesiology (the doctrine of the church).

In the summary that precedes his treatment of the doctrine of reconciliation Barth writes: 'The content of the doctrine of reconciliation is the knowledge of Jesus Christ who is (1) very God, that is, the God who humbles Himself, and therefore the reconciling God, (2) very man, that is, man exalted and therefore reconciled by God, and (3) in the unity of the two the guarantor and witness of

---

[17] *CD* I, 1, p.468.

our atonement. This threefold knowledge of Jesus Christ includes the knowledge of the sin of man: (1) his pride, (2) his sloth and (3) his falsehood – the knowledge of the event in which reconciliation is made: (1) his justification, (2) his sanctification and (3) his calling – the knowledge of the work of the Holy Spirit in (1) the gathering, (2) the upbuilding and (3) the sending of the community, and of the being of Christians in Jesus Christ (1) in faith, (2) in love and (3) in hope.'[18]

It will be obvious that here we can deal only briefly with some of the lines of this complex doctrine.

The first thing Barth says is that reconciliation is a *free act of God,*[19] in which he makes a completely new start. How do we know this? We can deduce it only from this act itself. It is impossible for us to deduce it from anything else. All we can say is: God *has* done it in Jesus Christ.

In the second place Barth emphasizes that *God* has done it. It is *God's* triumph in the antithesis, the opposition of man to himself. 'It is the lordship of His goodness *in medio inimicorum* – original, unilateral, glorious and truly divine – in which He acts quite alone, doing miracle after miracle.'[20] In reconciliation God himself crosses the frontier to man.

But does this mean that there is no room left to speak about *man?* Barth's answer is (and this is the third point he makes): we certainly must also speak about man. But *not* in the sense of man being a partner with God in the act of reconciliation. Man has a different place. We can speak about him only as the *object* and *result* of God's act of reconciliation, as the man who has been reconciled to God. Emphatically Barth says that this is the only way in which we may speak about man. We may no longer speak about him as the unreconciled man. For if God has reconciled man to himself, then man *is* reconciled. Henceforth we may understand man only in the light of Christ. Not only the believing man, but *all men.* 'In the atonement it is a matter of God and His being and activity for us and to us. And that means an alteration of the human situation, the result of which is *an altered being of man.* . . . Whatever we have to think and say of man, and not only of the Christian but of man in general, at every point we have to think and say it of his being as man reconciled in Jesus Christ.'[21]

But does this mean that there is no difference between the believer and the unbeliever? Barth believes there are *two points of difference.* First, the believer not only knows and experiences it, but it also becomes visible in his life. 'To the Christian it is a matter of experience and knowledge. He knows about Jesus Christ, and the reconciliation of the world to God made in Him, and therefore

---

[18] *CD* IV, 1, p.79. [19] *Ibid.,* p.79. [20] *Ibid.,* p.82. [21] *Ibid.,* p.91.

the new being of man in Him.' And second, 'The being of man reconciled with God in Jesus Christ is reflected in the existence of the Christian. That is something we cannot say of others.'[22]

The nature of reconciliation

How does the reconciliation of man to God take place in Jesus Christ? Especially here we see that Barth takes new roads. Traditional orthodox theology usually showed the following pattern.[23] First it offered a special doctrine of the person of Christ. Then there followed a discussion of his work, under the threefold heading of the *munus triplex* (threefold office): as prophet, as priest and as a king. To this was usually added a special doctrine of the two 'states' of Christ, his humiliation and exaltation.

Barth rearranges this system completely. He does maintain all the various aspects, but places them in a quite different order and inter-relationship. He divides the doctrine of reconciliation into three main aspects.

First we must say that Jesus Christ is *very God*. In terms of reconciliation this means: He is the *God who humbles himself,* the Lord who becomes a servant and therefore he is the reconciling God. Under this same heading Barth then discusses the *priestly* office and the state of humiliation.

In the second place we must say that Jesus Christ is *very man*. In terms of reconciliation this means that *man is exalted*: the servant becomes Lord. Under this heading Barth then discusses the *kingly* office and the state of exaltation. At first glance all this may not seem to be so very different from the traditional doctrine. But this is perhaps due to the fact that we are, almost naturally, inclined to assume that these two aspects follow each other. This, however, is expressly rejected by Barth. These two aspects are not successive, but *coincide*. The humiliation of God *at the same time* involves the exaltation of man! 'As in Him God became like man, so too in Him man has become like God. As in Him God was bound, so too in Him man is made free. As in Him the Lord became a servant, so too in Him the servant has become a Lord. That is the atonement made in Jesus Christ in its second aspect. In Him humanity is exalted humanity, just as Godhead is humiliated Godhead. And humanity is exalted in Him by the humiliation of Godhead.'[24]

But there is still a third aspect. Barth begins by admitting that actually nothing new can be added to the act of reconciliation. In the first two aspects everything has already been said. 'Everything that can be said materially concerning Jesus Christ and the atonement made in Him has been said exhaustively in the twofold fact . . . that He is very God and very man, *i.e.*, the

[22] *Ibid.*, pp.92f.   [23] *Ibid.*, p.123.   [24] *Ibid.*, p.131.

Lord who became a servant and the servant who became Lord, the reconciling God and reconciled man.'[25] And yet there is still a third aspect in which the unity and completeness of this history is viewed. Jesus Christ, the God-man, is himself also the *revelation* of this reconciliation. Here we get the third office, namely, the *prophetic* office, which does not add anything to the other two offices, but is their revelation.

It is evident that in this new structure of Christ's work, in particular in the coincidence of the two states, all emphasis is put on the *being* of Christ. Barth himself says: 'Jesus Christ is not what He is — very God, very man, very God-man — in order as such to mean and do and accomplish something else which is atonement. But His being as God and man and God-man consists in the completed act of the reconciliation of man with God.'[26] To be true, this statement is immediately preceded by the words: 'We hasten to explain that the being of Jesus Christ, the unity of being of the living God and this living man, takes place in the event of the concrete existence of this man. It is a being, but a being in a history', but it cannot be denied that the emphasis is on the very fact of his being God and man in one. This very combination means humiliation and exaltation at the same time and in this twofold fact we find the very heart of the atonement.[27]

Short evaluation

It cannot be denied that this is a grandiose conception. It offers an intricate, but also comprehensive doctrine of Jesus Christ and his work, in which many genuinely scriptural aspects are found. Nevertheless we have to hold this doctrine in the light of God's Word (as a matter of fact Barth would be the first one to agree with this!) and ask whether it is *fully* in agreement with the teaching of Scripture. On the basis of my own understanding of the Bible, I should like to make the following *critical remarks*.

1. The question may be asked whether Barth, with his strong emphasis on God himself as the subject of reconciliation and with his peculiar interpretation of God as humiliating himself, does not run the risk of falling into the old error of *Theopaschitism*. This, in fact, is *the* criticism G. C. Berkouwer levels against Barth's doctrine of reconciliation. 'When Barth speaks of the suffering of God and even of an "obedience of God", and this not as a bold manner of speaking but as an *essential* element in the being of God ... he exceeds the boundaries of the *revelation* which we have in Christ ... To conclude ... to a tension and an

---

[25] *Ibid.*, p. 136.   [26] *Ibid.*, pp. 126f.

[27] *Cf.* Robert W. Jenson, *Alpha and Omega, a Study in the Theology of Karl Barth* (Thomas Nelson, 1963), pp. 124ff.

obedience in God Himself, to an "above" and a "below" in Him, can only be characterized as speculation.'[28] The Christian church has always avoided this danger by speaking emphatically of the Son *in his human nature*. The contrast is not between Father and Son as such; it is not an intertrinitarian contrast or tension, but the Son *in his human form* subjects himself to the Father. This also explains such words as: 'The Father is greater than I' (Jn. 14:28), 'Not as I will, but as thou wilt' (Mt. 26:39) and even the most unfathomable of all Jesus' words: 'My God, my God, why hast thou forsaken me?' (Mt. 27:46).

2. My second point of criticism is Barth's *objectivism*. The reconciliation of man to God in Jesus Christ applies to *all people,* whether they believe in Jesus or not. The believers know it, the unbelievers do not know it; yet it is true of the unbelievers too. Man as such, every man, is now reconciled to God. All this is connected with Barth's supralapsarianism, which we mentioned before. In his doctrine of divine election Barth writes: 'In Jesus Christ God in His free grace determines Himself for sinful man and sinful man for Himself. He therefore takes upon Himself the rejection of man with all its consequences and elects man to participate in His own glory.'[29] Here too Barth intentionally speaks of 'sinful man' in general. Since Jesus Christ is the beginning of all God's ways and works, a decision has been taken about all men. In the doctrine of reconciliation this line of thought is carried on consistently.

The question has often been asked whether this view, if we take it seriously, does not lead to *universalism*.[30] It is interesting to note that Barth himself rejects the conclusion of an *'apokatastasis tōn pantōn',* although he does not exclude it! In other words, he wants to keep the question *open*. The reason he mentions is that we have to respect the freedom of God.[31] I am not so sure whether this argument is conclusive. Of course, we want to maintain, just as much as Barth, the divine freedom or the freedom of the divine grace. But we may not ignore the clear teaching of Scripture itself, which speaks of a final and definite judgment and of the condemnation of all those who have rejected the offer of God's grace in Jesus Christ. One could perhaps put it this way: Scripture takes man *in his unbelief more 'seriously'* than Barth does.

All this is confirmed by Barth's view of *preaching*. Within the whole context of his dogmatics, preaching becomes the proclamation of a changed state of affairs. In Jesus Christ the real sentence on man has been passed. Therefore, 'Jesus Christ is not simply one alternative or chance which is offered to

---

[28] G. C. Berkouwer, *The Triumph of Grace in the Theology of Karl Barth* (Paternoster, 1956), p.304.

[29] *CD* II, 2, p.94.

[30] *Cf.* Colin Brown, *Karl Barth and the Christian Message* (Tyndale Press, 1967), pp. 130ff.

[31] *CD* II, 2, p.417.

man . . . He is not put there for man's choice, *à prendre ou à laisser.'* And then Barth goes on to say that in the decision which has taken place in Jesus Christ, 'unbelief has become an objective, real and ontological impossibility and faith an objective, real and ontological necessity for all men and for every man'.[32] This does not mean that Barth denies the existence of unbelief. How could he? *But he does deny its decisive character,* for this is no longer possible after the cross and the resurrection. We believe that the Bible gives us a different picture. Proclamation is indeed the offer of grace *to all,* but this offer has to be accepted in faith and it can be rejected in unbelief. Rightly Berkouwer says: 'The New Testament speaks of belief and unbelief as a choice, a serious, if you will a *decisive* choice. Whatever the judgment as to the dogmatic place of belief and unbelief, we will in any case have to take as our point of departure the seriousness with which the New Testament takes the human response to the proclamation.'[33]

3. The third point I wish to mention is the *'one-dimensional' character* of Barth's doctrine of reconciliation. According to Barth there is *only one movement,* namely, *from God to man.* Barth bases this in particular on his exegesis of John 3:16 and 2 Corinthians 5:19 (where the verb *katalassein* is used).[34] Of course, there can be no doubt that these texts put all the emphasis on the fact that God is the source of reconciliation. We too believe that God is the primary subject. But is there not more in the Bible? We believe that the Bible still knows a second aspect, namely, Jesus acting *as our representative* before and over against God. We are thinking of the verb *hilaskesthai* (to expiate, to propitiate), of the wrath of God, of paying ransom, *etc.* The question may even be asked whether the same idea is not present in 2 Corinthians 5:19, where the apostle says that God was reconciling the world *'to himself'.* Related to all this is also the fact that Barth too quickly does away with the idea of 'satisfaction' and also with that of 'punishment'. Of the former he says that the thought of Jesus 'satisfying' or 'offering satisfaction' to the wrath of God is quite foreign to the New Testament. Concerning the latter he says that it does occur in Isaiah 53, but not in the New Testament. I wonder whether this can be maintained in the light of the frequent use Jesus and his apostles make of this central chapter of the Old Testament. Take only what Peter writes in 1 Peter 2:24: 'He himself bore our sins in his body on the tree . . . By his wounds you have been healed.'

4. Finally I want to draw attention to the way Barth sets the *two 'states'* *alongside each other.* I believe that this is a theological construction, which *does not do justice to the historical aspect* in the work of Christ. The question may even be asked whether in this way the incarnation itself becomes the focal point of

[32] *CD* IV, 1, p.747. [33] G. C. Berkouwer, *op. cit.*, p.270. [34] *CD* IV, 1, p.74.

the whole Christology, at the expense of cross and resurrection.[35] Is, in Barth's view, the incarnation the really crucial thing in reconciliation by which the gulf between God and man is bridged? Of course, Barth does not deny the reality of cross and resurrection. But in a sense they are relegated to a secondary place. The cross is only the consequence of the incarnation, showing us the depth of the humiliation of God, while the resurrection is the manifestation and revelation of the exaltation of man that has taken place. The resurrection is no longer a 'turning point', for there is no real historical progression.

In the Bible we find a different picture. The New Testament places the full emphasis on the temporal aspect involved in the progression from humiliation to exaltation.[36] Take only what Paul writes in Philippians 2: *'Therefore* God has highly exalted him and bestowed on him the name which is above every name . . .' (vv. 9ff.). The word *'therefore'* is very significant here, since it shows that there is a *historical* progression, and in this progression both cross and resurrection are indispensable and irreplaceable. The cross is *the* place of the atonement. Becoming obedient unto death, Jesus brings the supreme sacrifice of his life. Hence also Paul can summarize his whole preaching in the expression: 'the word of the cross' (1 Cor. 1:18; *cf.* 2:2). The resurrection is more than the unveiling, the revelation of the meaning of the cross and of the incarnation. It is *the* great reversal, the great *new* act of God, raising his Son to eternal life and thus bringing him to glory.

Much more could and should be said to do justice to Barth's doctrine of reconciliation and to his whole Christology. Moreover, we should not only be critical about it, but we should also appreciate its positive aspects. In the closing chapter of his book on the theology of Karl Barth, Robert W. Jenson quotes a few words from the farewell sermon of Eduard Thurneysen, Barth's life-long friend, in the Minster of Basel on June 21, 1959: 'And God be praised, today a theology has again been given us which "teaches rightly of grace".' Jenson makes these words his own and says: 'Here indeed is a theology which teaches of grace. And also those of us for whom Barth has not become the only master and teacher must join in thanking for this gift. There is too much theology which does not teach grace to do otherwise.'[37]

Indeed, there is too much theology that does not teach grace. There is too much preaching that is not born out of a theology of grace. For this reason alone the church will ever remain thankful to God for his gift of Barth. For whatever one may say in criticism of his theology (and much can be said here), one thing is certain: his theology is a theology of divine grace. That is why Berkouwer

---

[35] *Cf.* Fred H. Klooster, *The Significance of Barth's Theology* (Baker, 1961), p.95.
[36] G. C. Berkouwer, *op. cit.*, p.315.   [37] R. W. Jenson, *op. cit.*, p.146.

called his book on Barth's theology *The Triumph of Grace*. Barth himself was not entirely satisfied with this characterization of his theology and would rather summarize it in the well-known words of J. C. Blumhardt: *'Jesus ist Sieger'* (Jesus is victor). For 'we are concerned with the living person of Jesus Christ. Strictly, it is not grace, but He Himself as its Bearer, Bringer and Revealer, who is the Victory, the light which is not overwhelmed by darkness, but before which darkness must yield until it is itself overwhelmed.'[38] This is not only Barth's own summary of his *theology*, but it is also his *confession*, and we gladly join him in it.

[38] *CD* IV, 3, p.173.

THE KERYGMATIC CHRISTOLOGY
OF RUDOLF BULTMANN

H. D. McDonald

All the essays in the symposium, *Kerygma and History,* make it clear how central in Bultmann's theology is the issue of the interpretation of the *kerygma.*[1] Whether or not one accepts the claim made in the brochure of the Tübingen theological faculty that 'Bultmann is not the *cause* but rather the *symptom* of a crisis',[2] there can be no doubt that he became its focal point. About the middle of the present century the dominance of Karl Barth in the field of European theology yielded to that of Rudolf Bultmann, and for a number of years it was conceded that the latter held virtually undisputed sovereignty in the theological kingdom. Unlike Barth's, Bultmann's theology shows a steady consistency so that we are not confronted with an 'earlier' and 'later' Bultmann; and we have the advantage therefore of being able to refer to his work at any period of his activity without feeling that the idea either has been or might be abandoned later.[3] A reading of his first book which appeared in 1926[4] will reveal that the views expressed in his *Jesus Christ and Mythology* of 1958[5] were already present.

Bultmann's star began to rise with the publication of the symposium *Kerygma und Mythos* in 1948 which included his now famous essay, 'New Testament and Mythology'. This essay had, as a matter of fact, appeared some

[1] C. E. Braaten and R. A. Harrisville (eds.), *Kerygma and History: a Symposium on the Theology of Rudolf Bultmann* (Abingdon, 1962).

[2] *Ibid.,* p.10.

[3] 'The remarkable consistency with which Bultmann has developed his initial fundamental insights suggests that he made most of his germinal decisions during the crucial period represented by this collection and his intimacy with Heidegger.' R. Bultmann, *Faith und Understanding,* ed. R. W. Funk (SCM, 1966), Intro., pp.9f.

[4] ET *Jesus and the Word* (Nicholson & Watson, London, 1935).

[5] 'Indeed, the truth of the matter is that Bultmann has been expressing essentially the same position for over thirty years.' R. Bultmann, *Existence and Faith. Shorter Writings of Rudolf Bultmann,* ed. Schubert M. Ogden (Hodder, 1961), Intro., p.10.

seven years earlier but had remained almost unnoticed. In it Bultmann laid hold of the essential weakness of the Barthian theology and exploited it to the full to erect a theological system peculiarly his own. Thus could his views be regarded as complementary to, and yet as contrasting with, those of Barth. Bultmann took seriously the idea of faith as man's response to the Word of God encountered in Jesus Christ and the insistence that the Gospel records are not in any proper sense authentic *Historie*.

From different points of view, both Barth and Bultmann side-stepped history as significant for the disclosure of God. Barth sought to accentuate the uninhibited 'Godness' of God; Bultmann the existential 'manness' of man. Barth initiated the swing from historicism with the publication of his essay 'The Principles of Dogmatics according to Wilhelm Herrmann' in 1925. Herrmann had declared that 'we have no other means of knowing God except as he reveals *himself* to us ourselves by acting upon us'. There was ambiguity about the meaning of the phrase 'reveals himself to us ourselves by acting upon us' in the German original. What 'self' is to be understood by the 'himself'? Is the 'self' of the self-revelation God's or man's? Almost certainly Herrmann meant man's, and in this respect he is followed by Bultmann. But Barth took it as God's. Thus Barth gave the self a theological reference, Bultmann an anthropological. By underscoring the words 'by acting upon us' both cut loose from history. In spite of Barth's efforts to smuggle in a sense of objectivity, 'the later Barth', as Pannenberg observes, 'remains a disciple of Herrmann, as is Bultmann'.

Both Barth and Bultmann were able to buttress their thesis by strongly expressed propositions derived from elsewhere. Ranke had declared as a dictum that 'every epoch has an immediate relation to God'; and Kierkegaard the view that 'where the eternal is concerned there is only one time – the present'. Taken up into the context of theology, Barth conceived of divine revelation as an immediate act of being awakened by God – *himself* acting upon us. Bultmann interpreted faith as man's immediate awakening of *himself* to life's seriousness – *himself* acting in the decision of self-revelation.

Two broad features of Bultmann's theology
An interpretation of the Gospels in terms of existential philosophy
At the time when Barth was announcing his emancipation from existential categories, Bultmann, as is well known, was wedding himself the more closely to Heidegger's particular view of human existence. Bultmann proceeded on the presupposition, as Heinrich Ott says, that the mythological element of the New Testament could be 'totally eradicated by means of existential interpre-

tation'.[6] Bultmann unhesitatingly admits his heavy indebtedness to Heidegger,[7] although according to Karl Jaspers he limits himself to Heidegger's one early volume, *Sein und Zeit*;[8] Jaspers further contends that he 'misunderstands' Heidegger's work and would have surprised him by the way it is made the basis for a theology.[9] Bultmann was, of course, well aware that in seeking to recast the gospel message in the language of existential philosophy he was leaving himself open to criticism.[10] But this he sought to forestall by insisting that Heidegger provides 'the conceptuality in which it is possible to speak adequately of human existence and therefore of the existence of the believer'.[11] He is thus assured, he believes, of the right context for a non-mythological understanding of God.[12]

Bultmann was really led to adopt his existential stance as a consequence of the negative results yielded by the *Formgeschichte* methodology. He felt bound to conclude, as his own *Geschichte der synoptischen Tradition* makes clear, that no certain framework for the history of Jesus can be recovered from the Gospel records. 'In view of the tutelage under Harnack and Herrmann it is not surprising that as Bultmann comes to the dead-end of historicism's quest of the historical Jesus, he finds an alternative approach in the existentialist philosophy of Heidegger which, in its revolt against the objectification of historicism, is formally analogous to the Ritschlian emphasis of *Offenbarungswert*.'[13]

It does not belong to our purpose to attempt any exposition of Heidegger's philosophy here, but merely to note how Bultmann read him as providing those existentialist categories by which he thought to interpret the New Testament. In the series of lectures first delivered at Yale University Divinity School in October 1951, and subsequently at other theological centres in the

---

[6] 'Objectification and Existentialism', in H. W. Bartsch (ed.), *Kerygma and Myth* 2 (SPCK, 1962), p.307.

[7] R. Bultmann, *Essays Philosophical and Theological* (SCM, 1955); *Jesus Christ and Mythology* (SCM, 1960), pp.45, 77; *Faith and Understanding*, pp.324, 327; H. W. Bartsch (ed.). *Kerygma and Myth* 2, pp.138f.; H. P. Owen, *Revelation and Existence* (University of Wales, 1957), pp.9f., 38f. But see also E. M. Good, 'The Meaning of Demythologization' in C. W. Kegley (ed.), *The Theology of Rudolf Bultmann* (SCM, 1966), pp.28f.: 'Long before Bultmann wrote his essay "New Testament and Mythology" he was using the categories of Heidegger's *Sein und Zeit* to interpret the New Testament' (p.28).

[8] *Faith und Understanding*, p.9.

[9] 'Myth and Religion' in *Kerygma and Myth* 2, p.138. *Cf.* H. W. Bartsch, 'Bultmann and Jaspers', *ibid.*, pp.195ff.

[10] 'Reply to the Thesis of J. Schniewind' in *Kerygma and Myth* 1, pp.104f.; 'Bultmann replies to his Critics', *ibid.*, pp.191f.; 'The Case for Demythologizing: a Reply', *ibid.* 2, pp.181f.

[11] *Existence and Faith*, p.288.   [12] *Jesus Christ and Mythology*, pp.53f.

[13] J. G. Gibbs, 'Rudolf Bultmann and his Successors', *SJT* 18, no.4, Dec. 1965, p.397.

United States, Bultmann makes quite explicit his view that existentialism provides a medium by which to give a contemporary relevance to the Christian message.[14] Bultmann was deeply impressed by the way that the early Heidegger portrayed man as 'thrown' into existence in which he finds himself aware of his finitude and creaturehood, from which stems that 'anxiety' which characterizes the human predicament. Bultmann believes that the existential analysis of the human situation is true, but that existentialism does not itself offer an ideal pattern for human existence. It may indeed declare the factuality of human existence, but it cannot 'secure for man a self-understanding of his own existence'.[15] It may analyse but it can never actualize.[16] Thus, declares Bultmann, 'Existential philosophy, while it gives no answer to the question of my personal existence, makes personal existence my own responsibility, and by so doing it helps to make me open to the word of the Bible.'[17] Bultmann, noting Barth's reaction to this exposition, observes, 'Karl Barth rejects the view that a theological proposition can only be valid when it can show itself to be a genuine component of the Christian understanding of *human* existence... therefore... Barth contests my demand for an existential interpretation of Scripture.'[18]

The demythologizing of the gospel in terms consonant with
the discovery of authentic existence
The upshot of Bultmann's adoption of Heidegger's analysis of human existence is that the 'Christ-event' is considered in relation to the individual's existential situation and as having importance for his own self-understanding. 'If authentic human being is an existence in which man takes over himself and is responsible for himself, then authentic existence includes openness for the future or the freedom that becomes an event in the concrete present.'[19] In contrast with this there is what Bultmann calls 'the decisionless decision of an inauthentic human life'.[20] As a 'possibility of being', then, man is faced with decisions and choices which give him genuine existence.

It is at this point that Bultmann's demythologization programme enters. Modern man, he asserts, 'must be confronted with the issue of decision, be provoked to decision'.[21] Therefore the attempt to demythologize becomes

---

[14] *Cf. Jesus Christ and Mythology*, pp. 45f.   [15] *Ibid.*, p. 56.

[16] 'The *analysis* of the existential predicament is not also the *answer*. And all Bultmann claims to do with Heidegger is to use his phenomenology of man, his ontological analysis'. E. M. Good in C. W. Kegley (ed.), *The Theology of Rudolf Bultmann*, p.29.

[17] *Jesus Christ and Mythology*, p.56.   [18] *Essays Philosophical and Theological*, p.259.

[19] 'The Problem of Demythologizing', *Journal of Religion* 42, no.2, April 1962, p.97.

[20] *Ibid.*, p.98.   [21] *Kerygma and Myth* 2, p.183.

unavoidable. At its beginning Christianity was proclaimed in the context of a primitive mythological world-view which 'expresses a certain understanding of man'.[22] But this mythological New Testament world-view which articulated the *existentiell* has become obsolete and meaningless.[23] The demythologizing concern is then, according to Bultmann, a 'hermeneutical procedure that inquires about the reality referred to by mythological statements or texts'.[24]

We need not pursue in any detail the *apologia* Bultmann offers for his demythologizing thesis; the idea is now generally familiar.[25] It is enough to restate the point already made, that Bultmann set about demythologizing the New Testament to put its call – as he believes – for self-understanding, into modern terms. Bultmann was convinced that the response which man needs to make to the Christian proclamation to gain authentic existence has become virtually impossible, because the message continues to be wedded to Jewish and gnostic cosmological and apocalyptical ideas which the modern scientifically-minded man can no longer credit. It is not that Bultmann was content, like Origen, to allegorize the New Testament. When Brunner referred to Bultmann as 'a modern Origen, an allegorist of the Alexandrian school', he was being too kind. For Bultmann's programme is more radical than that. It is to strip the New Testament account of, for example, the virgin birth, the pre-existence of Christ, the miracles, the resurrection, of all objectivity and factuality. Thus the New Testament is reinterpreted in terms of a non-miraculous naturalism.

In this way Bultmann can assert that 'the right question to frame with regard to the Bible – at any rate within the Church – is the question of human existence'.[26] Yet Bultmann maintains that the process of demythologizing, which must now be undertaken in the most thorough manner because of the discrediting of the mythological structure of the universe in which the original message of the gospel was set forth, was in fact already begun within the New Testament itself, first with Paul and then, more radically, with John.[27] He can

---

[22] *Jesus Christ and Mythology*, p.19.

[23] *Cf.* 'The New Testament and Mythology' in *Kerygma and Myth* 1, p.3.

[24] *Cf. The Journal of Religion* 42, April 1962, pp.97f. *Cf.* also 'The real problem, in other words, is the hermeneutical one, *i.e.*, the problem of interpreting the Bible and the teachings of the Church in such a way that they may become understandable'. 'The Case for Demythologizing', in *Kerygma and Myth* 2, pp.184f.

[25] *Cf. e.g. Jesus Christ and Mythology*, ch. 1; 'The Problem of Hermeneutics', *Essays Philosophical and Theological*, ch. 12; *The Journal of Religion* 42, April 1962, pp.96-102; H. W. Bartsch (ed.), *Kerygma and Myth* 1, pp.1-44, 192-211; 2, pp.181-194.

[26] *Kerygma and Myth* 1, pp.191f.

[27] 'But very soon the process of demythologizing began, partially with Paul, and radically with John'. *Jesus Christ and Mythology*, p.32.

therefore declare that 'the religion of Paul could be described as a new self-understanding';[28] and so, too, is it with John.[29]

How thoroughly Bultmann carried through his programme comes out in his *Theology of the New Testament*. Bultmann virtually restricts the theology of the New Testament to that of Paul and John which he claims represents their own demythologization in terms of existential self-understanding meaningful for their day. He thus regards Paul's theology as an anthropology, and reads his Christology as a soteriology. John, who, he asserts, saw the *kerygma* from the perspective of a gnosticizing Judaism, in contrast to Paul's hellenistic Christianity, sought to 'demythologize' the gnostic cosmological dualism into a 'dualism of decision'.[30] From this standpoint, then, of existential translation, Bultmann's demythologizing purpose is, according to Fenton, to make the self-understandings which are recorded in the New Testament relevant and possible self-understandings for modern man. When this has been carried out, however, the result is only a 'this-worldly self-understanding which modern man finds acceptable'.[31] Put in Bultmann's own words this is to say that 'the question of God and the question of myself are identical';[32] for what the gospel gives me is a new understanding of myself.

Two significant aspects of Bultmann's Christology

It is within the context of the two broad features of his theology which we have outlined that we can best approach an investigation of Bultmann's Christology. For an understanding of this his answer must be sought to two questions. What place has the historical Jesus in the Christian message? How can Christ become the occasion for existential decision for us in our present?

Faith has no historical foundation beyond the mere 'thatness' of Jesus

In this statement we have a summary of Bultmann's answer to the first question. Bultmann does not, to be sure, say outright that the earthly life of Jesus had no interest for the early church. He is prepared to allow some connection between the historical Jesus and the preached Christ.[33] But he then virtually destroys the meaningfulness of the connection by declaring that it has

---

[28] *Faith and Understanding*, p.275.

[29] *Jesus Christ and Mythology*, p.33; *Faith and Understanding*, p.281.

[30] Cf. *The Theology of the New Testament* 1 & 2 (SCM, 1952, 1955).

[31] J. Y. Fenton, 'The Post-Liberal Theology of Christ without Myth', *Journal of Religion* 43, no.2, April 1963, p.96.

[32] *Jesus Christ and Mythology*, p.53.

[33] 'The Primitive Christian Kerygma and the Historical Jesus' in C. E. Braaten and R. A. Harrisville (eds.), *The Historical Jesus and the Kerygmatic Christ* (Abingdon, 1964), pp.17f.

little significance for the gospel as it is proclaimed to modern man. For what Jesus actually preached was displaced in the church's faith by what it believed and declared him to be.

In his early volume, *Jesus,* Bultmann asserts that while Jesus appeared as the proclaimer of the word of forgiveness actualized in those who responded to it, the first church did not continue his message. Rather it centred attention on Jesus, not as the proclaimer of God's act, but as himself the focal point of God's saving deed. Accordingly, there is, Bultmann asserts, nothing of Jesus' message in the church's kerygma; nothing beyond the bare fact of his 'thatness'. Therefore the faith of the church is the Easter faith; and the Christ of the church is the Christ of the resurrection perspective.

This summary statement of Bultmann's position regarding the historical Jesus is given explicit declaration throughout his numerous publications. In the introduction to *Jesus,* Bultmann made plain, at the very beginning of his theological career, the significance he attached to the 'historical' Jesus. He has, he says, no historical 'viewpoint' to defend, for he has no interest in the life and personality as such. He is emphatic, as he puts it in a much quoted statement, that 'I do indeed think that we can now know almost nothing concerning the life and personality of Jesus, since the early Christian sources show no interest in either'.[34] The only thing that we can know for sure is 'that Jesus like other agitators died on the cross as a Messianic prophet'.[35] Bultmann contends that to regard Jesus as 'an objectifiable phenomenon' is to misconceive his significance.[36] For him the almost total ignorance about the details of Jesus' history is no serious matter, certainly nothing to be deplored. A faith that needs the support of objective historical evidence is no true faith.[37] It is for this reason that Bultmann in a review of Emmanuel Hirsch's *Jesus Christus Der Herr* refuses to admit that Hirsch speaks 'theologically',[38] because what he 'paints is the "Christ after the flesh"'.[39]

Asserting that 'it is the Christ of the kerygma and not the person of the historical Jesus who is the object of faith',[40] the question may be asked of Bultmann, what, then, is the point of retaining the nebulous hold on the figure

---

[34] *Jesus,* p.8.   [35] *Ibid.,* p.26.

[36] *Essays Philosophical and Theological,* p.288.

[37] *Cf.* 'The attempt to demonstrate the legitimacy of the kerygma by scientific research serves a modern interest, for it puts to the kerygma a question with which it is not concerned. The kerygma is not interested in the "objective historicity" beyond the "that"...', *The Historical Jesus and the Kerygmatic Christ,* p.25.

[38] *Faith and Understanding,* p.129.   [39] *Ibid.,* p.126.

[40] *The Historical Jesus and the Kerygmatic Christ,* p.17.

of the historical Jesus for which he contends?[41] According to Bultmann, Jesus is the source and the first occasion of the kerygmatic event. 'And the Christian message is bound to a historical tradition and looks back to a historical figure only to the extent that it regards this figure as evidence of the Word of God.'[42] Jesus Christ is in some sense the occasion for man's existential decision for authentic existence. For he, as Jesus Christ, is the eschatological event by which the future comes into our present. He is the eschatological event 'as the man Jesus of Nazareth and as the Word which resounds in the mouth of those who preach Him'.[43] God encounters us in his Word; that is to say, in 'a particular Word, in the proclamation inaugurated with Jesus Christ'.[44] In the words of G. E. Ladd concerning Bultmann, 'The significance of the historical Jesus for us is that the intimacy existing between Jesus and His disciples led after His death to visions of Jesus alive from the dead and to the conviction of His resurrection. This in turn issued in the proclamation in the *kerygma* of Christ as the crucified and risen Lord.'[45] It is therefore with the kerygmatic Christ that we are to be concerned. 'Thus, theological thinking – the theology of the New Testament – begins with the *kerygma* of the earliest church and not before.'[46] Indeed 'over the figure of Jesus there hangs a mystery';[47] a mystery because Jesus cannot be uncovered by historical research, and because the Christ of faith can be only hesitatingly and uncertainly related to the Jesus-figure. So 'Bultmann's existential interpretation must be viewed as a variant of the kerygma-theology; it is concerned neither with the Christ idea nor with the personality of Jesus as accessible to historical research, but rather with the Jesus Christ proclaimed in the gospel.'[48]

The kerygmatic Christ – present as the proclaimed Christ
In this statement we have the answer to the second question to be asked of Bultmann. It is his contention that Christ comes when God's eschatological

---

[41] Cf. 'Despite certain statements suggestive of an alternative view, Bultmann believes that except for the cross and resurrection (the latter being no historical event) the historical form of the earthly Jesus is no longer essential to the kerygma. Moreover, this apparently means that insofar as this form seems to appear in the New Testament, especially in the synoptic gospels, it is either not historical or is of secondary importance (or both) and, strictly speaking, not necessary for the proper understanding and proclamation of the Gospel'. D. Moody Smith, 'The Historical Jesus in Paul Tillich's Christology', *Journal of Religion* 46, no. 1, pt. 11, Jan. 1966, p.133.

[42] *Kerygma and Myth* 2, p.193.   [43] *Essays Philosophical and Theological,* p.286.
[44] H. W. Bartsch (ed.), *op. cit.* 1, p.206.
[45] 'The Role of Jesus in Bultmann's Theology', *SJT* 18, no. 1, March 1965, p.61.
[46] *The Theology of the New Testament* 1, p.3.   [47] *Ibid.* 2, p.47.
[48] N. A. Dahl, 'The Problem of the Historical Jesus' in *Kerygma and History,* p.149.

event is encountered 'in the Word of preaching at any time'.[49] Thus, according to Bultmann, the enigma of New Testament theology is 'how the proclaimer became the proclaimed'.[50] Yet it is the proclaimed Christ who is the present Christ. It is the 'preached Christ', the kerygmatic Christ, that saves, for of the Jesus who is called Christ we know next to nothing. 'The real Easter faith is faith in the word of preaching which brings illumination. If the event of Easter Day is in any sense an historical event additional to the event of the cross, it is nothing else than the rise of faith in the risen Lord, since it was this faith which led to the apostolic preaching.'[51]

But is there any given content to the message by which it may be articulated in the present and be perpetuated into the future? Bultmann does not seem to allow for any. There is no 'given' revelation; no objectified facts: revelation is an act in the present,[52] a 'happening' in the moment the word is encountered. In an essay on 'The Word of God in the New Testament', Bultmann emphasizes that it is not the 'whatness' of preaching – not anything that Jesus said – but the 'thatness' of the proclaimed Christ which is decisive.[53] Thus elsewhere he observes, 'The proclaimer must be proclaimed, because it is the fact *that* he proclaimed which is decisive.'[54] So Bultmann affirms quite categorically 'that God meets us in His word, in a concrete word, the preaching instituted in Jesus Christ',[55] and 'the Word of God is what it is only in the moment in which it is spoken'.[56] By correlating the Word and faith in the way he does, Bultmann can affirm that 'Jesus Christ confronts men in the kerygma and nowhere else'. But it must be noted, as Robert W. Funk points out, that 'he does not say that Jesus of Nazareth is known only in the proclamation, but that Jesus as the *Christ* confronts man only there'.[57] The 'Christ-occurrence' which has put an end to history is not an event confronting us as an object over against a subject. It is rather an event which takes place in one's own self-understanding in relation to the summons to faith. The 'salvation-occurrence' is 'revealed as *proclamation*, in the Word'.[58] 'It is, as personal address, that the event of Jesus Christ becomes concretely present – present as an event that affects me in my own unique existence.'[59]

[49] *Essays Philosophical and Theological*, p.288.

[50] *Faith and Understanding*, p.283; *cf. The Theology of the New Testament* 1, p.33.

[51] *Kerygma and Myth* 1, p.42.

[52] *Cf.* 'Revelation in the New Testament', *Existence and Faith*, pp.58-91. *Cf.* also 'Revelation encounters man in the word – in the word that sounds forth in his present; and thereby actually happens to him whether he understands that it does or not'. *Ibid.*, p.79.

[53] *Faith and Understanding*, ch. 12.   [54] *Ibid.*, p.284.   [55] *Jesus Christ and Mythology*, p.78.

[56] *Ibid.*, p.79.   [57] *Faith and Understanding*, p.21.   [58] *Existence and Faith*, p.76.

[59] *Journal of Religion* 42, April 1962, p.102.

Reflecting on the two aspects of Bultmann's Christology outlined above, two consequences follow which Bultmann readily allows.

First, there is his insistence that New Testament pronouncements about Jesus are of his significance and not of his nature. He asks the pointed question, 'How far is a Christological pronouncement about him also a pronouncement about me? Does he help me because he is God's Son, or is he the Son of God because he helps me?'[60] Bultmann is sure that the latter is the case. Accordingly he asserts that for the apostles John and Paul, 'Christology is proclamation'.[61] It is indeed on this presupposition that Bultmann's theology of the New Testament is structured.[62] He is thus able to declare that what the New Testament has to say about 'Jesus' divinity or deity are not, in fact, pronouncements of his nature, but seek to give expression to his significance'.[63]

The second result following from the double aspect of Bultmann's Christology as presented above is that he regards historic pronouncements about Christ as 'very God' as inadmissible. In spite of what he has to say in the early part of his essay on 'The Christology of the New Testament' – in which he alleges that historical research presented a developmental Christology in which the man Jesus was endowed with old mythologies which enshrined ancient hopes and dreams[64] – his own reading of New Testament Christology is not all that different. For in his judgment, is not all that is said about the kerygmatic Christ mythological? In every one of his writings Bultmann reiterated the thesis that all that the New Testament writers said about Christ was of necessity mythological in nature, expressing how, in response to the proclamation of the Word, they had come to authentic existence; the mythological ideas concerning Christ grew as the success of the preaching advanced, calling as it did for fuller interpretation of his significance.

Nowhere is this more clearly set forth than in the way Bultmann deals with the question of our Lord's deity. Referring to the early Christian documents he says, 'As for *Christ's person,* the reflection about his relation to God which later occupied the ancient Church is still far off.'[65] This must be taken to mean that for Bultmann the first church did not view him in *essential* relation to God. This is, of course, the conclusion that Bultmann wished to make plain in his lecture delivered on 26 February 1951, at the conference of Swiss Liberal theologians

---

[60] *Essays Philosophical and Theological,* p.280; *cf.* R. Schnackenburg, 'Christology and Myth' in *Kerygma and Myth* 2, p.346.
[61] *Faith and Understanding,* p.281.   [62] *Theology of the New Testament* 1, pp.35f., 42f.
[63] *Essays Philosophical and Theological,* p.280.
[64] *Cf. Faith and Understanding,* pp.262ff., esp. p.264.
[65] *The Theology of the New Testament* 2, p.156.

in Aarau, on 'The Christological Confession of the World Council of Churches'. Bultmann's deliberate intention was to call in question the Amsterdam confession of Jesus Christ 'as God and Saviour'. He labours to show that Christ is not frequently designated 'God' in the New Testament writings. 'Neither in the Synoptic Gospels nor in the Pauline Epistles is Jesus called God', he contends.[66] The one 'certain passage', John 20:28, is referred to, but its implication is blunted with the remark that Jesus Christ always speaks of himself as subordinate to God. The title 'Son of God' is a mythological expression which merely elevates him to the status of 'a divine figure' — 'a god but not simply God'. References to him as Judge of the world and destined Lord of the universe are mythological expressions of later Judaism or of gnostic cosmology. So, Bultmann concludes, 'The formula "Christ is God" is false in every sense in which God is understood as an entity which can be objectified . . . It is correct, if "God" is understood here as the event of God's acting.'[67]

A comment

The teaching of Bultmann rallied a large following. But the Bultmannian camp broke into factions, mainly over Bultmann's failure to engage the historical background of the New Testament. Bultmann had among his students Dinkler, Käsemann, Fuchs, Ebeling, Kümmel, Bornkamm, Conzelmann, Metzger, to name but a few. Of these some have out-Bultmanned him and gone away ahead; others have turned back to walk no more with him; and a few have remained constant. Dinkler and Conzelmann are regarded by their former teacher as his 'genuine disciples', and they have his unqualified approval. Thus Conzelmann continues to insist that the mere fact that Jesus existed is the only historical datum that can be asserted with any show of certainty. With Bultmann, too, stand Metzger and Braun, the so-called 'Mainz radicals'; but they have his 'qualified approval' only. They both refuse to allow to faith any objective factuality and reject out of hand any idea of God's 'otherness' from the world. God is encountered always through personal relations — only through our neighbour. Braun would virtually eliminate altogether from the Gospels any serious Christology: 'The oldest stratum of the synoptics,' he declares, 'the one which reflects most accurately the views from the period of the historical Jesus, is without an explicit christology.'[68] The earthly Jesus preached. He did not teach anything theoretical. He was concerned rather that listeners accepted and obeyed his proclamation. It was the church,

---

[66] *Essays Philosophical and Theological*, p.275.   [67] *Ibid.*, p.287.

[68] H. Braun *et al.*, *God and Christ; Existence and Province* [sic], *Journal for Theology and the Church* 5, ed. R. W. Funk (Harper & Row, 1968), p.93.

influenced by Jewish apocalyptic and hellenistic gnostic ideas, which read the 'Jesus-event' in Christological terms.[69]

It was Ernst Käsemann's essay on 'The Problem of the Historical Jesus' which signalled the departure from the Bultmannian camp of many of his admirers. In his essay, Käsemann contended that Bultmann's lack of interest in the historical actuality of Jesus was nothing short of docetism. He charges Bultmann with being 'a man of the 19th century', and is said to inform his students that by substituting existential interpretation of the New Testament Bultmann is merely 'looking at his own navel'. The *Heilsgeschichte* school has reacted further from the apparent non-historical subjectivism of Bultmann and seeks for a firmer relation between history and revelation. Thus Kümmel, for example, although insisting that revelation exists only in response, yet contends that it is given not only in history, but even in historical events and the interpretation connected with them. It is the facts, not the kerygma, which evoke my response. Oscar Cullmann, too, emphasizes the need for the historical facts of Jesus' life and self-attestation.[70]

The result of the first considered reaction to Bultmann's theology was to bring into sharp relief the two prongs of his presentation which appeared to stand in opposition. On the one hand, there is his interpretation of the Christian faith in existential terms of man's decision for authentic existence; and, on the other hand, there is his evident desire to relate this as possible of actualization to the historical event of Jesus of Nazareth. It was right here that Bultmann's critics diverged. There are those on the left who reject the necessity of the event of Jesus and thus interpret Christianity completely in terms of existential anthropology. On the right are those who want to give greater weight to the historical reality of the Jesus-event in an effort to historicize the kerygma.[71]

On the farther right are those who write in conscious opposition to Bultmann's discarding of the historical in the Gospels. Stauffer, although he ignores Bultmann, is emphatic about the need to discover the historical Jesus. For him Jesus 'is the epiphany of a humanity not of this world'.[72] He must

[69] H. Braun, 'The Significance of Qumran for the Problem of the Historical Jesus', in *The Historical Jesus and the Kerygmatic Christ*, pp.69f.

[70] *Cf.* O. Cullmann, 'Out of Season Remarks on the "Historical Jesus" of the Bultmann School', *Union Seminary Quarterly* 16, no. 2, Jan. 1961, pp.131-148. Reprinted in H. K. McArthur (ed.), *In Search of the Historical Jesus* (SCM, 1970), ch. 30.

[71] *Cf.* 'It is itself a welcome development that precisely the students of Bultmann are re-opening the quest of the historical Jesus on the basis of form criticism'. O. Cullmann, *op. cit.*, pp.259f.

[72] E. Stauffer, 'The Relevance of the Historical Jesus' in *The Historical Jesus and the Kerygmatic Christ*, p.53.

therefore be authentically human – a reality of history.[73] Jeremias regards the study of the historical Jesus as the 'central task of New Testament scholarship'.[74] He contends that 'Every verse in the gospels tells us that the origin of Christianity lies not in the kerygma, not in the resurrection experience of the disciples, not in a "Christ-idea". Every verse tells us, rather, that the origin of Christianity lies in the appearance of the man who was crucified under Pontius Pilate, Jesus of Nazareth and his message.'[75] He contends that whatever statements of the kerygma we may care to examine, their origin is always to be found in the message of Jesus. He criticizes Bultmann on three counts: his lack of concern for the historical Jesus; his false view of the Jesus-figure as a sort of gnostic redeemer-myth; and his existential interpretation of the New Testament.

Kinder also, although ready to accept an existential interpretation of the gospel, is still sure about the need for fundamental historical facts. 'Faith knows that as faith it is created, supported, and fulfilled by facts.'[76] Walter Künneth takes an even stronger line; and his criticism of Bultmann is more direct. He questions Bultmann's thesis of a three-storeyed universe and his consequent reduction of the whole range of New Testament concepts to a mythology so as to explain it away. Künneth distinguishes between a world-picture and a world-view, and contends that faith or the interpretation of events in nature is not affected by the world-picture then in vogue. He stresses the historical nature of revelation. He sees in Christ the entrance of God into history; and he makes the point that, 'The more revelation is divorced from history, however, the more a new *Gnosis* remote from history becomes victorious. Bultmann's "theology" bears the stamp therefore of a new "Gnostic myth".'[77] In the end he finds Bultmann's theology neither genuine revelation, nor genuine decision, nor yet genuine faith.[78]

Those on the right who show an interest in the historical Jesus, more or less according to the measure of the church's influence they are prepared to allow, are Fuchs of Marburg, Ebeling of Zurich and Bornkamm of Heidelberg. They are ready to give concessions to Bultmann by accepting as mythological what those on the further right would regard as historical.

We all know well enough now that we cannot write a life of Christ. The old members of the Jesus of History school fondly imagined that it was possible to

---

[73] *Cf.* E. Stauffer, *Jesus and his Story* (SCM, 1960).

[74] *The Problem of the Historical Jesus* (Facet Books, Biblical Series 13, Fortress, 1964), p.21.

[75] *Ibid.*, p.12.

[76] 'Historical Criticism and Demythologizing' in *Kerygma and History*, p.75.

[77] 'Bultmann's Philosophy and the Reality of Salvation', *ibid.*, p.107.

[78] *Ibid.*, p.117.

strip away the drapery by which it was believed faith had enshrouded the Jesus-figure of the Gospel records, and set before us the real Jesus of Nazareth. They wanted a historical Jesus without a kerygmatic Christ. Barth wanted a kerygmatic Christ without a historical Jesus. Bultmann wants a kerygmatic faith, virtually without a kerygmatic Christ or a historical Jesus. (The 'new questers' want a kerygmatic Christ linked with a demythologized, but more or less historical, Jesus.)

But they all suggest that a wedge can be driven between the historical Jesus and the Christ of faith. They all seem to teach that what Jesus became to faith is not what Jesus was in historical actuality. But surely the records want to make clear precisely the opposite of this: namely, that the Christ of faith is none other than what was the Jesus of history. It is being unjust to the facts to suggest that the pre-Easter historical Jesus was somehow other than the post-Easter Christ. If John's Gospel was written that we might know that Jesus is Christ, then the Synoptic Gospels were written that we might know that Christ was Jesus and that the kerygmatic Christ did not displace the historical Jesus.

In all his theologizing Bultmann cannot avoid the appearance of subjectivity. He talks much of the cross; but his *crucis theologia* is interpreted in the context of a demythologized gospel. The cross is not the objective fact of the crucifixion of Jesus. It is the 'faith-event' which the primitive church discovered and related to a crucified Galilean. The cross is not therefore a 'once-for-all' act, but a repeatable event; a reality which each one makes actual for himself in the light of the resurrection. But by resurrection Bultmann does not mean a historical coming to life again of the crucified Jesus which can be established by external proofs. The resurrection, for Bultmann, is not in fact something done to Jesus, but something done in the disciples. The resurrection is, or rather was, a primitive way of saying that new life is possible to such as come alive to authentic existence through faith. Quite properly, then, does Paul Schilling liken Bultmann's view to the abstract art of Picasso or of Léger. The objects which provided the original stimulus have disappeared altogether in the abstract forms which alone are visible. On Bultmann's canvas the original Jesus of flesh and blood, the Christ of the Galilean road, has become an unknown, unknowable X, and the faith which he aroused is dissolved into mere abstraction and sheer subjectivity.[79]

Apart from this general dissatisfaction with Bultmann's theology, criticisms can be made of his detailed statements which render his Christology incoherent and unacceptable. It is not easy to see, for example, how the 'development' of Christology in the New Testament which necessitated an intensification of

[79] *Cf.* W. M. Horton, *Contemporary Continental Theology* (Norwood Editions, 1966), pp.97f.

mythology can be reconciled with his declaration that with Paul and John the process of demythologization was begun. The so-called 'Higher Christology' of these two would seem to demand more mythologizing, not less. Further, the question can be posed, as indeed it is by G. E. Ladd: Why must it be held that it was Jesus, and not, for example, John the Baptist, who was the first bearer of the Word? John, too, proclaimed the imminent coming of the Kingdom, and suffered a martyr's death. Why did not the kerygma arise around him? On Bultmann's presuppositions this question admits of no answer which does not appear to be utterly arbitrary. 'A similar faith, "authenticated" and "legitimatised" by the *Das* of the Baptist should be an equally Christian faith. But if it be answered that there was "something" in Jesus which was not in the Baptist, then the conclusion to be drawn undermines Bultmann's thesis. For in that case it follows that the kerygma was created not just because of the *Das* but also because of the *Was* of the Jesus of history.'[80]

According to Karl Barth an essential weakness in Bultmann is the way he states the relation between Christology and soteriology. It is, of course, right and proper to insist upon the unity of the two; but Bultmann, in Barth's judgment, has dethroned Christology and merged it into soteriology. But what becomes of Christology, asks Barth, if it is not so much a doctrine of Christ, but a doctrine of the happenings of the transition, which only had its beginnings in Christ, which only derives its names and titles from him? The end result of such a procedure must be that Jesus Christ becomes but an obscure and marginal figure. He would not be, Barth contends, the Christ of the New Testament, the Christ of historic Christian faith.[81] In Bultmann's theology, then, 'the *person* of Christ is obscured by the problematical relation between kerygma and history', and 'by the reduction of Christology to soteriology'.[82]

By his deliberate refusal to grant to Jesus Christ the appellation *God* in its fullest and authentic meaning, Bultmann presents us with a Christology which is anti-trinitarian, unbiblical and non-historical. It is hard, therefore, to resist the verdict of Käsemann, who, in his essay, 'The Problem of the Historical Jesus', states that Bultmann's theology is 'no longer Christian'.

[80] *Cf.* G. E. Ladd, 'The Role of Jesus in Bultmann's Theology', *SJT* 18, no. 1, p.66.
[81] K. Barth, 'Bultmann – an Attempt to understand him' in *Kerygma and Myth* 2, pp.96f.
[82] J. G. Gibbs, 'Rudolf Bultmann and his Successors', *SJT* 18, no. 4, Dec. 1965, p.403.

CAN ONE SAY 'JESUS IS GOD'?

Richard L. Sturch

In a symposium published in 1979[1] (to which frequent reference will be made in this essay), Don Cupitt set out to analyse the expression 'Jesus is God', on the ground that Christians were often thought to be people who believed that Jesus *was* God; but he added that few theologians would accept that formula without qualification. In this he was certainly correct. It is the object of the present essay to try and see why he was correct; what sort of qualifications might in fact be made by a theologian anxious to remain reasonably orthodox; and whether there could be evidence of a kind to justify him in asserting the truth of the expression once it had been qualified properly.

It is not simply a matter of finicky theologians being dissatisfied with plain and straightforward statements like 'Jesus is God'. This statement is nowhere to be found in the Bible itself, nor in any of the church's historic creeds, nor even in the confession of the Council of Chalcedon. The most celebrated of all assertions of our Lord's divinity, the prologue to John's Gospel, does not make any statement at all of which 'Jesus' is the subject; indeed, it does not use that name. It takes as subject a special term which it uses only in this passage, 'The Word', *Logos*; and it states, firstly, that this Word was in the beginning with God and was God, and, secondly, that this Word became flesh and dwelt among us, in, as rapidly becomes clear, the person of Jesus of Nazareth.

This indirect approach to the assertion of our Lord's divinity is in fact typical of the New Testament. Elsewhere we find that Jesus is addressed as 'God', or that the word 'God' is used in apposition to his name or an equivalent; we find that language used of God in the Old Testament is applied to Jesus in the New; we find that Jesus is described as one with God, and that God is said to be in him: but we do not find that the statement 'Jesus is God' is ever made. 'Jesus is

---

[1] M. Goulder (ed.), *Incarnation and Myth* (SCM, 1979), pp.31ff.

Lord', yes; but that is perhaps more an acclamation than a theological statement (though the mere fact that it is a proper acclamation for a Christian to make has distinct theological implications!).

In general, the church's liturgies and creeds have followed the biblical example. Christ is addressed as 'O Lord God, Lamb of God, Son of the Father' in the *Gloria in excelsis*; in the Nicene Creed 'God of God' appears in apposition to 'begotten of his Father before all worlds', which is itself adjectival to 'Jesus Christ'. But the blunt statement 'Jesus is God' is still avoided. And, as noted, even the great Christological definition of Chalcedon – perhaps one should say *especially* the definition of Chalcedon, with its care for absolute accuracy – avoided it: 'We teach men to acknowledge ... our Lord Jesus Christ, at once complete in Godhead and complete also in manhood, truly God and truly man.' The *Quicunque vult* comes nearest: 'We believe and confess that our Lord Jesus Christ, the Son of God, is God and Man.' The addition of 'and man' is not only sound doctrine, but also, we shall see, sound logic.

Now the question arises from all this: Is the reason for this strange linguistic habit the existence of a logical difficulty, or an impossibility rooted in the plain facts of the case? Is it *untrue* to say 'Jesus is God', as it would be untrue to say 'Richard Sturch is God', or is it *misleadingly expressed* to say it, as it would be to say 'Robert Boyle was the father of chemistry and brother of the Earl of Cork'?[2] This question might in fact be made into a kind of challenge to traditional orthodoxy, somewhat as follows: If the doctrine of the incarnation is false, it could well be that the authors of Scripture, and later Christian writers, insofar as they kept close to scriptural language, avoided saying that Jesus was God just as they avoided saying anything that was clearly untrue. But if the doctrine is not false, why did no biblical author ever use the expression, and why have so many later authors avoided it too? If no adequate reason can be given for the 'linguistic habit' on an orthodox basis, is not the natural conclusion that orthodoxy is wrong? We need therefore to look carefully into the possibility that there may be some sort of logical difficulty in the unqualified assertion that Jesus is God.

The most obvious possibility is that there is some sort of catch in the way the word 'is' was used. This word has a number of different uses with quite distinct logical features. Thus it may mean 'exists', as in 'There is no Loch Ness Monster'. It may be an 'is' of predication, as in 'Smith is dark-haired'. It may be an 'is' of identity, as in 'Smith is the man who mended my fence last week'. Discussion tends to be confined to these three, of which the first is clearly irrelevant to Christology and may therefore be left on one side, as is done by

---

[2] I owe this pleasant example to Ian Ramsey, *Religion and Science* (SPCK, 1964), p.78.

Don Cupitt.[3] But as a matter of fact a number of others exist. Thus I may point to a map and say 'This is Canterbury, and that is the M2 motorway', where 'is' means more or less the same as 'stands for' or 'represents'. Or I may see a fireworks display in the distance and say 'That is the Rotary Club celebrating Guy Fawkes night'. Or a critic of 'liberation theology' might say 'Advocating revolution is sheer Marxism', where obviously it is only a *part* of Marxism. No doubt others could be thought of too. So, although we are probably right to concentrate on predication and identity, the possibility must be kept in mind that one of these other kinds of 'is' might really be involved. (Thus someone who held that Jesus of Nazareth never existed at all might, I suppose, take the story of his life as allegorical, and say 'Jesus is God' in the sense 'stands for'. Anyone impressed by the Lord's life might say 'This is God!' meaning only 'God is at work here!', *i.e.* the 'fireworks' sense. And ordinary Trinitarians might well feel that even if 'Jesus is God' needs no other qualifications at all, still only God the Son was incarnate in him, so that the 'is' refers only to a part of God.)[4]

There are, irritatingly, certain difficulties in claiming either that the 'is' in 'Jesus is God' is one of identity or that it is one of predication. If it is one of identity, the statement should be reversible. The detective at the end of the whodunit may say either 'Sykes is the guilty party' or 'the guilty party is Sykes'; for the two assertions of identity have the same meaning, and if one is true the other must be also. But even someone willing to say 'Jesus is God' might well balk at saying 'God is Jesus'. 'God is *in* Jesus', yes; but 'God is Jesus' by itself suggests that there is no more to God over and above the man Jesus, which is not true.

This is no problem where predication is concerned. 'Smith is dark-haired' cannot be reversed so as to make 'dark-haired' the subject of the verb. So the natural way to take the 'is' in 'Jesus is God' must surely be as the 'is' of predication? But now we run up against a different snag. Surely 'God' is a proper name? And how can a proper name follow the 'is' of predication? It can follow that of identity easily enough, as in 'The guilty party is Sykes', but as it only names, and does not describe, it cannot be predicated of anything; with a predicative 'is' it can only be the subject.

However, perhaps 'God' is not a proper name after all. We remember Elijah's challenge on Mount Carmel: 'If the Lord is God, then follow him; but if

---

[3] Actually, Mr Cupitt adds a third, 'the "is" of acclamation'. But this is not really a new kind of 'is'; it is the whole sentence that is the acclamation and whose logic is affected by this.

[4] It could be that it is in this sense of the verb 'to be' that John can say 'the Word was God', or the Athanasian Creed 'The Father is God, the Son is God, and the Holy Spirit is God'.

Baal, then follow him.' Does not this make 'God' a descriptive phrase, equivalent to (say) 'the supreme being' or 'the only proper object of worship'? This seems fair enough; unfortunately, it turns out to raise just the same problem as treating 'God' as a proper name. The definite article picks out a single being or object; and a being or object, like a proper name, cannot be predicated of anything, it can only be identical with it. Nor will it help us to omit the definite article. That will enable us to use the word 'God' as a predicate, undoubtedly; but at the cost of saying only 'Jesus is *a* God'. A polytheist might accept this. I have seen a Hindu shrine which, among the images of Krishna and Śiva, included one of Christ on the cross; and I am sure the worshippers there would readily have agreed that 'Jesus is a God'. But that is not an option for us who are monotheists.

We cannot even escape by invoking the doctrine of the Trinity and saying that, although Jesus is not 'a God' in the sense of one god among many, yet he is one person of the Blessed Trinity among three. For this once again makes the 'is' one of identity, and so reversible; and this cannot be done. There is more to the person of God the Son, over and above the human Jesus – and more to the human Jesus than just the person of God the Son.

It seems, then, that the New Testament and the widespread tradition of later Christianity were right not to use the unqualified statement 'Jesus is God'; to do so lands one in serious logical and theological difficulties. But is this really an objection to incarnational theology? In order for it to be one, we should have to show not only that the expression cannot be used, but that incarnational theology requires that it *should* be used. And it is not at all clear that it requires any such thing.

In the first place, it asserts that Jesus is both God *and* man. Now this greatly reduces the difficulty we met in trying to make the 'is' one of predication. For that difficulty was, it will be remembered, that it could only be done by making 'God' a common or general term, so that 'Jesus is God' became in effect 'Jesus is *a* God'. And to the Christian, or to any other monotheist for that matter, the phrase 'a God' makes no sense; not only is there in fact only one God, there *can* be only one God. The 'is' could be made predicative only if Jesus' being (a) God were contrasted at least with the *possibility* that there might be other Gods. If one may illustrate the point with an analogy: there is at the time I write only one living emperor, Emperor Hirohito of Japan, and only one living pope, John Paul II. But it makes perfectly good sense to say 'Hirohito is a living emperor' (predicative 'is'), because, although there are in fact no other living emperors, there could be. On the other hand, it makes no sense to say 'John Paul II is a living pope', because there *can* be only one pope at a given time. Similarly, if there were only one God but others might have existed,

329

'Jesus is a God' would have made sense; but if there can be only one, it does not.

If, however, the correct expression is 'Jesus is both God and man', the predicative 'is' becomes possible after all. For the contrast is not now between one person to whom the predicate applies or conceivably might apply; it is a contrast between one predicate applying to a particular person and another predicate applying to the same person. It makes no sense to say 'John Paul II is a' [as opposed to 'the'] 'living pope', because 'a' here seems to imply that there could be other living popes, which there cannot. But it does make sense to say 'John Paul II is a living pope and a living Pole', because we are not interested here in the possibility of there being other popes but only in that of John Paul II's being something else as well as pope.

But we can go farther than that. Orthodoxy speaks of a joining of the two natures, divine and human, in the one person of Jesus Christ; to quote the Athanasian Creed again, 'One, not by conversion of the Godhead into flesh: but by taking of the Manhood into God'. It is not difficult to see that such a joining would lead to a situation requiring careful linguistic handling. Again, an analogy may help. Near the city of St. Louis, two of the world's great rivers, the Missouri and the Mississippi, join. The river below this junction is known by the name of one of these, the Mississippi, but is of course a combination of the two. Now it is interesting to note that a lot of the linguistic problems that arise if we try to say 'Jesus is God' *also* arise if we try to say 'This' (referring to the river below the junction) 'is the Missouri'. Clearly to *deny* that it is the Missouri would be even more misleading than to assert it; but equally clearly to assert it without qualification would also mislead. If we are thinking in the same sort of pattern as John in his prologue, we might say something like 'The Missouri turns south and is joined to the Mississippi'; if in the same sort of pattern as Thomas after the resurrection-appearance to him, we might address the combined river as 'My old friend the Missouri!'. Language applied to the Missouri above St. Louis may also be applied to the combined river (*e.g.* statements about its source, its total length, or the quantity of sediment it contains). Or the combined river could be said to be one with the Missouri; or the Missouri could be said to be in it. But the unqualified assertion 'This is the Missouri' could not be made without adding 'and the Mississippi'. Even so, it would not be correct to assert 'Jesus is God' without adding 'and man'.

In other words, the apparently perplexing difficulties over asserting that Jesus is God, and the reluctance of the New Testament to assert any such thing despite coming close to it at times, are precisely what we should expect if the orthodox doctrine of the incarnation were actually true. They cannot therefore be used as an objection to it. Of course, they do not prove that that doctrine *is* true. Other sets of circumstances might produce the same linguistic effects (though I am not sure what ones would) and there might be other reasons for rejecting the doctrine; but the coincidence is certainly interesting.

We have seen, then, why Don Cupitt was right to say that few theologians would accept the formula 'Jesus is God'. Incidentally, we have also seen what qualification needs to be added, namely 'and man'. This does not, of course, settle the ancient disputes between Nestorian, Chalcedonian and Monophysite, or their modern counterparts, that is, between people who would accept the qualification without any demur, but would then go on to argue about further refinements. It is not the purpose of the present essay to enter this field.[5]

But I think I can imagine a critic raising a new objection at this point. 'We are asked to say "Jesus is God" only if we add the qualification "and man". But surely we can say "Jesus is man" by itself, without qualification, and this without being in any way unorthodox. Why should orthodoxy require us to qualify only one of these two assertions? Ought there not to be more *symmetry* here?'

The answer to this is basically one of nomenclature. It is a long-established convention in Christendom to use the name 'Jesus' or 'Christ' to refer to the whole person or *prosōpon* of the incarnate Word, of whom it can properly be said that he is God and man, but not (without risk of being misleading) that he is God or man without the other term being added as a qualification. It is also correct to use the name 'Jesus' to refer purely to the human being who was crucified under Pontius Pilate, whether or not the speaker believes in the incarnation (or, indeed, in God). And in this latter case it is obviously quite correct to say 'Jesus is man' (or, more probably, 'Jesus was human') without qualification. The symmetry our imaginary critic wanted to see does in fact exist, for we can say 'The Son' or 'The Word is God' without any qualification at all, just as we can say 'Jesus was man' without any qualification at all. It is the double function that the name 'Jesus' has to fulfil in common Christian usage that has led to the objection.

It is, however, to this double function itself that Don Cupitt, if I understand him correctly, wishes to object.[6] The Fathers of the great councils, he says, 'were changing the logic of the name Jesus. It was ceasing to function primarily as the name of an historical individual, a man, and becoming a technical term in a mythical-dogmatic system of ideas'. There is perhaps some justice in this, though the Fathers in question might well have queried the term 'mythical'. But it is a lot older than the councils. Already in such passages as Ephesians

---

[5] I have endeavoured to discuss some of the problems in this area in 'The Metaphysics of the Incarnation', *Vox Evangelica* 10, 1977, pp.65ff.

[6] *Op. cit.*, p.37.

1:20-23 or Revelation 22:12–16 the name 'Jesus' or 'Christ' is being applied to the exalted Son as well as to the Galilean carpenter. It might perhaps have been convenient if some other term had been found to do the work – if, say, 'Jesus' had been used only for the manhood, 'the Word' for the Godhead, and 'Christ' for the Word incarnate, both during his lifetime on earth and since then in his exaltation in heaven. That did not in fact happen, however; 'Jesus' was used for both the first and the third of these. It is no more than an inconvenience. If you have a 'dogmatic system of ideas', you will need to use terms in it, and the use of 'Jesus' as a term has at least the advantage of driving home the fact that the system of ideas is not existing in a vacuum but is a system of ideas about 'an actual historical individual, a man', Jesus the son of Mary, of Nazareth in Galilee.

Once again our 'rivers' analogy may illustrate the point. The lower, combined river is known by the name 'Mississippi'. It need not have been. It might have been given some third name, but it was not. A geographical Don Cupitt might complain, 'They are changing the logic of the name "Mississippi". It is ceasing to function primarily as the name of a river flowing from northern Minnesota to St. Louis, and becoming a technical term used by Southerners to describe a much bigger river ending at New Orleans, quite different in speed, volume and appearance from anything in the Mississippi proper.' But of course there has been no change of logic at all. There is, rather, an additional fact, indeed two additional facts: the upper Mississippi has been joined by another great river, and the name of one of the two has continued to be used even in statements which apply only as a result of this confluence. Similarly, orthodox Christianity has believed in a certain fact about the man Jesus – that in him the Word became flesh and dwelt among us – and yet has continued to use the name 'Jesus' even in statements which apply only as a result of this incarnation. It means that we must be careful about what we say, if there is danger of our being misleading; but that is a good rule to follow at all times.

It would seem, then, that while there are indeed certain logical difficulties about the unqualified assertion 'Jesus is God', sufficient to explain why the Bible and subsequent theology have tended to avoid it, these difficulties are not indications of any logical incoherence in the doctrine of the incarnation, and are quite capable of arising in contexts which have nothing to do with theology at all.[7] Nevertheless, it could still be that there were other indications of logical incoherence in the doctrine, and to two arguments we may next turn which claim just this.

---

[7] In fairness to Mr Cupitt, I should add that though he rejects the doctrine of the incarnation, he does not regard it as self-contradictory: see his *The Debate about Christ* (SCM, 1979), pp.25f.

In another essay in the symposium already referred to,[8] Michael Goulder accuses modern defenders of orthodoxy, such as Professors Moule and Mascall, of what he calls 'mystification', that is, the propounding of a 'pseudo-paradox' which 'is in some radical sense unclear, and upon probing is found not to be capable of being stated at all'. It is a little unfortunate that Michael Goulder's illustrations of this concept leave it fairly unclear itself. Each is comprehensible enough in itself, but they seem to have little in common with one another. Thus the phlogiston theory of combustion (Michael Goulder's first example) would appear to be a straightforward case of a physical theory which turned out to be false. The fact that in its later years it involved assigning phlogiston a negative mass must have proved a serious strain on the *imaginations* of those who defended the theory (though scarcely less than that inflicted by a lot of more recent theories), but that can hardly be what Michael Goulder means. If the concept of something with negative mass could be fitted into the then current Newtonian physics (whether it could or not I have no idea), then no mystification was involved; if it could not, then there was a good reason to abandon the phlogiston theory (or Newtonian physics). It is true that *if* negative mass cannot be fitted into Newtonian physics, and *if* the believers in phlogiston also continued to believe in that physics, then they were guilty of self-contradiction; but this is not the same thing as a 'radically unclear' notion which 'cannot be stated at all'.

Much the same applies, though more clearly, to Michael Goulder's second example, the Dorze belief that leopards are Christians. Dorze Christians, it appears, fast on Fridays, while leopards do not; and the Dorze do not allow that leopards are undependable Christians or have a dispensation. This would seem to be a straightforward self-contradiction. It may be, however, that Michael Goulder, who is willing to allow paradoxes which take the form of apparent contradiction, but not those which take that of apparent nonsense, means simply that the Dorze belief that leopards are Christians is nonsense; but in that case why bring in the Friday fasts? (And he does accept that the story of the prince turned into a frog might make sense – though not of course that it was ever true!)

A little later in his essay Michael Goulder alludes to Professor Flew's celebrated accusation that some religious assertions die 'the death of a thousand qualifications' – that is, that certain terms in these assertions become so heavily qualified in the face of adverse criticism that they lose all meaning.[9] (Flew's illustration of this in a non-religious context was that of a gardener who is

---

[8] Pp. 51ff.

[9] In Flew and MacIntyre (eds.), *New Essays in Philosophical Theology* (SCM, 1955), pp.96ff.

asserted, as evidence against his existence piles up, to be invisible – unsmellable – intangible – 'eternally elusive' – by this stage, what on earth is meant by continuing to use the word 'gardener'?) This is much more intelligible, and one can see how it might have applied in the phlogiston controversy: once phlogiston was supposed to have negative mass, was the notion of it as a substance becoming vacuous? We may agree that it was heading in that direction, and would certainly have become vacuous if many more such qualifications had been needed. Perhaps the idea is that this is what happened during the great Christological debates of the early church. The ideas that Jesus was God pretending to be man, or a man specially favoured ('adopted') by God, or a human body inhabited by God instead of by a rational soul – each of which made some sort of sense – were one by one rejected. God and man were one in Jesus, but *not* as the Docetists, or the Adoptionists, or the Apollinarians, or the Nestorians, supposed. But what is then left of the original assertion that God and man were one in Jesus?

Well, the Fathers of Chalcedon thought that what was left was the assertion that God the Son and Jesus of Nazareth shared one and the same person or *prosōpon* and one and the same *hypostasis*. I have endeavoured elsewhere to suggest possible interpretations of this in more modern terms.[10] But clearly some positive content was left to the original assertion. Not all content had been taken from it by the qualifications. Indeed, the charge made against the heresies was that, so far from making the original assertion intelligible, they denied that it was true. Flew's gardener would not have died the death of a thousand qualifications if they had been merely denials that the 'gardener' was a postman, railway-worker or Member of Parliament.

In any case it is not clear that Michael Goulder is really wanting to take this line I have been suggesting and criticizing. He agrees that 'incarnation was not a mystification to Thomas [Aquinas]'; it seems that the 'mystifying' element has crept in more recently than Aquinas, and *a fortiori* more recently than Chalcedon. What bothers Goulder is not a shift in the position of the orthodox whereby they have moved from genuine assertions (true or false) to mystifications. It is a shift in vocabulary by humanity in general which he thinks the orthodox have refused to make, and thanks to which it is no longer possible to assert meaningfully what the orthodox still insist on asserting. The obvious retort – that this only means that Michael Goulder's vocabulary is impoverished, so that he is in the position of a deaf man despising music critics – he has anticipated: moderns, he says, use a different vocabulary for real reasons. Just as modern chemistry and physics have no room in their vocabulary for 'phlogiston',

---

[10] *Art. cit., Vox Evangelica* 10.

and are none the poorer for it, so modern language has no room for phrases like 'the human nature assumed by the Word' or discussions of the date at which Jesus received a human soul.

Now there is some truth in this. Words like 'nature' and 'soul' had a double function in patristic and medieval times. On the one hand, 'nature' had a perfectly ordinary usage which survives to this day ('it's against human nature to be that patient!'), while 'soul' had a religious usage, to refer to that aspect or part of a human being which was supposed (rightly or wrongly) to survive death of the body; and this, too, survives to this day, though I do not know whether Michael Goulder uses it or not. Both words, however, had also a quasi-scientific role to play. The *nature* of a class of being was supposed to be a fixed set of qualities from which could be deduced a great deal of what was true of members of that class; the description of such a 'nature' was roughly equivalent to a set of scientific laws today. The *soul* was supposed (by Aquinas and other Aristotelians at least) to be the 'form' of the body, the pattern in accordance with which it grew, developed and functioned.

The latter notions are both dispensed with by present-day science; they are as dead as phlogiston. It requires a considerable intellectual effort for a contemporary Thomist to find a place for both them and modern scientific concepts, and the result may possibly be what Michael Goulder calls 'mystification'. But the other uses of the words are not at all affected by scientific developments. Nor did they owe their appearance in Christian thought to Greek science. Paul, for example, uses 'nature' and 'soul' quite cheerfully without being suspected of Aristotelianism. And, as we have seen, both are used readily enough to this day, and by people who are no more Aristotelian than was Paul. Of course, it may be that there are, somewhere, real reasons for discontinuing these uses as well as the 'scientific' ones; but as far as I know none has been produced. (There are philosophers and theologians who deny the existence of a soul. But this, they would agree, is a matter of debate, and until it is settled decisively in their favour, if it ever is, we cannot rule out the use of the word 'soul'.)

It might be worth adding that in the case of 'nature' (not, I think, of 'soul') statements using the word in its non-'scientific' sense can almost always be rewritten without it. To say 'Jesus has a human nature' is exactly equivalent to saying 'Jesus is a human being'. Of course, such an expression as used by us today does not have the same content as it had to someone taking the quasi-scientific view of 'nature'. But then to him even 'Jesus is a human being' would have had overtones and implications that it does not have today. This would not alter the fact that its fundamental meaning was the same for both of us; and the same applies to the theologically important part of the content of 'Jesus has a human nature'. The Fathers of Chalcedon, in asserting the Two

Natures, were not insisting that their quasi-scientific theories were part of the dogma of the church; they were concerned simply to assert that Jesus was both man and God, and to reject certain views which were at the time expressed in 'nature' language. What they asserted can be equally well asserted today.

One more accusation of incoherence is made in the symposium *Incarnation and Myth* which may be dealt with more briefly. In discussing a contribution by Brian Hebblethwaite which defended a fairly traditional Christology, Don Cupitt concluded: 'The human Jesus' view of his own acts and experiences as a servant of God logically must be different from God the Son's view of Jesus' acts and experiences as acts and experiences of himself in a state of kenosis. Mr Hebblethwaite's theory leaves no-one in the position of being able to say "I am God in kenosis, suffering in and for man"; and if no-one can say that for himself, how can Mr Hebblethwaite say it of him?'[11]

This charge is certainly unfounded. The first sentence is true, but no objection; the human Jesus' view of his own acts and experiences, *e.g.* his view of the synagogue at Nazareth, was certainly distinct from God the Son's view of the same things; this is plainly implied by traditional Christology, and to deny it would be a form of Apollinarianism. Orthodoxy simply asserts that *both* views were held by the same person, which may be incoherent, but cannot be shown to be so simply by saying it. (Even human beings who are not God can have two different views of the same thing. Try looking at your nose with one eye shut!) The second sentence, on the other hand, would be a serious objection if it were true. But it is false. Firstly, because it *was* in fact possible for Jesus to know that he was God in kenosis, suffering in and for man; we shall come on to this later. Secondly, because even if it were not, Brian Hebblethwaite could still say it of him. 'In kenosis' here means simply that the human Jesus did not know all things, and, more specifically, did not (always) know that he was indeed divine. Since he did not know it, he could not say it. Nor could God the Son: for either his divinity was unaffected by the kenosis, in which case he could not say 'I am God in kenosis', or it was, in which case he was in precisely the same situation as the human Jesus. But we could still say it for him, as a simple analogy will show. It is not possible for me to say 'I am wearing odd socks while unaware of it'; but it may be true, and you can then say about me 'Sturch is wearing odd socks without being aware of it'. Similarly, it is not possible (with one reservation, to be discussed later) for the human Jesus to say 'I am God in kenosis', for this is equivalent to saying 'I am God and yet unaware of it'. Yet it may be true, and we may be able to say it of him.

---

[11] *Op. cit.*, p.45. Mr Hebblethwaite's article is on pp.87-100.

The heading of this essay is 'Can one say "Jesus is God"?'. I hope I have shown that there are no logical reasons for objecting to the statement in itself, provided that it is qualified by the addition 'and man'. But the question might be taken to mean, 'Can we have any reason to say it?' If Jesus *is* God in kenosis, are we justified in saying he is? The question would then be one about evidence rather than about logic; and to this possibility we must now turn. We are not concerned, I should make clear, with the question 'Does Scripture provide enough evidence for us to assert Jesus' divinity?' but with the significantly different one, '*Could* Scripture provide such evidence?'

The case for saying 'No' on purely *a priori* grounds would run, I imagine, somewhat as follows: The descriptions of Jesus' life in the Gospels are those of a *human* life. If at any point there is described an event which could not be part of a human life, either it did not really happen at all or we are landed with docetism. But if every event in Jesus' life was capable of being part of a human life, how can any such event be evidence for his being *divine*? If an archaeologist investigating a site finds that every item dug up is consistent with a third-century date for the site, how can any of it be evidence for a second-century date? The site may well have been occupied in the second century, but there is no way to prove it. Similarly, Jesus may have been divine, but if docetism is rejected there can be no way to prove it. Don Cupitt has used a rather similar type of argument[12] to refute the classical proof of Christ's divinity which says, 'Anyone who talked as Jesus did must have been either mad, a wicked deceiver, or God; but Jesus was neither mad nor wicked.' This, Don Cupitt argues, implies that Jesus' language was 'incompatible with normal human goodness and sanity'; it must therefore, to be good and sane, be non-human language, and we are back to docetism again. This particular formulation seems ill-constructed; all Don Cupitt has shown is that it is not *normal* human language, and this can be accepted without docetism. Jesus could be unique without ceasing to be human! But the general thrust of the argument does not incorporate so obvious a flaw, and must be met.

To make the argument more specific, consider the various elements in our Lord's life which have at times been used to 'prove' his divinity. The miracles are an obvious example. Could any human power have healed the sick, raised the dead, cleansed lepers and cast out demons as Jesus did? Assuredly not; but human beings acting by the power of God could, and if Scripture is to be trusted they did. Prophets before Christ's coming and apostles after it wrought miracles; Christ's miracles, therefore, can show no more than that God was at work in him. Lazarus and Jairus's daughter rose from the dead; Christ's

---

[12] *The Debate about Christ*, pp. 112-115.

resurrection can show no more than theirs did. The same applies to the goodness and holiness of his life (with the additional difficulty that most of his life is not recorded); God was its source, no doubt, but how could one show that it was God's own life?

Somewhat more difficult for the critic is the authority with which Jesus spoke, 'not as the scribes', and not even, it would seem, as the prophets. There is no 'Thus saith the Lord' prefixed to his words; on the contrary, we find the Law itself corrected with 'But I say unto you'. Related, of course, is the matter of Jesus' claims: most obviously, those in the Fourth Gospel, but also a good many in the Synoptics. Could these claims be made, and teaching be given with this sort of authority, by someone who was only a human being? Michael Goulder clearly thinks the answer is 'Yes': 'all the actions which to the Fathers give substance to the incarnation – the miracles, Jesus' memory of pre-incarnate life with God, "I and the Father are one", etc. – now find this-worldly explanations.'[13] Unfortunately, he does not go into details; possibly he means simply that Jesus never really made such claims, or that if he did he was mistaken. If so, the argument moves over into the field of New Testament scholarship and away from that of logic. But if we suppose that Jesus did make such claims, and did teach with such authority, and was not deluded or deceitful, are we not still left with docetism?

Taking a slightly different line of approach, Don Cupitt criticizes the 'argument from filial consciousness' by asking, 'Did Jesus really think of himself as divine?'[14] The evidence of the Fourth Gospel is, he thinks, of no value, and the Synoptists portray him (as indeed does John) as believing in and praying to God, with whom therefore he can hardly have thought of himself as identical. While if we want only to argue that he thought of himself as the *Son* of God, the son-father relationship is there in the Old Testament, applied to Israel as a whole or to Israel's king, and in any case unique sonship is not the same as divinity. There seems to be something a little disingenuous about this. Jesus' sonship was clearly not thought of as similar to that of Israel or the Davidic kings – it was, in Don Cupitt's word, unique; and while unique sonship is not indeed the same as divinity (as the existence of Arians and Jehovah's Witnesses reminds us), it leads to a series of theological problems which may be resolvable only by an assertion of divinity. However, this again moves us away from philosophical reasoning to biblical and theological; we had better return to the question of whether there can in principle be evidence for the incarnation.

[13] *Incarnation and Myth*, p.55.
[14] *The Debate about Christ*, pp.111f.

A number of the *Incarnation and Myth* symposiasts clearly felt that the crucial evidence for Jesus' divinity lay not in his words, actions or powers but in his *significance* – in particular, in his significance for the atonement.[15] This is not of course a new argument. 'If the properties of the flesh had not been ascribed to the Word,' said Athanasius, 'man would not have been freed.'[16] But that does not mean it is not a strong one. It is clearly evidence of a completely different *type* from the others we have been considering: it does not say 'Jesus would not have said *x* or done *y* if he had not been divine', but rather 'Jesus' life, death and resurrection would not have had the saving effects that they had and still have if he had not been divine'. This does not point to docetism; indeed, the same type of argument has of course also been used to prove the full *humanity* of the Lord. We might draw an illustration from the law. A document purporting to be an Act of Parliament is not shown to be such by any word it contains; its words must indeed exist and be used outside it for it to be an intelligible Act at all. It is shown to be a genuine Act by its effects on society. (It could also be known, of course, by its origins; but the corresponding element in the incarnation would be the mind of God, which is inaccessible to us.)

Of course, the effect of this approach is to shift the area of debate from incarnation to atonement. Is there reason to believe that God and man really have been made at one by Jesus Christ? The evidence for this would presumably lie partly in the experience of Christians down the ages and partly in the New Testament witness to Christ. But in mentioning the New Testament witness we have come close to a serious weakness in the whole earlier approach to the search for evidence. We have, at least until questions about the atonement were raised, been assuming that 'evidence' must consist of facts – facts about the earthly life of Jesus or perhaps about human conversions – from which we can infer another fact, that of the incarnation. Yet in the course of our lives we learn huge numbers of facts which would never normally be said to have been inferred in this way. I know the result of the 1980 presidential election in the U.S.A., but not as an inference from (let us say) the dejected air of my Democrat friends and the corresponding elation of Republicans; I know it because I have been told it, by press, radio, and the like. And the main reason that most Christians have for believing in the incarnation is, of course, that they believe it has been revealed to them by God – that they have, in fact, been told it. It could well be the case (indeed, I think myself it *was* the case) that the same held good of our Lord's own human knowledge of who he was: was it not to him that the voice of the Father said 'Thou art my beloved Son' (Mk. 1:11;

[15] *E.g.* Hebblethwaite, p.94; Moule, p.86; Sykes, p.126.
[16] *C. Arianos*, 3, 33.

Lk. 3:22)? (This does not rule out the possibility that he knew of this sonship already – again by revelation; *cf.* Lk. 1:35; 2:49.) Hence Don Cupitt's notion that the human Jesus could not be in a position to say 'I am God in kenosis', mentioned earlier, is not only irrelevant but mistaken. God in kenosis could not know his own divinity 'by nature', but could perfectly well know it by revelation.

Although of course the existence of a statement in the Bible (or for that matter in a daily newspaper) is itself a fact, and, strictly speaking, to go on from it to the further fact of which it speaks is to draw an inference, there is clearly an important difference between this and the kind of inference we were looking at earlier. The facts on which the earlier inferences were meant to be based had no 'intentional' side to them; they contained in themselves no reference to other facts or alleged facts. But the fact of a statement in the Bible, *e.g.* 'God was in Christ, reconciling the world unto himself' (2 Cor. 5:19), does have such a reference. It is not a question of guessing what may lie behind it, as in the case of, for instance, a miracle; it is simply a question of whether it is true or not. If it is, then what 'lies behind it' is given to us. Of course, we may also try to guess what else lies behind it. If we are going to ask questions about the theology of Paul, we shall have to do just that, and also, in a rather different way, if we want to discuss whether such Christological statements in the Bible imply an orthodox Christology rather than an Arian or Adoptionist one. But such questions about the implications of statements are obviously quite distinct from the question, 'Is the statement true or false?' Accept that the statements describing one of our Lord's miracles are true, and it still makes sense to say, 'Does this imply that God was in Christ?' Accept that the statement made in 2 Corinthians 5:19 is true, and it does not make sense to ask it any longer.

It is not practicable in this essay to begin discussing whether the biblical assertions about our Lord are in fact true or not, nor whether they do or do not imply the doctrine of the incarnation, though certainly I myself believe that the answer to both is 'Yes'. What I do hope I have shown is that there are no *a priori* reasons for saying they could not imply this doctrine, nor for denying that the doctrine makes sense. They can, and it does.

INDEX OF AUTHORS

DATE DUE